Peer Relationships and Social Skills in Childhood

Peer Relationships and Social Skills in Childhood

Edited by
Kenneth H. Rubin
Hildy S. Ross

Springer-Verlag New York Heidelberg Berlin

Kenneth H. Rubin
Hildy S. Ross
Department of Psychology
University of Waterloo
Waterloo, Ontario N2L 3G1, Canada

Library of Congress Cataloging in Publication Data
Main entry under title:
Peer relationships and social skills in childhood.
  Includes bibliographies and index.
  1. Social skills. 2. Friendship. 3. Age groups. 4. Social interaction. 5.
Child development. I. Rubin, Kenneth H. II. Ross, Hildy S.
HQ783.P43 1982   302.3   82-10550

With 3 Figures

Typeset by Publishers Service, Bozeman, Montana
Printed and bound by R.R. Donnelley & Sons Company, Harrisonburg, Virginia
Printed in the United States of America

9 8 7 6 5 4 3 2 1

ISBN 0-387-90699-1 Springer-Verlag New York Heidelberg Berlin
ISBN 3-540-90699-1 Springer-Verlag Berlin Heidelberg New York

To our best friends, Margo and Michael

Preface

Amy Rubin, the seven-year-old daughter of one of this volume's editors, was discussing with her close friend Kristin, her teacher's practice of distributing stickers to her classmates for completing their seat work. As the conversation continued, Joshua, Amy's two-year-old brother (although Amy would argue that he more often resembles an albatross around her neck) sauntered up to the older children. He flashed a broad smile, hugged his sister, and then grabbed her book of stickers.

Corey Ross, the nine-year-old son of the other editor was trying to plan a tobogganing party with his friend Claire. The problem facing Corey and Claire was that there were too few toboggans to go around for their grade four classmates. Jordan, Corey's younger brother had agreed to lend his toboggan. However, Harriet, Claire's younger sister and Jordan's close friend had resisted all persuasive attempts to borrow her toboggan. The older children decided that the best strategy was to use Jordan's friendship with Harriet and his good example of sibling generosity in presenting their case to Harriet.

Both of these anecdotes exemplify what this volume on peer relationships and social skills is about. Children have friends with whom they discuss issues of perceived social significance. During the early elementary school years, rather sophisticated conversations and debates concerning topics of reward distribution, altruism, person perception, social status, sibling relations, and cooperation can be overheard (especially by eavesdropping parents who have professional interests in such matters).

Moreover, very early in life, children have social repertoires far more complex than psychologists thought they did in years prior to the 1970s. Joshua, for example, attempted to solve his social problem by "setting up" his older sister. He smiled at and hugged her, knowing full well that she would warm to this social greeting. He then took her prized sticker book which, of course, elicited an unprintable response. Was he thinking that "hug + smile + grab" would lead to a higher probability of success than "grab" alone?

Given both the pervasiveness and the challenging complexity of peer interaction, it is clear why the number of researchers in this field has multiplied significantly in the past decade. This volume represents one attempt to capitalize on the fruits of their collective labors. We have compiled contributions from a number of eminent developmental psychologists whose work collectively concerns the study of infants, toddlers, preschoolers, school-aged children, and adolescents as well as several special populations. The topics of their research include a wide variety of social skills and peer relationships, and interestingly, the relations between social skills and relationships are discussed by many of the authors.

We hope that readers of this volume will be stimulated by both the wealth of theoretical insights and empirical observations provided by the authors herein.

Waterloo, Ontario   Kenneth H. Rubin
Canada   Hildy S. Ross

Contents

Contributors

Rona Abramovitch, Department of Psychology, University of Toronto in Mississauga, Mississauga, Ontario L5L 1C6, Canada

Steven R. Asher, Bureau of Education Research, College of Education, University of Illinois at Urbana-Champaign, Urbana, Illinois 61801, U.S.A.

Roger Bakeman, Department of Psychology, Georgia State University, Atlanta, Georgia 30303, U.S.A.

Thomas J. Berndt, Department of Psychology, Yale University, New Haven, Connecticut 06520, U.S.A.

John R. Brownlee, Department of Psychology, University of Utah, Salt Lake City, Utah 84112, U.S.A.

Susan B. Campbell, Department of Psychology, University of Pittsburgh, Pittsburgh, Pennsylvania 15206, U.S.A.

Michael Chapman, Laboratory of Developmental Psychology, National Institute of Mental Health, 9000 Rockville Pike, Bethesda, Maryland 20205, U.S.A.

Patricia Cluss, Department of Psychology, University of Pittsburgh, Pittsburgh, Pennsylvania 15206, U.S.A.

Carl Corter, Department of Psychology, University of Toronto in Mississauga, Mississauga, Ontario L5L 1C6, Canada

Anna-Beth Doyle, Department of Psychology, Concordia University, 1455 de Maisonneuve Boulevard West, Montreal, Quebec H3G 1M8, Canada

Carol O. Eckerman, Department of Psychology, Duke University, Durham, North Carolina 27706, U.S.A.

Connie Elliott, Department of Psychology, University of Waterloo, Waterloo, Ontario N2L 3G1, Canada

Dale F. Hay, Department of Psychology, State University of New York at Stony Brook, Stony Brook, New York 11794, U.S.A.

Ronald Iannotti, Laboratory of Developmental Psychology, National Institute of Mental Health, 9000 Rockville Pike, Bethesda, Maryland 20205, U.S.A.

Linda Rose Krasnor, Child Studies Program, Brock University, St. Catherines, Ontario, L2S 3A1, Canada

Susan P. Lollis, Department of Psychology, University of Waterloo, Waterloo, Ontario N2L 3G1, Canada

Henry Markovits, Department of Psychology, University of Quebec at Montreal, Montreal, Quebec H3C 3P8 Canada

Alison Nash, Department of Psychology, State University of New York at Stony Brook, Stony Brook, New York 11794, U.S.A.

Jan Pedersen, Department of Psychology, State University of New York at Stony Brook, Stony Brook, New York 11794, U.S.A.

Debra Pepler, Department of Psychology, University of Toronto in Mississauga, Mississauga, Ontario L5L 1C6, Canada

Peter D. Renshaw, Riverina College of Advanced Education, School of Education, P.O. Box 588, Wagga Wagga, New South Wales 2650, Australia

Hildy S. Ross, Department of Psychology, University of Waterloo, Waterloo, Ontario N2L 3G1, Canada

Kenneth H. Rubin, Department of Psychology, University of Waterloo, Waterloo, Ontario N2L 3G1, Canada

Robert L. Selman, Laboratory of Human Development, Harvard University, Larson Hall, Appian Way, Cambridge, Massachusetts 02138, U.S.A.

Jacqueline Smollar, Department of Psychology, Catholic University of America, 620 Michigan Avenue N.E., Washington, D.C. 20064, U.S.A.

Mark R. Stein, Department of Psychology, Duke University, Durham, North Carolina 27706, U.S.A.

Carolyn R. Stone, Graduate School of Education, Harvard University, Longfellow Hall, Appian Way, Cambridge, Massachusetts 02138, U.S.A.

F. F. Strayer, Department of Psychology, University of Quebec at Montreal, Montreal, Quebec H3C 3P8, Canada

Deborah Lowe Vandell, Department of Psychology, University of Texas at Dallas, P.O. Box 688, Richardson, Texas 75080, U.S.A.

Kathy Shores Wilson, Department of Psychology, University of Texas at Dallas, P.O. Box 688, Richardson, Texas 75080, U.S.A.

James Youniss, Department of Psychology, Catholic University of America, 620 Michigan Avenue N.E., Washington, D.C. 20064, U.S.A.

Carolyn Zahn-Waxler, Laboratory of Developmental Psychology, National Institute of Mental Health, 9000 Rockville Pike, Bethesda, Maryland 20205, U.S.A.

Introduction

Some Reflections on the State of the Art: The Study of Peer Relationships and Social Skills

Kenneth H. Rubin and Hildy S. Ross

The study of peer relationships and social skills in childhood has, after a lengthy period of relative hibernation, awakened to become, once again, a high-profile area in developmental psychology. During the 1930s and 1940s major theoretical, methodological, and empirical contributions were produced by such figures as G. H. Mead (1934), Piaget (1932), Parten (1932), Moreno (1934), and Lewin and his colleagues (Lewin, Lippitt, & White 1938). Researchers interested in children's peer relationships examined infant-infant interaction (Maudry & Nekula, 1939), social participation (Parten, 1932), and group dynamics (Lewin et al., 1938). Those interested in social skills investigated children's prosocial or sympathetic behaviors (Murphy, 1937), assertiveness and conflict (Dawe, 1934), and the correlates of individual differences in social competence (Jack, 1934; Koch, 1933; Lippitt, 1941; Neugarten, 1946).

In the 1940s, however, the study of peer relationships and social skills in childhood diminished. No doubt, the exigencies of the Second World War contributed to the decline of research in this area. In the 1950s, the Cold War fostered concern about academic prowess. With the launching of Sputnik by the Russians, the pressures to train children to become achievement oriented and skilled in the academic, impersonal domain turned developmental researchers away from their earlier focus on social relations.

In the 1960s, the rediscovery of Piaget led to a further disinclination to study children's peer relationships and social skills. According to many who read Piaget, "le patron" believed that young children are egocentric and that they tend to conceptualize their social worlds in terms of already existing ego-centered schemas. Given the assumption that infants, toddlers, and preschoolers are not socially oriented to begin with, it followed that it would profit us little to study the nature of children's peer relations. After all, children's peer relations and social skills were thought to resemble the Emperor's new clothes!

The sociopolitical "War on Poverty" and the resultant large-scale implementation of Head Start early intervention projects also conspired against the study of peer relations and social skills in the 1960s. The focus of these early intervention programs was clearly cognitive. For example, the cognitively oriented Montessori (1973) curriculum, long ignored for its total deemphasis of social developmental processes, regained high status among psychologists, educators, and parents. There was a proliferation of language (Bereiter & Englemann, 1966; Blank & Solomon, 1968) and cognitively oriented curricula (Kamii & DeVries, 1975; Lavatelli, 1970; Weikart, Rogers, Adcock, & McClelland, 1971), many of which were implemented in classrooms of middle- as well as lower class youngsters! Ironically, many of the cognitively oriented curricula were drawn from Piagetian theory, despite Piaget's premise that cognitive operations could not be taught. Moreover, the language-oriented curricula centered on syntactical and semantic concerns, ignoring the development of pragmatics both because of the concurrent focus in developmental psycholinguistics and because of the Piagetian conception of childhood egocentrism.

The turning point for research concerning peer relationships and social skills in childhood coincided with the publication of the third edition of *Carmichael's Manual of Child Psychology* (Mussen, 1970). In Volume 2 of the *Manual*, Hartup (1970), long the "Lone Ranger" of peer relations, reminded psychologists and educators alike that peers can play significant roles in child development. Hartup urged researchers to examine further the ways in which the peer group influences social, cognitive, and social-cognitive development. He also indicated that developmental data concerning peer relationships and social skills were sorely lacking.

Early in the 1970s, Roff, Sells, and Golden (1972) and Cowen, Pederson, Babigian, Izzo, and Trost (1973) reported that the quality of children's peer relationships is predictive of academic failure, antisocial behavior, and psychopathology in adolescence and adulthood. We came to realize that if children were rejected by their peers they might find school to be an aversive venue. As such, academic performance might suffer because of social rather than cognitive problems.

At about the same time, North American developmental psychologists began to read Piagetian theory and research with a more critical eye. Researchers indicated that young children are socially oriented and that they can communicate effectively on most occasions (Garvey & Hogan, 1973; Mueller, 1972). Infants and toddlers were found to seek social stimulation and to coordinate their interactions (Eckerman, Whatley, & Kutz, 1975; Mueller & Lucas, 1975). Fantasy play with peers, which Piaget considered lacking in adaptive significance, was found to be causally related to social and social-cognitive development (Rosen, 1974; Saltz & Johnson, 1974). Finally, Piaget's (1932) own premise that social-cognitive and social development are aided, in large part, by the young child's opportunities to engage in peer conversation, negotiation, and conflict became the rationale for studying peer relationships and social skills.

We are thus in a period of rapid acceleration of peer-related developmental research. This book represents a "state of the art" picture of the peer relationships and social skills literature as we enter the 1980s. The theoretical and research perspectives that are at the leading edge of the relevant literature are presented. It is our purpose to paint a fairly broad picture of how social skills and peer relationships develop in infancy through early adolescence. Our contributors provide us with a modernistic canvas: infants are drawn as stimulus-seeking characters who both influence and are influenced by their peers; toddlers are portrayed as both sociable and socially skilled; preschoolers and kindergarteners appear as social problem solvers; and older children and adolescents seem to have relatively sophisticated means of thinking about their friends.

Chapter Organization

The individual chapters make many unique empirical and conceptual contributions to the understanding of social skills and human relationships. The papers were brought together with the hope that the collection as a whole would reflect common themes that are significant across the span of childhood, from infancy to adolescence. In addition, it was our intention to include papers that represent both basic and applied research interests. Thus, a wide range of social skills and a variety of relationships among children who differ from one another along numerous dimensions are discussed. Our authors have used many methodological techniques, although, perhaps, the manipulative experimental design is relatively underrepresented.

The book is divided into three major parts. In Part I the authors' predominant concern lies with *social skills*. Specific chapter topics include social influence processes in infants (Hay, Pederson, & Nash, Chapter 1); cooperative play (Eckermen & Stein, Chapter 2) and communication in toddlers (Ross, Lollis, & Elliott, Chapter 3); rules that govern early conflict (Bakeman & Brownlee, Chapter 4); social negotiation and problem solving in preschoolers and school-age children (Krasnor, Chapter 5; Stone & Selman, Chapter 7); and the development of prosocial behavior (Zahn-Waxler, Iannotti, & Chapman, Chapter 6).

In Part II the predominant concern is with *peer relationships*. Authors contrast peer with parent-child relationships (Vandell & Wilson, Chapter 8; Smollar & Youniss, Chapter 12), and peer with sibling relationships (Pepler, Corter, & Abramovitch, Chapter 9; Vandell

& Wilson). Children's interactions with acquaintances, strangers, and friends are compared (Doyle, Chapter 10; Berndt, Chapter 11) and the processes of friendship formation are examined (Doyle; Berndt; Smollar & Youniss).

To some extent, the boundaries dividing Parts I and II are artificial and arbitrary, since in many cases the authors clearly deal with the interface between the two phenomena. For example, there are chapters in which social skills are viewed as developing more efficiently within certain relationships (Pepler, Corter, & Abramovitch; Doyle; Berndt; Smollar & Youniss). In other chapters a variety of relationships are studied in order to understand the sources or generality of social skills (Eckerman & Stein; Vandell & Wilson; Zahn-Waxler, Iannotti, & Chapman). In addition, in one chapter, the modulation of social strategies within different relationships is considered a skill in itself (Krasnor).

Finally, in Part III the authors deal with *individual differences* in peer relationships and social skill. In two cases the authors "target" their different groups by comparing the relationships and skills of children who vary with regard to physical (blind vs. sighted, Markovits & Strayer, Chapter 13) or behavioral (hyperactive vs. normal, Campbell & Cluss, Chapter 14) characteristics. In the remaining two chapters the authors' concern is with the development of social skills in children who differ with respect to the quality of their peer relationships (Rubin, Chapter 15; Renshaw & Asher, Chapter 16).

Some Common Themes

We have been struck, in our reading of these chapters, by both the similarities and differences that seem to exist among them. While our readers will no doubt focus on different issues, we thought that we would highlight some of the common themes.

One issue central to this volume is the conceptualization of social skill. All authors deal with the issue at least implicitly by virtue of the behaviors they choose to assess and the interpretations they offer concerning group or individual differences. One apparent emerging trend is the consideration of social goals or outcomes as essential features of the social skills concept. This theme is apparent in those chapters that deal most explicitly with the concept of social skills (Eckerman & Stein; Krasnor; Renshaw & Asher).

Eckerman and Stein define social skill as an ability to "achieve a variety of important social outcomes in approved ways." They offer a partial list of such outcomes and select one, cooperative play, for further scrutiny. Then they describe a number of particular skills that might further that outcome. One important aspect of Eckerman and Stein's research strategy is that they relate each potential social skill to the hypothesized outcome of cooperative play; thus, they seek validation of individual skills in relation to their social outcomes. Markovits and Strayer adopt a similar tactic in grouping and evaluating behaviors apparently lead to the goal of social cohesion.

Krasnor studies social problem solving, which she defines as "attempts to achieve personal goals within social interactions." She judges apparent goals and strategies from her observations of children interacting in preschool settings. Furthermore, Krasnor views the ability to differentiate both goals and strategies in relation to the physical and social characteristics of the "target" of the problem solving attempt as a skill in and of itself. While other researchers in the present volume document that children's social behaviors vary in different relationships (Berndt; Doyle; Pepler et al.; Vandell & Wilson; Zahn-Waxler et al.), none has taken this further step of viewing differentiation itself as a skill.

Renshaw and Asher consider social goals and strategies as two distinct components of social competence. In their interview procedures they find that children of different ages and social status view different goals as being appropriate in identical social situations. Stone and Selman are also concerned with social goals and strategies; they suggest that children's differing levels of interpersonal understanding predict their negotiation strategies.

Similarity among peers is a second theme that receives wide consideration by nearly all the authors in this volume, and yet it is the central focus of only Doyle's chapter. Recognition that another child somehow is similar to the self purportedly enhances attraction to that peer, increases interaction, and ultimately fosters the development of social skills. Thus, perceived similarity appears to play a significant role in social development.

The roots of perceived similarity may be planted during infancy and toddlerhood. They appear to emanate from early displays of similar behavior, or reciprocity. For example, Hay et al. find some evidence of behavioral reciprocity in both social distress and physical contact among 6-month-olds (but note that Vandell and Wilson do not find evidence of reciprocity in the first year). Ross et al. find similarity in the form and frequency of communicative overtures and responses in toddler dyads. Markovits and Strayer distinguish between behaviors likely to promote reciprocity (cohesive behaviors) and those likely to lead to differentiation (aggressive and competitive activities). The display of reciprocal behaviors in the early years may thus contribute to a sense of "feeling similar" or of "being like" the play partner.

Another contributing variable to the development of perceived similarity is drawn from actual physical or highly observable and salient characteristics of the social partner. Doyle, for example, finds that children evidence more mature social and cognitive play behaviors when they interact with acquaintances or with play partners of similar ethnic background as contrasted with unfamiliar or ethnically different partners.

Pepler et al. discuss similarity briefly with respect to differences in the extent to which children will imitate same-sex versus cross-sex siblings. Again, the source of perceived similarity in early childhood is taken from physical or concrete characteristics of the social partner.

As children grow older, the perception and significance of similarity is reflected in the increasingly abstract ways that they conceive of friendship. Smollar and Youniss report that children between 6 and 10 years of age feel that doing activities together (i.e., engaging in the same activity at the same time) leads to the formation of friendship. During the early teenage years, young adolescents actually suggest that the discovery of similarities between peers would lead to friendship formation. These perceived similarities between friends reported by Smollar and Youniss go hand in hand with Berndt's finding that young adolescent friends make more active attempts than nonfriends to create equality in the distribution of rewards. Moreover, they acknowledge that friends try to create equality (and hence similarity) of outcome.

Taken together, these reports point to the significance of the production of similar behaviors and the perception of similarity from toddlerhood until early adolescence. Several new avenues of research are suggested by this theme of similarity. For example, researchers might evaluate simultaneously the relations between perceived and actual behavioral similarity. Researchers might also manipulate behavioral or physical features of a social situation or, for that matter, of perceived similarity, in attempts to establish their roles as mediators of attraction, interaction, and friendship.

A third issue that permeates this volume concerns the source of social skills. Most of the authors seem to agree that social skills develop within social relationships; they develop first within more intimate relationships, where interaction is more frequent, and then are generalized to less intense relationships. This has led investigators of infant and toddler peer relationships to look, either directly or indirectly, to the mother-infant dyad (Hay et al.; Ross et al.; Vandell & Wilson) or to the sibling dyad (Pepler et al.) as sources of early social skill. Investigators who focus on older dyads consider friendships as the source of generalizable concepts of cooperation, interpersonal sensitivity, and justice (Berndt; Smollar & Youniss; Zahn-Waxler et al.).

Finally, many of the authors argue that social interaction with peers furthers the development of children's social skills (Bakeman & Brownlee; Berndt; Doyle; Eckerman & Stein; Rubin; Smollar & Youniss; Vandell & Wilson). This has led some researchers to be concerned with the fates of children who do not have normal interactive experiences or who are rejected by their peers (Campbell & Cluss; Renshaw & Asher; Rubin). One common intention of the latter group is to identify sources of and actual social skills deficits in order to plan intervention strategies, if required.

In summary, we have collected chapters written by many of the leading figures who study peer relationships and social skills throughout the years of childhood. Over the past decade, their individual contributions have been significant. Collectively, in this volume, their contributions provide the reader with an abundance of unique insights, findings, and suggestions for future research in this growing field of study.

References

Bereiter, C., & Engelmann, S. *Teaching the culturally disadvantaged child in the preschool*. Englewood Cliffs, N.J.: Prentice-Hall, 1966.

Blank, M., & Solomon, F. A tutorial language program to develop abstract thinking in socially disadvantaged children. *Child Development*, 1968, *39*, 379-390.

Cowen, E. L., Pederson, A., Babigian, H., Izzo, L. D., & Trost, M. A. Long-term follow-up of early detected vulnerable children. *Journal of Consulting and Clinical Psychology*, 1943, *41*, 438-446.

Dawe, H. C. Analysis of two hundred quarrels of preschool children. *Child Development*, 1934, *5*, 135-157.

Eckerman, C. O., Whatley, J. L., Kutz, S. L. Growth of social play with peers during the second year of life. *Developmental Psychology*, 1975, *11*, 42-49.

Garvey, C., & Hogan, R. Social speech and social interaction: Egocentrism revisited. *Child Development*, 1973, *44*, 562-568.

Hartup, W. W. Peer interaction and social organization. In P. H. Mussen (Ed.), *Carmichael's manual of child psychology* (Vol. 2). New York: Wiley, 1970.

Jack, L. M. An experimental study of ascendant behavior in preschool children. *University of Iowa Studies in Child Welfare*, 1934, *9*(3), 9-65.

Kamii, C., & DeVries, R. Piaget for early education. In R. Parker (Ed.), *The preschool in action*. Boston: Allyn & Bacon, 1975.

Koch, H. Popularity among preschool children: Some related factors and a technique for its measurement. *Child Development*, 1933, *4*, 164-175.

Lavatelli, C. S. *Piaget's theory applied to an early childhood curriculum*. Boston: American Science and Engineering, 1970.

Lewin, K., Lippitt, R., & White, R. K. Patterns of aggressive behavior in experimentally created "social climates." *Journal of Social Psychology*, 1938, *10*, 271-299.

Lippitt, R. Popularity among preschool children. *Child Development*, 1941, *12*, 305-332.

Maudry, M., & Nekula, M. Social relationships between children of the same age during the first two years of life. *Journal of Genetic Psychology*, 1939, *54*, 193-215.

Mead, G. H. *Mind, self and society*. Chicago: University of Chicago Press, 1934.

Montessori, M. *The Montessori method*. Cambridge, Mass.: Bentley, 1973.

Moreno, J. L. *Who shall survive? A new approach to the problem of human interrelations*. Washington, D.C.: Nervous and Mental Disease Publishing Co., 1934.

Mueller, E. The maintenance of verbal exchanges in young children. *Child Development*, 1972, *43*, 930-938.

Mueller, E., & Lucas, T. A. A developmental analysis of peer interaction among toddlers. In M. Lewis & L. A. Rosenblum (Eds.), *Friendship and peer relations.* New York: Wiley, 1975.

Murphy, L. B. *Social behavior and child psychology: An exploratory study of some roots of sympathy.* New York: Columbia University Press, 1937.

Mussen, P. H. (Ed.). *Carmichael's manual of child psychology* (Vol. 2). New York: Wiley, 1970.

Neugarten, B. Social class and friendship among school children. *American Journal of Sociology*, 1946, *51*, 305-313.

Parten, M. B. Social participation among preschool children. *Journal of Abnormal and Social Psychology*, 1932, *27*, 243-269.

Piaget, J. *The moral judgment of the child.* New York Harcourt Brace, 1932.

Roff, M., Sells, S. B., & Golden, M. M. *Social adjustment and personality development in children.* Minneapolis: University of Minnesota Press, 1972.

Rosen, C. E. The effects of sociodramatic play on problem-solving behavior among culturally disadvantaged preschool children. *Child Development*, 1974, *45*, 920-927.

Saltz, E., & Johnson, J. Training for thematic-fantasy play in culturally disadvantaged children. *Journal of Educational Psychology*, 1974, *66*, 623-630.

Weikart, D., Rogers, L., Adcock, C., & McClelland, D. *The cognitively oriented curriculum: A framework for preschool teachers.* Washington, D.C.: National Association for the Education of Young Children, 1971.

Part I
Social Skills

Chapter 1

Dyadic Interaction in the First Year of Life

Dale F. Hay, Jan Pedersen, and Alison Nash

The purpose of this chapter is to review existing information and to present some new evidence concerning human infants' interactions with other infants during the first year of life. This topic is of interest both for its practical significance and its theoretical import. In contemporary Western societies, early experience with peers can no longer be considered anomalous; day care, playgroup, or nursery school arrangements represent a familiar part of life for increasing numbers of infants and toddlers. Thus it is not surprising that developmental researchers have charted the structure and content of peer interactions in these settings (Field, 1979b; Finkelstein, Dent, Gallacher, & Ramey, 1978; Holmberg, 1980; Field & Roopnarine, Note 1). These naturalistic studies have been supplemented by attempts to specify the determinants of early peer interaction; such experiments have been conducted both in laboratory playrooms (Eckerman & Whatley, 1977; Jacobson, 1981; Vandell, Wilson, & Buchanan, 1980) and under controlled conditions in homes (Becker, 1977). Both types of studies have served to broaden the scope of current accounts of early development and to inform attempts by parents and educators to provide stimulating care for young children.

The study of infants' encounters with peers may also have relevance for more general issues concerning patterns and determinants of human interaction. Social psychological analyses of the interchanges of dyads and groups often seem to rest on the assumption that the actors in question are mature, cognitive organisms who make intentional, rational decisions to interact in certain ways. Much of human interaction is thought to depend not only on the participants' overt acts and responses, but also on the attributions each actor makes about the other's thoughts, intentions, and attitudes, that is, the meaning interactants perceive in their social situations (Brittain, 1973; Kelley, 1971). In the context of such views, what level of interaction would be expected of human infants? Their motoric, verbal, and cognitive limitations might severely

constrain their abilities to interact. For example, for about one-half of
the first year, infants cannot locomote and thus cannot exert direct
control over their locations in space. Throughout the first year, they
typically cannot speak; they do not even begin to use symbolic gestures
such as pointing until shortly before the first birthday. Their understanding of causal relationships is deficient, which may impede their
perception of connections between their own actions and those of their
peers. Only late in the first year do infants show the ability to use
varying means to obtain particular ends, and only then does their
behavior betray at least a rudimentary social intentionality.

Despite these limitations, however, infants characteristically engage
in harmonious interaction with adult caregivers; adult-infant exchanges
resemble the dialogues of older persons (for reviews see Cappella, 1981;
Schaffer, 1978). These interactions probably proceed so smoothly
because the adults involved play one-and-a-half roles per interchange;
they treat the infants as if the infants truly were responsive partners, and they interpret the infants' actions in terms of the concepts of
adult social life. What the interaction engaged in by two infants left to
their own devices might be like is quite another question. Such an
interaction might be random; it might resemble an encounter between
adults or older children; or it might follow primitive rules of its own.

In this chapter we attempt to explore the question of what infants'
interactions with peers are like, both by examining some existing
studies of peer relations in the first year of life and by reporting some
observations we have made of infants at the midpoint of that year,
when the capacity for interaction is first emerging. Our review is
restricted to studies that have tested infants 12 months of age or
younger; in some cases the infants concerned represent the youngest
age group in a cross-sectional study of toddlers' peer relations. Both in
reviewing the literature and in analyzing our own findings, we do not
describe encounters among more than two infants; rather, at the level
of dyadic interaction, we have sought answers to two general questions.
First, to what extent does the presence and activity of one infant
influence the behavior of a peer? Second, what factors facilitate or
constrain the extent of mutual influence between young peers?

Analyses of Influence Between Infant Peers

The concept of social influence is central to any discussion of early peer
interaction. Ever since Parten (1932) introduced the term "parallel
play" into the vocabulary of developmental psychologists, investigators
of social development have been at pains to determine whether or not
infants ever "truly interact," that is, whether they influence and are

influenced by other infants. Social influence, however, can be defined and recorded in various ways. Influence between two individuals can be described quantitatively or qualitatively, with respect to relatively short or relatively long time periods. We cannot ask infants directly if they are being swayed by the behavior of their peers, but rather must specify some criteria on which to base such an inference. Such criteria include topographical similarities, temporal contiguities, and statistical dependencies in the behaviors shown by two infants. In addition, an investigator may wish to determine whether the direction of influence is positive or negative, that is, whether the behaviors of one infant facilitate or inhibit the peer's responding, and whether the influence is direct or indirect (channeled through the agency of some third party). Conclusions regarding the extent and nature of peer influence in infancy obviously depend on the definitions and measurement techniques used to assess its occurrence. Thus we review studies of infants' interaction with peers with respect to the ways in which the occurrence of social influence was determined. We discuss some of the definitional issues raised by this review and describe some developmental trends that emerge in these studies.

Effects of the Presence and Actions of Infants on Peers

Early Responsiveness

Long before infants are capable of making deliberate overtures to their peers, they may respond to the general presence of other infants in more diffuse ways, as documented by researchers who observed infants reared in institutions in the company of other infants (Bridges, 1933; Bühler, 1935). For example, Bridges contended that even 2-month-old infants would attend to the movements of a peer in the next crib, but only 4- or 5-month-olds would react to a peer's vocalizations. In contrast, Bühler reported that the 4- and 5-month-old infants she observed were fairly oblivious to each other's presence, but that 6-month-olds actively solicited peer interaction.

More recently, the responsiveness of very young home-reared infants to peers, in contrast to other social stimuli, was assessed under controlled conditions. Fogel (1979) observed infants between the ages of 5 and 14 weeks who were tested under three conditions: when they were alone, while their mothers approached them, and while their mothers held them, facing another mother and infant. A variety of molecular measures of the infants' facial expression and gaze, arm and leg movements, and body postures were recorded in all three conditions. The first 10 seconds following each infant's first look at the mother or peer were examined in detail, in an effort to describe greeting responses. Discriminant analyses indicated that, when alone, infants were likely to show a relaxed, receptive posture; when the mother approached they were likely to smile, gesture, raise their eyebrows, and stick out their tongues; and when they were observed in the presence of another infant, they were likely to stare and strain forward, as if "to get a closer look at the other infant" (p. 220). During their second looks at the peers, infants were also likely to show abrupt head and arm movements, which Fogel suggested had "the quality of almost uncontrolled excitement" (p. 224). Thus, the infants' general level of activity and the specific locus and form of their actions appeared to differ among the three conditions.

In a similar study, Field (1979a) compared the reactions of 3-month-old infants to peers and to their own mirror images. The infants looked longer at themselves than at their peers, but were more likely to smile, vocalize, reach toward, and squirm when tested with peers than while looking in the mirror. (Girls were more likely than boys to smile and vocalize, whereas boys were more likely than girls to squirm). When compared with baseline levels, the infants' heart rate decreased significantly when they saw their own mirror images but increased when they saw their peers.

Peer-Directed Activity

Definitional issues. Somewhat older infants enact distinctive social behaviors in the presence of their peers; they show distal actions, such as smiles and vocalizations, and also contact their peers directly, by touching them, leaning on them, pulling their hair, etc. (Becker, 1977; Jacobson, 1981; Maudry & Nekula, 1939; Vandell et al., 1980). Some investigators have not considered such acts to be peer directed unless they are accompanied by visual gaze (Eckerman & Whatley, 1977; Jacobson, 1981; Vandell et al., 1980), whereas in other cases "chance contacts" have been differentiated from peer-directed actions on more subjective grounds (Maudry & Nekula, 1939). However, even when the more objective criterion is used, visual regard alone is not always sufficient for an act to be categorized as socially directed (as when an infant mouths a toy while watching the peer, as described by Vandell et al., 1980), and thus intuitive judgments are still being made. Given the problems inherent in assessing the intentions of preverbal infants, we find it preferable to view such actions as discrete indexes of the influence of a peer's presence; they may not necessarily qualify as purposive social acts. By enacting conventional social behaviors in the presence of peers, infants indicate that they recognize their peers as human beings. It is in this sense that we view these behaviors as social. However, to be consistent with the terminology used in the studies we are reviewing, we label such behaviors peer directed.

In addition to the differing criteria for labeling infants' actions as peer directed, comparison across studies is also rendered difficult by the fact that different investigators have used different units of analysis in recording these actions. Some have used fixed-interval time sampling procedures (e.g., Eckerman & Whatley, 1977; Field, 1979b), whereas others have tried to transcribe infants' actions into natural units (e.g., Becker, 1977; Maudry & Nekula, 1939). Similarly, the range of possible behavioral categories has differed greatly from study to study.

Developmental course of peer-directed behavior. Analyses of peer encounters in the second half of the first year have documented a number of developmental changes in peer-directed actions within this time period. In general, such actions are shown at a higher rate by older infants. In a classic, cross-sectional study of infants who were being temporarily cared for in institutions, Maudry and Nekula (1939) charted infants' reactions to being placed in a playpen with another infant. The behaviors shown by a group of target infants were summed across a number of encounters with different partners. The resulting records were divided into "impulses" on the part of each infant, defined as "items of behavior that show the same social tendency" (p. 204). Infants between 9 and 13 months of age showed a greater number of peer-directed impulses than did infants between 6 and 8 months, a total of 4106 versus 1092. More recently, Jacobson (1981), who observed pairs of home-reared infants at 10, 12, and 14½ months of age in free-play sessions in the laboratory, reported that the rate per minute of peer-directed behaviors increased linearly from 2.0 at 10 months to 3.8 at 14½ months.

Qualitative changes in peer-directed behavior over this period of time have been identified as well. For example, Vandell and her colleagues (Vandell, 1980; Vandell et al., 1980) observed the same pairs of first-born infants at 6, 9, and 12 months of age in free-play sessions. Across the entire age range, the most common type of socially directed act recorded was vocalization, followed by smiling at and touching the peer; vocalizations were reliably more frequent than any other type of act except for smiles. The frequency of approaching the peer increased with age, which is not surprising, given that many infants first begin to locomote during this time period; however, touching the peer declined in frequency during this time period. This finding might imply that a developmental shift from proximal to distal overtures to peers occurs around the end of the first year of life. However, evidence for such a shift is equivocal. Some investigators reported a continued decline in physical contact of peers following the first birthday (Bronson, 1981; Brooks-Gunn & Lewis, 1979; Finkelstein et al., 1978); in contrast, two cross-sectional comparisons of pairs of 12-month-olds with pairs of 24-month-olds did not detect reliable differences in the extent of physical contact of peers between these age groups (Eckerman & Whatley, 1977; Eckerman, Whatley, & Kutz, 1975). Furthermore, two groups of infants observed for several months showed more physical contact at the end of the observation period than at the beginning (Field, 1979b; Field & Roopnarine, Note 1). Thus, definitive evidence for a shift in the proximal versus distal mode of peer-directed behavior has not been obtained.

In general, it would seem from the lists of behavioral categories used in studies of infant peer relations that investigators have tried to identify actions shown by infants that resemble components of adult interaction. Hence, some attempts have been made to differentiate early forms of prosocial and antisocial overtures (Holmberg, 1980; Maudry & Nekula, 1939; Vandell et al., 1980). Such judgments have of course been made in terms of the form and consequences of the acts in question, not the intent of their agents. In keeping with this limitation, however, developmental changes in the "positive" or "negative" tone of peer-directed acts have been explored. For example, Maudry and Nekula (1939) noted that only 18% of the first reactions of 6- to 8-month-olds to being placed in playpens with their peers were directed to the peers themselves, but 87% of those were deemed to be positive in tone. About the same proportion of the initial reactions of 9- to 13-month-olds were directed explicitly to their peers, but only 54% of those were judged to be positive. Parallel results were obtained when the "impulses" throughout each trial, following the infants' first reactions, were categorized: 64% of the impulses of the 6- to 8-month-olds and 51% of those of the 9- to 13-month-olds were classed as positive. Taken together with the findings of studies in which 12-month-olds as well as older toddlers were observed (Bronson, 1981; Holmberg, 1980), these data suggest that a negative orientation to peers is not present at the outset, when peer-directed actions first begin to appear; rather, agonistic actions become more frequent toward the end of the first year (although they may still be primarily exploratory in nature) and continue to be demonstrated during the second.

In addition to the changes in the frequency and content of peer-directed acts over the course of the first year, there are corresponding changes in their structural complexity; as infants tested at 6, 9, and 12 months of age grew older, they were more likely to direct a combination of acts synchronously to the peers, for example, smiling at and gesturing toward their peers simultaneously (Vandell et al., 1980). In addition, the proportion of acts that adult observers judge to be intentional appears to increase with age. In Maudry and Nekula's (1939) sample, in absolute terms, 9- to 13-month-old infants showed more impulses that were categorized as "chance contact and interference without social intention" than did 6- to 8-month-olds (730 vs. 310 impulses being so categorized). However, chance contacts occurred *relatively* more often in the younger group, comprising 30% of their impulses, as opposed to 18% of those shown by 9- to 13-month-olds.

Occurrence of Interaction

Definitional issues. Some investigators of early peer relations have attempted not simply to describe behaviors evoked in the presence of peers, but to document the occurrence of patterned interaction between infants. In order to interact, infants must not only notice the general existence of other infants, but must adjust their behaviors—in terms of their content, frequency, duration, and distribution in time—in coordination with their peers' actions. Their ability to do so would imply the existence of more advanced social skills than simple recognition of each other as conspecifics. Thus it is important for investigators of infants' peer encounters to specify criteria for determining when interaction is taking place.

A number of methodological approaches have been taken to this problem. At an individual level of analysis, the interactive behaviors of particular infants (such as attempts to duplicate the peer's behavior or alternate one's actions with those of the peer) have been recorded, along with other forms of peer-directed actions (Eckerman & Whatley, 1977; Eckerman et al., 1975; Field, 1979b; Field & Roopnarine, Note 1). More commonly; however, the temporal and thematic relations between two infants' actions have been explored at a dyadic level of analysis, either by examining particular interactive episodes that resemble traditional categories of human interaction, such as conflicts or games (Brenner & Mueller, in press; Goldman & Ross, 1978; Maudry & Nekula, 1939), or by recording any of a variety of responses made by one infant within a certain time limit following another infant's actions (Becker, 1977; Finkelstein et al., 1978; Holmberg, 1980; Vandell et al., 1980). When the latter procedure has been used, the criterion time intervals have been 5 seconds (Finkelstein et al., 1978; Vandell et al., 1980), 8 seconds (Becker, 1977), and 10 seconds (Bronson, 1981; Holmberg, 1980). In only one case was the criterion interval chosen for theoretical reasons: Finkelstein et al. (1978) noted that their previous work on infants' contingency learning had indicated that infants themselves would not be likely to perceive a connection between two events separated by more than 5 seconds.

Interchanges identified on the basis of the temporal contiguity of two infants' actions have been further differentiated in terms of their complexity, intentionality, and meaning to adult observers and the infants themselves. With respect to the complexity of interchanges, Holmberg (1980) distinguished between simple interchanges (single action-reaction sequences) and elaborated ones (in which each partner took at least two turns, with the added requirement that the form of each infant's action vary from turn to turn; simple repetition of one's initial action would not suffice). With respect to the apparent intentionality of interchanges, each component of a sequence might or might not qualify as socially directed. For example, Vandell et al. (1980) noted that a socially directed behavior (i.e., one accompanied by visual regard of the peer) might be followed by an undifferentiated reaction by the peer; conversely, a socially oblivious action by one infant might evoke a socially directed response from the peer. In yet a third situation, a nonsocial act by one infant might be followed by a nonsocial act by the peer, within the designated time limit. Of course, under some circumstances, the latter pattern might still indicate a behavioral contingency in the actions of two infants, but only if the incidence of this pattern of actions exceeded that expected on the basis of chance alone. However, in Vandell's study (as in the others reviewed here), tests against a null hypothesis of random associations between actions or against autocorrelations of each individual's actions were not conducted. In view of the reliance on temporal contiguity to identify the occurrence of interaction, only those interchanges composed of at least one socially directed action of one infant followed by a socially directed response from the peer were considered instances of "true social interaction." In a similar analysis, Becker (1977) distinguished between simple action-reaction sequences and ones in which social actions were both stimulated and followed by the peer's behavior (i.e., were composed of at least three moves).

Finally, with respect to the thematic as well as temporal connection between the actions of two infants, Bronson (1981), who observed children longitudinally beginning at the age of 12 months, differentiated between "contact bursts," which met a temporal criterion but made little sense to adult observers, and "contact chains," which were judged to be thematically as well as temporally coordinated; only the latter qualified as "true" social interaction. This distinction is problematic; even adults interpret their own actions differently from the ones they watch other people perform (Jones & Nisbett, 1971), and thus it is possible that participants in contact bursts see connections in their actions that are not apparent to adult observers. A similar, but somewhat less restrictive, approach was taken by Brenner and Mueller (in press), who examined the content of action-reaction sequences. These sequences had already been judged to be temporally related and composed of socially directed actions by both partners. Each partner's role in these sequences was then classified with respect to a number of culturally recognizable themes such as "peek-a-boo" or "rough-and-tumble play." This analysis suggested that the structure and content of infants' interactions are separable phenomena; in more than one-half of the cases when one infant's act illustrated a certain theme, the partner's action expressed a quite different meaning or no meaning that was intelligible at all to the adult observers.

In view of the different assessment procedures and criteria for determining whether an interaction has taken place between two infants, as well as differences in the settings and characteristics of the samples tested, it is not surprising that the probability than an infant will enter into interaction in response to a peer's overture varies considerably from study to study (Table 1-1). There are some indications that the probability of a peer's response is a function of the content and complexity of the initiation. In a study of infants and toddlers in a day care center, the conditional probability of reacting to the peer's vocalization was .38, whereas the conditional probability of reacting to the peer's touch was only .01 (Finkelstein et al., 1978). In a study of pairs of 9-month-olds playing together in their homes, the probability that the peer would respond increased as a function of the number of components of behavior comprising the initiation, from .24 for initiations with a single component to .77 for initiations with four components (Becker, 1977).

Developmental course of peer interaction. The evidence for developmental change over the second half of the first year of life in the overall frequency with which infants respond to their peers' overtures is equivocal. In Maudry and Nekula's (1939) cross-sectional study, 56% of the 6- to 8-month-olds and 64% of the 9- to 13-month-olds responded to their peers' "social impulses"; 15% of the failures to react in both groups were judged to be due to the recipient's being engrossed in the play material. Among the pairs of infants observed by Vandell and her colleagues (1980) at 6, 9, and 12 months, the most common type of action-reaction sequence recorded at all ages (48% of all sequences) was that composed of a socially directed action followed by a socially directed reaction, the type described as being truly interactive. Neither the frequency nor the duration of interaction, nor the proportion of all sequences that contained three or more separate actions, increased reliably as the infants grew older. In contrast, Jacobson (1981) obtained evidence for reliably increased responsivity to peers over the last couple of months of the first year; infants who, on the average, had responded

Table 1-1. Percentages of Peers' Initiations Responded to by Infants

Investigators	Infants' ages (months)	Setting	Criterion interval (seconds)	%
Becker, 1977	9	Homes	8	67
Finkelstein et al., 1978	7-14	Day care	5	12
Holmberg, 1980	12	Day care	10	51
Jacobson, 1981	10	Laboratory	5	37
	12	Laboratory	5	52
Maudry & Nekula, 1939	6-8	Playpens	Not specified	56
	9-13	Playpens	Not specified	64

to 37% of the peers' overtures at 10 months responded to 52% when they were tested again at 12 months.

It is possible that infants' interactions with peers change qualitatively as well as quantitatively over this period of time. Maudry and Nekula (1939) examined two types of dyadic interchanges: games, which were defined as "the total of at least two impulses through which the same activity or activity with the same object is carried out by both children," and fights, defined as "the total of at least two impulses of negative social behavior" (pp. 209-210). This comparison extended their earlier analyses of the positive versus negative tone of particular peer-directed actions to the level of dyadic interaction. Fights occurred more frequently than games among both the 6- to 8-month-olds and the 9- to 13-month-olds (the rates per 10 minutes being 0.7 for games vs. 3.2 for fights in the younger group and 0.8 vs. 3.8 in the older group). Fights were more likely than games to be sustained across several impulses by each partner; however, the tendency to sustain both types of interchange was somewhat greater for the older infants.

Maudry and Nekula hastened to remark that the majority of these "fights" could not be viewed as deliberate, hostile acts of aggression; rather, the majority were described as "blind," in the sense that the infants seemed to stumble into conflicts in the course of playing near each other or seeking access to the same objects. Of the fights and games engaged in by the 6- to 8-month-olds, 90% and 100%, respectively, were classified as "blind." Most of the fights of the 9- to 13-month-olds were similarly classified; however, 34% of their games were judged to be "personal," encounters in which infants tried "to influence directly the partner's behavior, and modify their own reactions in order to have a mutual play situation" (p. 211). These findings suggest that the most important change over the first year is not in the incidence of interchanges that resemble games or fights, but in the extent to which such interchanges are sustained over time and in the growing intentionality and mutual awareness of the participants.

Developmental changes in both "positive" and "negative" interactions may depend to a large extent upon corresponding changes in infants' basic abilities to use objects as vehicles for interaction. The use of objects in the course of peer-directed activities increases between 6 and 9 months of age (Vandell et al., 1980) and seems to remain at a steady level throughout the rest of the first year; 9- or 10-month-olds and 12-month-olds seem about equally likely to incorporate objects into interaction with their peers (Jacobson, 1981; Vandell et al., 1980).

Summary

The preceding review suggests that infants under the age of 12 months are influenced by the general presence and particular actions of their peers. Distinctive social actions with peers first emerge around the midpoint of the first year. Both discrete peer-directed acts and the interchanges they comprise appear to change in form, number, and structural complexity during the succeeding months. In our own research (Hay, Nash, & Pedersen, 1981, Note 2) we have chosen to focus more intensively on the point at which this process begins, when infants are around 6 months of age. Our findings complement the data provided by previous studies; they also provide an illustrative example of ways in which social influence between infants can be examined at different levels of analysis and with respect to different theoretical questions. In particular, we have sought to chart interaction between previously unacquainted infant peers by examining statistical dependencies as well as topographical similarities and temporal contiguities in their behavior. Furthermore, we have tried to examine the content of infants' interchanges from the perspective of the adult social world.

Social Influence Between Six-Month-Old Peers

The preceding review suggests that infants under the age of 12 months are influenced by the general presence and particular actions of their peers. Distinctive social actions with peers first emerge around the midpoint of the first year. Both discrete peer-directed acts and the interchanges they comprise appear to change in form, number, and structural complexity during the succeeding months. In our own research (Hay, Nash, & Pedersen, 1981; Hay, Nash, & Pedersen, Note 2), we have chosen to focus more intensively on the point at which this process begins, when infants are around 6 months of age. In particular, we sought to chart interaction between previously unacquainted infant peers by examining statistical dependencies as well as topographical similarities and temporal contiguities in their behavior. Furthermore, we have tried to examine the content of infants' interchanges from the perspective of the adult social world.

We observed 12 pairs of 6-month-old infants who met for the first time in the presence of their mothers in a small, carpeted, brightly decorated playroom. The infants were observed during two 10-minute trials, in one of which several toys were present. The mothers had been instructed to chat together, responding to their infants' overtures, but not interfering with what the infants were doing except to prevent possible injury. If infants became distressed, the mothers were to comfort them in any way they naturally would.

Rather than searching blindly for all possible connections between two infants' behaviors, we simply asked how infants would respond when their peers engaged in either of two restricted classes of action: (1) a distal action, namely, the production of distressed vocalizations, and (2) a proximal action whereby one infant directly impinges on the other, namely, physical contact of the peer. Examination of these two behavior classes gave us opportunities to study influence between infant peers at several levels of analysis. Hence our findings illustrate a number of different techniques for determining that one infant has influenced the other. At the same time, both distress and physical contact of peers are of theoretical interest, insofar as they are analogous (if not homologous) to ways in which older individuals influence their companions. Affective displays, such as cries of sorrow or pain, and direct bids for intimacy, such as placing one's hand on a companion's arm or bestowing a kiss in greeting, are difficult for adults to ignore; are they salient for infants as well? Furthermore, an adult's reactions to such behaviors are governed by verbal norms and sanctions, which may possibly rest on more primitive, nonverbal response tendencies. By examining infants' responses to these two behaviors, we can determine not simply whether 6-month-olds can interact at all, but whether at this early age, when responsivity to peers is first emerging, they respond in consistent ways to these two common social dilemmas.

Reactions to a Peer's Distress

The direction of social influence can be positive or negative. Dependencies in the behaviors of two persons can theoretically take the form of matching, when an increase in one actor's behavior is paralleled by a corresponding increase in the equivalent behavior of the partner, or compensation, when an increase in the first actor's behavior is associated with a decrease in the partner's (Cappella, 1981). There were some indications in the literature on infant development that two infants might match each other in the extent to which they produced distressed vocalizations, both in the form of anecdotal reports (Darwin, 1877; Preyer, 1889) and experimental studies of newborns' reactions to tape-recorded cries (Sagi & Hoffman, 1976; Simner, 1971). Pilot observations in our laboratory had indicated that the 6-month-olds we observed might periodically start to fuss or cry, thus affording opportunities to measure their peers' reactions.

Distressed vocalizations, defined as sounds ranging from whimpers to loud, sustained wailing, were recorded from video tapes, using a continuous time sampling procedure based on 5-second time units. The impact of one infant's distress on the peer's likelihood of becoming distressed as well was examined both at a molar level of analysis (over the course of a 10-minute trial) and a more molecular one (at the exact time a distressed vocalizations occurred). No evidence for social influence was found at either level of analysis using conventional techniques. The frequency or extent of one infant's distress would not be predicted reliably (through intraclass correlations) from the peer's corresponding tendencies; the probability that an infant could fuss or cry within a given trial or, more stringently, within a given 5-second interval of a trial, was statistically independent of the peer's tendency to do so. Analysis of the transition probabilities of distress from interval to interval similarly did not indicate dependencies.

We reasoned, however, that an infant's distress might have cumulative effects on the peer that are not easily detected by the conventional interval-by-interval analyses. Such effects were apparent when toys were absent, when, on the average, in the six dyads where both infants eventually showed distress, the first infant to do so had cried during a reliably greater proportion of intervals than had the only infant to become distressed in five other dyads. More molecular analyses of the records of those 11 dyads in that trial indicated that the conditional probability for the second infant to become distressed in a given 5-second interval, given that the first infant had been distressed during *none* of the prceding k intervals, as k increased from 1 to 29, hovered around the level expected by chance alone ($p = .02$). In contrast, the conditional probability that the second infant would be distressed in a certain interval, given that the first infant had fussed or cried during *all* of the preceding k intervals, increased as the value of k increased, from $p = .04$ when $k = 1$ to $p = 1.00$ when $k = 28$. In other words, if the first infant fussed or cried long enough, the second infant would show distress as well. Thus social influence at this distal level did not take the form of precise matching of the extent or frequency of the peer's distress; rather, a cumulative pattern of influence was observed.

Physical Intimacy Between Infant Peers

We had expected to find some degree of matching in the distress of two infants; in contrast, we expected that compensation might occur when one infant touched the other. Adults have been characterized as abiding by an "equilibrium level" (Argyle & Dean, 1965) in their proximal interactions: When one adult draws closer to a new acquaintance, the latter is likely to withdraw, thus adjusting their degree of proximity back to equilibrium (for a review see Cappella, 1981). It is possible that the tendency to maintain a limited degree of intimacy with one's companions is already present when infants first begin to meet new peers. Thus we asked what would happen when one member of a dyad reached out and touched the partner. Would the peer respond by reciprocating, that is, touching the initiator in turn, and thus prolonging the contact? Or would the peer, as an adult would probably do, withdraw from contact and thus restore the level of intimacy back to equilibrium? Physical contact is a fairly common component of young infants' interactions with peers (Finkelstein et al., 1978; Vandell et al., 1980); however, it is not clear whether infants react in any consistent ways to these early bouts of contact. Finkelstein and his colleagues (1978) reported that physical contact was relatively ineffective in inducing a response from the peer; however, that observation was based on a combined sample of infants and older children.

Observers transcribed episodes of physical contact between the infants from videotaped records. Episodes were judged to begin when an infant touched the other and to end with the last contact by either partner that preceded a 5-second period in which no touching occurred. Each episode was subdivided into discrete bouts of touching separated by less than 5 seconds. This metric was then used to determine whether the initiator's touch had been reciprocated at any point in the episode and whether the initiator continued to touch the recipient after the first bout. In addition, the recipient's first reaction to being touched (i.e., the response to the first bout of touching in each episode) was classified as either passive responding (simply looking, smiling, and/or vocalizing), compensation (fussing or withdrawing physically), or reciprocation (reaching towards or touching the initiator in turn). Evidence for social influence was sought at three levels of analysis: within episodes, from episode to episode, and over the course of a trial.

Of 148 episodes initiated by a single infant, 27% contained reciprocation by the peer at some point in their course. Infants responded actively to the initiator's first touch on less than half the occasions; however, if they responded at all actively, they were reliably more likely to reach for or touch the initiator than to fuss or shrink away from contact. Within episodes, the peer's reaction to the initiator's first touch appeared to serve as feedback that influenced the initiator's subsequent behavior. When the recipient touched back, the initiator was about equally likely to continue touching or not; when the recipient did *not* touch back, the initiator was reliably less likely to continue.

A similar type of influence was seen from episode to episode. An infant who initiated one episode of peer contact was not reliably more likely than the recipient of that episode to initiate the next. However, *not* reacting in the course of one episode seemed to inhibit one's subsequent behavior. Infants who had not reciprocated their peers' overtures in one episode were reliably less likely than not to initiate the next.

Influence across the trial as a whole seemed situationally determined. We asked whether members of a given dyad were more similar to each other in the extent to which they initiated and reciprocated contact than they were to members of other dyads. Intraclass correlations for initiation and reciprocation of contact were reliable only in the trial in which toys were present.

Interrelations Between Peer Contact and the Peer's Distress

It is evident that a certain degree of influence between young peers occurs within each of the behavioral domains we have considered. To what extent is there influence that spans the two domains? That is, is there a relationship between one infant's production of distressed vocalizations and the peer's participation in episodes of physical contact? Because distress occurred infrequently in the trial when toys were present, we examined the relationship solely in the trial in which toys were absent. In that trial, infants were no more or less likely to be engaged in an episode of peer contact when one or both of them were distressed than when neither was distressed. The observed joint probability of distress and peer contact occurring simultaneously within a given 5-second interval of the trial was virtually the same as that expected by chance, $p = .03$ and $p = .04$, respectively. However, at a more molar level of analysis, and one focusing on individuals rather than on dyads, some evidence for social influence was obtained. The frequency with which infants initiated contact episodes was not reliably affected by whether they themselves were in distress, $r = -.04$, but *was* negatively related to the extent of their peers' distress, $r = -.45$, $p < .02$. This relationship remained the same even when the effect of the distressed infant's being held by the mother (and thus possibly out of the peer's reach) was controlled for.

Summary

The preceding analyses suggest that even 6-month-old infants, at least on occasion, are influenced by the distal and proximal actions of their peers. Our findings have extended previous observations of this age group (Maudry & Nekula, 1939; Vandell et al., 1980; Vandell et al., 1981) by demonstrating statistical dependencies as well as temporal contiguities in the actions of infant dyads. Furthermore, they underscore the fact that the extent of influence between young peers is not a unitary question; whether two infants will be said to be influencing each other's behavior will depend on the time frame used, the molecular or molar nature of the behavioral categories in question, whether the actions are characteristic of individuals or dyads, and whether inhibitory as well as facilitatory influence is being recorded. The second general question that we would like to raise concerns the factors that promote interaction among young peers. Here we discuss some potential determinants of early interaction and speculate about some other variables that may mediate their effects.

Constraints on Early Peer Interaction

Demographic, Experiential, and Situational Determinants

A search for possible determinants of the frequency and extent of infants' responsiveness to peers has been included in most studies of peer relations in the first year of life. Both internal and external, historical and immediate factors have been studied, and their effects have been examined both with respect to the acts of individual infants and the interchanges of dyads. The findings that have emerged from these studies can be summarized as follows (see Field & Roopnarine, Note 1, for another comprehensive review).

Subject Characteristics

Most investigators of early peer relations have reported considerable variability among individual infants and dyads they have tested; however, these individual differences cannot be accounted for completely in terms of the demographic characteristics of the infants. Information about the effects of gender and socioeconomic status on peer interaction in early life is inconclusive. Of 11 experimental or controlled observational studies of infants 12 months of age and younger (Becker, 1977; Brooks-Gunn & Lewis, 1979; Eckerman & Whatley, 1977; Eckerman et al., 1975; Field, 1979b; Finkelstein et al., 1978; Holmberg, 1980; Jacobson, 1981; Vandell, 1980; Vandell et al., 1980; Young & Lewis, 1979), only 1 reported main effects of the infants' gender: Jacobson (1981) observed girls to direct behavior to peers at a higher rate than did boys and to engage in more short interchanges than did boys. In 1 other study an interaction between gender and one other variable, maternal presence, was obtained (Field, 1979b). With respect to the socioeconomic status of the infants in these studies, peer-directed behavior has been recorded among infants from middle-class (Becker, 1977; Brooks-Gunn & Lewis, 1979; Eckerman & Whatley, 1977; Eckerman et al., 1975; Holmberg, 1980; Vandell, 1980; Vandell et al., 1980) and lower class (Becker, 1977; Finkelstein et al., 1978; Holmberg, 1980; Maudry & Nekula, 1939) backgrounds; however, no direct tests of the effect of socioeconomic status on peer interaction were reported in the studies reviewed here.

The subject variable that has been found to be most clearly associated with infants' interaction with peers is, not surprisingly, birth order. Birth order, of course, is a multifaceted variable that indexes the time in a family's development at which an individual is born, the type of relationship that child has with parents who may have more or less time to interact, and the opportunity to spend time with siblings, among other things. It seems, however, that the critical component of birth order with respect to early peer interaction is sibling experience. Vandell et al. (1981) compared the peer-directed behavior of previously unacquainted second-born infants who had preschool siblings with two groups of first-born infants: those who had frequent experience with preschool-age children and those who had only rarely interacted with preschoolers. (This comparison is somewhat problematic, in that the first- and second-born infants were drawn from different cohorts). The infants were observed at both 6 and 9 months of age. Differences among these groups were not observed at 6 months, but at 9 months first-borns with infrequent experience with preschoolers were more likely than infants in either of the other groups to show both simple and coordinated peer-directed acts and thereby to initiate interaction. Both groups of first-borns were more likely than second-borns to use objects socially. At a dyadic level of analysis, four different types of dyads were compared: those composed of two first-borns with infrequent experience with preschoolers, two first-borns who frequently interacted with preschoolers, two first-borns with differing experience in this regard, and two second-borns. Experience with preschoolers either in or out of the home again appeared to suppress infants' overtures to other infants: dyads in which one or both infants had not often met preschoolers engaged in more frequent interaction than the other two groups.

Despite the problem of possible cohort differences, these data call into question the generality of the findings of previous studies in which only first-borns were tested (Becker, 1977; Field, 1979b; Vandell, 1980; Young & Lewis, 1979). Furthermore, some of the prevalent individual differences observed in studies of early peer relations may be attributable to differing levels of experience with older children, including siblings. It is interesting to speculate, however, about what precise mechanisms account for the suppression effect. Do second-born infants have particularly punitive experiences when trying to interact with their older brothers and sisters? The fact that these differences appear at 9 months, when infants are beginning to locomote and investigate their siblings' possessions, gives credence to this possibility. However, it is also possible that infants might respond differently to their peers if they were tested in the presence of their siblings. The presence of preschool-age siblings facilitates infants' exploration of the physical world (Samuels, 1980), and might encourage them to investigate the social world as well.

Prior Peer Experience

Effects of prior experiences on interaction with new acquaintances. Experience with children of preschool age seems to depress infants' tendencies to interact with new infant acquaintances; would experience with children closer in age to the infants themselves do likewise? Vandell et al. (1981) also examined the interactive behavior of infants, tested at 6 and then again at 9 months of age, who had had prior experience either with toddlers or with other infants. Effects of experience with toddlers were found at the 9-month, not the 6-month, assessment, and paralleled the effects found for experience with preschoolers: both first- and second-born infants who had frequently interacted with toddlers were less likely to interact with the infants with whom they were tested. In contrast, prior experience with other infants did not have any effects on the infants' interaction at 9 months of age, and prior experience with agemates facilitated 6-month-old infants' interaction with new peers. On the average, 6-month-olds who had frequently met other infants succeeded in almost one-half (43%) of the initiations they made to peers in the test sessions, but 6-month-olds who had only rarely met infants succeeded in engaging peers in interaction only 25% of the time.

Effects of acquaintance between particular partners. One likely determinant of the extent and nature of social influence between persons would seem to be the extent of prior acquaintance that exists between two interacting partners. Young and Lewis (1979) studied a group of eight 12-month-old infants who each played consistently with another child, ranging anywhere from 7 to 22 months of age; the target infants were observed with their familiar partners and with unfamiliar peers who were matched on several characteristics to the usual partners. In both cases the infants were observed first when their mothers were attending to them and second when the mothers busied themselves reading magazines. The data were analyzed nonparametrically and separately by trial, and thus no main effects of familiarity across situations were reported. When mothers were watching, the 12-month-olds were more likely to contact and stay in proximity to familiar peers than unfamiliar children; however, when mothers were inattentive, the 12-month-olds were more likely to contact (with parts of their bodies other than their hands) unfamiliar peers. Although maternal attentiveness was confounded with order and length of trial, and thus these findings must be interpreted with caution, they raise an important point: in studies of increasing familiarity between infants, mothers are becoming acquainted as well. Their degree of acquaintance, at least when they are watching their infants closely, may mediate the extent of contact between infants.

More recently, Jacobson (1981) also compared the interactions of acquainted and unacquainted infant dyads. Forty-six infants were tested at 10, 12, and 14½ months of age; at each time of testing, the infants each participated in two play sessions. In one play session at each age each infant was observed with a familiar partner, an infant who the target child met about once a week throughout the course of the study. In the other session each infant was observed with an unfamiliar peer. The session with the familiar peer came first in the majority of cases, but the author reported that no order effects were observed. Surprisingly, the infants played more with toys and less with their peers when their familiar partners were present; in particular, the unacquainted dyads engaged in longer, more "sophisticated" social interchanges than did the acquainted pairs.

Somewhat different findings have been obtained when the acquaint-ance process itself has been studied in familiar settings, either infants' own homes (Becker, 1977) or the day care center they attend (Field & Roopnarine, Note 1). Becker examined familiarization between infants by comparing two groups of 9-month-olds. The first was composed of 16 pairs who met for 10 play sessions, alternating between each other's homes. The second group, composed of 16 matched dyads, was observed twice, with the visits separated by the number of days that had elapsed between their matched partners' first and tenth sessions. The frequency of peer-directed action increased over sessions for the experimental dyads. When they met new peers in an 11th session, peer-directed behavior was somewhat less frequent than it had been in the 10th session with their original partners, but more frequent than it had been in the very first session. The complexity of peer-directed behavior, as well as its frequency, also increased with acquaintance; overtures to peers that contained two, three, or four behavioral components increased over sessions, whereas those composed of single behavioral components did not. Equivalent changes over trials were not observed for the matched control infants. At a dyadic level of analysis, infants in the experimental group engaged in progressively more interactions (action-reaction sequences) as their acquaintance proceeded. The proportion of three-unit interchanges increased most sharply over days, but the proportion of two-unit sequences increased as well. The percentage of infants' acts that did not lead to interaction remained constant at about 33% throughout the play sessions. Equivalent changes were not observed for the control dyads.

Field and Roopnarine (Note 1) extended Becker's findings by examining the effects of increasing acquaintance over a longer period of time (an academic semester) and within a larger circle of acquaintances. They observed 11 infants and 11 toddlers in the course of their day care center activities for 1 month at the beginning and 1 month at the end of a semester. The infants were reliably more likely to watch, display distal overtures, and contact their peers in the second observa-tion than in the first. More importantly, these changes did not seem to be purely maturational; infants were more likely to show these peer-directed behaviors at the end of the semester than the toddlers had been at its beginning. Thus it appears that in familiar settings infants' peer interchanges may profit from their increasing acquaintance, as do the interactions of older toddlers (Mueller & Brenner, 1977). However, in novel settings, infants' attention may be drawn to other aspects of the situation, especially new and attractive toys; a partial explanation of Jacobson's (1981) findings may lie in Becker's (1977) report that, despite overall positive effects of increasing acquaintance, infants directed more behavior to peers when the peers were visiting them than when they were visiting their peers. In the latter case, in which a novel environment was available for exploration, toys received the bulk of their attention.

Situational Variables

Effects of the social setting. With the exception of Maudry and Nekula's (1939) observations of pairs of infants alone together in playpens, information about infants' overtures to their peers has been collected in settings where parents or other adult caregivers are present. There are some indications that the behavior of adults present and their identity may affect the frequency and nature of infants' interactions with peers. As mentioned earlier, the effect of familiarity of infant peers may be mediated by the behavior of the infants' mothers (Young & Lewis, 1979). Furthermore, infants may display different types of actions toward their peers when their mothers are present than when they are absent. In a longitudinal study of an infant playgroup (Field, 1979b), infants could be observed both when their mothers were in the room and when they were absent (the mothers of playgroup members took turns supervising the group's activities such that each mother was present 50% of the time). When their mothers were absent, infants were more likely to watch, smile at, vocalize to, and touch other infants, in general displaying their better natures; in contrast, when their mothers were present, they were reliably more likely to cry and take toys from their peers.

The presence of other persons in settings in which infant peers are observed implies that these persons may also serve as recipients of the infants' social acts. For example, in the study just described (Field, 1979b), when mothers were in the room, infants were more likely to vocalize to, touch, and approach their mothers than other infants or the other mothers. Similarly, observations of 7- to 14-month-old infants in a day care center indicated that 42% of the infants' social behavior was directed to teachers whereas only 6% was directed to other infants (Finkelstein et al., 1978). In contrast, when pairs of infants were observed at home with their mothers present, a greater proportion of their behavior was reported to be peer-directed: Becker (1977) noted that an average of 33% of the behaviors recorded per play session were directed to the peer, 9% to the mother, and 8% to the peer's mother. Over the course of 10 such play sessions, behavior to the peer increased, behavior to the mother remained constant, and behavior to the peer's mother declined (although the latter finding was accounted for solely by female infants paired with male playmates, tempting us to draw conclusions about the lack of responsiveness to girls on the part of mothers of boys).

Vandell (1980), as part of her longitudinal study of infants between 6 and 12 months of age, systematically compared peer- and mother-directed behavior. She noted that three theoretical positions could be taken on the possible relations between these sets of behaviors: they might be unrelated, each serving different functions and deriving from different experiences; they might be basically quite similar, a view set forth by Vandell herself in the past; or the behaviors directed to peers might generalize from those shown to the mother, in which case mother-directed behavior would be expected to appear earlier in an infant's development. In an effort to examine these positions, Vandell compared developmental trends, overall frequencies, interrelations, and sensitivity to subject characteristics and situational determinants of selected behavioral categories that could be directed either to mothers or to peers. With increasing age, infants were more likely to vocalize to and look at both their mothers and their peers; however, with increasing age they were more likely to touch their mothers without looking at them, but less likely to do so to their peers. Vandell noted that "no behavior was directed first to mother at 6 months and only later to peer" (p. 358). In terms of the overall frequencies of the behaviors, infants looked and vocalized more to peers than to their mothers, but touched their mothers without looking at them more than they did their peers. With respect to correlations among the measures, vocalization and smiling to mothers were each related to the equivalent behaviors to peers; however, the frequency of touching the mother was negatively related to the frequency of touching the peer. No reliable cross-lagged relationships were noted. Finally, behavior to both partners increased in the absence of toys, although this finding may be an artifact of the investigator's decision to double the scores for the 5-minute trial without toys; it seems likely that if the trial had gone on for a full 10 minutes, the duration of the trial with toys, and the infants began to fuss (the likelihood of which was discussed by Vandell et al., 1980), they might have directed more behavior to their mothers and less to their peers. The infants' gender was reliably associated only with behavior to the mother: girls were more likely than boys to smile at their mothers and less likely than boys to touch them.

Vandell concluded that the evidence supported her original position of similarity between infants' behavior to mothers and peers, but acknowledged that a fair test of the generalization hypothesis might require the study of younger infants and a broader set of dependent measures. Observations of 3-month-olds' tendency to show conventional social behaviors such as smiling and vocalizing in the presence of their mothers but more diffuse arousal in the presence of their peers (Fogel, 1979) do in fact appear to support the generalization viewpoint. Furthermore, it seems likely that parents themselves play a role in regulating and interpreting their infants' overtures to other infants, as when a 6-month-old presses down on a peer's scalp with her palm and her mother says, "O.K., now, make nice." Thus the similarities between peer- and adult-directed behavior may at least partially result from parents' placing a social construction on infants' undifferentiated actions with their peers.

Interaction between persons depends not only on each actor's production of social acts, but each person's attention and responsiveness to acts produced by the partner. It is possible that infants may direct actions equally frequently to peers and adults, but respond more predictably to overtures from the adults. This possibility, however, is not supported conclusively by the available evidence, which is derived from studies of infants in day care centers. In one center, infants between 7 and 14 months of age were not much more likely to respond to overtures from their caregivers than to those from their peers, responding to 16% of the former and 12% of the latter (Finkelstein et al., 1978). However, they were reliably more likely to be observed in the midst of interaction with caregivers than with peers, a finding that emphasizes the degree of responsibility taken by adults in maintaining their interaction with infants. In contrast, observations in other day care centers indicated a greater degree of responsiveness to adults on the part of 12-month-old infants, who responded to 54% of their caregivers' initiations and to 33% of their peers' initiations (Holmberg, 1980). Curiously, the adults' responsiveness matched that of the infants; the adults responded to 52% of the infants' initiations to them. The difference between these two sets of findings is probably at least partially attributable to the differing definitions of what constituted initiation and response, and the different time criteria used to determine that a response had been made.

Effects of the physical setting. Infants' behavior toward their peers has been assessed in laboratory playrooms, which range in area from 8.1 m^2 (Eckerman et al., 1975) to 25.7 m^2 (Eckerman & Whatley, 1977), day care centers, and private homes. Becker (1977) reported that infants were reliably more likely to direct behavior to peers when in their own homes, and were more likely to pay attention to toys when in the peer's home. This difference underscores the importance of one of the most consistent findings of early peer relations: the presence of toys in general tends to depress the frequency of interaction among infants.

In their analysis of infants' first reactions to various experimental situations, Maudry and Nekula (1939) noted that, in the absence of toys, 42% of 6- to 8-month-old infants' first overtures were to their peers; the comparable percentage for 9- to 13-month-olds was 45%. All such reactions were judged to be positive in tone. In contrast, in situations where toys were presented directly to the target infants themselves, only 10% of the first reactions by the younger infants and 23% of those by the older group were peer directed, and most of these were deemed to be negative. When toys were presented to the peers, the target infants differed in their reactions, depending on their age: younger infants directed positive overtures to peers with toys on 17.3% of the occasions and negative ones on only 1.3%, whereas 9- to 13-month-olds directed positive reactions to peers with toys on 3.4% of the occasions and negative ones on 17%. When toys were present in the playpen but not offered directly to either infant, 9% of the younger infants' reactions were peer directed, with positive reactions predominating; 20% of the first reactions of the older group were peer directed, about equally divided between positive and negative ones.

Maudry and Nekula's observations have been corroborated by several more recent studies. Ramey, Finkelstein, and O'Brien (1976) observed six infants between the ages of 6.5 and 11.5 months in an infant nursery in which toys were usually present. After baseline measures of contact between infants were taken, the toys were removed. Peer contact increased reliably over baseline levels; moreover, it persisted at this higher level even after the toys were returned. In a laboratory of previously unacquainted 10- to 12-month-old and 22- to 24-month-old infants, Eckerman and Whatley (1977) observed that infants of both ages who met without toys were more likely to watch, stay near, and show both distal signals to and physical contact with the peers than were those who met with toys present. As the authors remarked, "the presence or absence of toys provided a greater change in the frequency of peer-directed behaviors than did a difference in age of 12 months" (p. 1652). The change in frequency of these categories of behavior was primarily accounted for by peer-directed activity that was composed of two or more behavioral components; thus, the presence of toys appears to depress the incidence of complex overtures to peers. In addition, attempts to duplicate the peer's actions were more frequently made when toys were absent, suggesting that the possibilities for social learning between peers may be greater in that condition.

Similar results were found in a longitudinal study of younger infants (Vandell et al., 1980). Pairs of infants were observed at 6, 9, and 12 months of age, for 10 minutes with toys present and 5 minutes with them absent, in counterbalanced order. Reliably more fussing and crying occurred when toys were absent, a tendency uncovered in pilot testing that led the investigators to adopt the shorter trial length for that condition. (In contrast, Eckerman and Whatley had reported that, among the older infants they observed, very little fussing occurred and it was equally distributed between the two conditions). Nonetheless, despite their increased likelihood of becoming distressed when toys were absent, in that condition infants were reliably more likely to approach, smile at, vocalize to, gesture toward, and touch their peers. When toys were absent, interactions occurred more frequently and lasted longer. At these ages, both simple and complex overtures to peers were facilitated by the absence of toys; however, toy absence was especially conducive to engagement in interchanges that were complex (i.e., composed of three or more separate acts).

Summary

In summary, infants seem most likely to be influenced by the presence and behavior of their peers in the absence of other distractions, such as toys or attentive mothers. Experience with infants in general and with the actual partner in particular may also promote interaction, although this effect seems tempered by the age of the infants involved and the novelty of the setting in which they are tested. In contrast, however, experience with older children, especially preschool-age siblings, decreases the likelihood that infants will interact with other infants. The majority of the evidence suggests that girls are no more or less likely than boys are to influence and be influenced by their peers; the influence of other demographic and personality characteristics on early interaction is not yet known.

Direct Versus Indirect Determinants

The preceding review indicates that among the possible determinants of peer interaction in the first year, situational factors are the most influential. This general proposition received additional support from the observations we made of 6-month-olds who were tested in the presence and absence of toys (Hay, Nash, & Pedersen, 1981; Hay, Nash, & Pedersen, unpublished manuscript). None of the interactive measures we described earlier were affected by the infants' gender, but many were influenced by the presence of toys. For example, when toys were absent, infants were reliably more likely to become distressed, and the cumulative effects of a peer's distress were only clearly seen in that condition. When toys were absent, infants touched their peers more frequently and were more likely to reciprocate touches by their peers. These findings corroborated those of earlier studies (Eckerman & Whatley, 1977; Maudry & Nekula, 1939; Vandell et al., 1980). In contrast to the findings reported by Ramey et al. (1976), however, we found no evidence for persisting effects of having interacted with peers without toys; there were no reliable effects of the order in which toy absence and toy presence were experienced.

We wished to extend these findings further by searching for some possible mechanisms that might underlie the impact of toys on early interaction. This question in turn bears on another central issue: Just how social is the social influence detected between infants under 1 year of age? In particular, to what extent do situational factors such as the presence of toys affect infants' individual states and activities and the ways in which infants' mothers respond to them? If such changes in the broader social setting are taking place, they may completely account for the observed changes in the interactive measures; the absence of toys in the environment may promote certain activities on the part of individual infants and their mothers that may create an illusion of peer interaction.

We examined this issue in two steps. First we measured the effects of the presence of toys on a number of measures of the infants' individual behavior and on their mothers' tendencies to intervene in their activities. None of these measures were reliably associated with gender nor with the order in which they experienced presence and absence of toys. However, when toys were absent, individual infants were reliably more likely to show distress and to engage in gestural activity, and individual mothers were reliably more likely to intervene in their infants' activities. (Surprisingly, however, the extent of maternal intervention was not reliably associated with the extent of an infant's distress).

In view of the finding that infants and mothers alike responded differently when toys were present than when they were absent, we next sought to determine whether information about an individual infant's state and activity and his or her mother's behavior could be used to predict the extent of initiation and reciprocation of contact with peers. When toys were absent, the frequency with which infants initiated peer contact was reliably predicted by the extent of gestural activity they engaged in; addition of measures of the infants' own distress and the frequency of maternal interventions did not increase predictability. Reciprocation of peer contact in the trial when toys were absent could not be predicted reliably by any of these measures. This is not surprising, in that an infant's tendency to initiate contact with the peer was not reliably associated with his or her tendency to reciprocate the peer's overtures.

For the analysis of the trial in which toys were present, the predictor variables included gestural activity, distress, maternal interventions, and extent of toy contact. None of these measures reliably predicted either initiation or reciprocation of peer contact. Curiously, however, when toys were present, the extent of initiation and reciprocation of contact were reliably and positively related.

These analyses indicated that peer contact was related to an individual infant's overall tendency to gesture; nonetheless, a perfect relation was not found. The extent to which an infant engages in peer contact cannot be completely accounted for by an overall tendency to be active. This finding gives credence to the notion that contact of peers is not completely serendipitous. Similarly, a perfect negative relationship was not found between the extent to which an infant contacted toys and the frequency with which that infant initiated contact of the peer. However, this finding led us to wonder whether or not peer contact when toys were absent might be *positively* related to toy contact when toys were present. If both were indices of a general exploratory tendency on the part of individual infants, a positive association would be expected. Additional regression analyses did not, however, confirm this supposition; toy contact did not reliably predict either initiation or reciprocation of contact with peers when toys were absent. In passing, these analyses also indicated that the frequencies of initiation and reciprocation of contact were not at all stable across trials, a finding that again demonstrates the susceptibility of early peer interaction to situational rather than dispositional determinants.

In general, then, these findings suggest that individual variables and the behavior of the mothers may contribute to the occurrence of interaction between peers, but they do not completely account for it. Rather, these analyses convince us even more strongly of the fundamentally social status of contact episodes between young peers.

Conclusions

Studies of peer relations in the first year of life suggest that the capacity for reciprocal interchange predates locomotion, speech, and the mature cognitive skills that permit persons to plan ahead and to assess the consequences of their actions. Infants can obviously interact more smoothly with socially skilled, caring adults than they can with other infants; nonetheless, two young infants, each with limited skills and resources, can and do interact. Even 6-month-olds are sensitive both to their peers' distal affective displays and to direct peer contact. Given their general capacities to influence and be influenced by their peers, however, infants do not always choose to interact. The extent to which interaction takes place seems to depend in infancy, just as it does in adulthood, on situational constraints and enhancements and on the degree of acquaintance that exists between potential partners.

The evidence for interactive abilities in very early life raises more general questions about the process of social development. It is not at all apparent that the early development of peer relations should be characterized as a process of response learning, whereby discrete classes of social behavior are acquired (cf., Becker, 1977, for some similar thoughts); rather, the presence and activity of a conspecific seems to evoke some degree of reaction, even in early life, before these conventional classes of social action are differentiated. Even 3-month-olds are reported to react to the presence of their peers (Field, 1979a; Fogel, 1979). As infants grow older, their reactions increasingly resemble ones shown in company with adults (Vandell, 1980). Furthermore, with increasing development, as infants become able to locomote and to appreciate the relations between events in their lives, the actions evoked in the presence of peers become more coordinated, intentional, and verbal. They become more likely to be coded symbolically into categories such as "being friendly," "being competitive," "being mean," and the like, first by parents who comment on their children's actions and later by the children themselves. It seems likely that a process of reification is at work: classes of action that we have words for may seem more easily differentiable than those for which we have no words.

Thus it seems likely that infants do not have to learn to interact with peers per se; they try their hands at peer interaction from the first few months of life on. As time goes on, however, they gradually learn to abide by certain rules and conventions governing the frequency, duration, and permissible content of all social interactions in which they engage. Social learning in this general sense involves perceptual and symbolic learning, as well as the acquisition of discrete responses. It is a long, complicated process that proceeds throughout childhood and must be undertaken again and again, in the course of forming new relationships. Even for adults, learning to interact with new acquaintances is no easy task. Fortunately, our eventual abilities to do so rest on the firm foundations of young humans' decided interest in and responsivity to their peers.

Acknowledgments

Preparation of this chapter was facilitated by National Science Foundation Grant BNS-8025474 to Dale Hay. We thank Suk-hang Chin, Dennis Clarke, Peter Hayward, and Rosemary Krawczyk for their assistance.

Reference Notes

1. Field, T., & Roopnarine, J. Infant peer interaction. In T. Field et al. (Eds.), *Review of human development*. New York: Wiley, in preparation.
2. Hay, D. F., Nash, A., & Pedersen, J. *Characteristics and determinants of peer interaction between 6-month-old infants*. Unpublished manuscript.

References

Argyle, M., & Dean, J. Eye contact, distance, and affiliation. *Sociometry*, 1965, *28*, 289-304.
Becker, J. M. T. A learning analysis of the development of peer-oriented behavior in 9-month-old infants. *Developmental Psychology*, 1977, *13*, 481-491.
Brenner, J., & Mueller, E. Shared meaning in boy toddlers' peer relations. *Child Development*, in press.
Bridges, K. M. B. A study of social development in early infancy. *Child Development*, 1933, *4*, 36-49.
Brittain, A. *Meanings and situations*. London: Routledge & Kegan Paul, 1973.
Bronson, W. Toddlers' behaviors with agemates: Issues of interaction, cognition, and affect. *Monographs on Infancy*, 1981, *1*.
Brooks-Gunn, J., & Lewis, M. The effect of age and sex on infants' playroom behavior. *Journal of Genetic Psychology*, 1979, *134*, 99-105.

Bühler, C. *From birth to maturity: An outline of the psychological development of the child.* London: Routledge & Kegan Paul, 1935.

Cappella, J. N. Mutual influence in expressive behavior: Adult-adult and infant-adult dyadic interaction. *Psychological Bulletin*, 1981, *89*, 101-132.

Darwin, C. A biographical sketch of an infant. *Mind*, 1877, *2*, 285-294.

Eckerman, C. O., & Whatley, J. L. Toys and social interactions between infant peers. *Child Development*, 1977, *48*, 1645-1656.

Eckerman, C. O., Whatley, J. L., & Kutz, S. L. Growth of social play with peers during the second year of life. *Developmental Psychology*, 1975, *11*, 42-49.

Field, T. Differential behavioral and cardiac responses of 3-month-old infants to a mirror and a peer. *Infant Behavior and Development*, 1979, *2*, 179-184. (a)

Field, T. Infant behaviors directed toward peers and adults in the presence and absence of mother. *Infant Behavior and Development*, 1979, *2*, 47-54. (b)

Finkelstein, N. W., Dent, C., Gallacher, K., & Ramey, C. T. Social behavior of infants and toddlers in a day-care environment. *Developmental Psychology*, 1978, *14*, 257-262.

Fogel, A. Peer- vs. mother-directed behavior in 1- to 3-month-old infants. *Infant Behavior and Development*, 1979, *2*, 215-226.

Goldman, B. D., & Ross, H. S. Social skills in action: An analysis of early peer games. In J. Glick & K. A. Clarke-Stewart (Eds.), *The development of social understanding.* New York: Gardner Press, 1978.

Hay, D. F., Nash, A., & Pedersen, J. Responses of six-month-olds to the distress of their peers. *Child Development*, 1981, *52*, 1071-1075.

Holmberg, M. C. The development of social interchange patterns from 12 to 42 months. *Child Development*, 1980, *51*, 448-456.

Jacobson, J. L. The role of inanimate objects in early peer interaction. *Child Development*, 1981, *52*, 618-626.

Jones, E. E., & Nisbett, R. E. *The actor and the observer: Divergent perceptions of the causes of behavior.* Morristown, N. J.: General Learning Press, 1971.

Kelley, H. *Attribution in social interaction.* Morristown, N. J.: General Learning Press, 1971.

Maudry, M., & Nekula, M. Social relations between children of the same age during the first two years of life. *Journal of Genetic Psychology*, 1939, *54*, 193-215.

Mueller, E., & Brenner, J. The origins of social skills and interaction among play-group toddlers. *Child Development*, 1977, *48*, 854-861.

Parten, M. B. Social participation among preschool children. *Journal of Abnormal and Social Psychology*, 1932, *27*, 243-269.

Preyer, W. *The mind of the child.* (H. W. Brown, trans.) New York: Appelton, 1889.

Ramey, C. T., Finkelstein, N. W., & O'Brien, C. Toys and infant behavior in the first year of life. *Journal of Genetic Psychology*, 1976, *129*, 341-342.

Sagi, A., & Hoffman, M. L. Empathic distress in newborns. *Developmental Psychology*, 1976, *12*, 175-176.

Samuels, H. The effect of an older sibling on infant locomotor exploration of a new environment. *Child Development*, 1980, *51*, 607-609.

Schaffer, H. R. Acquiring the concept of the dialogue. In M. H. Bornstein & W. Kessen (Eds.), *Psychological development from infancy: Image to intention.* Hillsdale, N. J.: Erlbaum, 1978.

Simner, M. L. Newborn's response to the cry of another infant. *Developmental Psychology*, 1971, *5*, 136-150.

Vandell, D. L. Sociability of peer and mother during the first year. *Developmental Psychology*, 1980, *16*, 335-361.

Vandell, D. L., Wilson, K. S., & Buchanan, N. R. Peer interaction in the first year of life: An examination of its structure, content, and sensitivity to toys. *Child Development*, 1980, *51*, 481-488.

Vandell, D. L., Wilson, K. S., & Whalen, W. T. Birth-order and social-experience differences in infant-peer interaction. *Developmental Psychology*, 1981, *17*, 438-445.

Young, G., & Lewis, M. Effects of familiarity and maternal attention on infant peer relations. *Merrill Palmer Quarterly*, 1979, *25*, 105-119.

Chapter 2

The Toddler's Emerging Interactive Skills

Carol O. Eckerman and Mark R. Stein

A socially skilled toddler might well be described by parents and teachers as a child who can achieve a variety of important social outcomes in ways approved of by such socialization groups as the family, school, and neighborhood playgroup. Attaining attention, comfort, affection, praise, information, and help from others, giving the same to others, cooperating with others in performing tasks, engaging in conventional games, carrying on conversation, generating games of pretend, resolving disputes, and forming and maintaining friendships might be among the important social outcomes mentioned. Reasonable as such a description of social skill may appear, our current knowledge of early social behavior falls far short of providing answers to the questions generated by such a description: How does the young child attain important social outcomes? How do the skills involved develop? How may the development of social skill go awry? The aims of the present chapter are three: (1) to provide a conceptualization of the type of skills required for attaining important social outcomes; (2) to summarize current knowledge about one set of such skills, that involved in cooperative play; and (3) to explore two research strategies for discovering and assessing the social skills of toddlers. First, however, a brief summary of other lines of research on early social development is required, since the present efforts rest upon these past accomplishments.

Since the late 1800s, baby biographers, psychologists, and pediatricians have engaged in tracing the emergence of new elements in the child's social repertoire. Although social behavior has proved elusive of definition, there has been scant difficulty in pointing out behaviors of the child that have social impact. Other humans treat a variety of emerging behaviors as having social meaning, and it is these behaviors that have been the focus of study. Although the rough form of the young child's social repertoire has been known for some time (Bayley, 1933; Bühler, 1930, 1933; Dennis & Dennis, 1937; Gesell & Thompson,

1934), marked advances have been made recently in understanding the social repertoire of the newborn (Schaffer, 1977; Trevarthen, 1979) and in tracing the emergence of conventional communicative behaviors (e.g., pointing, language) in the older infant and toddler (Bates, 1979; Lock, 1978).

Even the very young child possesses a rich social repertoire, and that repertoire expands rapidly and in a predictable order over the first 2 years of life. The newborn, for example, looks toward and away from others (Stern, 1971), smiles, coos, and shows "prespeech" movements of the mouth (Trevarthen, 1979), and shows facial expressions connoting pleasure, anger, sadness, and surprise (Field & Walden, in press; Trevarthen, 1979). By 3 months of age, the infant coos and smiles more strongly and emits more distinct prespeech movements (Trevarthen, 1979), shows well-aimed visual orienting to the mother's eyes (Trevarthen, 1979), laughs (Washburn, 1929), babbles (Wolff, 1969), and reaches toward others in anticipation of being lifted (Bayley, 1969). During the next 6 months, the infant comes to reach more readily and distinctly toward others, approaches and follows others, cries when separated from specific others, and greets these others when they return (Stayton, Ainsworth, & Main, 1973). By 12 months of age, the infant points out objects to others (Leung & Rheingold, 1981), offers and shows objects (Escalona, 1973; Hay, 1979), hugs and kisses others (Escalona, 1973), initiates well-practiced games such as peek-a-boo (Ratner & Bruner, 1978), expresses a wish or demand to others (Bates, 1979; Escalona, 1973), imitates others (Eckerman, Whatley, & Kutz, 1975; Eckerman, Whatley, & McGehee, 1979), and complies with requests (Escalona, 1973; Stayton, Hogan, & Ainsworth, 1971). During the second year of life, the child acquires new forms of verbal communication (Brown, 1973; Dore, 1974), requests information through gestures and language (Escalona, 1973), structures cooperative interchanges around new material (Hay, 1979; Ross & Goldman, 1977), and inflicts hurt in an intentional way (Escalona, 1973).

Although charting changes in the young child's social repertoire may provide a useful starting point for examining changes in the child's social skill, examining changes in the child's use of his or her social repertoire should prove even more informative. Much prior work, too, has focused upon tracing developmental changes in infants' discriminative use of their social repertoire. In attempts to trace the young infant's emerging discriminations among people and the infant's changing emotional responses to people, investigators (e.g., Ainsworth, 1973; Lamb, 1976; Schaffer, 1971) have contrasted how often the child directs social behaviors to different social partners (e.g., to mothers vs. unfamiliar adults, to mothers vs. fathers, and to parents vs. peers) and to the same partner under different conditions (e.g., to a mother when the child is frightened vs. at ease, or to the mother when the mother remains near the child vs. when she returns after an absence of a minute or so, and to a stranger when the stranger stays at a distance vs. picks up the child). The resulting picture of the young infant's differential responding to the different people is much too detailed to summarize briefly here. For our purposes, it is sufficient to note first that these contrasts have amply demonstrated the young child's discriminative use of his or her social repertoire; second, that even from very early in life, the frequency with which the infant looks, smiles, and babbles to people varies with the person and the person's behavior; and third, that these contrasts were not meant to nor did they generate a picture of how children behave during the moment-by-moment flow of social interaction. The contrasts have been undertaken largely to establish and elaborate the constructs of *attachment* and *fear of strangers*, constructs which summarize the young child's emotional reactions to caregivers and unfamiliar persons beginning in the second half-year of life. Attachment and fear of strangers serve to abstract and highlight certain phenomena thought to mark healthy infant development and to hold strong predictions for the quality of later functioning. They call attention to phenomena that hold across the young of diverse species and that within the human species distinguish different developmental periods and different individuals at a given period. Their utility thus rests in their power to predict other developmental outcomes for the human and in their highlighting of possible evolved paths of development, not in the precision with which they describe the infant's current functioning in social encounters or the process of social development.

To understand how the young child comes to skillfully generate cooperative play with others, converse with others, resolve disputes, and attain help or information, we must push toward a more molecular analysis of the child's use of his or her social repertoire. Cairns (1972) makes similar points while discussing differing levels of analysis of social functioning. Cairns suggests a necessary conflict between economical constructs (such as attachment) and unitary constructs, those that deal with a unitary attribute of behavior and thus permit the detailed tracing of clear antecedents and consequences of the behavior. Attachment meets the need to distill vast numbers of observations into a small number of dispositional variables; it serves the useful function of identifying developmental and individual difference consistencies that may not be easily seen at a more molecular level of analysis. Cairns proceeds to argue, as do we, that in order to understand the details of social functioning and achieve potent explanatory mechanisms for development, constructs such as attachment must be complemented by a more molecular level of analysis. Cairns proposed a psychobiological and social learning analysis of the behaviors used to index attachment; we will argue for a similar detailed analysis of component social interactive skills.

The Concept of Interactive Skills

Central to the present approach to social skill and its development is the concept of interactive skills. An interactive skill is a systematic way that the young child relates his or her own behavior, both in form and in timing, to that of a social partner. It is a way of behaving during the moment-by-moment flow of social encounters which functions to facilitate the attainment of important social outcomes (e.g., generating a social game or obtaining help). At a quite rudimentary level, an interactive skill may consist of timing a social overture so that it occurs when one's partner is attentive. Observations of encounters between unfamiliar 10-month-olds, for example, yield instances of apparent mistiming of overtures. A quite young child may hold out a toy to another, but to the other's back. Nothing in the offering child's behavior indicates any awareness that an offer has to be attended to in order to have a social effect. Such mistimings, however, rarely occur in the encounters of older infants. The offering child either offers an object when the partner is already attending or accompanies the offer with exclamatory sounds, which elicit attention. It is this systematic relationship between the occurrence of an overture and the partner's attentional state that we call an interactive skill.

At quite a different level of sophistication, an interactive skill may consist of forming a social overture so that its content matches the partner's current interests. For a partner setting a table in a game of "house," an overturing child might assume the role of the father returning home from work at dinnertime rather than overturing by throwing a ball toward the child and yelling "catch." The former manner of approach would be expected to lead more often and readily to cooperative play. The relevance of the latter interactive skill to classical conceptions of role taking is readily apparent. Although we cannot move from existing notions of roletaking to specifying how young children actually behave in social encounters, we can move from documented interactive skills to reasoning about the young child's emerging role-taking abilities.

The emphasis upon interactive skills and their centrality for understanding social skill has been prompted both by our observations of the successes and failures of early peer encounters and by the burgeoning literature describing early mother-infant interaction. Observing the encounters between unfamiliar infant peers during the second year of life led us to conclude that infants often seem very interested in one another (Eckerman et al., 1975, Eckerman & Whatley, 1977). Even the youngest infants observed (10-month-olds) smiled and vocalized to one another, approached and followed each other about, offered and exchanged toys, imitated each other, and often ended up close together in space manipulating the same play material. Despite such apparent interest, however, what transpired between the infants often had an unpredictable sequential nature, unpredictable at least in the sense of not conforming to the patterns of interaction characteristic of parent-infant interaction or later peer interaction. Each infant's actions often seemed unrelated, or unconnected, to the actions of the partner. Against this backdrop of unpredictableness, the occurrence by 2 years of age of infrequent but discernable repetitive patterns of interaction stood out, prompting the speculation that the second year of life is a period rich in the development of the interactive skills required to generate even the most basic patterns of social interaction.

Concurrently, students of the mother-infant dyad had been examining, often in minute detail, the patterns of interaction generated by mother and infant. From the resulting literature (Brazelton, Koslowski, & Main, 1974; Ratner & Bruner, 1978; Schaffer, 1977; Stern, 1977; Trevarthen, 1979), one can glean a speculative picture of the infant's developing social skill that both points toward interactive skills as major achievements of infancy and emphasizes how the infant and mother together construct experiences conducive to the acquisition of such skills.

In outlining this speculative picture, we begin at the birth of the child, for from birth infants behave in ways that facilitate interactions with others. They are attentive to the stimulation that people provide, looking selectively at visual arrays with the amounts of contour change, brightness, and movement provided by human faces and appearing particularly attentive to sounds with the characteristics of human speech. They also emit behaviors that evoke characteristic responses from caretakers: cries bring people to their side; later, smiles keep them there and prompt them into answering smiles and talk; and looks toward or away from others seem to function to increase or reduce the stimulation others present. Recent observers of early mother-infant encounters have suggested that almost any distinctive behavior by the infant (a kick, a yawn, a gurgle, or an opening of the mouth) may be treated by the mother as if it were a communication and that such actions prompt her answering reactions. Furthermore, infants may come with temporal regularities, or cycles, to their behavior that affect the timing of others' behaviors toward them. In all such ways, newborns appear to facilitate interactions with others: some of their behaviors bring others to their side; selective attention to and orienting toward the stimuli these others provide set the stage for others interacting with them; and newborns' ways of behaving in the presence of others mold in part how others behave with them.

From birth, too, infants find themselves participants in patterned social interaction. They are born into a social environment that provides them with repeated experience with basic patterns of social interaction. The adults who care for them and play with them adjust their behavior to the infant's so as to repeatedly produce temporal patterns of interaction such as those called *coaction* and *dialogue*. In coaction, the adult matches his or her behavior to the child's both in time, intensity, and sometimes form, thereby producing bouts of mutual gazing or vocalizing, synchronous alternating cycles of approach and withdrawal, or synchronous cycles of building excitement and affectivity. At other times, the mother responds to her infant as if the infant were communicating with her; she fits "answering" behaviors into the pauses left in the infant's stream of behavior to produce a turn-taking dialogue.

At first, the infant plays a limited role in structuring such patterns of interaction. It is the partner who appears to continuously adjust his or her behavior to that of the infant and thus structure the interaction. But the infant also comes capable of learning. Since patterned interaction characterizes much of the infant's social experience, it is important raw material for that learning. Infants, for example, may learn the social meanings of their behavior in this context. They may develop expectations concerning how others behave. They may learn how to produce these expected behaviors more and more efficiently. They learn how to adjust their behavior in timing and in form to that of the mother. In time, they come to act toward their mother as she has repeatedly acted toward them; they reverse roles with her. They learn rituals of play. Perhaps the infant abstracts the more general "rules" (e.g., turn taking) that underlie the patterned interaction he or she repeatedly experiences.

With development, then, the infant gradually acquires interactive skills—ways of behaving with others that enable him or her to participate more fully in structuring the interactions repeatedly experienced with others. At first, the infant may become a full participant only in structuring well-rehearsed routines of interaction with familiar partners. Later, the infant becomes able to generate new patterns of interaction with these familiar partners and able to engage new partners in familiar routines. Still later perhaps, he or she becomes able to generate new dialogues or new forms of coaction with new partners, and, thus, able to readily achieve a variety of valued social outcomes with a variety of social partners.

The above picture of development points to interactive skills as basic building blocks of social skill. It is the sum of such skills and their integration that transforms the neonate into the child who actively participates in the generation of social games, who converses and argues with others, and who helps and shares. Each such skill, then, warrants discovery and careful scrutiny. What is the behavioral form of the skill? How does the skill function in social encounters? What conception of others is implied by the skill? What interactive experiences provided by others facilitate the development of this skill? How may skills acquired earlier in development prod the acquisition of later skills? What uniformities exist across children in the order in which skills emerge?

Analysis of social behavior at the level of component interactive skills is especially useful for developmental inquiries. The component interactive skills required for a given social outcome develop at different times and often in a predictable order, and earlier occurring interactive skills may well function in the development of later occurring skills. Analysis of social encounters at the level of interactive skills also serves to highlight how the child's own ways of behaving potently shape his or her own social experiences and hence opportunities for learning. For example, a child who offers toys to an attentive partner produces different social experiences than a child who offers when partners are inattentive. The child's interactive skills also provide an anchoring point for attempts to understand how major variations in social experience (e.g., group day care vs. rearing within a nuclear family, sensitive vs. intrusive mothering, or the absence vs. presence of siblings) affect the development of social skill. The critical questions become the following: "How do these major variations translate into interactive experiences important in the development of interactive skills? How do these major variations impinge upon the child, given his or her current level of interactive skill? Understanding the basic interactive skills most children develop during their first few years of life also holds promise for understanding the inability of some young children to interact successfully and for conceptualizing the component skills to be developed through special experiences. Finally, interactive skills are behaviorally and functionally defined. They do not presuppose knowledge (which we do not have) about the young child's intentions or social understandings, but rather provide us with a window to the infant's growing understanding of others and the processes of social interaction.

Interactive Skills and Cooperative Play

Current knowledge of interactive skills is sparse. Rather than attempt a discussion of the different skills involved in different social outcomes, pointing to a skill here and there, we focus our inquiry here upon the skills involved in one valued social outcome, cooperative play. Our knowledge of interactive skills is perhaps best developed for cooperative play and the phenomenon of cooperative play between peers has guided our own recent research efforts. Despite the formidable history of difficulty in defining "play" and "cooperation," a working definition is required. For our purposes, the essential characteristics of cooperative play within a dyad are as follows: (1) the engagement of both members of the dyad with one another; (2) a meaningful relationship between the behaviors of the two participants, such that each participant appears to be responding to the other's actions and both appear to be about a jointly understood and agreed upon endeavor; (3) an affectively neutral or positive tone to the encounter; and (4) the apparent engagement in the interchange for its own sake. Each requirement, of course, is problematical; yet there exist encounters which can be agreed upon as fulfilling these requirements. Mutual engagement can be indicated by mutual visual regard and laughter punctuating the exchange. A common endeavor appears clear when two children alternate in stacking blocks upon a common tower or when two children verbally note to one another "We are playing house, right?" An affectively positive tone can be ascertained in encounters marked with laughter and smiles, or even in "mock fighting" accompanied by mutual glee. Engagement in the interchange for its own sake can become apparent through prolonged repetition of the acts or the statement "Let's pretend..." Our aim in proposing a definition of cooperative play is not to divide all of social interaction into "cooperative play" and "not cooperative play," but rather to point to an important social phenomenon that can guide the search for component interactive skills.

The definition proposed is broader than that for "social play" presented by Garvey (1974) for older, preschool children, and than that for "game" elaborated for both mother-infant and peer interaction by Ross and her colleagues (Goldman & Ross, 1978; Ross, 1982). Social play, characterized by "alternating, contingent behaviors and nonliteralness of those behaviors," and games, defined as "extended and structured forms of cooperative interaction..." characterized by "the mutual involvement of two partners and the repeated enactment of game roles in a turn-alternation pattern" are examples of cooperative play, but cooperative play need not conform to a turn-alternation pattern. For example, imagine two toddlers chasing after one another around a table, laughing, and periodically glancing over their shoulders at the child behind. Such an episode is marked by mutual involvement, positive affect, a meaningful relationship between the two children's behaviors, and a discernible common endeavor, but not by a repetitive alternation of turns. We anchor our inquiry about cooperative play rather than the construct of social play or game specifically to ask whether or when turn-alternation patterns characterize cooperative play. A broader net, too, may be necessary to capture the developmental precursors of the full-fledged game.

That cooperative play, social play, or games are valued social outcomes few would question. Such interchanges have variously been described as forums for learning to involve and influence others and for learning that social interaction in general is rule governed (Ross & Kay, 1980), as a prime medium for language acquisition (Bruner, 1977; Ratner & Bruner, 1978), as a forum for practicing motor patterns modeled by the parent (Crawley, Rogers, Friedman, Iacobbo, Criticos, Richardson, & Thompson, 1978), as opportunities for prosocial learning (Hay, 1979), and as important in the child's construction of social schemas (Lee, 1975).

That cooperative play occurs from early infancy is undeniable. Cooperative play has been described between mothers and their infants during the first half-year of life (Crawley et al., 1978; Ratner & Bruner, 1978), between fathers and infants (Power & Parke, Note 1), between unfamiliar adults and infants (Ross & Kay, 1980), between young siblings (Dunn & Kendrick, 1979), and between infant peers (Bühler, 1933; Eckerman, et al., 1975; Goldman & Ross, 1978; Maudry & Nekula, 1939; Vincze, 1971), Furthermore, cooperative play takes multiple forms during the first 2 years of life. Infants in Western culture engage with adults in such conventional or ritualized games as "peek-a-boo," "I'm gonna get you," "catch," "chase," or "stack and topple." At other times, cooperative play appears a novel construction, generated upon the spot, as when two toddlers take turns licking a table, jumping from a step into a laundry basket only to tip it over and roll out, or throwing a bean bag through the skylight of a playhouse. Cooperative play takes both a turn-taking structure, as in the above examples, or a coaction structure, as in wrestling or simultaneously chasing one another. The type of meaningful relationship between the behaviors of the two partners also varies: a mother waddles, quacking like a duck, and her infant reacts with laughter (an actor-audience relationship); a mother throws a ball into a basket and her infant throws a ball into the basket too (an imitative relationship); a mother throws a ball into the basket and her infant retrieves it and hands it back to her (a complementary relationship); or a mother throws a ball to her infant who catches it and throws it back to the mother (a reciprocal relationship).

Cooperative play thus occurs from early in infancy, and it occurs with a variety of social partners and in a variety of forms. What then do we know about how infants and toddlers generate cooperative play with others? The studies of cooperative play with adults have generally had different foci of concern than the studies of cooperative play between young peers, and as a result the two sets of studies have yielded somewhat divergent views of the young child's skills in generating cooperative play.

Cooperative Play with Adults

Students of cooperative play with adults (usually the mother) have focused upon ritualized or conventional games, and traced through development the participants' changing ways of playing these games and the changing types of conventional games played. The result has been an emphasis upon the parent's role in structuring the game and in skillfully changing his or her participation in line with the child's developing abilities. The parent at first controls the game, scaffolding the child's efforts, and sometimes performing both roles in the game. In so doing, the parent is seen as providing the context in which the child gradually becomes a more skilled partner. With development the child changes from playing a fairly passive role in these games to actively anticipating the parent's actions, to initiating the game and eventually to performing what was originally the parent's role in the game (Ratner & Bruner, 1978; Ross & Kay, 1980). The games played, too, change from ones requiring only a passive, audience role to those requiring more active involvement by the infant (Crawley et al., 1978; Gustafson, Green, & West, 1979).

Although they point to the infant's changing ability to initiate such games and reverse roles, the descriptions of parent-infant games give few hints about specific interactive skills of the child. How do children initiate these games? When do they initiate? Do they time their initiations with respect to their parent's ongoing activities? Do they repeat or elaborate their initiatives if their parents fail to take up the game? Do they pause after their own action, leaving space for their parent's action, signaling a change of turns? And so on. Furthermore, the focus upon ritualized games leaves unaddressed the skills involved in generating games with new content, where the intentions of each partner are not understood on the basis of a long history of prior experience with specific play actions.

Cooperative Play Between Young Peers

Studies of encounters between young peers provide both counts of how frequently cooperative play occurs at different points in development and descriptions of the forms cooperative play assumes. A few studies (Bühler, 1930; Maudry & Nekula, 1939; Shirley, 1933; Vincze, 1971) have reported games between peers less than 1 year of age, but the definitions employed are unclear, leaving uncertain the issue of whether these early games share the features of the games more clearly and often described for older children. Cooperative play with peers (indexed by the existence of games, as defined by Ross and her colleagues, or by repetitive turn-alternating sequences of meaningfully related behaviors) occurs with increasing frequency during the second year of life (Eckerman & Whatley, 1977; Ross & Kay, 1980; Ross, 1982). Even at 2 years of age, however, cooperative play is a relatively infrequent occurrence between peers, with some dyads failing to generate any cooperative play at all. Nevertheless, the fact that cooperative play occurs at all between unfamiliar peers attests to the considerable skill of at least some toddlers.

Counting changes in the frequency of occurrence, of course, yields little information about the skills involved. Speculations about relevant skills arise from descriptions of cooperative play between young peers. Existing descriptions emphasize the generative nature of the play, a turn-taking structure, and the occurrence of imitative, complementary, and reciprocal relationships between the two participants' behaviors (Eckerman & Whatley, 1977; Goldman & Ross, 1978; Ross, 1982). Young peers have been described as taking turns kicking a radiator, patting a wall, shaking hands at one another, throwing themselves into a mother's lap, throwing a ball to one another, and as exchanging objects and engaging in games of peek-a-boo. Furthermore, a developmental progression from imitative to complementary to reciprocal relationships between the two participants' behaviors has been proposed, although not convincingly demonstrated (Mueller & Lucas, 1975; Ross, 1982).

The existence and descriptions of cooperative play between peers have prompted speculations about the relevant skills of the toddler. Often these speculated skills have been described only in such general terms as coordinated socially directed behaviors and role-reversing abilities (Mueller & Brenner, 1977; Mueller & Lucas, 1975). Ross and her colleagues, however, have been more explicit about the behavioral forms such skills might take. For example, detailed examination of 28 games generated by 18-month olds with a 12- or 24-month-old partner (Goldman & Ross, 1978) led to speculations about how toddlers initiate games and manage their turn-taking structure. Among the ways of behaving implicated in initiating games were (a) accompanying an overture to the peer with smiles and/or laughter, (b) using an overture whose content was part of a familiar, conventional game (e.g., throwing a ball) or whose content had little relevance in literal interaction (e.g., foot tapping), and (c) repeating the overture to signal game intentions and that an imitation game was intended. Implicated in managing turn alternation were such behaviors as (a) looking to the partner after one's turn, often while remaining immobile, (b) withdrawing from the object involved in the game and alluding to the content of the partner's turn (e.g., looking back and forth between the partner and the object or holding up the arms ready to catch the object), (c) withdrawing and looking to the peer in instances where simultaneous turns had been initiated, and (d) repeating one's own turn and yielding again when the peer fails to take his or her turn. Although descriptions of how children behave in successful games may prove a fertile discovery ground for interactive skills, such descriptions by themselves cannot answer a number of important questions: How often and under what conditions do young children exhibit the proposed skill? Do the proposed skills actually aid in the generation of cooperative play? How successful are such skills and under what conditions are they successful? When and how do such skills develop? The examination of failures in generating cooperative play may also be required to open our eyes to still further interactive skills.

Thus, students of cooperative play between young peers have documented both that cooperative play does occur between children 2 years of age and younger and that the cooperative play appears largely generative in nature, rather than a reenactment of specific games learned with more adept partners. In so doing, they have painted a picture of considerable skill for the 2-year-old and a picture of greater skill than have students of parent-infant interaction. Interactive tasks which the 2-year-old appears to master with someone no more skillful than he or she have been highlighted, and some specific interactive skills have been proposed. The proposed skills, however, await scrutiny, and still other skills undoubtedly await discovery.

Discovering and Assessing the Toddler's Interactive Skills

For the past 3 years, we have been exploring techniques to discover and assess the toddler's interactive skills. Our efforts began with the skills involved in cooperative play and an attempt to conceptualize the task demands of cooperative play in a manner that could guide our search for interactive skills. Our conceptualization of the tasks of cooperative play has undergone much revision and undoubtedly will continue to do so, since the dual tasks of discovering interactive skills and discovering the interactive tasks they accomplish proceed hand in hand.

Interactive Tasks of Cooperative Play

Currently, we see cooperative play as involving at least six sets of tasks: (1) establishing joint agreement on a topic, (2) assuming related roles in acting upon the topic, (3) managing the temporal structure of cooperative action, (4) handling interruption, (5) communicating about the state of joint endeavor, and (6) varying the topic. Although we shall describe the tasks as if they occurred in sequential order, the negotiation of several tasks probably proceeds concurrently.

As Bruner (1977) has aptly noted, a basic task of communication is to indicate to each other, and to mutually understand and agree upon, a topic around which a subsequent exchange can take place. Cooperative play is no exception. There is a theme or topic for the cooperative venture that must be jointly understood and agreed upon. Often the topic for the toddler appears to be an object or an array of objects. An object may serve as the topic in much the same way as we might summarize the topic of a verbal conversation as "trees" or "school." Reaching agreement about a topic for interaction would appear to place helpful constraints upon the subsequent interaction and increase the likelihood of the partners assuming meaningfully related roles in a cooperative venture.

Beyond establishing the topic, however, the children must also establish how they are to deal with the topic. In verbal conversation, children may deal with the topic of school in various ways—for example, by listing in turn the things they like or dislike about school, or by asking and answering questions about school. Likewise, in cooperative play, the choice of a topic (e.g., an object) may constrain the nature of the cooperative endeavor, but still one kind of cooperative endeavor among the several possible must be negotiated. The participants must agree upon meaningfully related roles with respect to the topic. On the topic of "blocks," for example, two toddlers could stack the blocks together or both could throw them into a basket (assume imitative roles), or one could stack them and the other knock them down (complementary roles), etc. The possibilities are many. Furthermore, the roles may be renegotiated during the course of cooperative play, as when stacking blocks together into a tower evolves into one stacking the tower and the other knocking it down. Assuming meaningfully related roles and maintaining them even through variation, thus, are critical interactive tasks.

A third task involves managing the temporal structure of the cooperative play. In turn-taking interchanges, temporal coordination is required in both the yielding and taking of turns. Simultaneous attempts at turns as well as prolonged delays in the taking of a turn may hinder the cooperative venture. Goldman and Ross (1978) have highlighted the importance of this interactive task for games and suggested a variety of interactive skills that may serve to manage the task. Cooperative play with a coaction structure, however, may require even more precise temporal coordination, as when two children standing in a large basket act jointly to gradually tip the basket over and roll out. To accomplish this smoothly, both must continually monitor the pace of the other's actions.

A further set of interactive skills seems to address the task of handling interruptions in the cooperative play. Interruptions may result from motor difficulties of a partner, as when a child repeatedly drops a ball and retrieves it on the way to deposit it in a basket. Interruptions may also arise from the intervention of others into the game, such as a mother insisting a child blow his or her nose or other children attempting to engage one or both partners. Interruptions may also arise from the temporary distraction of one member or both from the cooperative endeavor. Different types of interruptions may well call for different types of skills, but waiting even for long periods for the partner to complete his or her action, and gesturing or vocalizing to the partner to reengage appear to be basic skills.

Communicating about the achieved state of joint endeavor also appears to be an important task, serving to maintain and extend the joint endeavor. Mutual visual regard at set points in the joint endeavor has been considered a way of acknowledging that the interactive partners are engaged in a joint enterprise or of checking upon the existence of such shared involvement (Bruner, 1977). Laughter and

smiles may also serve in such communication, as well as verbal statements acknowledging the joint enterprise ("*We* are playing house"; "*We*
are playing"). Newman (1978) has suggested that young children may
repeat part of their partner's prior utterance both to maintain contact
and a sense of common engagement and to demonstrate to others that
they form a social unit.

The final task of cooperative play to be considered is that of varying
the topic. In verbal conversations topics change, sometimes abruptly
and sometimes gradually by one topic evolving into another; so too in
cooperative play, the topic must eventually change. Some skills may
involve adding variations to the existing joint endeavor to sustain
interest in the endeavor over prolonged periods of time; others involve
changing one topic to another topic (shifting, for example, from a game
of catch to building a tower of blocks); still others may involve termi-
nating the state of joint engagement.

This scheme of interactive tasks now guides our search for the young
child's developing interactive skills. Critical to the enterprise, too, is the
development of research strategies and analytical tools that can serve in
both the discovery and assessment of interactive skills.

Strategies for Assessing the Toddler's Interactive Skills

The paucity of knowledge about the young child's interactive skills
results in part from difficulties inherent in assessing an individual's
contribution to a social product. Cooperative play is a social product, a
construction built by both participants. By definition, each actor is
continuously influencing the other. If we observe natural encounters
between the young child and a parent, an older sibling, or any adult,
how can we disentangle the child's skills from those of the more adept
social partner? Despite the various analytic procedures proposed and
tried, the basic confound between the partner's behavior and that of the
child remains. Do infants, for example alternate their play actions with
their mothers or do they only appear to do so because their mothers
skillfully insert their own actions after the child's action, before the
child can act again? Or, when mothers act more quickly after their
infants than vice versa, can we conclude that the infant is unable to
manage turn taking or only that the mothers are so attentive that they
give their infants little chance to show or exercise such skills? Descriptions of naturally occurring cooperative play between infants and more
adept partners can suggest some infant interactive skills, but to discover
others and rigorously assess these skills, further research strategies
are needed.

One promising strategy uses natural social encounters between near
equals in interactive skill. Whatever forms of cooperative play peers
manage to generate must be attributed to the interactive skills of

children of their own developmental level. There is no more skillful partner to carry the burden of the interaction. Of course, young children may possess more interactive skills than they show clearly in their peer interactions. The relative lack of skill in a partner can reduce one's own level of skillful performance. Peer interaction perhaps is best thought of as a harsh or strong test of interactive skills. Still, young peers during the second year of life do generate a number of patterns of cooperative play, attesting to the variety of interactive skills potentially discoverable in peer interaction. These skills largely still await discovery. Although the phenomenon of cooperative play has been defined, counted, and described for young peers, the development of sequential analytic procedures to assess the skills shown in peer interaction has barely begun. The likelihood of a socially directed behavior of one child being followed by that of another child has been assessed in the work of Mueller and Vandell and their colleagues (e.g., Mueller & Brenner, 1977; Vandell, Wilson, & Buchanan, 1980), but socially directed behavior is too broad and mixed a category of behavior to address the questions about interaction raised here.

A second promising research strategy for assessing interactive skills consists of programming the behavior of the child's social partner so as to probe for the existence of a hypothesized skill. To assess, for example, whether toddlers signal their partner to act in turn-taking games, one could instruct the partner to act only when the toddler gives a specified signal, or to pause 10 seconds to set the occasion for such a signal (cf. Ross & Kay, 1980). By programing the partner, the confound between his or her behavior and that of the child can be broken or ameliorated. Considerable art, of course, is involved in programming portions of the partner's behavior without destroying the social phenomenon itself. Explicit ideas about the specifics of the toddler's interactive skills also are required to guide the manipulations. Using a programed partner thus is a technique for assessing interactive skills rather than for discovering them.

Illustrative findings from two recent studies explore the utility of these two research strategies for assessing interactive skills and of the concept of interactive skill itself.

Illustration 1: Reaching Agreement on a Topic

In the first study we examined freely occurring peer interactions and explored primarily the skills involved in reaching agreement about a topic for cooperative play. Previous descriptions of peer encounters as well as everyday observations of toddlers' encounters with parents and siblings highlight how often toddlers go to the objects others are using —to the play materials of peers and siblings or the household objects of parents. Going to the objects others are using appeared to us an excellent all-purpose strategy for achieving a joint focus of attention (the object) about which a social exchange could occur. The resulting social exchange might evolve into cooperative play, or perhaps into struggles, didactic conversations, or simply an exchange of the object. Others have suggested that following the partner's line of gaze similarly serves the function of achieving joint attention to a common reference point (Scaife & Bruner, 1975). For the locomoting infant, however, going to the partner's object may not only achieve a joint focus of attention, but also possess the additional advantages of signaling interest in acting together on that object and of placing the infant beside the object, facilitating his or her acting upon the joint topic.

A prior study using a programed adult partner documented that 1-year-old infants did systematically approach and contact the toy an adult manipulated (Eckerman et al., 1979). Furthermore, they tended to smile and vocalize to the adult as they contacted the toy, giving a social flavor to this way of behaving. Since the adult partner was programed only to manipulate the toys in set ways and in a set order, we were unable to explore further in this study the potential social consequences of going to another's object. A further study therefore was undertaken to assess these social consequences, replicate the basic finding with another social partner (an unfamiliar peer), and trace the development of this potential interactive skill.

Twelve pairs of same-sex peers, half 18 months of age and half 24 months of age, met under conditions designed to facilitate their generation of cooperative play. The children, drawn on the basis of age from the population of white infants born and residing in a southern industrial and university city of moderate size (Durham, North Carolina), were primarily from homes with above-average levels of parental education. Children, paired on the basis of age, sex, and a common meeting time, were unacquainted with one another prior to the study.

The study setting contained toys thought conducive to cooperative play—a platform for climbing on and jumping off, a playhouse with door and window, a large box into which a ball could be inserted at the top of one side to reappear at the bottom of the opposite side, a set of foam blocks, and a large laundry basket. During the week prior to the peer encounter, each child came to this play setting with his or her mother. The mother and child played alone in the setting for 10 minutes and then were joined by an unfamiliar adult female who engaged the child in four specific games involving the toys. The games consisted of jumping off the platform in turn, engaging in peek-a-boo through the playhouse window, the child inserting the ball into the chute and the adult retrieving it and handing it back to the child, and gathering the blocks into a tower to be knocked down by the child. The first visit both familiarized the children with the playsetting and provided some common experiences in using the play materials in cooperative play.

Within 1 week, each pair of peers met in the play setting for 20 minutes. The mothers sat on floor cushions and talked with one another; they responded simply to the children's overtures, but neither directed their activities nor played with them. They intervened only rarely, in cases of physical danger or rapidly escalating conflicts.

Different observers for each child used a keyboard connected to a multiple-channel event recorder to generate a timed listing of the child's looks toward the peer and each social signal directed toward the peer. The social signals were 26 predefined types of vocalization (e.g., cry, laugh, vocalize), conventional gesture (e.g., offer, point, take, brush aside), and physical contact (touch, strike), each thought to hold the potential for contributing to social interaction. The observers coded the occurrence of a social signal. The type of signal and the objects contacted by each child were coded later from videotaped records. The resulting record listed, along a common time line, each child's looks to the partner, social signals directed at the partner, and contacts with play material. This listing allowed assessments of the temporal relationships existing between different behaviors by the same child as well as between behaviors of the two children. Interobserver agreement at both stages of coding averaged above 85%.

To assess whether toddlers did systematically go to each other's play material, the timed records were searched for each instance of a child making contact with an object not already contacted by the peer, and the time elapsing before the peer contacted that same object was noted. Figure 2-1 shows how often and how rapidly the children contacted each other's play material. Plotted is the cumulative probability of the second child contacting the same object as the first as a function of the number of seconds since the first child contacted the object. For both ages, the resultant curve deviates markedly from the straight line function expected if the children were not influencing each other's choice of objects. The chance probabilities used to generate the straight line function were computed using for the initiating child the probability of initiating contact with a specific toy when the peer was not already contacting that toy, and for the responding child an unconditional probability of initiating contact with that toy based upon how often he or she had initiated contact with that toy during the 20-minute session. The joint probabilities for each specific object were then summed. Computations of all probabilities were done separately for each child of a pair and the results averaged across the dyad for use in group summaries and statistical comparisons.

To highlight the temporal parameters of the phenomenon of going to the peer's object, statistical tests were performed contrasting the obtained probability during each successive 10-second period (not the cumulative probability) to the chance probability. At both ages, the difference was reliable for the first 10 seconds [18 months, $t(5) = 4.32$,

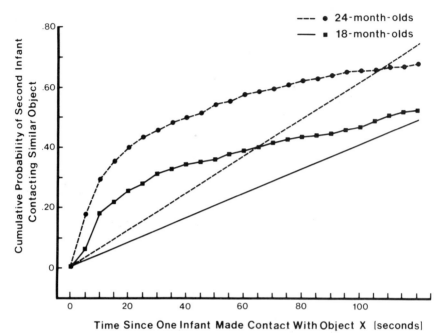

Fig. 2-1. Frequency and speed with which 18- and 24-month old peer partners contact each other's play material. Connected symbols represent the cumulative obtained probability of contacting the partner's object for increasing time intervals. Unconnected symbols represent computed chance probabilities.

$p < .01$; 24 months, $t (5) = 6.92, p < .01$]. For the younger dyads, the difference was also reliable during the third 10-second period [$t (5) = 2.59, p < .05$] and approached significance for the second 10-second period, reflecting perhaps a slower pace of locomotion for the younger toddlers.

As Figure 2-1 shows, the older toddlers contacted their partner's object both more quickly and more often than the younger toddlers. These differences may result both from their faster pace of locomotion and the greater number of times the older toddlers initiated object contacts, resulting in a greater chance probability of going to the same object (mean .06 vs. .04 in 10 seconds). To assess whether the older toddlers showed a greater tendency to go to their partner's object which could not be attributed to these two factors, we contrasted for the two ages the extent to which the observed probability exceeded the chance probability for increasing time intervals. These contrasts yielded a reliable difference only for the 0-10 second period [$t (10) = 2.23, p < .05$] and not for the 0-20 second period or the 0-30 second period, confirming the conclusion that the two age groups did not differ in their readiness to go to their partner's object but only in the speed with which they did so and their overall frequency of moving from object to object.

Does going to the peer's play material facilitate the reaching of a topic for interaction? Is it an interactive skill? Going to another's object would seem to provide the interactors with a common reference point (the object) about which to send messages and with which to reply; thus, the first step in asking about social consequences was to assess whether going to another's object did result in a common reference point. If a common reference point is indicated by simultaneous contact of the same play material, then going to the peer's play materials within 20 seconds did result in a common reference point over two-thirds of the time for both age groups. The older toddlers who went to the peer's object more often, spent almost one-half of the session in joint object engagement (simultaneous contact of the same play material); the younger toddlers spent reliably less of the session in this manner, roughly one-quarter of the session [mean 554 vs. 319 seconds; $t(10) = 3.50, p < .05$].

Did the common reference point, the object, appear to facilitate communication between the peers? Table 2-1 contrasts the frequency of occurrence of several types of social signals for periods of joint object engagement versus periods of solitary object engagement (either or both were not contacting an object or each contacted different objects). For each dyad, the probability of occurrence of a social signal was greater during periods of joint object engagement than during solitary object engagement. Children of the two ages did not differ reliably in the overall frequency of signals, the frequencies of specific types of signals, or the frequency contrasts between joint and solitary object engagement. Thus, to assess which types of signals occurred more often during joint object engagement, data were collapsed across the two age groups to increase the number of dyads showing each specific type of signal. During joint object engagement, vocalizations, touches, and takes (actual takes, attempts to remove an object from the peer's hand, and more distant reaching gestures toward the peer's object) occurred reliably more often. (Note that "takes" were not restricted by definition to joint object engagement. When a child had not previously been contacting the same material as the peer, moves or gestures to take the peer's object occurred during solitary object engagement.) Protests, strikes, pointing, and sharing (showing, offering, or throwing an object to the peer) also occurred more often during joint object engagement but not reliably so; and the remaining signals occurred too infrequently to allow a reliable contrast.

A still stronger test of communication during joint object engagement, however, lies in assessing whether the toddlers "answered" one another's signals. Table 2-2 summarizes the data leading to the conclusion that only the older toddlers appeared to answer each other's signals and that they did so only during joint object engagement. The probability that the social signal of one child was followed within 3 seconds by a social signal from the peer (an "answer") was contrasted

Table 2-1. Frequency of Social Signals per 10 Seconds of Joint or Solitary Object Engagement

Social signal	18-months-olds		24-months-olds	
	Joint	Solitary	Joint	Solitary
All combined	.76 (6)[a]	.41 (6)	.82 (6)	.47 (6)
Vocalize	.43 (6)	.30 (6)	.42 (6)	.33 (6)
Protest	.01 (2)	.01 (3)	.05 (3)	.01 (1)
Cry	.00 (0)	.00 (0)	.00 (0)	.00 (0)
Laugh	.01 (1)	.01 (2)	.05 (2)	.00 (1)
Touch	.11 (4)	.01 (2)	.08 (5)	.02 (3)
Strike	.10 (2)	.04 (3)	.08 (4)	.02 (1)
Request Object	.00 (0)	.00 (0)	.01 (2)	.00 (0)
Take Object	.06 (4)	.03 (5)	.09 (5)	.04 (3)
Share Object	.01 (2)	.02 (6)	.06 (5)	.03 (5)
Point	.02 (3)	.02 (4)	.06 (4)	.03 (3)

[a]Number of dyads emitting at least one instance of the specified social signal is shown in parentheses.

to the unconditional probability of a social signal by the peer occurring during a 3-second period. The resulting difference scores for the two children of a dyad were averaged, making the dyad the basic unit of analysis. The probability of an answering signal was reliably greater than expected only for the older dyads and only for these dyads

Table 2-2. Answers to the Peer's Social Signal

Answer parameters	18-month-olds		24-months-olds	
	Joint	Solitary	Joint	Solitary
Probability of answer	.12	10	.33	.17
Meaningful relationship between signal and answer	81%	69%	82%	72%
Type of relationship Vocalization→vocalization	11	4	15	6
Gesture→complementary gesture	3	6	19	1
Gesture→negating gesture	3	1	4	4
Contact→contact	4	0	7	2
Unclear	5	5	10	5

during periods of joint object engagement [t (5) = 2.96, $p < .05$].

To evaluate further whether the signals occurring within 3 seconds could be thought of as answers, the relationships in form between the initial signal and the following signal were examined. Four types of apparently meaningful relationships were found: (a) a vocalization with or without accompanying signals was followed by a vocalization; (b) a gesture with or without accompanying signals was followed by a complementary gesture (e.g., offer-accept, reach to take-relinquish, reach for-throw to); (c) a gesture with or without accompanying signals was followed by a negating gesture (move to take-gesture peer away, request-shake head "no", attempt to take-resist); (d) a physical contact with or without accompanying signals was followed by the peer making physical contact, The remaining relationships could well be meaningful given their context, but a meaningful relationship was not apparent from their form alone. At both ages meaningful relationships were found for a greater proportion of the answers during joint versus solitary object engagement, and in joint object engagement at least 80% of the answering signals appeared meaningfully related to the prior signal.

Taken together, the data on going to a partner's object, joint object engagement, and communication suggest that going to a partner's object does indeed facilitate the reaching of a topic around which communication occurs. Joint object engagement facilitates both the toddler's sending of communicative signals to a partner and his or her answering the partner's signals. Furthermore, the interactive skill of answering a partner's signals appears later than that of sending signals, and its development may well be facilitated by the interactive experiences characterizing joint object engagement. The toddler, at least, first evidences this skill with peers during bouts of being together and contacting the same play material.

Examination of the toddlers' visual regard of one another reinforces these conclusions. Mutual visual regard was more likely during joint object engagement than during solitary object engagement [18 months, t (5) = 3.93, $p < .02$; 24 months, t (5) = 2.80, $p < .05$]. Since mutual visual regard has been considered a way of acknowledging a joint enterprise or of checking upon such shared involvement (Bruner, 1977), its greater occurrence during joint object engagement confirms the view that going to another's object facilitates reaching a common topic for a social exchange. Furthermore, it was during bouts of joint object engagement that the older toddlers appeared to look toward one another in unison, evidencing further awareness of the joint enterprise. The older toddlers more often than the younger toddlers looked toward one another virtually simultaneously (within 1 second of each other), but only during joint object engagement (2.2 vs. 1.3 such occurrences per minute).

Illustration 2: Assuming Related Roles in Acting Upon the Topic

Although approaching and contacting a partner's object may bring about a common topic for a social exchange, simply contacting the object does little to elaborate upon the topic or to generate the cooperative endeavor forming the heart of cooperative play. A second major task facing the child is to develop a way of acting with respect to the topic which is meaningfully related to his or her partner's actions on the topic. For the primarily nonverbal toddler, such roles must be negotiated largely through motoric action rather than through verbal means. A second, longitudinal study, which is still in progress, allows an examination of the young child's skills in assuming a role related to that of his or her partner. Seventeen pairs of initially unfamiliar peers are being observed interacting with one another, with their mothers, and with a programed adult partner at 16, 20, 24, 28, and 32 months of age. Preliminary analyses of interaction with the adult for the 6 pairs seen through 24 months will serve to raise a number of questions about how the young child comes to relate his or her behavior meaningfully to that of an unfamiliar partner.

The children were observed in a setting thought to be conducive to interactive play. The room, the playhouse, ball and chute, and platform were the same as in the prior study; but the laundry basket and blocks were replaced by a freestanding low wall (a gigantic busy box) containing four equally spaced activity centers: a recessed mirror covered by a towel that can be raised and lowered, a large bicycle horn, an animal with a rotating telephone dial belly, and a hole into which bean bags can be inserted to drop out a second, lower hole.

During a first visit at each age, each child came to the playroom with a parent. The parent and child played together for 8 minutes before being joined by a relatively unfamiliar adult partner. The parent then was asked to sit on a floor cushion and assume an observer's role, responding simply to the child's overtures without actively playing with or directing the child. The adult proceeded in a set order to three play centers in the room. The adult's behavior at each was programed to mimic a well-formed play overture of the type toddlers direct toward one another (cf. Ross, 1982). At each play center, she performed a set play action and then stepped back from the play material, paused and looked toward the child. If the child smiled or vocalized to the adult, the adult replied in kind. The adult repeated her play overture as soon as the child acted upon the same play material in an imitative or complementary manner or after 10 seconds without a relevant action by the child, and continued in this manner for 90 seconds at each of the play centers. The play overtures consisted of inserting the ball into the chute and saying "down it goes" as it rolled out the other end; knocking on the outside of the playhouse before inserting her head into the window and saying "hello, there"; and stepping up onto the low platform and jumping off while saying "jump." The verbal component of each overture increased the attention-eliciting aspects of the adult's behavior, marked the end of the adult's "turn," and also allowed the child to respond with a related verbal utterance.

The adult's behavior was programed to probe both for the child's readiness to join the adult at the play material and for the child acting upon the play material in a manner meaningfully related to the adult's action. With the ball and chute, for example, the child could insert the ball into the chute (imitative relationship), retrieve the ball and hand it to the adult (complementary relationship), or take the ball away from the adult (interfering relationship). The child, of course, could also laugh at the adult's antics (audience relationship) or tell or gesture her to do it again (directive relationship). Furthermore, if the child joined the adult and assumed a related role with the play material, the child's skills in repetitive turn taking could also be assessed. The adult and child could generate a sustained turn-taking game. The role of the adult in this effort, however, was circumscribed, leaving to the child a considerable burden in generating cooperative play.

At all three ages (16, 20, and 24 months), most of the toddlers joined the adult at the play material she was acting upon. If we consider each of the adult's actions upon the play material as starting a trial, then the children joined the adult (came to or remained within 2 feet of her play material) during an average of 43% of the trials. The frequency of joining did not differ reliably among the three ages. At each age, 2 or 3 of the 12 children never joined the adult, but these were not the same children across ages.

For each trial during which the child joined the adult, the relationship between the child's actions at the play material and the adult's programed action was characterized as either imitative (performing the same action), complementary (facilitating or complementing the adult's action), audience (laughing at the adult after her action), directive (pointing to the adult and vocalizing or verbalizing to her), interfering (restricting the adult's access to the play material), tangential (acting upon the play material but in a way unlike the above relationships), or none (acting upon different play material or no action at all). Clear reciprocal relationships were not found, nor were they actively probed for in the choice of play material and play overture. The various types of observed relationships were grouped into three categories on the basis of their apparent consequences for cooperative play. Cooperative relationships (audience, directive, imitative, and complementary) are those thought to facilitate cooperative play. The interfering relationship is viewed as acting against the generation of cooperative play, and the obscure relationships (tangential, none) are viewed as neither acting against cooperative play nor probably aiding in its generation. At best, such relationships might maintain engagement between the partners until some more cooperative relationship occurred.

Table 2-3 summarizes the changes with age in how the toddlers related their actions to the adult's play overtures. For the present analysis, each trial was characterized by one type of relationship, and the frequencies are given as percentages of the total number of trials during which the child joined the adult. Audience and directive relationships frequently accompanied complementary and imitative relationships, but they were used to characterize a trial only when they were the only cooperative relationship that occurred. Friedman two-way analyses of variance by ranks, comparing the frequencies of obscure, interfering, and cooperative relationships at an age, indicated reliable differences in frequency at each age (16 months, χ^2_r = 6.95, $p < .05$; 20 months, χ^2_r = 8.45, $p < .02$; 24 months, χ^2_r = 9.39, $p < .01$). Subsequent sign tests indicated that at the youngest age, interfering relationships occurred less often than obscure or cooperative relationships and that the frequency of obscure and cooperative relationships did not differ reliably. At both 20 and 24 months, however, cooperative relationships reliably outnumbered both obscure and interfering relationships, and the latter two types of relationships did not differ reliably in frequency.

Further assessments of changes with age in the frequency of types of relationships were complicated by the fact that 6 of the 12 toddlers did not join the adult at one of the three ages. Sign tests contrasting the frequencies at successive ages for all subjects providing data at these ages, however, indicated two major changes: (a) obscure relationships decreased in frequency from 16 to 20 months ($p = .008$), and (b) cooperative relationships increased in frequency between the same two ages ($p = .004$). The frequency of interfering relationships did not differ reliably across the ages.

Table 2-3. Relationship Between Child's Actions and Partner's Action

Relationship	16 months (n = 10)	20 months (n = 10)	24 months (n = 9)
Obscure	45.8[a](10)[b]	17.8 (7)	5.1 (3)
Tangential	26.6 (8)	12.1 (4)	2.5 (2)
None	19.2 (5)	5.6 (5)	2.6 (2)
Interfering	14.2 (6)	9.9 (6)	15.3 (2)
Cooperative	40.0 (8)	72.3 (10)	79.6 (8)
Audience	5.0 (2)	2.7 (2)	8.7 (4)
Directive	0.8 (1)	2.0 (1)	0.0 (0)
Imitative	18.7 (4)	34.0 (8)	54.0 (8)
Complementary	15.4 (6)	33.6 (8)	16.9 (5)

[a]Percentage of trials with specified relationship.
[b]Number of subjects showing specified relationship at least once is shown in parentheses.

Inspection of Table 2-3 suggests further qualifications upon the age changes in cooperative relationships. Audience and directive relationships by themselves occurred infrequently at all ages. Imitative relationships, however, showed a marked and progressive increase with age; while complementary relationships increased from 16 to 20 months and then decreased from 20 to 24 months. Given prior speculations of a developmental progression from imitative relationships to complementary relationships, these apparently conflicting data warranted further scrutiny. Sign tests provided no evidence for a differential frequency of imitative and complementary relationships at 16 months (p = .50). However, at 20 months, there was a tendency for complementary relationships to occur more often than imitative ones (p = .09), whereas at 24 months imitative relationships clearly occurred more frequently (p = .004). Of the 7 children contributing data at both 20 and 24 months, 6 showed a change from more complementary relationships at 20 months to more imitative relationships at 24 months; the remaining child showed the same shift between 16 and 20 months and an intensification of the greater frequency of imitative relationships at 24 months.

The different play materials and overtures elicited different characteristic types of cooperative relationships. If we define a characteristic relationship as one shown by at least one-half of the toddlers joining the adult at a given age, then the ball and chute elicited both complementary (giving the ball to the adult) and imitative relationships at 20 months and imitative relationships at 24 months. At each age, the playhouse characteristically elicited complementary relationships (entering the house to wait for or peer out at the adult), and the platform elicited imitative relationships. Additionally, at 24 months the platform elicited audience relationships. The differences with age in the frequency of different types of relationships, however, cannot be attributed to changes in the type of play material engaged. Similar numbers of toddlers across age joined the adult at each of the three sets of play material.

Individual children, too, often showed multiple types of cooperative relationships, even from the youngest age studied. At 16 months, 4 toddlers showed multiple types of cooperative relationships (3 showed both imitative and complementary and 1 showed imitative, audience, and directive relationships), while 4 others showed single cooperative relationships (2 complementary, 1 imitative, and 1 audience). By 20 months, 8 of the 10 toddlers joining the adult showed multiple cooperative relationships.

The data reported so far speak clearly for the toddler's developing skills in responding to a partner's play overture with actions that are meaningfully and cooperatively related to the partner's actions. But what of the toddler's skills in maintaining the meaningfully related roles? Given an obliging and skillful adult partner who inserted her play action immediately after the child's imitative or complementary action and waited at least 10 seconds for the child to act, even the youngest toddlers participated in games (turn-taking sequences with at least two repetitive enactments of the same related actions by each participant). Five of the ten 16-month-olds joining the adult generated at least one complementary or imitative game with her for a total of 7 games (3 complementary, 4 imitative). By 20 months, 8 of the 10 toddlers generated a total of 14 such games (8 complementary and 6 imitative); and at 24 months, 8 of the 9 toddlers who joined the adult generated 14 games (6 complementary and 8 imitative). Sign tests comparing the frequency of games between two ages for those toddlers joining the adult at both ages indicated a reliable increase in games from 16 to 20 months of age (p = .01) and from 16 to 24 months (p = .03), but not from 20 to 24 months. The increased frequency of games between 16 and 20 months probably resulted more from the increased likelihood of assuming imitative or complementary roles between these ages than from any increased tendency to repeat such a role across trials once it had been assumed. The probabilities of repeating an assumed imitative or complementary role from one trial to the next were comparable for all three ages (ranging from .50 to .57). Furthermore, there were no differences among the ages in the average number of "turns" taken by the toddler in the games (mean 3.6).

Despite the apparent skill of these toddlers in generating "games" with an unfamiliar adult partner, the toddlers also behaved in several ways that might well prove problematical with a less obliging partner. Often they left the area of the game during its progress, returning to the parent or visiting another play area briefly (12 games), and often they intermixed other, tangentially related or unrelated acts with their cooperative acts during the same "turn" in the game (7 games). A detailed examination of such problematic behaviors, as well as facilitating behaviors (e.g., verbal directions to the partner, standing back and pausing for the partner's action, and laughter) awaits the completion of our observations on the full sample of toddlers.

The preliminary data presented on toddlers' skills in relating their own actions to an adult's play overture both confirm and extend those reported earlier for freely occurring peer interactions. Throughout the second year of life, toddlers readily approach and contact the play material manipulated by others. Older toddlers do not differ from younger toddlers in their readiness to go to another's play materials; rather, they differ in their behavior once they and their partner are engaging the same play material . The earlier analyses showed that older toddlers are more likely to respond to a peer's social signal with an answering signal. The present analyses extend these findings: older toddlers also are more apt to act upon a partner's play material in a way that is meaningfully related to the partner's own actions and in a way that would appear to facilitate reaching agreement about a cooperative endeavor. Older toddlers imitate or complement their partner's actions more often; these ways of behaving appear time and again in the descriptions of toddler cooperative play. Younger toddlers more often behave in unrelated or only tangentially related ways.

Although the older toddler appears clearly more skillful in relating his or her own behavior meaningfully and cooperatively to that of a social partner, no support was found for the proposed developmental progression from imitative to complementary role relationships. Instead, both complementary and imitative role relationships were shown by even the youngest toddlers studied. By 20 months of age, imitative and complementary relationships occurred frequently and with near equal frequency. Furthermore, in contrast to the speculated progression from imitative to complementary relationships, by 24 months imitative relationships occurred reliably more often than complementary relationships. The generality of these developmental trends, of course, has yet to be established; but such findings fuel the speculation that similar, perhaps identical, abilities are required for the toddler to assume both imitative and complementary roles and that these abilities emerge during the second year of life. The role of imitation in the toddler's development of interactive skills may lie less in its facilitation of the development of the abilities to assume more complex, complementary roles, and more in its widespread applicability. Imitating another's actions seems an excellent, all-purpose strategy for meaningfully and cooperatively relating one's own actions to those of a partner. As such, it may be especially useful with new partners with whom the toddler does not yet have a well-practiced set of complementary interchanges and with largely nonverbal partners. Virtually all of a peer's playful actions can be imitated by a toddler; relatively few suggest a complementary action to the adult observer and, we suspect, to the toddler. As we continue to observe these toddlers into their third year of life, rapid changes in their verbal communication and in fantasy play may well result in the occurrence of more complementary relationships and fewer imitative ones. Verbal communication in combination with fantasy play may increase the ability of the young child both to specify a complementary role to his or her partner and to understand and assume such a role with respect to that partner.

The analyses to date provide little insight into the toddlers' increasing skills in *maintaining* cooperative role relationships. With an obliging, skillful, adult partner, 16-month-olds were as likely to reenact a complementary or imitative role relationship as were 24-month-olds. Comparing the same toddlers in interaction with a peer partner versus the adult partner may aid in teasing apart which of the component skills required for maintaining cooperative play develop during the second year of life. Difficulties in managing the temporal structure of the interaction may well mask the toddler's ability and willingness to repeat acts cooperatively related to his or her peer's actions.

Evaluation

The interactive skills so far isolated and examined for the toddler are few, but their implications are far reaching. Throughout the second year of life, going to another's object can be viewed as a way of achieving a shared topic (the object) about which two persons can communicate. Skills in relating one's own actions on the object meaningfully and cooperatively to those of a partner develop during the second year of life, increasing the toddler's ability to generate cooperative endeavors with others. Imitating another's action can be thought of as a generative strategy for expressing agreement about a topic and for specifying the form a cooperative endeavor may take. Skills in "answering" a peer's vocalizations, gestures, and physical contacts and in looking at one another in unison also emerge during this developmental period in the context of a common topic, increasing the toddler's abilities to communicate about that topic and to communicate about the joint endeavor itself.

Each of these interactive skills is a basic achievement on the road to social maturity. Each facilitates interpersonal communication and the achievement of important social outcomes. Each indicates the child's growing understanding about persons and the process of communicating with another. Perhaps most importantly, each such skill shapes the toddler's social experience. Going to another's object results in different experiences than staying at a distance. Behaving in a way that is cooperatively related to another's actions prompts different reactions than unrelated or interfering actions. Looking at one's partner at particular points in the interaction results in jointly initiated bouts of regard. Through their interactive skills, toddlers contribute potently to their own social experience and development.

Reference Notes

1. Power, T. G., & Parke, R. D. Toward a taxonomy of father-infant and mother-infant play patterns. Paper presented at the biennial meeting of the Society for Research in Child Development, San Francisco, March 1979.

References

Ainsworth, M. D. S. The development of infant-mother attachment. In B. M. Caldwell & H. N. Ricciuti (Eds.), *Review of child development research* (Vol. 3). Chicago: University of Chicago Press, 1973.

Bates, E. *The emergence of symbols: Cognition and communication in infancy.* New York: Academic Press, 1979.

Bayley, N. *The California first-year mental scale.* Berkeley: University of California Press, 1933.

Bayley, N. *Manual for the Bayley Scales of Infant Development.* New York: Psychological Corporation, 1969.

Brazelton, T. B., Koslowski, B., & Main, M. The origins of reciprocity: The early mother-infant interaction. In M. Lewis & L. Rosenblum (Eds.), *The effect of the infant on its caregiver*. New York: Wiley, 1974.

Brown, R. *A first language*. Cambridge, Mass.: Harvard University Press, 1973.

Bruner, J. S. Early social interaction and language acquisition. In H. R. Schaffer (Ed.), *Studies in mother-infant interaction*. London: Academic Press, 1977.

Bühler, C. *The first year of life*. New York: Day, 1930.

Bühler, C. The social behavior of children. In C. A. Murchison (Ed.), *A handbook of child psychology* (Vol. 1). New York: Russell and Russell, 1933.

Cairns, R. B. Attachment and dependency: A psychobiological and social-learning synthesis. In J. L. Gewirtz (Ed.), *Attachment and dependency*. Washington, D.C.: Winston, 1972.

Crawley, S. B., Rogers, P. P., Friedman, S., Iacobbo, M., Criticos, A., Richardson, L., & Thompson, M. A. Developmental changes in the structure of mother-infant play. *Developmental Psychology*, 1978, *14*, 30-36.

Dennis, W., & Dennis, M. G. Behavioral development in the first year as shown by forty biographies. *Psychological Record*, 1937, *1*, 349-361.

Dore, J. A pragmatic description of early language development. *Journal of Psycholinguistic Research*, 1974, *3*, 343-350.

Dunn, J., & Kendrick, C. Interaction between young siblings in the context of family relationships. In M. Lewis & L. A. Rosenblum (Eds.), *The child and its family*. New York: Plenum Press, 1979.

Eckerman, C. O., & Whatley, J. L. Toys and social interaction between infant peers. *Child Development*, 1977, *48*, 1645-1656.

Eckerman, C. O., Whatley, J. L., & Kutz, S. L. Growth of social play with peers during the second year of life. *Developmental Psychology*, 1975, *11*, 42-49.

Eckerman, C. O., Whatley, J. L., & McGehee, L. J. Approaching and contacting the object another manipulates: A social skill of the 1-year-old. *Developmental Psychology*, 1979, *15*, 585-593.

Escalona, S. K. Basic modes of social interaction: Their emergence and patterning during the first two years of life. *Merrill-Palmer Quarterly*, 1973, *19*, 205-232.

Field, T. M., & Walden, T. A. Perception and production of facial expressions in infancy and early childhood. In H. Reese & L. Lipsitt (Eds.), *Advances in child development and behavior* (Vol. 16). New York: Academic Press, in press.

Garvey, C. Some properties of social play. *Merrill-Palmer Quarterly*, 1974, *20*, 163-180.

Gesell, A., & Thompson, H. *Infant behavior: Its genesis and growth*. New York: McGraw-Hill, 1934.

Goldman, B. D., & Ross, H. A. Social skills in action: An analysis of early peer games. In J. Glick & K. A. Clarke-Stewart (Eds.), *The development of social understanding*. New York: Gardner Press, 1978.

Gustafson, G. E., Green, J. A., & West, M. J. The infant's changing role in mother-infant games: The growth of social skills. *Infant Behavior and Development*, 1979, *2*, 301-308.

Hay, D. F. Cooperative interactions and sharing between very young children and their parents. *Developmental Psychology*, 1979, *15*, 647-653.

Lamb, M. E. (Ed.). *The role of the father in child development*. New York: Wiley, 1976.

Lee, L. C. Toward a cognitive theory of interpersonal development. In M. Lewis

& L. A. Rosenblum (Eds.), *Friendship and peer relations*. New York: Wiley, 1975.

Leung, E., & Rheingold, H. L. Development of pointing as a social gesture. *Developmental Psychology*, 1981, *17*, 215-220.

Lock, A. (Ed.). *Action, gesture and symbol: The emergance of language*. London: Academic Press, 1978.

Maudry, M., & Nekula, M. Social relations between children of the same age during the first two years of life. *Journal of Genetic Psychology*, 1939, *54*, 193-215.

Mueller, E., & Brenner, J. The origins of social skills and interaction among playgroup toddlers. *Child Development*, 1977, *48*, 845-861.

Mueller, E., & Lucas, T. A developmental analysis of peer interaction among toddlers. In M. Lewis & L. A. Rosenblum (Eds.), *Friendship and peer relations*. New York: Wiley, 1975.

Newman, D. Ownership and permission among nursery school children. In J. Glick & K. A. Clarke-Stewart (Eds.), *The development of social understanding*. New York: Gardner Press, 1978.

Ratner, N., & Bruner, J. Games, social exchange and the acquisition of language. *Journal of Child Language*, 1978, *5*, 391-401.

Ross, H. S. Establishment of social games among toddlers. *Developmental Psychology*, 1982, *18*, 509-518.

Ross, H. S., & Goldman, B. D. Infants' sociability toward strangers. *Child Development*, 1977, *48*, 638-642.

Ross, H. S., & Kay, D. A. The origins of social games. In K. H. Rubin (Ed.), *Chilren's play: New directions for child development* (Vol. 9). San Francisco: Jossey-Bass, 1980.

Scaife, M., & Bruner, J. S. The capacity for joint visual attention in the infant. *Nature*, 1975, *253*, 265-266.

Schaffer, H. R. *The growth of sociability*. Harmondsworth, England: Penguin, 1971.

Shaffer, H. R. *Studies in mother-infant interaction*. London: Academic Press, 1977.

Shirley, M. *The first two years: A study of twenty-five babies* (Vol. 2). Minneapolis: University of Minnesota Press, 1933.

Stayton, D. J., Ainsworth, M. D. S., & Main, M. B. Development of separation behavior in the first year of life: Protest, following, and greeting. *Developmental Psychology*, 1973, *9*, 213-225.

Stayton, D. J., Hogan, R., & Ainsworth, M. D. S. Infant obedience and maternal behavior: The origins of socialization reconsidered. *Child Development*, 1971, *42*, 1057-1069.

Stern, D. N. A microanalysis of mother-infant interaction. *Journal of the American Academy of Child Psychiatry*, 1971, *10*, 501-517.

Stern, D. *The first relationship: Mother and infant*. Cambridge, Mass.: Harvard University Press, 1977.

Trevarthen, C. Communication and cooperation in early infancy: A description of primary intersubjectivity. In M. Bullowa (Ed.), *Before speech: The beginning of interpersonal communication*. Cambridge, England: Cambridge University Press, 1979.

Vandell, D. L., Wilson, K. S., & Buchanan, N. R. Peer interaction in the first year of life: An examination of its structure, content, and sensitivity to toys. *Child Development*, 1980, *51*, 481-488.

Vincze, M. The social contacts of infants and young children reared together. *Early Child Development and Care*, 1971, *1*, 99-109.

Washburn, R. W. A study of the smiling and laughing of infants in the first year of life. *Genetic Psychology Monographs*, 1929, *5-6*, 397-537.

Wolff, P. H. The natural history of crying and other vocalizations in early infancy. In B. M. Foss (Ed.), *Determinants of infant behaviour* (Vol. 1). London: Methuen, 1969.

Chapter 3

Toddler–Peer Communication

Hildy S. Ross, Susan P. Lollis, and Connie Elliott

Communication is the foundation of social interaction. People do not merely act synchronously or direct behavior to their social partners in some temporally organized manner; rather, they send and receive meaningful messages, interpret one another's behavior, and react in appropriate ways. Furthermore, their communicative actions, gestures, and words reflect the assumptions that social partners can understand and may comply to requests contained within such overtures. In this chapter we consider the peer interaction of toddlers within a communicative framework.

Communication has been studied by those interested in mother-child interaction and also by those interested in the peer interaction of preschoolers. Students of mother-infant interaction have recognized the importance of early communication patterns for the development of language and of social relations (Bruner, 1977; Greenfield & Smith, 1976; Ryan, 1974; Schaffer, Collis, & Parsons, 1977; Snow, 1977; Trevarthen, 1980; Zukow, Reilly, & Greenfield, 1980). They have focused explicitly on the communicative assumptions mothers make concerning their infants, the conversational context of language acquisition and interaction, the comprehension of maternal gestures and language by infants, and the beginnings of intentional communication in the early years. The methodological problems of dealing with intention and meaning have proven difficult, but not insurmountable (Bruner, 1974; Greenfield, 1980). Furthermore, students of peer relations among preschool-age children have dealt directly with the communicative competence of their young subjects (Garvey, 1975; Levin & Rubin, in press; Mueller, 1972; Spilton & Lee, 1977; Wellman & Lempers, 1977), considering, for example, requests and directives, the adequacy of responses, and the modification of initial overtures in relation to listener feedback. Thus, precedent exists in the literature for considering communication both during the first 2 years of life and

with peers. In studies of *toddler-peer* interaction, however, questions of
the meaning of children's actions and gestures, and of the appropriateness of peer interpretations and responses have rarely been directly
addressed.

Three basic approaches characterize recent studies of toddler-peer
interaction. In the first, observations are made of the *frequency* of
particular forms of peer-directed behavior (Eckerman & Whatley, 1977;
Eckerman, Whatley, & Kutz, 1975; Rubenstein & Howes, 1976).
Communicative actions are recorded within the response categories in
these studies; they include vocal and affective signals, and shows, offers,
or other gestures. Usually, the meanings of such actions play a role in
the interpretation of the findings; however, recording is often limited to
one child at a time, and so the social consequences of such acts are
unknown.

In other work, explicit attention is paid to the *consequences* of
socially directed behavior. Researchers examine whether peers respond
to social overtures with socially directed activities, whether interaction
chains develop, and how long such interchanges last (Mueller & Brenner,
1977; Vandell, Wilson, & Buchanan, 1980). One might assume that
these interactive sequences contain many instances of toddlers directing
meaningful overtures to their peers, who, in turn, comprehend and
react appropriately. In much of this work, however, the nature of the
socially directed behavior is not a focus, and so the meaning of the
actions or the relation between the actions and responses generally
cannot be evaluated.

One exception to this generalization is Bronson's (1981) recent
monograph in which overtures were considered either positive or negative and responses were classified as passive, negative, or positive
reactions; negative and positive reactions were further classed as either
related or not related to the overture and as brief or sustained. The
match of positive overtures with positive responses (especially positive, sustained, and related responses) and of negative overtures with
active negative responses was taken as evidence of comprehension and
appropriate responding. Bronson found very little evidence of comprehension and compliance, especially for positive overtures. Her criteria
may have led her to underestimate the extent of appropriate peer
reactions (see Ross, Borwick, Goldman, & Hay, in press): for example,
passive responses (such as accepting a proffered toy) could give evidence of both comprehension and compliance, and negative reactions
to positive overtures could in some cases signal comprehension, but
were not considered as such. Finally, the classification of overtures into
positive and negative specifies little about the meaning of such actions.
Hence, a more direct approach to each incident might be more profitable.

A third research approach has been to *isolate interaction sequences*
within the flow of peer activity, such as games, conflicts, or thematic

interchanges, and to focus on communication and mutual comprehension within these. In this way, the role of communicative gestures in
instigating and maintaining games (Mueller & Lucas, 1975; Goldman &
Ross, 1978; Ross, 1982), the use of communication to further goals
within conflict (Hay & Ross, 1982), and the sharing of meaningfully
related play themes (Brenner & Mueller, in press) have been explored.
These studies establish both the use of communication in peer interaction and the appreciation of the meaning of peer-directed behavior
within the context of sustained interaction; they encourage the broader
based description of toddler-peer communication, including analysis of
both overtures and responses, that we have attempted here.

In the current analyses we consider the communicative means that
toddlers adopt when attempting to influence the behavior of their
peers, and the social consequences of the communicative overtures. We
ask the following questions: When and how do toddlers communicate
with their peers? Are there patterned relationships among the communicative attempts? Do toddlers comprehend the meanings intended
by their peers? Do they comply with the implicit or explicit requests
contained within peer overtures? What influences the extent of comprehension or compliance? Later in this chapter, we examine the role of
interpersonal relationships in the development of patterns of peer
comunication. Do particular dyads develop characteristic patterns of
communication? Do the responses the toddlers receive from one
another influence subsequent communicative endeavors?

Definition of Communication

What actions might be considered communicative in toddler-peer
interaction? The results of this investigation will depend, as in any
research, on the definitions adopted at the outset and will need to be
interpreted within the context of our initial assumptions. This is particularly so in a study of toddler-peer communication, as different approaches may guide the selection of definitional criteria. Several approaches to this problem were rejected as being either too broad or too
restrictive. For example, any action by a child could be considered
communicative as it carries and imparts information to the peer,
without specifically being directed toward the peer. Such a definition
would include all actions by each child and the peer's responses would
be very difficult to judge, especially as the occasion for response
would not be set by a peer-directed overture. A narrower definition
might include only intentional communicative patterns, which have
been defined in the past by the presence of (a) visual regard of the
partner accompanying the action, (b) an identified goal, (c) sustained
direction of behavior in the form of repetition, amplification, and
substitution when unsuccessful in reaching the goal, and (d) termi-

nation of the communication when the goal is reached (Bruner, 1974). The first two criteria are part of our current definition; however, the third and fourth criteria, which serve well to identify the onset of or the capacity for intentional communication, cannot be applied to evaluate whether each and every action is communicative. Actions that do not meet with failure (and therefore offer no clear evidence of sustained direction) or actions that the initiating child decides for some reason to abandon (and therefore show no evidence of repetition or termination upon reaching the goal) may not, in themselves, provide palpable evidence of intentional communication (Greenfield, 1980) but might still have been intended to communicate with a social partner.

Because we have chosen to focus on the interacting dyad, our definition of communication is based on consideration of the action from the viewpoint of the recipient as well as the viewpoint of the child initiating the signal. *Our first criterion is that communicative overtures appear to be directed toward the peer and to invite the peer's involvement.* Direction toward the peer is indicated by actions accompanied by visual regard of the peer, or by actions embedded within a sequence of peer interaction and not directed elsewhere (e.g., as an aside comment to the mother). Intent to involve the peer is indicated by both directing the overture to the peer and waiting, for at least a brief period, for the peer's response. *Second, communicative overtures must be potentially capable of imparting information concerning the goals of the overturing child.* The particular goals inferred and thus the form of peer involvement requested depend upon the overture and will be discussed later. *Third, communicative actions are restricted to those that would require the peer's comprehension and compliance to meet their goals* (although, in fact, evidence of comprehension and compliance are not always present).

An example might help to clarify the third criterion: If one child wanted a toy held by the other, he or she might approach, grab, and tug at the toy while watching the peer. If this action succeeded in meeting its goal, it might be because of the strength of the initiating child, who could wrest the object from the peer. Another means of achieving the same goal might be to approach, reach toward the toy, exclaim "mine ball" and watch the peer. If this child succeeded, the partner would have had to recognize the action as a request for the toy, and comply by giving it to his or her peer. The first course of action would not be considered communicative in this research. Although it does communicate the interest of the actor in possessing the toy held by the peer, the partner need not comprehend the message nor comply to the request in order for it to succeed. The second set of actions, on the other hand, meets the definition of communicative acts adopted here. In addition, it reflects an important but possibly implicit assumption made by the initiator of the request, namely, that the partner is capable of comprehending and responding to this less direct means of achieving a goal.

This assumption might be incorrect—toddler peers may lack such under-standing; nonetheless, it seems unlikely that a child would repeatedly use communicative means to influence a peer unless these were expected to have at least the potential to achieve the goal.

Method

The 48 children who participated in this study were all between 20 and 22 months of age. The children, accompanied by their mothers, came to a university laboratory, where they played with partners of the same sex in a brightly decorated playroom for 15 minutes on each of 3 consecutive days. There were 12 pairs of boys and 12 of girls. The members of each pair had not met prior to the study, but the same pairings were retained for the 3 days.

The mothers remained with their children throughout the play sessions. They were seated near one another, and could talk or respond to the children fairly naturally, but were asked to refrain from directing the children's play, initiating or fostering extensive interaction with the children, or intervening in the children's exchanges except when there was the possibility of injury. Many age-appropriate toys (108 if all separable parts were counted) were available for the children, rang-ing in size and type from a large plastic wash tub to wheelbarrows, balls, pull toys, hats, dolls, sets of building blocks, dishes, and tiny cars. These were arranged around the room on the floor and on or in several brightly colored hollow plastic toy boxes. All sessions were recorded on videotape with two cameras (one stationary, one moving and re-motely controlled) mounted near the ceiling in the playroom, enabling coverage of virtually the entire room.

Measures of Communication

Transcriptions of the videotapes were prepared based on the agreement of two observers working together. These included an account of events preceding, during, and following each instance of communicative behavior. The categories of communicative acts were developed from the first six records transcribed and modifications of the categorization system continued as new situations arose. All sessions were later re-viewed by another observer who verified the descriptions and the consistency of the categorization. Interobserver reliability was estab-lished based on independent transcripts for nine sessions; exact agree-ment averaged 82% for the descriptions and categorization of communi-cative overtures and responses.

Nine categories of communicative overtures were identified: *showing, giving,* and *offering* objects to the peer; *requesting* objects of the peer; *declarative* statements; *expressive* actions or words; *invitations to play;*

attempts to join peer play; and *protests* of peer's actions (Table 3-1).

All of these communicative actions serve to establish a topic of joint reference to either an object or an activity of one of the partners. Showing, offering, and giving have been considered means whereby a child can establish joint reference to an object, and as precursors to declarative statements (Bates, 1976). Moreover, many of the communicative actions went further, with additional comments that might be considered elaborations on the focus of attention. For example, invitations to play generally included both an object to play with and the display of appropriate actions with that object; requests for objects accompanied by the word "mine" drew attention both to the object and to the alleged ownership by the requestor.

These communicative signals have imperative qualities as well, making it possible to categorize the appropriateness of the peers' responses. Objects shown should be looked at and those offered or given, accepted. Declaratives and expressives are less explicit in terms of an appropriate response, but can be acknowledged by further pertinent conversation or reciprocating expressive actions. A peer invited to play is expected to respond by adopting appropriate actions in a play context (often with imitative or complementary acts), and a child might be expected to acknowledge the peer's joining play by facilitating continued mutual play. Finally, protests of a peer's actions and object requests have very clear imperative messages: peers are expected to cease actions protested and to give objects requested.

When a peer complies appropriately to a communicative gesture (*compliance*) we may assume that the gesture has been understood; but in many cases active *noncompliance* may also give evidence of comprehension. When a requested object is withdrawn with an assertion "No, mine!", or a proferred object is pushed away and labeled "too heavy", comprehension of the communicative overture is apparent. For some overtures, it is also possible for peer reactions that are neither compliant nor noncompliant to offer evidence of comprehension (*other*). Therefore, evidence for comprehension was sought directly by examining the responses to communicative gestures in their immediate context (Table 3-1). However, it could not be concluded that a gesture was not understood when the peer did not respond or when the response failed to offer evidence of comprehension; hence a more tentative category, *no evidence of comprehension* was adopted for such cases. A child's response offered no evidence of comprehension if the communicative act was apparently perceived but the child failed to perform any action that conveyed comprehension: this included occurrences of simply looking at the peer or at a referent object (except for show), as well as other communicative acts that may have conveyed understanding of the social nature of the peer's act but gave no evidence of comprehension

Table 3-1. Communicative Overtures and Responses

Show: point to or hold up an object; verbal "look" or "see"
  Compliance: look at or approach the referent object
  Noncompliance: protest; turn away or fail to look[a]
Give: throw, drop, or place an object near the peer or in an object the peer is playing with
  Compliance: take the object; verbal "thanks"
  Noncompliance: verbal protest; push or throw object away
Offer: hold object out toward peer
  Compliance: reach for or take the object
  Noncompliance: protest; push object away; turn away[a]
Request object: reach toward or touch object; verbal request such as "want it"
  Compliance: give or offer object to peer
  Noncompliance: protest or withdraw object
Declarative: all intelligible verbal utterances, except those otherwise classified (e.g., as show); vocalizations that are meaningful in context (e.g., "hmm?" or "oh! oh!")
  Compliance: a meaningful and pertinent declarative reply
  Noncompliance: none
  Other: perform an action related to peer's vocalization such as looking at named object
Expressive: laugh, smile, pat, kiss, name peer, greet, approach face-to-face, point to peer, call peer "baby"
  Compliance: perform a related, reciprocating expressive
  Noncompliance: protest; withdraw self
  Other: perform an unrelated social act that reciprocates the social intent of the peer's overture
Invitation to play: perform actions watched by the peer and follow with a pause or signal for the peer to join
  Compliance: join peer's play with a related action
  Noncompliance: protest; refuse to participate[a]
  Other: join the peer, but with an unrelated action
Attempt to join play: manipulate an object in the peer's possession without attempting to exclude the peer; imitate or perform an action complementary to the peer's
  Compliance: continue to play, and acknowledge and encourage peer's participation; perform a further invitation to play
  Noncompliance: protest; refuse to participate[a]
Protest action: screech, fuss, or whine; verbal "no" or "don't"; make a threatening gesture; withdraw self or object slightly
  Compliance: interrupt and cease action protested
  Noncompliance: protest; perform an act of physical aggression; resume protested action[a]
  Other: redirect peer's attention

---

[a]When scored noncomply, these responses occurred in the context of immediately prior compliance to similar overtures, giving the impression of active refusals to comply.

of the intent or content of the particular communicative act (e.g.,
smiling at the peer's face with no attention to the object in response to
a show). A fifth category of response was *unaware*, recorded when the
respondent did not see the peer's act and the act contained no clear,
attention-getting vocalizations. Finally, a response could also be considered a communicative overture if it met the three criteria outlined
above.

Communicative Overtures

Communicative gestures, actions, and words were frequent in this
sample. In all, there were 1,821 such overtures. This averaged 76 for
each pair, or 25.3 within a single 15-minute session.

The nine categories of communicative acts listed in order of total
frequencies for the toddlers in this study are as follows: attempt to join
play (315), expressive (247), invitation to play (216), show (206),
protest action (200), request object (186), offer (180), declarative
(176), and give (95). All but one of the categories (give) had total
frequencies of more the 175, yielding average frequencies of 7.3 or
more acts per category for each pair across the three sessions.

The number of pairs who used each category of communicative
overture ranged between 18 (75%) for protest action to 22 (92%) for
show. Of the 24 dyads, 11 used all classes of communicative overtures
at least once over the three sessions; 10 additional pairs used six or
more categories, 2 used four, and 1 pair used only two categories in the
45-minute time period. Thus, 88% of the pairs used six or more different types of communicative overtures in the sessions.

Variability Among the Dyads

Considerable variability among the pairs was displayed in the number of
communicative acts. At one end of the distribution, four pairs used
fewer than 20 communicative gestures, while at the other end of the
distribution, nine pairs exhibited more than 100 such acts, four of
whom used communicative actions more than 160 times in the three
sessions.

In addition, there were striking individual differences in the patterns
of communicative gestures in the different pairs. Examples of this
variability are shown in Figure 3-1. Three of the five dyads with the
greatest number of communicative acts are included; their total frequencies of each type of act, summed across the 3 days, are graphed.
Pair 20, the dyad with the greatest overall number of communicative
overtures, used many expressives and protests of the peer's actions;
they used few offers, invitations to play, and attempts to join play. In
contrast, pair 5 had extremely high numbers of play invitations and

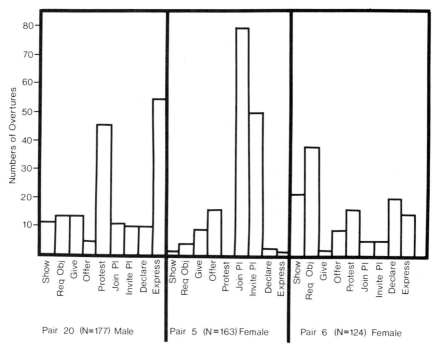

Fig. 3-1. Patterns of communicative gestures in three different pairs.

attempts to join play, and low numbers of all other categories but offer. The pattern of overtures in pair 6 was different again, with high numbers of request object, show, and declarative, and rather low numbers of invitation to play, attempt to join play, and give.

Patterns of Communication

The differing patterns and the considerable variability among certain dyads suggest that, more generally, particular communicative overtures may tend to co-occur, creating different patterns of communication among the dyads. Cluster analyses were therefore used to explore the patterns of use of different types of communicative overtures (Johnson, 1967). This analysis groups together variables with the highest relationships; new variables enter the group or cluster at the point of their average correlation with the other variables already in the cluster (the average distance method). The maximum and minimum distance methods were also used with very little deviation from the pattern shown by the average distance method. The results of the cluster analysis are presented in Figure 3-2.

The analysis revealed three pairs of communicative overtures that were highly related. The first cluster was formed by the two most strongly related variables, attempt to join play and invitation to play. This initial cluster was later joined by two other variables, give and

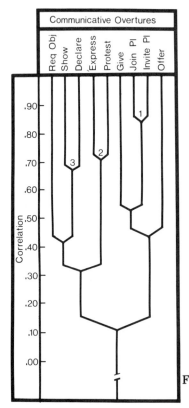

Fig. 3-2. Cluster analysis of communicative overtures by the average distance method.

offer, at a lower level of relatedness. Give preceded offer, indicating
that it was more closely related to the other two variables than was
offer. In addition, give was more closely related to the two joint play
categories than it was to offer. Expressive and protest action formed a
second cluster of responses that were highly related. A third cluster was
formed by show and declarative, with request object entering that
cluster at a point of modest relationship. The latter two clusters join
with average correlations between .30 and .40, and then the first cluster
joins to form a general cluster of all variables at a point of very low
average correlations (.10). Thus, particular overtures tend to co-occur
and discernible patterns of communicative overtures differentiate the
peer dyads.

Integration of Communicative Overtures and Meaningful Utterances

Thus far, our analysis indicates that frequent, varied, and patterned
communication exists between toddler peers. Children used actions and

gestures as well as words to convey information to their agemates. The rich variety of actions used suggests that actions, like words, are productive forms of communication wherein children can form new messages to meet their communicative needs. Nonetheless, language can be singled out as a communicative form; toddlers are in the process of learning language that will eventually add great power to their communicative capacities. Furthermore, it has recently been argued that language derives meaning from the context in which it is embedded and that language learning is made possible by the contextual embeddedness of early language (Bates, 1976; Carter, 1978; Clark, 1978; Lock, 1980; Zukow et al., 1980). In these data it was possible to examine the overlap between communicative actions and meaningful vocal utterances, and in this way to explore the relation between language and context in early peer communication.

We found that 43% of all communicative overtures either consisted of (n = 370) or were accompanied by (n = 418) meaningful vocal utterances. The distribution of such vocal utterances across the categories of action is presented in Table 3-2. Some categories seldom involved meaningful utterances (give, offer, attempt to join play, invitation to play), while other categories frequently did so (show, request object, protest action, expressive). Declaratives, by definition, were always meaningful verbal utterances without accompanying communicative gestures. Excluding declaratives, there were reliable relations between the category of communicative action and the frequency with which it was either expressed with, χ^2 (7) = 180.2, p <.001, or accompanied by, χ^2 (7) = 308.9, p <.001, a meaningful utterance.

Meaningful vocalizations were classified into eight categories: names of objects (166), statements of possession (106), verbal expressives (97), references to the state of an object (59), negatives (50), imperatives (48), miscellaneous words (138), and miscellaneous vocalizations (124). Some of the verbal utterances fell into certain overture categories by definition when they occurred alone; "look" or "see" were always classified as shows, "no" was most often a protest of peer's action, "mine" was generally a request of an object, and greetings were always classified as verbal expressives. Other potential relations between the communicative action and the accompanying vocalization were not determined by the category system itself (although without analyzing the vocalizations in the absence of visual cues it is not certain that this categorization was entirely independent of accompanying gestures). Nonetheless, it was possible to determine whether relations existed between the two category systems to see if meaningful verbal utterances were used within appropriate contexts. Categories of vocalizations and three categories of communicative actions (show, request object, and

Table 3-2. Use of Meaningful Utterances to Express or Accompany Communicative Overtures

Category of overture	Total overtures (no.)	Expressed by a meaningful utterance (%)	Accompanied by a meaningful utterance (%)	Without a meaningful utterance (%)
Show	206	5	65	30
Give	95	0	11	89
Offer	180	0	20	80
Request object	186	27	22	51
Declarative[a]	176	100	—	—
Expressive	247	24	23	52
Invitation to play	216	6	11	83
Attempt to join play	315	3	9	88
Protest action	200	24	41	35

[a]The distribution of declaratives is a function of the definition adopted.

protest action) that were frequently accompanied by meaningful vocalizations were analysed (Table 3-3).[1] The overall relationship was reliable, χ^2 (12) = 171.5, p <.001, and individual cells deviated markedly from chance expectations.[2] Negatives and miscellaneous vocalizations were used most often with protest action, possessives with object requests, and object names and imperatives with shows. Negatives and possessives were used less often with shows than might have been expected by chance; the name of the object was used less often than expected when children protested the actions of their peers. These findings suggest that verbal utterances were used meaningfully in context; the name of the object is a frequent accompaniment of shows (Leung & Rheingold, 1981), negatives are sensible vocal accompaniments to protests, and possessive statements righteously justify object requests. Furthermore, the angry tone of the miscellaneous vocalizations that accompanied protests presumably gave these their meaning within the interactive context.

---

[1] The fourth category with frequent accompanying utterances, expressives, was not included in this analysis as most (82%) accompanying vocalizations fell into the category "verbal expressive".

[2] Throughout this chapter, when individual cells are described, the value of chi square associated with that cell would have been sufficient, in itself, to reach accepted levels of statistical significance.

Table 3-3. Association of Meaningful Utterances with Three Communicative Overtures

Category of accompanying utterance	Category of overture		
	Show	Request object	Protest action
Imperative	25	0	5
Negative	0	1	29
Possessive	7	19	13
Name object	54	7	3
Describe state of object	11	6	0
Miscellaneous words	26	4	5
Miscellaneous vocalizations	13	3	28

Responses to Communicative Acts

Relation Between Overture and Response

Responses to communicative acts were categorized in a hierarchical system reflecting awareness, comprehension, and compliance. The distribution of responses in relation to the category of communicative action is shown in Table 3-4. Overall, in only a small percentage (4%) of the responses to specific actions did the partner appear unaware of the overture. Three communicative acts—shows, expressives, and declaratives—accounted for the greatest percentage of responses coded as unaware (7%, 9%, and 10% respectively), while other actions had fewer than 2% of their responses coded as unaware (Table 3-4). The distribution of responses coded as aware or unaware was significantly different from expected frequencies based on chance, χ^2 (8) = 61.2, $p < .001$; expressives and declaratives deviated most strongly from chance expectations.

Of the 1747 responses in which awareness of the partner's behavior was present, 61% showed some evidence of comprehension of the action, while 39% showed no evidence of comprehension (Table 3-4). Two categories of actions, expressive and declarative, accounted for the lowest percentage of responses offering evidence of comprehension; their respective rates were 35% and 18%. All other categories had comprehension rates ranging from 60% (show) to 79% (request object). The distribution of responses showing or failing to show evidence of comprehension was significantly different from the expected distribution based on chance, χ^2 (8) = 272.9, $p < .001$. Declaratives and expressives showed markedly less comprehension than would have been expected, whereas request object, protest action, and offer exceeded chance expectations of the frequency of comprehension.

Table 3-4. Responses to Communicative Overtures

Category of overture	Aware of communicative act					Total aware	Unaware
	Evidence of comprehension			Total comprehension	No evidence		
	Comply	Non-comply	Other				
Show	94	20	0	114	77	191	15
Give	55	15	0	70	24	94	1
Offer	112	19	0	131	47	178	2
Request object	19	125	0	144	38	182	4
Declarative	0	1	27	28	130	158	18
Expressive	7	57	15	79	145	224	23
Invitation to play	85	47	1	133	79	212	4
Attempt to join play	142	73	0	215	94	309	6
Protest action	41	108	5	154	45	199	1
Total	555	465	43	1068	679	1747	74

Evidence of comprehension was provided by compliance in 52% of cases; 43% of comprehended responses met with noncompliance; and 5% fell within the "other" category (Table 3-4). Other responses were made almost exclusively to expressive and declarative overtures, but the small number of such responses prevented statistical analysis. In addition, once other responses were eliminated, only one response to a declarative remained, and so this category could not be considered further in comparisons of compliance and noncompliance.

The variation in the proportion of compliance for individual categories was dramatic, ranging from 85% for offers to only 9% for expressives. The relation between the category of action and the responses of compliance and noncompliance was statistically significant, χ^2 (8) = 311.9, p <.001. Object requests, protests, and expressives met with higher rates of noncompliance, whereas shows, gives, and especially offers met with more compliance than would have been expected based chance distributions.

Gestures, Utterances, and Peer Responses

Analysis of the responses given to communicative overtures was extended by examining whether accompanying meaningful vocalizations aided the comprehension or altered the responses to communicative acts. The three categories of overtures that were frequently accompanied by vocalizations were examined: namely, show, object request, and protest action. Within these classes it was possible to determine whether vocal utterances which occurred alone were comprehended (and thus likely to produce redundant or additional information when combined with gestures) and whether the combination of gesture and utterance influenced the pattern of responding. In addition, the data allowed us to explore the relations of particularly appropriate utterances, given the context, and the responses of the peer. The response categories of compliance, noncompliance, and no evidence of comprehension were used in this analysis.

When shows, object requests, or protests were expressed vocally, evidence of comprehension by the peer equaled or exceeded 60% (Table 3-5). Nonetheless, evidence of comprehension was more common with request object and with protest action when nonvocal gestures were used either alone or combined with utterances. In the case of request object, the association of the type of act (i.e., with or without gestures) and of response was reliable, χ^2 (2) = 9.04, p <.02. More responses showed no evidence of comprehension when only an utterance was used. Similar analyses for show and protest action did not result in reliable associations.

Given the reasonably high rates of comprehension of utterances that occurred alone, it seemed reasonable to expect that they would produce

Table 3-5. Relation of Peer Responses and the Use of Utterances in Communicative Overtures

	Responses (%)		
Form of overture	Comply	Noncomply	Evidence of comprehension
Show			
Utterance only	60	0	60
Gesture only	52	6	58
Gesture & utterance	47	13	60
Request object			
Utterance only	8	57	65
Gesture only	13	71	85
Gesture & utterance	8	78	85
Protest action			
Utterance only	13	57	70
Gesture only	24	61	86
Gesture & utterance	23	49	72

either redundant or additional clarifying information when combined with communicative gestures. This might then alter the pattern of responses by decreasing the percentage showing no evidence of comprehension and increasing either compliance or noncompliance, depending upon which of the two was the more prevalent response. The analyses of these data failed to produce any evidence of the influence of an accompanying vocalization, however. Few differences were evident in the patterning of responses in Table 3-5. The one trend, noted in protest action, was not reliable and was in a direction opposite to that expected: evidence of comprehension in the form of noncompliance was more frequent when the gesture was not accompanied by a meaningful utterance.

When particular types of vocalizations were examined, the general results held: the name of the object did not change the pattern of responses to shows; the use of possessives did not alter the responses to object requests; and neither negatives nor miscellaneous vocalizations influenced the responses to protest actions.

Determinants of Peer Responses

The peer's responses to communicative overtures provide evidence of virtually universal awareness, frequent comprehension, and substantial rates of both compliance and active noncompliance with the imperative intent communicated. Thus the communicative overtures both transmitted information and fostered interaction between the toddlers.

The category of the communicative overture strongly influenced the peers' responses. Expressives and declaratives met with very limited evidence of comprehension. This might be attributed to a genuine lack of comprehension of the meaning of the actions or utterances used, as the children are still limited in their knowledge of language and possibly in the full range of affectionate expression. Alternatively, they may not feel the same pressures as adults do to respond to conversational gambits, greetings, or affectionate declarations; the imperative quality of expressive and declarative overtures may be embedded within a cultural system (Goffman, 1981) that these young children have yet to acquire.

Among those types of communicative overtures that evoked comprehension, most were met with compliance, and only two, request object and protest action, were frequently met with active noncompliance. The differences in the responses seem to be related to the nature of the demands made by the peer, rather than the ability to comply, since offering or giving objects as well as ceasing actions are well within the capacities of these toddlers. Object requests and protests of action are both requests to give something up, either an object or an activity of current interest; all other gestures offer either objects to see or hold, or activities to share. Thus self-interest seems to explain the peers' responses to communicative overtures.

Finally, the redundant or additional information provided by the combination of gestures and utterances does not influence the pattern of responding, despite the comprehension of both utterances and gestures when they occur alone and the apparent appropriateness of combinations within their contexts. This finding presents an additional puzzle in understanding the development of peer communication: If the combination of gesture and utterance has no influence on the effectiveness of the overture, why are the two combined? We shall return to that question later in this chapter.

Interpersonal Influence in Communication

In the final sections of this chapter we explore processess of interpersonal influence on the communicative patterns within the dyad. Much of the power of a communicative system comes from its applicability across different social partners. The 21-month-olds in this study had obviously developed a variety of communicative overtures that were effective in other social situations and these were used to communicate their desires and intentions to the new agemates they met in the laboratory playroom. Nonetheless, we might expect some continuing development of communicative skills within each new relationship. For example, in initial meetings with new peers, children might first evaluate whether these other people could be influenced by communicative means. Can they understand indirect signals and actions? One clue to the overtures that might be understood is provided by those the peers use themselves. In this way children might use overtures that their peers have used, and the communicative means used by each member of a pair would become more like those of the partner. In addition, the outcome of initial influence attempts might affect the subsequent use of similar communicative overtures. The children might evaluate the effectiveness of their communicative overtures in terms of their social consequences: whereas gestures complied with might be deemed effective and employed often, gestures ignored, or especially those protested, might decline in frequency. Hence the effective means of influencing the peer might be refined, and different aspects of a general communicative system applied within a particular relationship.

Influence of the Peer's Overtures

Intraclass correlations were conducted to determine whether the communicative overtures of one member of the dyad influenced those of the partner. This is basically an analysis of variance procedure in which subjects are nested within pairs and the variance attributable to pairs is evaluated. Intraclass correlations were statistically significant for the total frequency of communicative acts, $F(22, 24) = 5.43, p <.001$, for the proportion of acts complied with, $F(18, 19) = 4.36, p <.001$, and for the proportion of acts receiving a noncompliant response, $F(18, 19) = 3.95, p <.002$.[3] In addition, four of the individual categories also yielded reliable intraclass correlations: show, $F (22, 24) = 2.33, p <.023$; give, $F (22, 24) = 2.16, p <.034$; attempt to join play, $F (22, 24) = 7.89, p <.001$; and invitation to play, $F (22, 24) = 2.19, p <.032$. Four other measures yielded intraclass corelations with probabilities ranging from .16 to .30; while these were not significant, they were also not low enough to conclude that the data from each subject were independent of that of the peer. These categories were declarative, $F (22, 24) = 1.52, p <.16$, offer, $F (22, 24) = 1.32, p <.25$, protest action, $F (22, 24) = 1.30, p <.27$, and request object, $F (22, 24) = 1.24, p <.30$. The expressives of one member of the dyad appeared to be independent of those of the peer, $F (22, 24) = .88, p <.62$.

Consequences of Communicative Success and Failure

A learning analysis concerning the expression of communicative gestures in the peer dyad would predict that those gestures that receive a high proportion of compliance would increase over time, whereas those that are met with active noncompliance would decrease over time. To test these hypotheses the linear component of the Day 1 to Day 3 trends for each gesture was correlated with the proportion of those

---

[3] The number of pairs in the latter two analyses was reduced to 19 in order to exclude pairs with very few communicative acts since, in these cases, stable estimates of compliance and noncompliance were not possible.

gestures that met with compliance and with the proportion that met with noncompliance. These proportions were not merely the reciprocals of one another, as a third category (no evidence of comprehension) was also possible. Predictions were sufficiently specified to allow the use of 1-tailed tests. Only those pairs with four or more communicative acts of a given type were included, as fewer acts in the pair would not have provided a stable estimate of compliance or noncompliance, nor a basis for learning the probable outcome of a given communicative act. The number of pairs included in each analysis ranged from 12 to 19 (Table 3-6).

In general, the correlations for the seven communicative acts tested were low. Five of the seven correlations with compliance were positive, but only one (attempt to join play) was statistically significant, and one other (expressive) approached accepted levels of significance (Table 3-6). Correlations of linear trends and noncompliance were even more variable; three of the seven correlations were in a direction opposite to that predicted, and only the correlation with attempt to join play was strong enough to be considered a trend.

To explore further the relation of attempt to join play and the peer's response, we asked if compliance and noncompliance differed in the extent to which they were followed by immediate repetitions of the same actions. The 19 subjects whose attempts to join play were met at times by compliance and at times by noncompliance repeated the attempt more often following compliance, M = 2.3 and 1.4, respectively, T = 4.5, p <.01 by the Wilcoxan test. Six subjects had only compliant responses to their attempts to join play and six met with only noncompliance from their peers; these could not be used within the statistical analysis reported above, but their mean scores reinforce the

Table 3-6. Relation of Compliance and Noncompliance to Linear Trends of Communicative Overtures

Category of overture[a]	Number of dyads included	Correlations with linear trends	
		Comply	Noncomply
Show	14	-.13	.04
Offer	15	.01	-.02
Request object	13	.02	-.06
Expressive	15	.43*	.16
Invitation to play	12	-.07	-.24
Attempt to join play	19	.41**	-.30*
Protest action	12	.19	.25

[a]Give and declarative were not included in these analyses as fewer than one-half of the dyads met the criterion for inclusion.
*p <.10.
**p <.05.

trends: subjects who experienced only compliance repeated their attempts to join play more often than the others ($M = 3.4$), whereas those who experienced only noncompliance repeated their attempts less often than the others ($M = .2$).

Interpersonal Influences

The consequences of communicative overtures thus failed, generally, to have predictable effects on the subsequent use of similar communicative means. Attempts to join play were the one exception to this general pattern: increases in attempts to join play across sessions were reliably related to the proportion of such overtures that met with compliance within the dyad, and attempts to join play that met with compliance were repeated more often within a session than those that met with noncompliance.

Interpersonal influence was not absent from these interactions, however. The overtures of both members of the dyad tended to be similar in both form and frequency, as was the prevalence of compliant and noncompliant reactions to the peer's communicative attempts. As both compliance and noncompliance comprised a variety of individual responses depending upon the nature of the initiating act, the achievement of reciprocity in this regard gives evidence of a fairly abstract level of interpersonal influence: children were not imitating compliant or noncompliant responses, but sharing a more general spirit of cooperation or resistance.

Conclusions

We have taken a first step toward a direct communicative analysis of toddler-peer interaction. The rich yield of initial findings confirms the value of this approach. Communicative overtures occurred with sufficient frequency in dyadic play between 21-month-olds to form the basis of meaningful data analysis. A variety of communicative forms were used, each appearing to express a different type of interpersonal goal. Most of the communicative overtures were present in a majority of the dyads; nonetheless, there were differences among individual dyads in both the amount of communicative interaction and the types of messages most often conveyed. These differences were characteristics of the dyads; the overtures used by both partners within each dyad tended to be similar. Furthermore, there were related clusters or associations among the types of overtures the individual dyads used. The associations can be sensibly interpreted in the light of our general knowledge of interpersonal communication and in light of other findings from this study.

The first cluster consisted of invitations to play, attempts to join play, gives, and offers. These first two classes of overtures are alternative ways of becoming involved or involving others in joint play. The fact that gives and offers also entered the first cluster indicates that these responses might also serve to foster joint play in the peer dyad. The second cluster, expressives and protests, reflects the fact that expressives were often actions that met with protest (i.e., noncompliance) and often seemed to be repeated in the face of protest. Since expressives were the one class of overtures in which the frequencies of action by the two dyad members were independent, it is likely that this pattern results from basically complementary roles of expressive assault and protest. Declaratives and shows formed the nucleus of the third cluster; of all communicative actions, shows were most frequently accompanied by declaratives, and declaratives that occurred alone often named objects. Both may serve to indicate a topic of mutual attention. While Bates (1976) has classified both shows and offers as precursors of declarative intentions (protodeclaratives), the current analysis fails to support the inclusion of offering and giving within this functional category; rather, requests for objects were more closely related to shows and declaratives than were offers. This relationship is consonant with Leung and Rheingold's (1981) analysis of pointing and reaching, which resemble each other in their development in mother-infant interaction. In addition, sophistication in linguistic abilities seems unrelated to initiations of interactive play: different pairs seem to excel in these two clusters of responses.

Communicative overtures were not only prevalent and patterned, but were also frequently effective. A substantial number of overtures conveying an imperative request appear to have been understood and to have been met with peer compliance. In fact, there was enough evidence of comprehension and compliance to raise the suspicion that when no such evidence was present it was often a matter of disposition rather than capacity. In other words, the failure might as readily be attributed to a lack of desire to comply or show comprehension as to an inability to understand or to meet the demands of the peer. Two additional findings are consonant with this view: first, the presence of redundant information in an overture (i.e., the combination of words and gestures) did not alter the pattern of responses. Such combinations would be expected to enhance the clarity of the message, and hence peer comprehension, rather than the peer's willingness to respond. Second, the partners' own self-interest seemed related to their rates of compliance to particular overtures: object requests and protests of action, both attempts to induce a partner to give something up, met most frequently with noncompliance, whereas all other comprehended overtures, all of which offered activities of objects to share, met most often with compliance.

One exception to this overall pattern of peer comprehension is worthy of some note: a conspicuous failure to communicate occurred in the case of declarative statements. Although the children did use meaningful verbal and vocal utterances that appeared to be used in appropriate nonverbal contexts, and utterances which served as shows, object requests, or protests were comprehended, the children did not carry on verbal conversations with one another—they did not respond to declarative statements with a pertinent verbal comment. Perhaps the more concrete context of gesture and action still may be needed at 21 months for successful interpersonal communication, or, as suggested previously, the norms that impel adults to respond to one another's comments with further conversation may not yet be present.

In our examination of interpersonal influences on peer communication we found that both children within a dyad came to use the same types of overtures, but the response received to each overture did not generally influence the subsequent frequency of similar overtures. Similarly, the peers' responses to communicative overtures were influenced by the types of overtures (what was demanded) but not by the apparent clarity of the messages (the appropriate combinations of words and gestures). These findings are fairly consistent with other research (Becker, 1977; Bronson, 1981; Garvey & Ben Debba, 1974; Krasnor, 1981). Both Becker, studying 9-month-olds, and Krasnor, studying preschoolers, found that responses to peer overtures did not influence the subsequent frequency of similar peer-directed action. Becker also found that the frequency of peer-directed behavior was associated for two infants playing together, and Garvey and Ben Debba reported a similar finding for preschool-age dyads. Bronson observed that the type of overture influenced the peer's response.

In addition, these findings can be interpreted within the framework of contemporary social learning theory (Bandura, 1977; Cairns, 1979). According to this theory, response consequences do not influence subsequent responding unless the pattern of outcomes is perceived, remembered, and integrated with other information to form an expectancy of future outcomes that might guide behavior. "People do not learn much from repeated paired experience unless they recognize that events are correlated" (Bandura, 1977, p. 165). Observational learning and a related tendency to reciprocity within social interchanges are considered more potent determinants of learning and action. Observations of the activity of others can provide information concerning response outcomes, but it can also act more directly to suggest both precise forms and more abstract modes or styles of interactive behavior. Furthermore, when beliefs about the consequences of action conflict with actual outcomes, the prior beliefs or theory concerning the behavior-consequent relationships that exist have a powerful influence on both the relationships perceived and on the behavior that results (see also Nisbitt & Ross, 1980).

Our current findings give evidence of the powerful effect of peer observation and reciprocal influence within the dyad. In addition, abstract as well as concrete patterns of action were based on the models provided by peers. We also find, for the most part, that response consequences have no detectable influence on subsequent responding. Nisbitt and Ross (1980) suggested that adults have great difficulty seeing relations between behavior and its consequences if, among other things, the interval between successive pairings of events is not brief and if early reinforcement is not consistent. These circumstances certainly characterize our peer sessions. In this light, it seems rather remarkable that there was a relationship between peer responses to attempts to join play and subsequent increases in these overtures. This class of overture was most frequently displayed and was often repeated when the peer complied. In addition, 40% of the children showed a consistent pattern of responses to such overtures, that is, when they showed evidence of comprehension they either always complied or always did not comply to the peer's request. These factors may have been sufficient to produce the correlation of .41 between the compliance rate and the trend to increase attempts to join play.

This one positive finding encourages us to be cautious in interpreting the general thrust of these results. It is possible that with more extensive experience with particular agemates toddlers might begin to modify their actions in response to the consequences of their behavior. It is also possible that within individual dyads some overtures may have been sufficiently consistent for such effects to have occurred within the sessions of this study, without resulting in reliable general effects when all data were combined. In summary, these data are consistent with, but do not firmly establish the view that positive or negative consequences have a limited impact on toddlers' social overtures to their peers.

In addition, we propose that the development and utilization of communicative overtures is predicated on the assumption, probably generalized from other social contacts, that toddler peers are independent agents who are capable of perceiving, understanding, and potentially complying with indirect overtures. If this assumption is elaborated to include the corollary that, as independent agents, others may sometimes be inattentive, momentarily obtuse, or resistant to proposed plans of action, then it becomes highly resilient. The frequent use of communicative overtures by so many of the toddlers observed in this study implies that they do make such assumptions concerning the capacities of their unfamiliar agemates. It appears unlikely that they carefully test the limits of their assumptions with each newly met peer; if such testing had occurred, then the consequences of communicative overtures should have had greater impact. Instead, the refutation of such assumptions is more likely to require dramatic, consistent, and repeated evidence and would possibly lead to new assumptions that could accommodate the exceptions.

Finally, the results of this research depend upon the initial conceptualizations built into the categorization system. This is not a unique situation since all findings depend, in part, on what one chooses to measure and how that measurement is carried out. We have anchored our categorization system in terms of observable behavior and specifiable contexts; however, we have also made inferences concerning the imperative intention of an overturing child in order to define the appropriateness of the responses received. The concepts of comprehension, compliance, and noncomplinace are built on these initial assumptions, and hence our attributions of intention could have far-reaching effects. We do not feel that this issue can be easily resolved, but it is likely that focused attention on particular communicative patterns, especially in experimental situations where inferred intentions are misconstrued or violated, will provide additional useful information for evaluating their validity. In the meantime, we are encouraged by the positive results of the current analyses that provide at least preliminary verification of some of our assumptions. We seem to have arrived at a reasonable understanding of the social function of attempts to join play, as evidenced by the relation of this diverse class of overtures to outcome. The general character of compliance or noncompliance seems to fit well with the nature of the overtures that received one or the other of these responses predominantly: when children were asked to give up an object or activity, they objected; when offered an object or activity, they complied. The children also seemed to influence one another to adopt similar communicative forms and to adopt joint patterns of cooperation or resistance to communicative influence. The overtures themselves were organized into seemingly sensible patterns of interaction. Thus, our initial inferences have been useful and now await more detailed evaluation; the analysis of toddler interaction in terms of peer communication seems to be profitable.

Acknowledgments

This research was supported by a Social Sciences and Humanities Research Council of Canada Grant, a Canada Council Grant, and a University of Waterloo Grant. At the time of this research Susan P. Lollis was supported by a Social Sciences and Humanities Research Council of Canada Doctoral Fellowship and Connie Elliott by the Gladys Raiter Bursary offered by the Imperial Order of the Daughters of the Empire. We thank Cindy Seibel, Mary Hamilton, James Bouquin, Marie Bountrogianni, Donna LaFlamme, and Karen Luks for the long hours spent observing and recording the interaction. The data were originally collected for a collaborative project with Dr. Dale Hay, and independent analyses of these videotapes form the basis of a joint paper (Hay & Ross, 1982). We also appreciate the efforts of our colleagues, Diane Borwick, Barbara Goldman, and Ken Rubin, who read and commented on earlier versions of this chapter. Finally, we thank the children and their mothers, who devoted a week to helping us with this study.

References

Bandura, A. *Social learning theory*. Englewood Cliffs, N. J.: Prentice-Hall, 1977.

Bates, E. *Language and context: The acquisition of pragmatics*. New York: Academic Press, 1976.

Becker, J. M. T. A learning analysis of the development of peer-oriented behavior in 9-month-old infants. *Developmental Psychology*, 1977, *13*, 481-491.

Brenner, J., & Mueller, E. Shared meaning in boy toddlers' peer relations. *Child Development*, in press.

Bronson, W. C. Toddlers' behaviors with agemates: Issues of interaction, cognition, and affect. In L. P. Lipsitt (Ed.), *Monographs on infancy* (Vol. 1). Norwood, N.J.: Ablex, 1981.

Bruner, J. S. The organization of skilled action. In M. P. M. Richards (Ed.), *The integration of a child into a social world*. Cambridge, England: Cambridge University Press, 1974.

Bruner, J. S. Early social interaction and language acquisition. In H. R. Schaffer (Ed.), *Studies in mother-infant interaction*. London: Academic Press, 1977.

Cairns, R. B. *Social development: The origins of plasticity of interchanges*. San Francisco: Freeman, 1979.

Carter, A. L. From sensori-motor vocalizations to words: A case study of the evolution of attention-directing communication in the second year. In A. Lock (Ed.), *Action, gesture and symbol: The emergence of language*. New York: Academic Press, 1978.

Clark, R. A. The transition from action to gesture. In A. Lock (Ed.), *Action, gesure and symbol: The emergence of language*. New York: Academic Press, 1978.

Eckerman, C. O., & Whatley, J. L. Toys and social interaction between infant peers. *Child Development*, 1977, *48*, 1654-1656.

Eckerman, C. O., Whatley, J. L., & Kutz, S. L. Growth of social play with peers during the second year of life. *Developmental Psychology*, 1975, *11*, 42-49.

Garvey, C. Requests and responses in children's speech. *Journal of Child Language*, 1975, *21*, 41-60.

Garvey, C., & Ben Debba, M. Effects of age, sex, and partner on children's dyadic speech. *Child Development*, 1974, *45*, 1159-1161.

Goffman, E. *Forms of talk*. Philadelphia: University of Pennsylvania Press, 1981.

Goldman, B. D., & Ross, H. S. Social skills in action: An analysis of early peer games. In J. Glick & K. A. Clarke-Stewart (Eds.), *Studies in social and cognitive development* (Vol. 1): *The development of social understanding*. New York: Gardner Press, 1978.

Greenfield, P. M. Toward an operational and logical analysis of intentionality: The use of discourse in early child language. In D. R. Olson (Ed.), *The social foundations of language and thought*. New York: Norton, 1980.

Greenfield, P. M., & Smith, J. H. *The structure of communication in early language*. New York: Academic Press, 1976.

Hay, D. F., & Ross, H. S. The social nature of early conflict. *Child Development*, 1982, *53*, 105-113.

Johnson, S. C. Hierarchical clustering schemes. *Psychometrika*, 1967, *32*, 241-254.

Krasnor, L. R. *An observational study of social problem solving in preschoolers*. Unpublished doctoral dissertation, University of Waterloo, Waterloo, Ontario, Canada, 1981.

Leung, E., & Rheingold, H. L. Development of pointing as a social gesture. *Developmental Psychology*, 1981, *17*, 215-220.

Levin, E., & Rubin, K. Getting others to do what you want them to do: The development of children's requestive strategies. In K. Nelson (Ed.), *Child Language* (Vol. 4). New York: Gardner Press, in press.

Lock, A. *The guided reinvention of language.* New York: Academic Press, 1980.

Mueller, E. The maintenance of verbal exchanges between young children. *Child Development*, 1972, *43*, 930-938.

Mueller, E., & Brenner, J. The origins of social skills and interaction among play-group toddlers. *Child Development*, 1977, *48*, 854-861.

Mueller, E., & Lucas, J. A developmental analysis of peer interaction among toddlers. In M. Lewis & L. A. Rosenblum (Eds.), *Friendship and peer relations.* New York: Wiley, 1975.

Nisbitt, R. E., & Ross, L. *Human inference: Strategies and shortcomings of social judgment.* Englewood Cliffs, N.J.: Prentice-Hall, 1980.

Ross, H. S. The establishment of social games amongst toddlers. *Developmental Psychology*, 1982, *18*, 509-518.

Ross, H. S., Borwick, D. M., Goldman, B. D., & Hay, D. F. Review of *Toddlers' Behaviors with Agemates: Issues of Interaction, Cognition, and Affect* by W. C. Bronson, *Journal of Developmental Psychobiology*, in press.

Rubenstein, J., & Howes, C. The effects of peers on toddler interaction with mother and toys. *Child Development*, 1976, *47*, 597-605.

Ryan, J. Early language development: Towards a communicational analysis. In M. P. M. Richards (Ed.), *The Integration of a child into a social world.* Cambridge, England: Cambridge University Press, 1974.

Schaffer, H. R., Collis, G. M., & Parsons, G. Vocal interchange and visual regard in pre-verbal children. In H. R. Schaffer (Ed.), *Studies in mother-infant interaction.* New York: Academic Press, 1977.

Snow, C. E. The development of conversation between mothers and babies. *Journal of Child Language*, 1977, *4*, 1-22.

Spilton, D., & Lee, L. C. Some determinants of effective communication in four-year-olds. *Child Development*, 1977, *48*, 968-977.

Trevarthen, C. The foundations of intersubjectivity: Development of interpersonal cooperative understanding in infants. In D. R. Olson (Ed.), *The social foundations of language and thought.* New York: Norton, 1980.

Vandell, D. L., Wilson, K. S., & Buchanan, N. R. Peer interaction in the first year of life: An examination of its structure, content, and sensitivity to toys. *Child Development*, 1980, *51*, 481-488.

Wellman, H. M., & Lempers, J. D., The naturalistic communicative abilities of two-year-olds. *Child Development*, 1977, *48*, 1052-1057.

Zukow, P. G., Reilly, J., & Greenfield, P. M. Making the absent present: Facilitating the transition from sensorimotor to linguistic communication. In K. Nelson (Ed.), *Children's language* (Vol. 3). New York: Gardner Press, 1980.

Chapter 4

Social Rules Governing Object Conflicts in Toddlers and Preschoolers

Roger Bakeman and John R. Brownlee

As adults we often regulate our dealings with others by social rules—generally understood conventions—and so usually we face the front in an elevator, go to the end of a line, etc. Such rules serve to minimize the number of conflicts that otherwise might engage us and generally make our behavior more predictable to others. They appear to be learned, and indeed the explicit teaching of rules is often regarded as an important responsibility of socializing agents. It may be, however, that early in life some social rules emerge quite spontaneously in the context of peer play, not as a result of cultural intervention, but simply as a consequence of a fundamental human propensity to regulate social interaction in a ruleful manner. Independent of explicit adult teaching, even very young children may be capable of developing rules to regulate interaction with their age-mates.

Even a decade ago the idea that toddlers and preschoolers could be rule users might have seemed farfetched to many psychologists. Indeed, if we view young children as socially blind and egocentric, then it makes sense to predict that conflicts among peers would be decided simply by physical power or adult intervention. However, a growing body of research suggests that children from the second year of life on are far more socially skilled and socially aware than psychologists have traditionally claimed (Eckerman & Whatley, 1977; Ross & Goldman, 1977; Rubenstein & Howes, 1976; Wellman & Lempers, 1977). This makes us think it at least plausible that some kinds of conflicts among quite young peers might be regulated by social rules. We think of such rules as being shared by group members and affecting expectations about others' behavior even if they cannot be articulated. (For a discussion of the distinction between inarticulate "practice" and articulate "theory" see Shotter, 1978.)

As a means of exploring the possibility that very young children might use social rules to regulate peer conflicts, we chose to study possession episodes, that is, times when one child tried to take an object from another. Possession is highly regulated by both legal and informal means in adult life and appears to be an important theme to young children as well (Furby, 1978). The idea of "mine" appears early in life and, as though testing the limits of that idea, possession struggles are frequently observed in young children (Bronson, 1975; Dawe, 1934; Eckerman, Whatley, & Kutz, 1975; Hay & Ross, 1982). Moreover, such disputes are frequently the occasion of adult intervention and rule stating. For all these reasons, we thought that if young children have any social rules at all, they might very possibly involve possessing.

Preliminary work with a group of nine children in their third year of life suggested that a rule did indeed exist (Brownlee, 1977). It seemed that when "takers"—those children who were attempting to gain possession of an object from another child—had played with that object at some point in the recent past, their take attempts were more likely to succeed. We termed this the "prior possession rule" because these children behaved as though prior possession of an object conferred some sort of current right.

Both Bronson (1981) and Furby (Note 1), in their studies of children in the second year of life, reported results consistent with the notion of a prior possession rule. They recorded the length of prior possession for the current "possessor" or "holder," not whether the "taker" had had prior possession. Both researchers reported that the taker was more likely to be successful if the holder had been playing with the contested toy only a short while and was less likely to be successful if the holder had been playing with the contested toy for some time. Taken together, these studies suggest that children in their second year of life may already have some appreciation of their own possession rights. However, as Bronson notes, this could be only a personal and not a shared perception. None of these studies, including our preliminary study, demonstrates that young children appreciate the possession rights of others. Such a demonstration is required to infer a shared social rule.

Perhaps we should examine the holder's resistance or lack of it and not just the taker's success. If takers who previously have played with an object typically succeed in their take attempts, their successes might be due simply to vigorously pressing their claims. However, if takers who can claim a prior possession right typically meet less resistance in their take attempts than takers who lack such a claim, then it seems possible to argue that the claim is recognized by the holder as well. Moreover, if over the many possible dyadic combinations in a peer group prior possession is systematically related to a lack of resistance, then it seems reasonable to argue that a prior possession rule is at work regulating possession conflicts in that group.

Settling possession conflicts on the basis of prior possession would seem to be a rather fair and egalitarian way to approach the matter.

However, there is another possible basis—dominance; as Strayer and Strayer (1976) have demonstrated, dominance can also affect the interaction of preschoolers. Perhaps some children are simply more powerful than other children and systematically win conflicts with those to whom they are "dominant," unaffected by prior possession.

Even if a dominance ordering could be demonstrated for any given group, this does not necessarily mean that the children appreciate their dominance relations and use their relative status as a rule to regulate possession conflicts. If certain children usually win conflicts with other children, this could mean simply that they are more powerful. However, if children deemed dominant to other children on the basis of their wins are also less likely to encounter resistance when dealing with less dominant children, then we would appear to be on firmer ground in arguing that a shared dominance rule is at work. Our assumption is that if a rule—either a prior possession rule or a dominance rule—is a shared and not just a personal matter, then it should affect not only the outcome of a conflict, but also the initial negotiation of that conflict.

When we designed this study our first concern was to determine whether the finding from the preliminary study—that the taker's prior possession affected his or her success—would hold for slightly younger and slightly older children (children in the second and in the fourth year of life). We were also concerned with dominance and how effectively it might account for the outcome of possession conflicts. More broadly, we wondered if any behavioral evidence would support the notion of shared social rules regulating interaction in groups of very young children. With these concerns in mind, we observed two groups of children, one consisting of children in the second and one consisting of children in the fourth year of life. When we observed one child attempting to take an object from another child, we noted whether the taker had played with the contested object at some point in the recent past, whether the take attempt met with any resistance initially, and whether the take attempt ultimately succeeded.

Method

All children regularly attending the toddler class (six boys, five girls, mean age 18.4 months, range 12-24 months) and one preschool class (six boys, seven girls, mean age 44.4 months, range 40-48 months) at a day care center were observed during indoor free play several times over the course of 6 weeks during the spring of 1979. Both classrooms were about 6 × 8 m² in size and were attractively furnished with a wide range of age-appropriate toys. The day care center consisted of an almost even mixture of low-income and middle-class children, but because we were only allowed to observe, we have no background information or test scores on individual children.

Each day several children ("target" children) were observed in a random order for periods of 5 minutes each. Because free play periods usually lasted longer for the toddlers, they were observed an average of 113 minutes each, while the mean observation time for the preschoolers was 77 minutes. Two observers rotated between the two classrooms; together they observed 20.7 hours in the toddler class and 16.6 hours in the preschool class.

As we defined it, a *possession episode* required physical contact with the contested object by both children. The *holder* had to be holding or touching the object and the *taker* had to touch the object and attempt to remove it from the holder's possession. Incidents in which a child simply held out his or her hand to another child were not regarded as possession episodes. Each time the current target child was involved in a possession episode, the observer recorded: (1) the name of the child attempting to take the object (the taker) and the name of the child currently possessing the object (the holder); (2) whether the taker had been playing with the object within the previous 1 minute (the time was estimated, but see the agreement data); (3) whether the holder resisted the take attempt (refusing to release the object, fighting back, showing distress, or soliciting help from others); and (4) whether the take was successful, unsuccessful, or indeterminate (because either peers or adults intervened).

At the end of training and before data collection, interobserver agreement was assessed. The two coders observed until one had recorded 50 episodes; 44 (88%) of those episodes were also noted by the other observer. For the episodes observed in common, there was no disagreement about the children involved, and agreement about prior possession, resistance, and success was .91, .78, and .79, respectively, as determined by Cohen's kappa (Cohen, 1960; Hollenbeck, 1978). This statistic corrects for chance agreement; thus, for a given level of agreement, kappa scores are lower than the percentage agreement scores commonly reported.

Results

Possession episodes in the toddler class were more frequent than in the preschool class (mean rates per hour 11.7 vs. 5.4) and were more likely to end in intervention (20% vs. 11%). However, here we are interested specifically in what happens when children work out their possession episodes themselves, and for that reason the analyses reported below are based on the 192 episodes in the toddler class (9.3 per hour) and the 79 episodes in the preschool class (4.8 per hour) that did not occasion intervention.

Dominance Hierarchies

There was some evidence for a dominance hierarchy in both the toddler and the preschool classes, at least with regard to possession struggles. Following Strayer and Strayer (1976), we found the rank ordering for the children in each class that produced the "best" dominance matrix. (Rows and the corresponding columns are labeled with the children's names. Rows represent "winners" and columns represent "losers." If child A wins over child B in one episode, then a tally is entered in the cell defined by the Ath row and the Bth column. The "best" dominance matrix is produced by the ordering of children that maximizes tallies in cells above the diagonal.)

Given this matrix, two aspects of the dominance ordering can be quantified: linearity and rigidity (Strayer & Strayer, 1976). Given a perfectly linear ordering, if A wins over B and B wins over C, then A should win over C. If not, that would represent a "relational reversal." Linearity is then defined as the number of dyads that engaged in episodes, minus the number of relational reversals, divided by the number of dyads that engaged in episodes. Similarly, given a perfectly rigid dominance structure, if A is dominant to B, then A should win all episodes with B. If not, then each episode B wins over A would represent an "episodic reversal." Rigidity is then defined as the number of episodes, minus the number of episodic reversals, divided by the number of episodes.

Linearity was 83.0% for the toddlers and 76.9% for the preschoolers. Rigidity was 68.8% for the toddlers and 60.8% for the preschoolers. These values are considerably lower than those reported by Strayer and Strayer (1976). Nevertheless, we think they indicate that the children in these two classes were organized into moderately linear but not especially rigid dominance hierarchies. These dominance orderings were used for analyzing the individual possession episodes, as described below.

Log-Linear Analyses

The possession episodes were classified by dominance (Was the taker dominant to the other child?), prior possession (Had the taker played with the contested object within the previous 1 minute?), and success (Did the taker gain possession of the object?) and also by dominance, prior possession, and resistance (Did the taker encounter resistance?) for the toddlers and the preschoolers separately. This resulted in four 2 by 2 by 2 contingency tables (Tables 4-1 and 4-2). We regarded dominance and prior possession as antecedent or "explanatory" variables and success and resistance as consequent or "response" variables. Because we wanted to examine the effects of the explanatory variables on each response variable separately, we did not construct tables with both a resistance and a success dimension; and because we thought the

Table 4-1. Success in Relation to Dominance and Prior Possession

		Success			
Dominant	Prior possession	Yes		No	
Toddlers					
Yes	Yes	21[a]	(22.2)[b]	5	(3.8)
	No	50	(48.8)	22	(23.2)
No	Yes	12	(10.8)	8	(9.2)
	No	21	(22.2)	53	(51.8)
Preschoolers					
Yes	Yes	10	(9.4)	1	(1.6)
	No	11	(11.6)	12	(11.4)
No	Yes	9	(9.6)	5	(4.4)
	No	9	(8.4)	22	(22.6)

[a] Number of observed episodes.
[b] Expected values appear in parentheses. They were generated by the [DS][PS] [DP] model (see text) and computed by Goodman's ECTA program.

results would be clearer and more straightforward if data for the two age groups were analyzed separately but in parallel, we did not construct tables with age as a dimension.

The four contingency tables were analyzed using techniques developed by Goodman and others (for references, see Feinberg, 1977) and described for the nonstatistician by Feinberg (1977) and Davis (1978). These techniques are designed to analyze multidimensional contingency

Table 4-2. Resistance in Relation to Dominance and Prior Possession

		Resistance			
Dominant	Prior possession	Yes		No	
Toddlers					
Yes	Yes	19[a]	(16.2)[b]	7	(· 9.8)
	No	42	(44.8)	30	(27.2)
No	Yes	16	(16.4)	4	(3.6)
	No	61	(60.6)	13	(13.4)
Preschoolers					
Yes	Yes	6	(6.2)	5	(4.8)
	No	18	(19.2)	5	(3.8)
No	Yes	8	(7.8)	6	(6.2)
	No	27	(25.8)	4	(5.2)

[a] Number of observed episodes.
[b] Expected values appear in parentheses. They were generated by the [DR][DP] model for the toddlers and by the [PR][DP] model for the preschoolers (see text) and were computed by Goodman's ECTA program.

tables, are simple and flexible to use, produce results that can be expressed in analysis of variance-like terminology, and make few assumptions about the data. For all these reasons, their use here seemed recommended, but because they are not yet commonly used by psychologists, some general comments about them may be in order; these comments are necessarily brief and apply primarily to the case at hand. (The interested reader is urged to consult Feinberg, 1977.)

For each of these four contingency tables, a set of hierarchial models can be defined (Feinberg, 1977, Chapter 3). The simplest model—the null or equiprobable model—contains no terms at all and generates the same expected value for each cell. The most complete or saturated model would contain sufficient terms to generate expected values that are identical to the observed ones. The idea is to find the least complex model that nonetheless generates expected values not too discrepant from the observed ones, as determined by a goodness-of-fit test. Usually one begins with the null or some other simple model. If that fails to generate data that fit the observed data, more complex models are tried. If all else fails, the saturated model will always fit the observed data.

The simplest example of this logic is provided by the familiar chi square test of independence. The model typically tested first—the just main effects model—contains two terms, one for the row variable and one for the column variable. This model generates expected values that are constrained by the row and column totals. In introductory statistics, students almost always learn how to compute these expected frequencies, although they rarely learn to think of them as generated by this particular model. If these estimated values do not fit the observed ones, the value of chi square will be large and this model is rejected. In the case of a 2 by 2 table, only one more complex model remains; this is the saturated model, which contains, in addition to the main effect terms, an interaction term as well. Hence, if the value of chi square is sufficiently large, we are forced to accept a model which includes an interaction term. This is the substantive result usually desired.

Each term of a model imposes constraints on the expected cell values. For example, in the case of a two-dimensional table and the just main effects model discussed above, the cell values were constrained to reflect the R (row) and the C (column) marginals. Following notational conventions, this would be the [R][C] model; the expected values are easily computed from the row, column, and grand totals. (The saturated model would be represented by [R][C][RC]. This is usually written just [RC] because the lower level terms, [R] and [C], are implied by the higher level [RC] term.) In the case of multidimensional tables, the matter is more complex. For example, if S stands for success, D for dominance, and P for prior possession, then the [S][DP] model states that the expected values, when classified by success and when cross-classified by dominance and prior possession, must agree with the observed ones. In this case, indeed in all but the two-dimensional case described above, computing expected values is not a simple or straight-forward affair. Usually computer programs are used.

In analysis of variance terms, the [S][DP] model and the [R][DP] model (where R stands for resistance) are the "no effects" models for our 2 by 2 by 2 tables. As stated above, dominance and prior possession are regarded here as explanatory variables (although they were not manipulated), and so the [DP] term merely states the design, while the[S] term or the [R] term indicates that the explanatory variables do not affect success or resistance (Feinberg, 1977, Chapter 6). When success is analyzed, a main effect for dominance would be indicated by the [DS][DP] model, a main effect for prior possession by the [DS] [DP] model, main effects for both by the [DS][PS][DP] model, and a dominance by prior possession interaction by the [DPS] or saturated model. (As above, the implied lower level terms are omitted. This abbreviated form for hierarchical models is discussed by Feinberg, 1977, Chapter 3.)

For each of our four 2 by 2 by 2 tables, the "no effects" model generated data that failed to fit the data we observed (Table 4-3). We then proceeded to add terms, selecting first the term that resulted in the greatest reduction in chi square, the next greatest reduction, and so forth, until there was no term left whose addition would result in a further significant reduction in chi square. The results of this "stepping"

Table 4-3. Log-Linear Models for Success and Resistance

Model	df	χ^2	$\Delta\chi^2$
Success, toddlers			
[S][DP]	3	35.5****	
[DS][DP]	2	7.9**	27.6****
[DS][PS][DP]	1	0.9	7.0***
Success, preschoolers			
[S][DP]	3	15.4****	
[PS][DP]	2	4.6*	10.8***
[DS][PS][DP]	1	0.5	4.1**
Resistance, toddlers			
[R][DP]	3	11.3**	
[DR][DP]	2	1.9	9.4***
Resistance, preschoolers			
[R][DP]	3	7.2*	
[PR][DP]	2	0.8	6.4***

Note. Maximum likelihood ratio chi square values are presented. Goodman's ECTA program was used to compute these statistics.
$*p < .10.$
$**p < .05.$
$***p < .01.$
$****p < .001.$

procedure are presented in Table 4-3; the expected values generated by the models so selected are given in Tables 4-1 and 4-2; and the results for the two response variables are described below.

Success. For both the toddlers and preschoolers, there was a main effect for both prior possession and dominance when success was analyzed. In other words, both prior possession and dominance appear to have independently regulated the success of the toddlers and the preschoolers. To predict success accurately for either the toddlers or the preschoolers, we need to know whether the taker was dominant and whether he or she had had prior possession. The probability that a toddler taker would be successful was .54; this increased to .72 when the taker was dominant and also to .72 when the taker had had prior possession. For the preschoolers, the probability that a taker would be successful was .49; this increased to .62 when the taker was dominant and to .76 when the taker had had prior possession.

Resistance. When resistance was analyzed, there was a main effect for dominance among the toddlers but a main effect for prior possession among the preschoolers. In other words, dominance determined resistance only among the toddlers, while prior possession determined resistance only among the preschoolers. For the toddlers, the probability that a taker would meet with resistance was .72; this was .76 when the taker had had prior possession but decreased to .62 when the taker was dominant. For the preschoolers, the probability that a taker would meet with resistance was .75; this was .71 when the taker was dominant but decreased to .56 when the taker had had prior possession.

Sex effects. No sex effects were detected. Boys and girls were distributed quite evenly throughout the dominance ranks (a runs test was not significant), and neither boys nor girls were more likely to have their take attempts resisted or to have their take attempts succeed.

Discussion

Given these data, we can describe some specific features of possession struggles among very young children. Perhaps more interestingly, we can also speculate about general features of peer conflicts and their regulation by social rules.

If the taker was dominant to the other child, then his or her take attempt was more likely to succeed. This is an artifact, however; after all, dominance rank was defined using the outcome of possession episodes and so there is some circularity here. What is noteworthy is that prior possession mattered as well, and for both the toddlers and preschoolers. Even with its circularity in this analysis, dominance alone is insufficient to predict whose take attempt will succeed. We need to know whether the taker had prior possession too. These results, coupled with those from our pilot work, indicate that the outcome of possession episodes among children in the second, third, and fourth year of life is not simply a matter of individual power, but can be at least partly explained by reference to the prior possession rule.

This rule is "social" in the sense that it can account for systematic features of observed social interaction. It is not necessarily "social" in the sense of being a convention "understood" and upheld by the participants. The individual toddler and preschool takers may have believed that prior possession gave them a right to the contested object, but that right may or may not have been recognized by the other child. Perhaps the other only acquiesced to the taker's "vigor of righteousness."

Still, there is some evidence that the prior possession rule was social, in the sense of being shared, for the preschoolers if not for the toddlers. First, possession episodes were almost twice as frequent among the toddlers, reflecting perhaps a greater uncertainty as to how possession should be resolved and a need to explore each possible conflict to see how it would end. Second, toddlers were as likely to resist a taker who had had prior possession as not, while preschoolers were less likely to resist a taker who had had prior possession. This suggests that among the preschoolers the prior possession claim may have been recognized by both children, at least at a point sufficiently early in the taking so that active resistance was less likely.

The toddlers were guided by a dominance rule. Toddlers were less likely to resist a dominant taker than a subordinate one, while preschoolers were as likely to resist a dominant as a subordinate taker. (It makes sense to pay attention to this dominance effect, because resistance does not suffer the circularity problem success does.) Our argument, here and in the previous paragraph, is that the holder's lack of resistance indicated recognition of the taker's right and suggests the existence of a shared rule. This is an arguable proposition, but if we accept its logic and its implications, then the following question arises: Why should the rule change from dominance for toddlers to prior possession for preschoolers?

One simple and basic distinction that can be made about rules is the following: some rules, such as dominance, depend on the particular persons involved, while other rules are based on situational characteristics and apply to all individuals equally. For example, it is not the biggest or most powerful car that goes through the traffic light; usually it is the car with the green light. We might term the first type status rules or rules of power and the second type egalitarian rules or rules of law.

The use of these two types of rules would seem to require somewhat different cognitive capacities. Rules of power require that children remember relationships between enduring and often perceptual attributes of their partners and the outcomes of past actions in similar encounters. Rules of law require that children attend to more than just the specific stable characteristics of their social partners; they must also attend to and comprehend the role the partner is playing in the current episode. According to this analysis, it is not at all surprising that we observed a developmental progression, albeit cross sectional, from a dominance to a prior possession rule. Applying a dominance rule requires little more than social memory, but applying a prior possession rule requires taking into account fluid, role-based aspects of the social partner.

Nevertheless, applying either type of rule requires an appreciation of rules, and the interpretation we have offered above is that our data reveal shared rules at work; but is the notion of shared rules required to account for the behavior we observed? Furby (Note 2) would argue not necessarily—that there is at least one plausible alternative explanation. When children have played with a toy recently, that *could* indicate that, for the moment at least, they prefer that toy to others and hence would expend more effort in its recovery. If so, other children might eventually acquiesce to this assumedly more vigorous onslaught, which we suggested could be called the "vigor of righteousness" but which Furby might term simply the "vigor of desire." Later, children may come to resist the prior possessing taker less, not because they have accepted a social rule, but only because they have learned about the negative consequences often associated with this situation.

This social learning perspective satisfactorily explains how an apparent prior possession rule (with respect to both resistance and success) might arise among the preschoolers. It also explains how a dominance rule might arise. It does not, however, explain very well why dominance would affect resistance only among the toddlers and not among the preschoolers. After all, dominance affected success among the preschoolers, so presumably they had had some experience of the negative consequences of losing to dominant children. More detailed data about possession episodes, coupled with longitudinal designs, might provide a basis for a better understanding of these issues. However, it is probably unreasonable to expect data alone to provide a basis for definitively deciding between a "social learning" and a "shared rule" interpretation. We suspect that the difference between these two interpretations may be more apparent than real, more a matter of using different terms than of uncovering fundamentally different phenomena.

There seems to be no reason to doubt that individual children learn rules for regulating social interaction, such as the prior possession rule suggested here, from their interactive experience with others. In addition, they may readily generalize to other children "rules" they may have formed after interacting with specific children. Nevertheless, the rules that develop in a group of children often vary little from child to child. This we attribute to two factors: first, similarities between children far outweigh their differences—they are after all members of the same species and share a common phylogentic history—and so they tend to provide similar interactive experiences to each other; and second, a particular species characteristic of humans is the tendency both to form and to follow rules (Fishbein, 1976).

The conceptual orientation we find most helpful in thinking about these matters is suggested broadly by Waddington (1957) and is explicitly applied to children's social development by Fishbein (1976). Very young children readily acquire social rules that regulate interaction because they are designed by their long evolutionary past to do so. Such rule acquisition is a heavily canalized characteristic requiring only moderate encouragement from the environment. From this point of view, young children are neither nasty brutes who must have rules imposed upon them nor noble savages who come with a built-in sense of equity; rather, they are adaptive, socially sensitive organisms trying to get along in a social world full of conflicting needs and limited resources. They may have a far greater capacity for ruleful regulation of their social affairs than we usually grant them, a capacity which only careful observations of young children playing with their age-mates is likely to reveal.

Some students of early infant-mother interaction claim that "knowledge itself originates within an interaction process . . . between the infant himself and other, more mature, human individuals who already possess shared understandings with other communicating beings" (Newson & Newson, 1975, p. 438). The idea is that human understanding arises from a process of negotiation between two or more individuals, a process that the term "intersubjectivity" is meant to suggest. Most researchers and writers in this tradition have stressed the role of adults, typically the mother (e.g., Trevarthen & Hubley, 1978); but we think it likely that as early as the second or third year of life peers are capable of constructing intersubjective worlds among and for themselves and that attempts to study this phenomenon would expand our understanding of early peer relations.

Reference Notes

1. Furby, L. *An exploratory analysis of possessive behavior in toddlers.* Unpublished manuscript, 1980.
2. Furby, L. Personal communication, September 1980.

References

Bronson, W. C. Development in behavior with age mates during the second year of life. In M. Lewis & L. A. Rosenblum (Eds.), *Friendship and peer relations.* New York: Wiley, 1975.

Bronson, W. C. Toddlers' behavior with agemates: Issues of interaction, cognition, and affect. In L. P. Lippsitt (Ed.), Monographs on Infancy (Vol. 1). Norwood, N.J.: Ablex, 1981.

Brownlee, J. R. *The interactive function of hits and takes: An ethological study of two year olds.* Unpublished masters thesis, Georgia State University, 1977.

Cohen, J. A coefficient of agreement for nominal scales. *Educational and Psychological Measurement*, 1960, *20*, 37-46.

Davis, J. A. Hierarchical models for significance tests in multivariate contingency tables: An exegesis of Goodman's recent papers. In J. Magidson (Ed.), *Analyzing qualitative/categorical data: Log-linear models and latent-structure analysis.* Cambridge, Mass.: Abt Books, 1978.

Dawe, H. C. An analysis of two hundred quarrels of preschool children. *Child Development*, 1934, *4*, 139-157.

Eckerman, C. O., & Whatley, J. L. Toys and social interaction between infant peers. *Child Development*, 1977, *48*, 1645-1656.

Eckerman, C. O., Whatley, J. L., & Kutz, S. L. Growth of social play with peers during the second year of life. *Developmental Psychology*, 1975, *11*, 42-49.

Feinberg, S. E. *The analysis of cross-classified categorical data.* Cambridge, Mass.: MIT Press, 1977.

Fishbein, H. D. *Evolution, development, and children's learning.* Pacific Palisades, Cal.: Goodyear, 1976.

Furby, L. Possessions: Toward a theory of their meaning and function throughout the life cycle. In P. B. Baltes (Ed.), *Lifespan development and behavior* (Vol. 1). New York: Academic Press, 1978.

Hay, D. F., & Ross, H. S. The social nature of early conflict. *Child Development*, 1982, *53*, 105-113.

Hollenbeck, A. R. Problems of reliability in observational research. In G. P. Sackett (Ed.), *Observing behavior* (Vol. II): *Data collection and analysis methods.* Baltimore: University Park Press, 1978.

Newson, J., & Newson, E. Intersubjectivity and the transmission of culture. *Bulletin of the British Psychological Society*, 1975, *28*, 437-446.

Ross, H. S., & Goldman, B. M. Establishing new social relations in infancy. In T. Alloway, L. Krames, & P. Pliner (Eds.), *Advances in communication and affect* (Vol. 3). New York: Plenum Press, 1977.

Rubenstein, J., & Howes, C. The effects of peers on toddler interaction with mother and toys. *Child Development*, 1976, *47*, 597-605.

Shotter, J. The cultural context of communication studies: Theoretical and methodological issues. In A. Lock (Ed.), *Action, gesture and symbol: The emergence of language.* London: Academic Press, 1978.

Strayer, F. F., & Strayer, J. An ethological analysis of social agonism and dominance relations among preschool children. *Child Development*, 1976, *47*, 980-989.

Trevarthen, C., & Hubley, P. Secondary intersubjectivity: Confidence, confiding, and acts of meaning in the first year. In A. Lock (Ed.), *Action, gesture and symbol: The emergence of language.* London: Academic Press, 1978.

Waddington, C. H. *The strategy of genes.* London: Allen and Unwin, 1957.

Wellman, H. M., & Lempers, J. D. The naturalistic communicative abilities of two-year-olds. *Child Development*, 1977, *48*, 1052-1057.

Chapter 5

An Observational Study of Social Problem Solving in Young Children

Linda Rose Krasnor

Social problem-solving (SPS) behaviors are attempts to achieve personal goals within social interaction. In one recently observed preschool incident, for example, "Gretel" attempted to solve the problem of getting her classmates, "Samantha" and "Hecate," to stop being witches. Her first strategy was to touch each witch on the arm, saying "If you be the witch, I'm not your friend." They looked at her and then resumed their role play. Gretel made a second, slightly modified, attempt. This time she held up her wrist and said, "If you play witches, I won't let you wear my watch." The second attempt was more successful. "Alright," Hecate responded, "we won't play witches. Let's go to a party." Gretel and the two ex-witches walked to the playhouse together and began to dress for a ball at the castle.

SPS attempts, such as those described above, are common in everyday interaction and encompass a wide variety of personal goals (e.g., attaining assistance, eliciting cooperation, obtaining information, stopping another's action). Many different strategies (e.g., crying, asking, hitting) can be used to achieve a given goal, and an SPS attempt may consist of more than one specific strategy. In Gretel's second attempt, for example, there were two strategies (showing and threatening). An individual's success in achieving personal goals is a measure of social effectiveness and has been considered by many researchers to be a central aspect of social competence (Foster & Ritchey, 1979; O'Malley, 1977; Trower, Bryant, & Argyle, 1978; Weinstein, 1969; White & Watts, 1973).

Several basic assumptions underlie this view of competence. First, social behavior is assumed to be organized and goal directed, although not necessarily at a conscious level (Langer, 1978). Second, it is assumed that the strategies used to attain these goals can be judged as successes or failures on the basis of their environmental impact. Thus, there can be no a priori definitions of what constitutes effective or competent social action. These assumptions clearly outline a functional approach to social competence, in which assessment is made in specific situations or contexts.

Solving social problems effectively appears to be a complex "multi-disciplinary" skill. Relevant research has come from a wide range of fields, including studies in information processing (e.g., Schank & Abelson, 1977), sociolinguistics (e.g., Ervin-Tripp, 1977), ethnology (e.g., Harré, 1974), clinical psychology (e.g., Spivack & Shure, 1974), and ethology (e.g., Blurton-Jones, 1972). Integration of these diverse areas, however, has been difficult and largely post hoc in nature. The need for a theoretical model that could encompass differing perspectives and guide further research is clearly indicated.

There have been several recent attempts to construct integrative models of social action that would be consistent with an SPS framework (Harré, 1974; Schank & Abelson, 1977; Spivack & Shure, 1974; Trower et al., 1978). Krasnor and Rubin (1981) proposed a multistep model that was specifically designed to be compatible with observational methods. In this model, a social goal is set; attaining this goal defines the social problem. The first step in solving the problem is to gather relevant task information from the social environment. Relevant items may include, for example, information about the mood of the target (the person to whom the SPS attempt is directed), the objects available in the physical setting, the nearness of an adult, or the direction in which the target is looking (c.f., Lee, 1975). Second, one or more social strategies are selected. The selection process utilizes information about the current social situation, information retrieved from long-term memory, and/or any available SPS algorithms, heuristics, or "scripts" (Schank & Abelson, 1977). In the third step, the social strategy is attempted. Finally, the impact of the strategy on the environment is evaluated. On the basis of this evaluation, decisions regarding subsequent SPS behavior are made.

This hypothetical model identifies aspects of social behavior which are potentially important in the SPS process. A descriptive analysis of these SPS components could establish a normative data base, and ideographic assessments may prove useful in predicting individual SPS success. Four major areas of assessment are suggested within the model (Krasnor & Rubin, 1981): (a) the child's sensitivity to social task variables; (b) the quantity and quality of the child's repertoire of social strategies which can be employed to solve social problems; (c) the degree to which the child "matches" a strategy to a specific situation, reflected both in the effectiveness of the strategy in achieving the goal and in the social acceptability of the strategy; and (d) the child's sequencing of SPS attempts after failure. In this chapter, I focus on the first assessment area and concentrate on examining observed SPS behavior for sensitivity to social task features during naturalistic preschool interaction. The remaining three assessment areas have been considered in a more extended treatment of these data (Krasnor, 1981).

Sensitivity to Social Task Features

The impact of setting or situation on social behavior has long been recognized (Heider, 1958), although its importance has often been underestimated (Mischel, 1973). The importance of situation in determining behavior is stressed in the work of ecologists (e.g., Barker & Wright, 1955), ethnologists (e.g., Harré, 1974), and behaviorists (e.g., Patterson, 1979). Social behavior should vary as the "rules" or the contingencies of situations vary.

A basic premise of SPS theory is that information contained in the social situation will be important in the selection of effective and appropriate strategies. Extracting information from the social world is difficult, however, since socially derived evidence is often shifting, ambiguous, and inferential (Lee, 1975; Trower et al., 1978). Nevertheless, an analysis of the social situation is presumed to be important for the production of socially effective behavior (Argyle, 1979).

One way of discovering those features of specific situations that are important in determining behavior is to examine how behaviors change with situational variance. For example, if social strategies change as the relative distance between problem-solver and target changes, then it could be inferred that physical distance from the target is relevant to the SPS process. Alternatively, if no differences are found in social strategies directed to curly versus straight-haired targets, it could be concluded that curliness of hair is an irrelevant bit of social information (at least with respect to choosing social strategies). There is considerable evidence that children at surprisingly young ages do predictably vary their social behavior in response to situational features. Most of the research has focused on analyses of target features. Some of the specific target characteristics associated with changes in social behavior include sex of partner (Jacklin & Maccoby, 1978), age of partner (Whiting & Whiting, 1975), popularity (Putallaz & Gottman, 1981), and peer familiarity (Doyle, Connolly, & Rivest, 1980).

The impact of situational influences on behavior is one-half of an ongoing "situation versus trait" debate in the social psychological literature (Bowers, 1973; Mischel, 1973). The "trait" side of this issue emphasizes individual consistency in behavior across situations, rather than situational consistency across individuals. In general, the data have not clearly supported either position. It appears that individuals, in fact, differ in the extent to which they change their behavior across situations (Bem & Allen, 1974; Bowers, 1973; Mischel, 1973; Snyder, 1979).

These individual differences in situationally based variations may be due to differences in the way social information is processed. Variation in behavior across situations would depend first on the ability to identify social features and then to use this information to choose situationally appropriate social action. Children who process social information would then be expected to be more situationally "variable." A child who is sensitive to changes in social features (e.g., mood of target) may show corresponding changes in behavior as those features change across situations. His or her social behavior will show more situational differentiation. On the other hand, a child who does not process social information should show less behavioral variation across situations; his or her behavior would therefore be less well differentiated with respect to those social features.

At present, there is little evidence directly relevant to this issue. Snyder's (1979) recent work investigating "self-monitoring" adults has applicability. Highly self-monitoring individuals were defined as those who were aware of the social appropriateness of actions and were concerned with their personal social "image" and the social impact of their acts. Snyder found that high self-monitors had better memory for social information and made more accurate inferences concerning the emotions of others. High self-monitors also reported greater situational variability in their behavior than did the low self-monitors. The high self-monitors acted in ways they perceived as appropriate for given situations, while low self-monitors reported greater consistency of actions across a variety of different situations.

It is a reasonable hypothesis that competent behavior will vary across situations (Nakamura & Finck, 1980). Some behaviors will be more effective and/or appropriate in some situations than in others. Socially competent children should then show higher differentiation of behavior across social situations, if the requirements for socially effective responses also vary. This would mean, then, that socially competent children should be more aware of social features and show more situationally based variation in behavior. Evidence for either factor is very scant.

Recall of social features is one way of assessing the degree to which information from the social situation is processed. In one recent study (Ince, Messé, Stollack, & Smith, Note 1), first- and third-grade children who were rated as socially competent by their teachers had more accurate recall of a videotaped sequence of social behavior than less competent peers. It should be noted, though, that both groups of children were equally accurate in recalling child behavior sequences; differential recall was shown only for adult social behavior. These findings indicate that the high- and low-competence children did not differ in overall recall, but rather the difference was specific to a target feature.

Nakamura and Finck (1980) hypothesized that children rated by their teachers as "effective" would appropriately vary their behavior in response to changes in the requirements of specific situations. These authors found that effective children were able to perform a greater variety of behaviors appropriate to different phases of a block-building task, compared to less effective peers.

The importance of sensitivity to situational factors is stressed in the Krasnor and Rubin (1981) model of SPS behavior described briefly earlier. Awareness of and responsivity to social environmental features may be necessary for the development of effective SPS skills. An indirect assessment of this responsivity can be made by observing covariation of SPS components and features of the social situation. Two hypotheses follow from these considerations. First, predictable variation exists in SPS across target variables; second, there is a relationship between behavioral differentiation across situations and observed social success.

Hypothesis 1: Preschool children will show predictable variation in the SPS components of goal and strategy in response to "naturally" occurring variation in SPS targets. This variation will be interpreted as indirect evidence of the processing of social task information during social interaction. Variation of goal and strategy components in response to target features would indicate that target information is relevant to the SPS process. Existing evidence of social variation in response to sex and age differences in targets suggests the potential importance of these target dimensions for the selection of SPS strategies and goals.

Hypothesis 2: Behavioral differentiation of goal and strategy across targets will be positively related to observed SPS success among preschool children. The ability to solve social problems effectively is assumed to rest partly on the ability to discriminate social features and to use them to select appropriate SPS behaviors. In addition, effective social behavior is assumed to vary with social task features. Thus, children who show greater differentiation across targets should also be more effective in their SPS attempts.

Method

Children

Eight children (four boys and four girls) between the ages of 3½ and 4½ years were randomly selected from each of two preschools in southwestern Ontario. One of the girls moved from the area and was dropped from the study. At the start of the observations, the remaining 15 children had a mean age of 48.5 months. There were no significant school or sex differences in age.

Observational Procedure

The observational method was designed to collect extended samples of naturally occurring SPS behavior during free-play interactions. A focal individual sampling procedure was used. Each of the 15 children was observed in random order for a total of ten ½-hour sessions. Observations were generally made in each school for 3 days per week during the 4½ months of the study (except for school holidays and field trips).

The observer positioned herself in an unobtrusive place in the playroom and carried a battery-powered audiotape-recorder, equipped with a timer which recorded a tone onto the tape every 10 seconds. Observation began once the observer had located the focal child in the playroom and positioned herself approximately 5 feet from the child. The observer then described the focal child's behavior into a microphone. The behaviors directed to the focal child by others were also described. The observer moved with the focal child, if necessary, in order to maintain contact.

Coding of Transcripts

The narrated tapes were transcripted and the 10-second intervals were marked on the written transcripts. Three a priori criteria were used to identify SPS attempts. The behavior: (a) had to be socially oriented, as indicated by visual gaze toward another or an attention-getting verbalization (e.g., "Hey John"); (b) had to include a directive component (Ervin-Tripp, 1976), such as a command or agonistic action, or constitute an initiation of an interaction; and (c) had to be initiated by the focal child. If an action met all three criteria, it was coded as an SPS attempt.

Once identified, these attempts were coded for four main variables: goals, strategy, outcome, and target. Coding definitions for the strategy, goal, and outcome categories are presented in Table 5-1. The targets were coded first as individuals and then by target group (teacher, girl, boy, or multiple targets)

During reliability sessions, two observers independently narrated the behaviors of the same focal child. This procedure was used with six children during the first third of the study and a different six children during the last third. The independently recorded observations (a total of 6 hours) were transcribed and then separately coded by the two observers. Reliability was assessed by comparing the two sets of codes from the separate transcripts for the 12 reliability sessions. Intraclass correlations were calculated for the categories coded by each observer. The correlation for total SPS attempts was $r = .97$, $p < .01$. Intraclass correlations for the strategy categories ranged from .67 to .91, $M = .84$; for the goal codes, the correlations ranged from .68 to .97, $M = .87$. The intraclass correlations for success and failure codings were .77 and .95 respectively. All intraclass correlations were significant ($p < .05$). Three coding categories had insufficient data in the reliability transcripts to perform the intraclass correlations; these were playnoise, affection goals, and partial success outcomes. Percentage agreements for these codes were 71%, 100%, and 85%, respectively.

Individual Difference Measures

Intelligence. The Peabody Picture Vocabulary Test (Form A) was administered to each child since a significant relationship between IQ and SPS effectiveness was expected. This expectation was based on the relationship between IQ and the ability to solve hypothetical social problems (Spivack & Shure, 1974) and that between social and cognitive competencies (White & Watts, 1973).

Two children refused to be tested on the intelligence test. The IQ scores for the remaining 13 children ranged from 82 to 139, $M = 113.8$. Age, school, and sex differences in IQ were all nonsignificant.

Effectiveness. Effectiveness in SPS was measured by percentage success in observed SPS interactions. This percentage was calculated by dividing the number of observed successes by the total number of SPS attempts made by each child. Percentage success ranged from 35% to 64%, $M = 56\%$. There were no significant age, sex, or school differences in percentage success.

Behavioral differentiation index. An index was needed to measure the extent to which an individual's SPS behavior showed differentiation across targets. This differentiation would be reflected in interdependency between relevant distributions, and in how accurately one could predict the social goal or strategy from knowledge of the target. For example, the greater the interdependency between strategy and target distributions, the more accurately one could predict strategy if the target was known (and vice versa) compared to predictions made from the baseline probabilities of the strategy categores alone. Suppose "Jack" and "Jill" both used the strategies of hitting, grabbing, and asking at the same overall rates. Jack's strategies, however, were highly differentiated by target; he only hit boy targets, grabbed from girls, and asked his teachers. Jill, on the other hand, used the three strategies randomly across targets and showed no target-specific differentiation. Knowing that Jack's target was a girl would enable us to predict more accurately his strategy. Knowing the target of Jill's SPS attempt,

Table 5-1. Categorization of Social Problem-Solving Attempts

Category	Definition
Strategy	
Directives	Personal need statements, direct imperatives, imbedded imperatives, permission directives, bribes/threats
Suggestions	Propositions, want questions
Statements	Descriptions of objects, persons, events, etc.
Claims	Assertive statements which claim ownership (Dore, Gearhart, & Newman, 1978)
Interrogatives	Direct questions, rhetorical questions, titles or greetings
Play noise	Nonword or playful vocalizations during play
Unintelligible	Inaudible vocalizations
Orienting acts	Actions which direct attention to an object, event, or person (e.g., showing, pointing)
Object agonistic	Use of force or threatened force directed at object
Person agonistic	Use of force or threatened force directed at person
Affiliative	Positive, nonforceful contact with another (e.g., hugging, holding hands, giving object)
Goal	
Stop action	Attempts to prevent or stop the action or intended action of another
Self-action	Attempts to obtain permission or to perform an action made by the focal child (e.g., to join ongoing play)
Other action	Attempts to elicit an active response from another not otherwise coded
Object acquisition	Attempts to gain sole possession of or access to an object or activity
Attention/ acknowledgment	Attempts to direct another's attention to a concrete object, event, or person
Affection/ comfort	Attempts to elicit or give positive, prosocial, physical or verbal affection
Information	Attempts to elicit information, clarification, or agreement not otherwise coded
Nonspecific initiations	Attempts to initiate interaction (no interaction with target within the full 10-second interval preceding the attempt) not otherwise coded
Outcome	
Success	Action specified in the attempt is performed by the target with the 10-second interval following the interval in which the attempt occurred *and* prior to the next related attempt; when an object is taken from the target without a contingent response, the outcome is judged successful if the focal child retains the object for 10 seconds; similarly, if the goal is stop action, the specified action must be stopped for a full 10-second interval

Table 5-1. (continued)

Category	Definition
Partial success	Target specifically indicates a need for clarification or performs part of the specified act within 10 seconds of the focal child's attempt and before the next related attempt
Failure	Focal child performs the act himself; nontarget other performs the act; target performs act after the 10-second period; all other noncompliance circumstances
Uncertain	Either the goal is unknown or the target response is not observed or is unintelligible

however, would not lead to a strategy prediction which would be any more accurate than that made using the baseline probabilities of her strategies alone.

The increase in predictability of strategy category over baseline, given knowledge of target, is reflected in the amount of shared information, $T(x,y)$, between the distributions of target (x) and strategy (y). More precisely, $T(x,y)$ is the difference (expressed in bits of information) between the information value of knowing the baseline probabilities of strategy categories and the conditional probabilities of each strategy, given that the target is known (Steinberg, 1977). The greater the value of $T(x,y)$, the greater is the relationship between the two variables, and the greater the accuracy of predicting the strategy from knowledge of the target (compared to predicting from baseline alone).

$T(x,y)$, like chi square, is calculated from contingency tables. A goal by target contingency table was constructed for each child, and individual $T(x,y)$ indices were calculated. This statistic was used as a measure of how much each child differentiated *goals* across targets. In addition, $T(x,y)$ indices were calculated for each child from individual strategy by target contingency tables. This index reflected how much each child's *strategies* were differentiated by target.

Results

Sensitivity of SPS Components to Target

Goal and target distributions. A total of 6,338 SPS attempts was identified from the written transcripts. Goal and target could be identified for 6,282 of these attempts. The observed frequency of SPS goals directed at each target group is presented in Table 5-2 for both schools combined. The goal and target distributions were significantly interdependent, χ^2 (21) = 827.0, $p < .01$. The distribution of goals was therefore contingent upon the target of the SPS attempt (and vice versa).

A nonparametric chi square analysis was one of the several possible approaches to the assessment of behavioral differentiation. The results of the chi square analysis can only be considered approximations, however, since the cell frequencies were not independent but were summed across all children. In addition to violating one of the chi square assumptions, this procedure also may result in a bias toward the contributions of the more socially active children. For these reasons a second set of analyses was computed. The same data were subjected to a repeated-measures analysis of variance, in which goals and targets were considered as repeated measures. The latter approach compensated for individual variation in frequency of SPS attempts.

A sex (2) by school (2) by goal (8) by target (4) repeated-measures analysis of variance was therefore calculated for frequency of SPS attempts. Consistent with the chi square analysis, the goal by target interaction was significant, F (21, 231) = 10.24, $p < .05$.[1] The finding was also significant with reduced degrees of freedom, df = 1, 11, allowing for possible heterogeneity of variance (Greenhouse & Geisser, 1959).

Thus, both the chi square analysis and analysis of variance indicated that target distribution varied with goal category (and vice versa). The joint distribution of goal and target will be examined from both the row and column perspectives of Table 5-2. The row percentages reflect the distribution of SPS attempts among the target groups for each goal; these will be compared to the marginal percentages for all goals combined. The column percentages reflect the relative distribution of goals within each target group; these will be compared to the marginal percentages for all targets combined.

As shown in Table 5-2, 37.8% of all SPS attempts were directed to boy targets. This percentage varied across goals, however. Boys received a relatively high proportion (65.8%) of all stop-action goals and a relatively low proportion (17.1%) of affection goals. Girl targets received 29.4% of all SPS attempts. They had relatively high proportions of affection (53.7%) and information (39.4%) goals, but low proportions of attention (17.7%) goals. Teachers received 28.9% of all SPS attempts. Self-action, attention, and nonspecific initiation goals accounted for relatively high percentages of the goals directed at teachers (41.4%, 47.5%, and 41.0% respectively), while other-action (19.0%),

---

[1] Although the goal by target interaction is most directly analogous to the chi square analysis, it should also be noted that there were significant main effects for goal and target frequencies, as well as for sex by target and sex by target by goal interactions. No significant school differences were found in the analysis of variance.

Table 5-2. Goal by Target Distribution of SPS Attempts

Goal	Target				Total frequency
	Boys	Girls	Teacher	Multiple	
Other action	586 (40.3)[a] (24.7)[b]	522 (35.9) (28.3)	276 (19.0) (15.2)	71 (4.9) (28.6)	1,455 (23.2)
Stop action	466 (65.8) (19.6)	196 (27.7) (10.6)	26 (3.7) (1.4)	20 (2.8) (2.9)	708 (11.3)
Object acquisition	171 (40.4) (7.2)	160 (37.8) (8.7)	83 (19.6) (4.6)	9 (2.1) (3.6)	423 (6.7)
Self-action	125 (29.3) (5.3)	108 (25.3) (5.9)	177 (41.4) (9.8)	17 (4.0) (6.9)	427 (6.8)
Attention	318 (31.1) (13.4)	181 (17.7) (9.8)	485 (47.5) (26.7)	37 (3.6) (14.9)	1,021 (16.2)
Affection	7 (17.1) (0.3)	22 (53.7) (1.1)	12 (29.3) (0.7)	0 (0.0) (0.0)	41 (0.1)
Information	305 (31.9) (12.8)	377 (39.4) (20.4)	243 (25.4) (13.4)	31 (3.2) (12.5)	956 (15.2)
Initiation	396 (31.7) (16.7)	279 (22.3) (15.1)	513 (41.0) (28.3)	63 (5.0) (25.4)	1,251 (20.0)
Total frequency	2,374 (37.8)	1,845 (29.4)	1,815 (28.9)	248 (3.9)	6,282

[a] Row percentage.
[b] Column percentage.

object acquisition (19.6%), and stop-action (3.7%) goals were attempted with relative infrequency. Multiple targets received 3.9% of all SPS attempts; this percentage showed little variation across specific goal categories.

A comparison of the column percentages for each goal among the target groups provides a different perspective of the goal by target interaction. In general, the relative proportion of goals directed at boy targets approximates the marginal proportions for all targets combined. A similar pattern is apparent for the goal distribution of SPS attempts directed at girls. The relative goal distribution for teacher targets, however, shows that although stop-action goals accounted for 11.3% of all SPS attempts, they accounted for only 1.4% of those directed at teachers. On the other hand, the proportion of attention goals directed at teachers (26.7%) exceeded the proportion of attention goals for all targets combined. It should also be noted that teachers received a higher proportion of nonspecific initiations (28.3%) than did boy or girl targets (16.7% and 15.1% of SPS attempts directed at boys and girls, respectively). Finally, the distribution of goals directed at multiple targets generally followed the overall goal distributions for the targets combined, except for stop-action goals. Multiple targets received relatively fewer stop-action goals (2.9%) than reflected in the marginal percentage (11.3%) for all targets combined.

Strategy and target distributions. The frequency of strategies used with each of the target groups is presented in Table 5-3. A total of 9,066 strategies was identified from the 6,282 SPS attempts. A significant chi square value was found for the distributions in the contingency table, $\chi^2(30) = 547.2, p < .01$.

The relationship found in the chi square analysis was supported by a sex (2) by school strategy (11) by target group (4) repeated-measures analysis of variance. There was a significant strategy by target interaction, $F(30, 330) = 7.23, p < .01$, indicating that the frequencies of strategies varied with the target group.[2] This was also significant with reduced $df = 1, 11$.

As indicated in Table 5-3, 38.1% of all SPS strategies were directed at boy targets. Using this percentage as a reference point, boys received relatively high proportions of claims (61.5%), play noises (61.6%), object agonistic strategies (63.2%), and person agonistic (61.4%) strategies. Girls received a relatively high proportion of suggestions (44.1%) but a low proportion of play noises (12.0%), compared to the 30.4% of all SPS strategies which had girl targets. Teachers received 27.5% of all strategies. Callings (41.4%) and orienting acts (39.5%) accounted for a relatively high proportion of strategies directed at teachers; suggestions (12.5%), claims (5.4%), play noises (16.0%), person agonistic acts (1.8%), and object agonistic acts (4.7%) accounted for relatively low proportions. Four percent of all SPS strategies had multiple targets. This percentage remained relatively consistent across all strategy categories for this target group.

Few differences emerge when the column percentages of each target group are compared either to the marginal percentages or to each other. This indicates that the relative proportions of strategies *within* target groups were similar for the four target groups.

---

[2] This analysis of variance also yielded significant main effects for target and strategy, as well as a sex by strategy by target interaction. No school differences were significant.

Table 5-3. Strategy by Target Distribution of SPS Attempts

Goal	Target				Total frequency
	Boys	Girls	Teacher	Multiple	
Directives	860 (39.2)[a] (24.9)[b]	682 (31.1) (24.8)	565 (25.8) (22.6)	84 (3.8) (23.0)	2,191 (24.2)
Suggestions	165 (38.9) (4.8)	187 (44.1) (6.8)	53 (12.5) (2.1)	19 (4.5) (5.2)	424 (4.7)
Descriptions	828 (36.0) (24.0)	645 (28.0) (23.4)	719 (31.2) (28.8)	110 (4.8) (30.1)	2,302 (25.4)
Claims	91 (61.5) (2.6)	44 (29.7) (1.6)	8 (5.4) (0.3)	5 (3.4) (1.4)	148 (1.6)
Questions	386 (31.4) (11.2)	468 (38.1) (17.0)	325 (26.5) (13.0)	49 (4.0) (13.4)	1,228 (13.5)
Callings	110 (33.2) (3.2)	75 (22.7) (2.7)	136 (41.1) (5.4)	10 (3.0) (2.7)	331 (3.6)
Play noises	77 (61.6) (2.2)	15 (12.0) (0.5)	20 (16.0) (0.8)	13 (10.4) (3.5)	125 (1.4)
Object agonistic	215 (63.2) (6.2)	105 (30.9) (3.8)	16 (4.7) (0.6)	4 (1.2) (1.1)	340 (3.8)
Person agonistic	70 (61.4) (2.0)	41 (36.0) (1.5)	2 (1.8) (0.1)	1 (0.9) (0.3)	114 (1.3)
Orienting	438 (31.8) (12.7)	393 (24.1) (14.3)	545 (39.5) (21.8)	63 (4.6) (16.8)	1,379 (15.2)
Affiliative	212 (43.8) (6.1)	158 (32.6) (5.7)	107 (22.1) (4.3)	7 (1.4) (1.9)	484 (5.3)
Total frequency	3,452 (38.1)	2,753 (30.4)	2,496 (27.5)	365 (4.0)	9,066

[a] Row percentage.
[b] Column percentage.

Behavioral Differentiation and SPS Success

Differentiation of goal by target. Individual goal by target contingency tables were constructed. A $T(x,y)$ index was calculated for each child from these tables. These indices ranged from .057 to .340 (M = .158, SD = .065). In order to determine the relationship between differentiation of goal over targets and social effectiveness, a correlation was calculated between each child's $T(x,y)$ index and his or her percentage success. This correlation was positive but nonsignificant, r (13) = .35. A significant positive relationship between $T(x,y)$ and percentage success was found, however, when the variance due to IQ was partialed out of both variables, r (12.3) = .64, $p < .05$.

Differentiation of strategy by target. A strategy by target matrix was constructed for each child. Individual $T(x,y)$ indices were calculated from these tables, reflecting each child's differentiation of strategy by target. These indices ranged from .040 to .220 (M = .091, SD = .051). As with the goal by $\times$ target matrices, the first-order correlation between these $T(x,y)$ indices and percentage success across individual children was nonsignificant, r (13) = .36. When the effects of IQ were partialed out of both variables, however, the partial correlation was both positive and significant, r (12.3) = .59, $p < .05$.

Discussion

Social problem solving has been defined as the process of influencing others in order to attain personal goals. Behavioral responsivity to "key" situational or task features was hypothesized to be an important SPS ability. In particular, information about the social target was considered important in decisions about both goal and strategy.

Sensitivity of SPS Components to Target

Two different analytic approaches were used to test the interdependencies between goal and target and between strategy and target distributions. Both the chi square analysis and analysis of variance indicated significant interrelationships between strategies and targets and between goals and targets. Thus, the two SPS components of goal and strategy did vary predictably with the target. Some selected aspects of these interactions are discussed below.

The results indicate that preschoolers do not tend to tell their teachers what to do; they especially do not tell them what *not* to do. There were also relatively few attempts to acquire objects from teachers; teachers received low percentages of agonistic acts and claims. These findings parallel those of Holmberg (1980) and Whiting and Whiting

(1975), who found less assertive interactions with older social targets. It appears safe to conclude that when preschoolers show assertive SPS behaviors, the targets are most likely to be age-mates.

Teachers, however, were relatively more often the targets of nonspecific initiations and attention goals; together these two goals accounted for well over one-half of all teacher-directed SPS attempts. Conversational initiations and attention/ acknowledgment were thus found to be one of the most frequent child-initiated adult functions in SPS interactions, in contrast to other potential functions which may be served by an adult among preschool children (e.g., giving assistance, providing objects, giving affection). Whether or not adult attention or conversation functions *should* be primary for teachers is an important programing consideration. The specification of teacher roles is a critical aspect of any curriculum model. In a program which emphasizes self-directed, independent, task-oriented behaviors (e.g., Montessori curriculum), it would be expected that relatively low proportions of teacher-directed attention and nonspecific initiation goals should be found during free-play interactions. In more traditionally oriented preschools, which tend to emphasize a more emotionally supportive and play-oriented teacher role, relatively higher proportions of nonspecific initiations, attention, and affection goals would be expected to have teacher targets. The relative frequencies of SPS goals can reflect curriculum philosophy and, if used formatively, can provide a guide to program improvement consistent with that philosophy.

Predictable differentiation of SPS strategies over targets was also found. Claims and antagonistic strategies, for example, tended to be more often directed to boy targets. The use of these strategies with boys may have been associated with the higher frequency of stop-action goals directed at boys, since these strategies would be likely to be used for such purposes. The greatest differentiation of strategies directed at teachers for 7 of the 11 strategy categories showed considerable deviation from the marginal percentages. This may indicate that monitoring strategy use with teachers may be more important than with other target groups. This is consistent with the finding by Ince and his colleagues (Note 1) that memory for adult behavior differentiated competent from less competent children.

It should be noted carefully that not all goals showed equal differentiation across targets. Little difference was found, for example, in the proportions of other-action goals directed to boy and girl targets, unlike the pattern found for stop-action goals. Certain goals may be equally appropriate for a variety of targets (e.g., initiating conversation), while other goals may be more specific to the target (e.g., affection). Goals that are highly differentiated by target may depend more on the specific social role of the target (e.g., caretaker) or the control of relevant resources (e.g., toys).

Similarly, some strategies may be effective and/or appropriate for any or all targets; other strategies may be more specific in application. Directive forms, for example, have been found to vary with the relative social status of the target (Mitchell-Kernan & Kernan, 1977). Gretel's threats to Samantha and Hecate, as described at the beginning of this chapter, would most likely have been both inappropriate and ineffective with teacher targets. The differentiation of SPS behavior across social situations may therefore be characteristic only of certain social tasks or specific social actions.

The first hypothesis, that predictable variation in SPS goals and strategies across targets would be found in the social interactions of preschoolers, was thus supported. The second hypothesis, in which the relationship between behavioral differentiation and SPS effectiveness was addressed, is considered next.

Behavioral Sensitivity and SPS Success

It was hypothesized that goal and strategy differentiation would be positively related to observed SPS effectiveness. This hypothesis received qualified support. Significant positive relationships between differentiation of goal and social success and between differentiation of strategy and social success were found, but only after IQ was partialed out of both differentiation and effectiveness variables. It appeared, then, that among children of similar IQ levels, those who showed greater differentiation of SPS components across targets tended to be more successful in their SPS attempts than those who did not. Children whose behavior shows this contingent variation in goals and strategies may be engaging in more "sensitive" processing of social information during interaction.

This differentiation in social behavior across targets was distinct from and uncorrelated with IQ; its relationship to social effectiveness was independent of the contributions of general intelligence (as measured by the Peabody Picture Vocabulary Test). However, the strong and positive relationship between intelligence and observed success tended to overshadow the relationship between differentiation and success. Several speculations may be offered to explain why the first-order relationship between differentiation and observed effectiveness was not as strong as expected.

Target group membership (boy, girl, teacher, or multiple targets) is a rather global categorization of targets. It is likely that more specific information about targets may be considerably more important in determining SPS behavior. This specific information may include relationship variables that apply only to particular pairs (or groups) of individuals. Masters and Furman (1981), for example, found that the selection of a particular peer on a sociometric test was related to specific interactions between the peer and the selecting child, and not related to the overall social behavior of the selected child. The specific degree of acquaintanceship has also been found to be related to social influence attempts (Gottman & Parkhurst, 1980). Greater specificity in the categorization of targets may lead to a differentiation index that correlates more highly with overall success than the index based on the general category of target group.

In addition, target information is only one part of the available social data. There are many other dimensions of social information that may be critical in determining effective and appropriate social action. One dimension concerns the physical setting itself, including available resources and restraints (e.g., knowledge as to which toys are available as "bribes" to elicit action, or whether an escape route exists, if necessary). A second dimension concerns culturally defined "rules" which may be operating in standard social interactions (Harré, 1974, 1979). Introduction rituals (i.e., who gets introduced to whom and in what order) are a general example; the specific subculture rules are also important for the problem-solver to identify (e.g., in which of the houses on the block one must remove one's shoes before entering). In addition, the specific phenomonological meaning which targets ascribe to an interaction may be an important source of social information in planning SPS behavior (Weinstein, 1969). Thus, it may be critical to know whether a target considers the problem-solver to be a friend or an enemy, or whether he or she considers the situation to be one which threatens his or her self-esteem or one which is essentially nonthreatening. It is clear that much more extensive investigation is necessary to ascertain which types of social information are relevant to effective SPS.

It should also be remembered that these findings are based on observations of a relatively small number of basically homogeneous children. Although the generalizability of the findings may therefore be limited and await replication, the analysis demonstrates the feasibility of an observational analysis of situationally relevant SPS behavior.

The findings summarized in the preceding pages indicate that preschool children predictably varied goals and strategies over target groups during SPS interactions. The content of SPS attempts differed among targets, as did the means the children used to attain personal goals in social interaction. This differentiation, as reflected in variations in observed behaviors in naturalistic settings, was significantly related to observed success, once the effects of IQ were removed. Finer grained analyses of social information may be necessary in order to demonstrate a stronger relation between behavioral differentiation and social effectiveness. Differentiation of goals and strategies across targets was not equal for all goal and strategy categories, indicating that some goals and some strategies may have more generality across targets than others.

Little is known about the sources of individual differences in how behavior varies across situations. We do not yet understand the determinants, correlates, and consequences of such variability, nor do we understand its role in development. Does variability and situational differentiation increase with age and experience as behavior becomes more consolidated (Cairns, 1979) or "scripted?" Is it also possible that with age and experience, relatively few "multipurpose" and generally effective strategies may be found and used over and over in a variety of social situations? How does behavioral differentiation across social features relate to indices of competence other than observed effectiveness (e.g., peer popularity, self-report of adjustment, teacher ratings)? Finally, can we increase competence by increasing behavioral differentiation during social interaction, perhaps by facilitating conscious processing of "critical" social information? The answers to these and other questions will require a coordinated program of research which includes both cognitive and behavioral components, both observation and interview, and integrates the rich mix of perspectives relevant to the SPS process.

Reference Notes

1. Ince, R., Meesé, L., Stollack, G., & Smith, H. *Person perception and psychosocial competence in children.* Paper presented at the annual meeting of the American Psychological Association, Montreal, August 1980.

References

Argyle, M. Sequences in social behavior as a function of the situation. In G. Ginsburg (Ed.), *Emerging strategies in social psychological research.* New York: Wiley, 1979.

Barker, R., & Wright, H. *Midwest and its children.* New York: Harper & Row, 1955.

Bem, D., & Allen, A. On predicting some of the people some of the time: The search for cross-situational consistencies in behavior. *Psychological Review*, 1974, *81*, 506-520.

Blurton-Jones, N. Categories of child-child interaction. In N. Blurton-Jones (Ed.), *Ethological studies of child behavior.* London: Cambridge University Press, 1972.

Bowers, K. Situationalism in psychology: An analysis and a critique. *Psychological Review*, 1973, *80*, 307-336.

Cairns, R. *Social development.* San Francisco: Freeman, 1979.

Dore, J., Gearhart, M., & Newman, D. The structure of nursery school conversation. In K. Nelson (Ed.), *Children's language* (Vol. 1). New York: Gardner Press, 1978.

Doyle, A., Connolly, Jr., & Rivest, L. The effect of playmate familiarity with the social interactions of young children. *Child Development*, 1980, *51*, 217-223.

Ervin-Tripp, S. Is Sybil there? The structure of some American English directives. *Language in Society*, 1976, *5*, 25-66.

Ervin-Tripp, S. Wait for me, roller skate! In S. Ervin-Tripp & C. Mitchell-Kernan (Eds.), *Child discourse.* New York: Academic Press, 1977.

Foster, S., & Ritchey, W. Issues in the assessment of social competence in children. *Journal of Applied Behavioral Analysis*, 1979, *12*, 625-638.

Gottman, J., & Parkhurst, J. A developmental theory of friendship and acquaintanceship processes. In W. Collins (Ed.), *Minnesota Symposium in Child Development* (Vol. 13). Hillsdale, N.J.: Erlbaum, 1980.

Greenhouse, S., & Geisser, S. On methods in the analysis of profile data. *Psychometrika*, 1959, *24*, 95-112. (Cited in B. Winer, *Statistical principles in experimental design* (2nd ed.). New York: McGraw-Hill, 1972.)

Harré, R. Some remarks on "rule" as a scientific concept. In T. Mischel (Ed.),
Understanding other persons. Oxford: Blackwell, 1974.

Harré, R. *Social being*. Oxford: Blackwell, 1979.

Heider, F. *The psychology of interpersonal relations*. New York: Wiley, 1958.

Holmberg, M. The development of social interchange patterns from 12 to 42
months. *Child Development*, 1980, *51*, 448-456.

Jacklin, C., & Maccoby, E. Social behavior at thirty-three months in same-sex and
mixed-sex dyads. *Child Development*, 1978, *49*, 557-569.

Krasnor, L. *An observational study of social problem solving in preschoolers*.
Unpublished doctoral dissertation, University of Waterloo, Waterloo, Ontario,
Canada, June 1981.

Krasnor, L., & Rubin, K. The assessment of social problem-solving skills in young
children. In T. Merluzzi, C. Glass, & M. Genest (Eds.), *Cognitive assessment*.
New York: Guilford Press, 1981.

Langer, E. Rethinking the role of thought in social interactions. In J. Harvey, W.
Ickes, & R. Kidd (Eds.), *New directions in attribution research* (Vol. 2). Hillsdale, N.J.: Erlbaum, 1978.

Lee, L. Toward a cognitive theory of interpersonal development: Importance of
peers. In M. Lewis & L. Rosenbaum (Eds.), *Friendship and peer relations*. New
York: Wiley, 1975.

Masters, J., & Furman, W. Popularity, individual friendship selection and specific
peer interaction among children. *Developmental Psychology*, 1981, *17*, 344-
350.

Mischel, W. Toward a cognitive social learning reconceptualization of personality.
Psychological Review, 1973, *80*, 252-283.

Mitchell-Kernan, C., & Kernan, K. Pragmatics of directive choice among children.
In S. Ervin-Tripp & C. Mitchell-Kernan (Eds.), *Child discourse*. New York:
Academic Press, 1977.

Nakamura, C., & Finck, D. Relative effectiveness of socially oriented and task
oriented children and predictability of their behavior. *Monographs of the Society for Research in Child Development*, 1980, *45* (3-4, Serial No. 185).

O'Malley, J. Research perspective on social competence. *Merrill-Palmer Quarterly*,
1977, *23*, 29-44.

Patterson, G. A performance theory for coercive family interaction. In R. Cairns
(Ed.), *The analysis of social interactions: Methods, issues and illustrations*. Hillsdale, N.J.: Erlbaum, 1979.

Putallaz, M., & Gottman, J. Social skills and group acceptance. In S. Asher & J.
Gottman (Eds.), *The development of friendship: Description and intervention*.
New York: Cambridge University Press, 1981.

Schank, R., & Abelson, S. *Scripts, plans, goals and understanding*. Hillsdale, N.J.:
Erlbaum, 1977.

Snyder, M. Self-monitoring processes. In L. Berkowitz (Ed.), *Advances in experimental social psychology* (Vol. 12). New York: Academic Press, 1979.

Spivack, G., & Shure, M. *Social adjustment of young children.* San Francisco: Jossey-Bass, 1974.

Steinberg, J. Information theory as an ethological tool. In B. Hazlett (Ed.), *Quantitative methods in the study of animal behavior.* New York: Academic Press, 1977.

Trower, P., Bryant, B., & Argyle, M. *Social skills and mental health.* London: Methuen, 1978.

Weinstein, E. The development of interpersonal competence. In D. Goslin (Ed.), *Handbook of socialization theory and research.* Chicago: Rand McNally, 1969.

White, B., & Watts, J. *Experience and environment. Major influences in the development of the young child* (Vol. 1). Englewood Cliffs, N.J.: Prentice-Hall, 1973.

Whiting, B., & Whiting, J. *Children of six cultures: A psychocultural analysis.* Cambridge, Mass.: Harvard University Press, 1975.

Chapter 6
Peers and Prosocial Development

Carolyn Zahn-Waxler, Ronald Iannotti,
and Michael Chapman

Piaget (1965) described children's social interactions, particularly during the middle years of childhood, as essential to the development of mature, relativistic moral thought. During middle childhood, there was hypothesized to be a decline in egocentrism, an increase in role-taking skills, and heightened sensitivity to the experiences of others. A primary catalyst for these changes was thought to be the increased reciprocity and egalitarianism that comes to characterize peers' social interactions. Piaget's observations have been interpreted by some investigators as indicating that peer relations in the elementary school years also may be particularly important for the development of altruism. From a psychoanalytical perspective, Sullivan (1953), too, emphasized the value of friendships between preadolescents for the organization and consolidation of prosocial patterns of interaction.

The focus of this chapter is on the multiple roles that peers play in children's emerging abilities to comfort, help, share, and cooperate. Our goal is to learn more about peers as recipients and stimulators of prosocial behavior and about the peer culture as a context for the emergence of altruism. The definition of peers used here includes not only age-mates, but also children or siblings who differ in age by more than 1-2 years.

There are many reasons to assume that peers are important in children's prosocial development and that their roles do not simply duplicate parental or adult functions. Mutual influence should occur more readily between persons who are relatively more equal in their power relations than, for example, are parent and child. Interactions between children often provide many natural opportunities for acts of altruism that differ in frequency and form from interactions with adults, for example, sharing play materials, and collaborating or cooperating in the context of fantasy play, games, and task assignments. Physical aggression or rough-and-tumble play, which typify peer interactions more than child-adult relations, increase the likelihood that a given child will be hurt and show distress. This provides unique occasions for potential acts of altruism, expressed as reconciliation or reparative behavior if the attacker atones, or as an act of compassion by an onlooker. Furthermore, some distresses of children (e.g., crying and pain) are expressed with more salience and intensity than characteristically would be seen in adults.

As bystanders to others' distresses, children may make different decisions about intervening depending upon whether they are alone or with peer companions (Staub, 1970), and depending upon the convictions of their peers. Children's reactions could be altered by a peer's comments (e.g., "He's crying because he's a dumb sissy; let's leave him alone"), as well as by a peer's level of affective arousal (e.g., standing next to a trembling friend while witnessing an accident). Peers could potentially function as models, teachers, reinforcers, and punishers and hence serve as socializers of altruism.

Peers may thus have unique capabilities for helping children channel aggressive impulses and develop concern for others. It is not necessary to wait until the middle years of childhood to see reciprocal, coordinated interactions between peers. Mueller and Rich (1976), and others as well, have characterized the second year of life as the ideal time to study the emergence of social interactions among peers. Prosocial actions are also present by this time. Thus, the special contributions to children's altruism that derive from peer interactions can be studied in very early stages of development. We begin with an account of the precursors and origins of altruism, considering the role that peers might play in early developmental processes. Subsequent sections provide other perspectives on the determinants of altruism: these include (a) characteristics of peers as elicitors and recipients of altruism, (b) cognitive and affective mediators of children's prosocial behavior toward peers and nonpeers, and (c) peers as socializers of altruism.

Development of Altruism

Altruism is defined as regard for or devotion to the interests of others. We will be indexing altruism based on a review of naturalistic and laboratory studies of children that cover a range of prosocial behaviors: helping, sharing, comforting, sympathizing, protecting, and cooperating. A caveat is necessary: the behaviors may not always be principally motivated by concern for the other person. For example, a prosocial act could result from self-interest. A critical and difficult research question pertains to the developmental delineation of different forms of altruism and different motives for altruism. Empathic arousal may be one primary motivator of prosocial behavior. Here we consider the possible origins of altruism mediated by empathy and the role that peers may play in this process.

Newborns' affective arousal in response to the cries of other infants suggests very early sensitivity to the distress of peers. Bühler and Hetzer (1928) and Bühler (1930) exposed newborns to a crying infant. They reported evidence for contagious crying, with frequencies varying across studies and conditions of exposure. Such crying may be a precursor or early sign of empathy. On the other hand, the crying may reflect fear, irritability, a physiological reaction to an aversive stimulus, or a coincidental response.

Simner (1971) compared infants' responses to the distress cries of other newborns with several other experimental conditions: a 5½-month-old's cry, synthetic (computer) cries, white noise, and a silent control. Babies cried most often in response to the newborn cry. Reflexive crying may indicate a rudimentary capacity for responding to peer-generated social stimuli. Hoffman (1975) has described this affective arousal in conjunction with the infant's inability to differentiate self from others as a first stage in the development of empathy.

It is difficult to infer the infant's experiential state when it responds affectively to the cry of another infant. Hence, it would be informative to trace this phenomenon developmentally. Hay, Nash, and Pederson (1981) examined distress responses of 6-month-old children to the distresses of their peers in dyadic play interactions in a laboratory setting. Distress stimuli ranged from whimpers and fusses to fullblown cries. Under these circumstances, there was little evidence for reflexive crying in response to peers' distress.

Naturalistic, longitudinal studies of the origins of altruism (Radke-Yarrow & Zahn-Waxler, 1978; Zahn-Waxler & Radke-Yarrow, in press) indicate that crying in response to others' distress is still present by the end of the first year of life. In one study, 24 mothers were trained to observe children's responses to others' distresses (reported in detail in Zahn-Waxler & Radke-Yarrow, in press.) Children were in one of three age cohorts. Children in Cohort A (four boys and four girls) were first observed at 10 months of age, in Cohort B (four boys and five girls) at 15 months, and in Cohort C (three boys and four girls) at 20 months. Each child was studied for 9 months. Thus, developmental changes in affective arousal and prosocial acts could be assessed within and across age cohorts.

Mothers provided daily reports on children's responses as bystanders to distresses experienced by others. The situations included events in which anger, fear, sorrow, pain, or lethargy (or any other negative emotion) was expressed by someone in the child's presence. Mothers also reported on children's responses to others' positive emotions, to provide a comparative base. They gave a detailed narrative, tape-recorded description of each affective event describing (a) the emotions and behaviors of the person(s) expressing the distress, (b) the child's affective, verbal, and behavioral responses to the emotion, and (c) the responses of mother (and others) to the child. Mothers and home visitors also collected data on children's responses to emotions by functioning as experimenters. They simulated specified distresses according to a script. Simulations also provided bases for reliability assessments; data indicated that mothers' observations were as reliable as those of trained research assistants (Cummings, Zahn-Waxler, & Radke-Yarrow, 1981). Approximately 2,000 incidents were reported by the 24 mothers.

Developmental analyses were conducted to examine the course of crying in response to other's distress in relation to other emerging response patterns. The response categories relevant to issues of prosocial development are presented in Table 6-1; the table indicates the average percentage of occasions on which children in different cohorts and at different ages within a cohort responded to another's distress by (a) crying, (b) seeking out their caregiver, and/or (c) making a prosocial intervention. Reliabilities based on comparisons of mothers' and home visitors' reports of children's responses to simulated distresses were 100% for crying, 67% for seeking caregiver, and 86% for altruistic interventions. Coder reliabilities based on dual assessments of mothers' naturalistic reports were in the 80s and 90s.

Crying in response to naturally occurring distresses was prominent at Time 1 in Cohort A, but it decreased significantly with age. Children first showed an increase, then a decrease with age in the extent to which they actively sought out the caregiver during both natural and simulated distresses. With age, children became significantly more likely to make prosocial interventions on behalf of the victim in response to both naturally occurring and simulated distresses.

The first prosocial interventions of children occurred shortly after the first year of life. They took the form of positive, physical contacts on behalf of victims, expressed as direct affectional displays (e.g., hugging, patting) or mediated through objects. During the second year of life, these contacts became more elaborated and differentiated. For example, direct help, sharing, indirect help, making suggestions, rescue attempts, verbal sympathy, mediation of fights, and protecting the victim occurred with significant frequency. (See Zahn-Waxler & Radke-Yarrow, in press, for more detailed developmental analyses.) Most of the different forms of prosocial behavior were seen in 80% or more of the children by the time they reached the ages of 1½-2 years. Sometimes multiple prosocial attempts were made within single incidents.

In summary, children's early responses to distress most often consisted of affective arousal and lack of interactive engagement with victims; they cried or, a little later in time, they sought their caregiver. The self-oriented affective reactions were replaced developmentally by

Table 6-1. Average Percentage of Distress Incidents to Which Children Responded

Responses	Cohort A		Cohort B		Cohort C	
	Time 1 (38-61)[a]	Time 2 (62-85)	Time 1 (62-85)	Time 2 (86-109)	Time 1 (86-109)	Time 2 (110-134)
To natural distresses						
Distress cries [b]	28	14	16	12	5	10
Seeking caregiver [c]	2	10	26	25	11	18
Prosocial intervention [d]	11	11	16	30	39	32
To simulated distresses						
Distress cries	5	4	9	3	4	2
Seeking caregiver [c]	19	30	48	29	22	26
Prosocial intervention [d]	4	5	19	30	33	33

[a] Age of children in weeks.
[b] Crying in response to others' distress emotions decreases significantly with age.
[c] A significant curvilinear relationship exists between age and seeking caregiver.
[d] Prosocial interventions increase significantly with age.

more focused efforts to interact positively with victims in distress. Affective arousal diminished in intensity but did not disappear with age. Mothers' often reported that their "older" children looked worried or concerned while watching a victim.

The transition from self-distress to active concern for the other, possibly mediated by dependency bids to the caregiver, can be viewed as a landmark in social development. Children's prosocial instrumental responses to others' distress may in some way derive from the earlier emotional reactions. We do not yet know whether early self-distress and later prosocial behavior are on a continuum developmentally or whether they are conceptually distinct response entities. A related question concerns the meaning of the early affective arousal: Does it represent fear, empathy, aversion, or even more complex affective blends?

The peak in dependency bids at the point of transition from a self-orientation to an other-orientation is provocative. There may be intimate links between self-distress, help-seeking, and help-giving early in life. The seeking of caregiver could result from self-distress as the child looks for some reassurance. Children also may be seeking information about the nature of the distress and how to intervene. Finally, what is traditionally interpreted as a dependency bid, children may be trying to get the caregiver to help the victim. We would assume, then, that the caregiver plays a critical, pivotal role at this point of transition. Differences in what the caregiver models, teaches, and generally communicates affectively and cognitively about distress may result in very different patterns of reaction by the child (Zahn-Waxler, Radke-Yarrow, & King, 1979). The following mother's reports illustrate one child's transition from self-distress to active prosocial engagements with a distress victim and the role that this particular mother played.

Betty at 70 weeks: Betty and I went to a friend's house to baby sit. Their 5-year-old was downstairs and she played with him for awhile. Then, I heard the little baby crying upstairs. He cried quite loudly and intensely. I started to go upstairs and when Betty heard him crying she stood very still and looked around, quite alarmed. She looked around the room and then toward me with a look of fear on her face and confusion. She started to cry very hard. I brought the baby downstairs and when she saw us she wasn't the least bit consoled. She looked at him and back at me and continued to cry. She stuck very close to me.

Betty at 77 weeks: Another toddler from down the street stayed here while his mother went to run some errands. He cried and screamed and was almost hysterical from the moment she shut the door. He laid down on the floor and began to pound his fists. From experience I've known not to pick him up; it seemed to upset him more. Betty, when she saw him do that, looked quite alarmed, and her body stiffened, and she looked at him, frightened. Then she looked at me questioningly. I put my hand on her shoulder and drew her closer to me and tried to explain that it was all right. Betty continued to look very worried. Her eyebrows were up and she made one or two moves to walk towards him and then back toward me. She kept looking over her shoulder at him, and every once in a while she'd walk over to him and reach out with a very worried look on her face. A little later she reached down to a Kleenex box and took out a Kleenex. She looked very worried still; not as alarmed as she had been in the beginning. She brought the Kleenex over, and she put her face down quite close to his, and began to wipe his nose.

Betty at 82 weeks: I was baby-sitting for a neighbor. Betty and I were downstairs for about half an hour and then the baby woke up. When I brought him downstairs he was crying. I held him, rocked him for awhile. Betty at first didn't pay any attention to him at all. She was exploring new toys. After about 10 minutes, I had put him down on the couch, she crawled up beside him. He was still crying. She had a blanket with her that's one of her favorites and she reached down and pulled that up beside her, and she looked very pleased with herself. Then she began to look at him more carefully. She looked from his face to mine, back and forth. She didn't look upset. Then she reached over and began to pat his knee. It didn't have any effect. After several moments of that, his face was quite wet, so I wiped his face with a towel. Betty immediately picked up her blanket and began to try to wipe his face, too. I didn't want to say no to her, but I kind of gently moved her away because I was afraid she would frighten him. She continued to watch him very intently. After a few more moments I picked him up and put him on my lap. Betty came over and stood at my knee and tried to stroke his arm, and she patted him, continued to look very concerned, but not frightened. Again she took her blanket, this time without my having wiped his face, and tried to wipe his face. I smiled at her and acted like that was a very nice thing to do.

Children's responses to peers' and adults' distresses were combined in the statistical analyses of developmental transitions presented in Table 6-1. All forms of crying (i.e., crying in response to any type of distress) were combined, as were different categories of prosocial interactions. Patterns of crying in response to others' distresses differed depending upon whether the victim was a peer or adult and upon the particular distress emotion expressed. Crying that resulted from other children's distresses usually was in response to a crying child. Of 89 incidents in which children cried in response to other children's distresses, 86% of those distresses involved crying victims. This is the naturalistic condition most parallel to experimental studies of infants' reflexive crying. There was little contagious crying in response to crying adults. Of 62 incidents in which children cried in response to adult distresses, only 10% of those distress events involved crying adults. Children did not see adults cry frequently, and when they did, they generally did not respond with contagious crying. When children cried in response to adult distresses, the stimuli tended to consist of angry interactions, such as fights between parents.

The evidence that affective arousal differs depending upon the type of distress and type of victim suggests that there are different motives for altruism. Under some circumstances affective arousal may be equivalent to empathy. *Affective empathy* has been defined as experiencing the emotional state of the other. Empathy has often been hypothesized as a mediator of prosocial interventions, particularly those acts that are accompanied by compassion or sympathy. In perhaps no other situation is the potential for this transmission of feeling states from one organism to another so fully realized as when one child cries in response to another child's cry. Affective empathy between age-mates may implicate peers in a unique way in the process of early prosocial learning.

Although many forms of prosocial acts were similarly directed toward peers and nonpeers, some appeared more frequently in response to peers' distress. Sometimes a child gave that which would comfort her/himself to the victim, for example, a bottle or a pacifier; this was done almost exclusively with peers. This suggests a primitive level of understanding of what is differentially appropriate help for peers versus adults. Children also distinguished between adults and young children as recipients of aid when witnessing a fight between a parent and another child. Altruism did not occur frequently, but when it did children invariably came to the defense of the child rather than taking sides with the parent. Children were more likely to use indirect help with child than with adult victims (e.g., bringing a mother to intervene).

Most of children's prosocial reactions to adults were expressed toward their own parents. For example, they rarely showed altruism to home visitors, but frequently comforted their mothers under parallel distress conditions (Zahn-Waxler & Radke-Yarrow, in press). Prosocial reactions toward peers, on the other hand, included a greater range of protagonists—babies, age-mates, older children, familiar and unfamiliar children, siblings. One might hypothesize that generalized prosocial responding may be more likely to develop from peer interactions.

The balance of prosocial responses toward peers and adults differed markedly depending upon the particular family constellation and the extent to which parents chose to include playmates in children's developing social networks. Some children virtually never had opportunities to show empathy toward other children, some children directed most of their compassion toward parents, and still others did so toward their siblings. A few children were, by age 2 years, extensively involved in caregiving of their baby brothers and sisters. Children's prosocial patterns later in life may sometimes be linked to the early variations in opportunities and interactions with peers. In a 5-year follow-up study (Radke-Yarrow, Zahn-Waxler, & Cummings, Note 1) certain individuals have shown continuity from their early experiences. One child who was initially one of the most intensely empathically involved with her peers was also the most self-sacrificial at follow-up; for example, she gave her own sandals to a barefoot friend as they walked on a hot sidewalk. At the other extreme was a child with little initial exposure to, or prosocial interactions with, playmates; he was also pathologically avoidant of peers' distresses 5 years later.

We have focused on the development of one form of prosocial behavior (children's altruistic responses to someone in distress) in considering the role of peers in the child's affectively based prosocial learning. The second year of life is a time of transition from affective arousal to active prosocial engagements with others in distress. This time period may have particular theoretical significance because it is when children's social interactions with peers and prosocial potentials both become manifest to a significant degree. These issues are being explored further in ongoing research with a second sample of 28 families. The children are first seen at 1 year of age. In addition to the longitudinal, parental reporting of children's responses to emotions, each child is seen at ages 2-3 years with a same-age friend in laboratory sessions in order to assess prosocial and aggressive response patterns between peers.

Other forms of prosocial behavior that occur in nondistress situations are also present by the second and third years of life. Rheingold, Hay, and West (1976) reported evidence for children's sharing behaviors toward adults in laboratory studies. Stanjek (1978) has demonstrated sharing between peers. Other investigators have identified cooperative behaviors in 2-year-olds not only between the children and adults (Hay, 1979), but between children and their peers as well (Eckerman, Whatley, & Kutz, 1975; Ross & Goldman, 1977). Further signs of a large repertoire of prosocial behaviors between peers (e.g., help, cooperation, sharing, sympathy) come from many naturalistic studies of preschool-age children (Iannotti, 1981; Marcus & Jenny, 1977; Murphy, 1937; Radke-Yarrow & Zahn-Waxler, 1976; Strayer, 1980; Strayer, Wareing, & Rushton, 1979). There are significant individual differences in the frequency of young children's prosocial behaviors. Undoubtedly, there are differences in motives and intentions as well. We emphasize this point because it is the middle years of childhood that are most frequently considered in theories of the origins and development of altruism, the formation of peer friendships, the emergence of role-taking abilities, and the interactions of these variables. However, different children come to this period of childhood with different established prosocial patterns and social experiences, and hence with different receptivities and sensitivities for further development.

The Role of Peers in Eliciting Altruism

The nature of children's social relationships with peers and nonpeers is explored in terms of children's altruistic interventions toward (a) adults and children, (b) friends and strangers, and (c) children of different ages. Characteristics of peers that foster or discourage altruistic acts on their behalf are also considered. One major theme concerns the role of friendship and reciprocity in children's prosocial behaviors.

Children's Social Relationships

Altruism toward peers and adults. Freud and Dann (1951) provide vivid illustrations of children whose early life experiences caused them to direct their altruism almost exclusively toward peers. Six 3-year-old German-Jewish children were found living by themselves (i.e., peer reared) in a concentration camp. They were then cared for in a relocation center. Their attachments were exclusively to each other. Furthermore, their compassion and care giving toward each other was frequent and intense.

In a naturalistic study of nursery school and kindergarten children, Stith and Conner (1962) compared dependency and helpfulness directed toward peers and adults. Helpfulness was significantly greater toward peers than adults. Helpfulness toward both peers and adults increased with age. In interactions with adults, children were more likely to seek help than to give help. Children were as likely to give help to peers as to receive help from them. These findings nicely illustrate the reciprocal nature of early peer interactions. Different patterns toward children and adults were also found by Strayer et al. (1979), who coded acts of sharing, helping, cooperation, and comfort in nursery school children. Approximately 60% of prosocial behaviors were directed toward peers and 40% toward teachers. Interrelations of different prosocial behaviors showed more consistency for peer-directed than for teacher-directed altruism. There were few relations between peer-directed and teacher-directed prosocial behaviors.

We have assessed children's responses to adult versus child victims in two laboratory studies. The purpose was to examine cognitive and affective correlates of prosocial behaviors. (Details on procedures, coding, etc. are given later in this chapter.) Children were seen individually in play and task-oriented activities in a 1½-hour session. Batteries of measures of altruism, perspective taking, and affective arousal in response to distress were administered. Study 1 included 60 children, ages 4-5, 6-7, and 10-11 years (20 children per age group). Study 2 included 22 children 6-7 years old. Experimental simulations of distress were carried out and responses were videotaped from behind a one-way mirror. In Study 1, each child was exposed to an adult who injured her back while demonstrating a physical exercise. Later the child met a mother and her infant who had just been overheard crying in the next room (a tape-recording). The mother was looking for the baby's bottle. (Due to scheduling problems, 5 children did not experience this condition.) In Study 2 each child was exposed to the injured adult. Later the child encountered an upset same-age peer, just injured on a ladder in the next room.

Children's prosocial reactions toward each of the different victims were scored on four measures (interrater agreements are in parentheses): (a) verbal sympathy, e.g., "it's too bad you fell" (79%); (b) indirect help, e.g., telling someone else to help (81%), (c) physical help, e.g., bringing the bottle, rubbing the adult's back (93%); and (d) a composite rating of altruism. In Study 1, summing across ages, children were significantly more likely to help the infant peer (M = 3.16) than the adult (M = 2.14) on the composite rating measure, t (54) = 3.65, p < .001. Children showed more verbal sympathy to the adult (M = 1.27) than to the infant (M = 1.01), t (54) = –3.93, p < .001. Children favored the infant for physical help (M = 1.35 and M = 1.09 for the infant and adult, respectively), t (54) = 3.42, p < .001, and indirect help (M = 1.56 and M = 1.05 for the infant and adult, respectively), t (54) = 6.59, p < .001. There were some interesting developmental trends: On the composite rating, children in the youngest group were significantly more prosocial to infants (M = 2.65) than adults (M = 1.60), t (19) = 3.42, p < .01, as were children in the middle age group, (M = 3.39 and M = 1.75 for the infant and adult, respectively), t (17) = 6.38, p < .001. In the oldest group, however, the difference between prosocial behavior to peers (M = 3.52) and adults (M = 3.25) was not significant, t (16) = 0.63. In Study 2, children were marginally significantly more likely to show altruism to the peer (M = 2.77) than to the adult (M = 1.95) on the composite rating of altruism, t (21) = 1.80, p < .10.

In none of the studies, laboratory or naturalistic, are the distress stimuli equated or necessarily comparable across victim types, creating interpretive problems. At the same time, this confounding reflects the realities of the environmental distresses with which children contend. Findings from several studies do indicate that children are more often involved in helping other children than adults. An important process variable is suggested in a laboratory study of sharing by 5- to 6-year-olds and 8- to 9-year-olds (Willis, Feldman, & Ruble, 1977). Children in both age groups showed more generosity toward crippled children than crippled adults, possibly motivated by feelings of greater similarity to the child than to the adult.

The sex of the child represents one particular case in which perceived similarity of self and other may facilitate altruism. Relationships between same-sex peers are usually characterized not only by greater physical similarity, but also by greater familiarity and experience than those with opposite sex peers. Several investigators (e.g., Feshbach & Roe, 1968) have found more empathy in laboratory studies when the pictured distress stimulus was the same sex as the subject child. In some observational studies of preschool children (Eisenberg-Berg & Hand, 1979; Marcus & Jenny, 1977), prosocial interactions were much more frequent between children of the same sex than between children of opposite sexes. These differences may also reflect corresponding differences in friendship patterns.

Friendship patterns and altruism. Friends are ordinarily defined as people who seek the company of one another, spontaneously and apart from strong social pressures to do so. Friendships often occur with persons similar in age, interests, and goals. Are interactions between mutual friends marked by a high incidence of reciprocity, empathy, and helping? Mannarino (1976) studied the altruism of sixth-grade boys who did or did not have an intimate friend. Boys with a good friend showed higher levels of social responsibility and cooperation toward others than boys without such a friend. Gottman and Parkhurst (1980) conducted a naturalistic study of pairs of best friends, between the ages of 2 and 9 years, playing together in the home of one member of the pair. Sympathy and sensitivity often characterized the interactions of these playmates—interestingly, more so in the younger pairs of children. In a study of extensiveness of social contacts (not of friends per se), Keasey (1971) found that preadolescent children who belonged to relatively many clubs and social organizations had higher moral judgment scores than children who were members of fewer organized groups. Could extensiveness of organized social contacts between peers also be related to children's prosocial behaviors? Currently, in our own culture, smaller families and fewer families with young children make social contacts between children more difficult and sometimes less spontaneous. This may have implications for the development of altruism.

In laboratory studies of children's sharing and helping responses toward friends or nonfriends, results are mixed. Mann (1974) and Staub and Sherk (1970) found more sharing between friends than nonfriends. Wright (1942), Fincham (1978), and Sharabany and Hertz-Lazarowitz (1981) found more generosity with nonfriends than with friends. Prosocial behaviors in laboratory settings sometimes may provide a means for the nonfriends to establish a relationship– a first step in working together on the prescribed tasks and one that is not necessary for friends.

In a nicely designed series of laboratory studies of sharing and helping of elementary school children (see Chapter 11, this volume) Berndt (Note 2) found that pairs of friends were relatively more prosocial than nonfriends when participating in tasks that involved mutually satisfying outcomes. Friends were less prosocial than nonfriends when the task involved competition. The findings on competition were particularly pronounced for boys.

Is a child prosocial because he or she has well-established friendships or are the friendships formed because the child is prosocial? Or, as is most likely the case, are these factors interdependent? Recent work by Dodge (Note 3) is innovative and exemplary in design because it provides a means for posing causal questions and studying processes associated with the development of social relations and prosocial interactions. Dodge brought together 48 7-year-old boys who were placed in 6 playgroups of 8 boys each. The children had had no prior experience with each other. The playgroups met for 1 hour per day for 8 days over a 2-week period. An adult group leader was present, but for most of the session the children were free to play as they wished. Social interactions were observed and at the end of the study each boy was interviewed to determine sociometric status. Significant changes in social behaviors occurred across sessions that were predictive of whether a boy developed many friendships or became isolated. Boys who became popular were more frequently involved in cooperative play and social conversation and were more likely to refrain from aggression than boys who became rejected or isolated. Thus, prosocial behavior may be part of a social engagement strategy that fosters the establishment of friendships. Parallel research with girls is needed. In addition to well-documented sex differences in patterns of aggression, friendship patterns of boys and girls also differ in terms of intimacy, number of friends, and so forth (Sharabany, Gershone, & Hoffman, 1981; Berndt, Note 2).

The concept that peer friendships are important for the establishment of altruism is hard to test empirically. Friendship is difficult to define, measure, and influence both outside and inside the laboratory setting. It is an oversimplification to assume that friendship is a necessary prerequisite for altruism or that it inevitably facilitates altruism. The data on the early origins of altruism suggest that stable prosocial patterns may appear before stable friendship patterns develop. Dodge's (Note 2) data indicate that prosocial modes of interaction with peers may facilitate the development of friendship, rather than the reverse. We have seen in Berndt's (Note 2) data that friendship can result in competition as well as cooperation and sharing.

Friendships are not always characterized by mutuality or harmonious functioning. Dominance hierarchies among children in groups and in pairs indicate asymmetries and individual differences in children's interpersonal relations. Conceptual and methodological refinements are needed in further attempts to reliably index social relations. If a child has a close friend, is he or she likely to behave more benevolently to the world at large, or is the compassion mostly directed toward the friend? Friendships also have the potential for exclusionary behavior. In the future, researchers might consider how to foster prosocial interactions between peers when the potential recipient of altruism is quite dissimilar and unfamiliar to the child. Often these other victims are the truly less fortunate (e.g., poor children, sick children, retarded children, problem children). Research by Peterson (1974) on attitudes toward retarded children and by Lambroso, Tyano, and Apter (1976) on attitudes toward the mentally ill indicates that children's views of such groups were more favorable if they were provided contacts with these populations. It would be illuminating to explore whether children's prosocial behaviors (rather than attitudes) could be similarly influenced.

Altruism directed toward peers of similar and different ages. We have considered arguments that children's associations with age-mates should maximize the likelihood of altruism. There is also a case to be made for heterogeneous age groupings as facilitators of altruism. Suomi and Harlow (1972) demonstrated that cross-age peer contact between isolated rhesus monkeys and younger age-mates could help to remediate the deleterious effects of maternal deprivation and social isolation. The monkey "therapists" were undoubtedly not motivated by compassion, but the outcome of their helpful behavior suggests the possible beneficial effects of heterogeneous age groupings. Benefits may also derive from peer tutoring in which older children help younger children to learn. Declining school enrollments of recent years have resulted in heterogeneous age groupings in classrooms (much like that in the old country schools); children's social interactions in these newly constituted environments are of special interest. Bizman, Yinon, Mivtzari, and Shavit (1978) hypothesized that children in age-heterogeneous kindergartens would show more altruism that children in age-homogeneous kindergartens. Heterogeneity should create more opportunities for older children to help younger children and a less competitive environment. The authors found that children of the same ages helped and shared more in age-heterogeneous than in age-homogeneous classrooms.

Social interactions between siblings of homogeneous and heterogeneous ages also have been studied. Whiting and Whiting (1973) demonstrated that in some cultures in which children are given responsibility for child care within the family they show more altruism. Whiting and Whiting (1973) noted that in highly industrialized, achievement-oriented societies there is often a failure to provide the child with opportunities to contribute to the welfare of the family and hence to learn altruism. They also suggested that third and fourth graders could be taught to take care of younger children as part of the school curriculum.

Age differences between peers may cause their interactions to resemble those of parent and child (Hartup, 1980). Observational studies of sibling interactions confirm the potential prosocial function of older siblings. Cicirelli (1973) reported that younger siblings were more likely to accept help or direction from an older sibling when the age interval between siblings was large. Furthermore, younger siblings were more likely to accept help from older sisters than older brothers. Abramovitch, Corter, and Lando (1979) studied families in which the younger siblings averaged 20 months of age and the age interval between siblings was either large (2½-4 years) or small (1-2 years). Older girl siblings were more likely to engage in nurturing behaviors than were older boys or younger "older" children. Dunn and Kendrick (1979) reported that in 16 of 20 families observed when the younger child was 14 months old, the older child (3-5 years of age) showed empathic concern for the younger child. Bryant and Crockenberg (1980) studied prosocial interactions between elementary school-age female siblings in seminaturalistic structured settings in the home. Helpfulness between children occurred, with the older child more often helping the younger child. Helping by the older child also correlated with anger in the younger child. Such help may have been motivated less by generosity than by a need to control or dominate. Acts of altruism thus can occur for a variety of reasons, and the intentions and emotions underlying prosocial acts need exploration.

Cues of the Victim that Alter the Probability of Altruism

How the child behaves in circumstances of distress may figure importantly in whether or not he or she receives help from peers. We hear of children who are said to "invite" abuse. Who are the children who invite altruism? There is considerable evidence to suggest the reciprocal nature of altruism even by the preschool years. In other words, children who help will receive help back (Marcus & Jenny, 1977; Staub & Sherk, 1970; Strayer et al., 1979), although in some instances nonsignificant associations have been reported (Bryant & Crockenberg, 1980). Such reciprocation should increase the likelihood of future altruism.

We know little about what further helps or hinders a child if he or she is being aggressed against or victimized. Some children may exaggerate their distress, dramatizing their plight by sulking or behaving like martyrs. Others may be stoic and seldom signal a need for help. Ginsberg (1977) studied children's altruistic responses to a victimized peer from a sociobiological perspective. He observed fights between elementary school boys on the playground. Ordinarily, when one boy showed signs or submission (cues usually took the form of diminished body stature), aggression would cease. Violation of this biosocial norm (by continuing to attack) was the cue for other children to intervene. It would be intriguing to explore individual differences in the ways in which children turn off aggression and do, or do not, direct help toward themselves. It would be important to study girls as well. The organization of aggression, submission, victimization, and altruism in girls and boys may be quite different.

Radke-Yarrow and Zahn-Waxler (1976) have studied children as recipients of aggression and have considered the implications of victimization for children's prosocial initiations. The relations of naturally occurring prosocial behaviors (helping, sharing, and comforting) with aggression given and aggression received were examined in a group of preschool children. For highly aggressive children there were no significant associations between victimization and prosocial behavior. For less aggressive children prosocial behavior increased as aggression experienced from others increased. If a child enjoys reasonably good peer relations (i.e., is not too aggressive), aggressions experienced may contribute to the child's own developing sensitivity and empathy toward others.

Internal Mediators of Altruism

Children's cognitive and affective understanding of another's experiences have both been implicated as mediators of altruism. The ability, cognitively, to put one's self in the place of another and understand that person's internal state is characteristically defined as perspective taking or role taking. Affectively experiencing what the other is experiencing is typically defined as empathy. Prosocial acts may have both affective and cognitive components. Empathy provides the motivation to act, while cognition provides the knowledge base. However, in many studies that relate perspective taking or empathy to prosocial behavior, the cumulative results are less than illuminating (reviewed by Radke-Yarrow, Zahn-Waxler, and Chapman, in press).

Sometimes significant associations between perspective taking, empathy, and altruism are obtained, but often not. The reasons are difficult to disentangle (Kurdek, 1978). One set of issues concerns the procedures devised to assess cognitive and affective variables. For example, sometimes measures (especially cognitive measures) are not appropriately adapted to the child's developmental level nor are they closely aligned with real-life experiences (Iannotti, 1981; Rubin & Everett, 1982). Moreover, the targets of empathy, altruism, and role taking have not been delineated sufficiently. For example, peers and adults have typically been treated as equivalent stimuli, which they undoubtedly are not. One focus of our research has been the relations between social cognition, affective responsiveness, and altruism toward peers and those toward adults. Prosocial responses to the two distress incidents described earlier in Study 1 were examined in relation to measures of empathic arousal and perspective taking to determine the best predictors of altruism.

Empathic arousal was assessed by rating the child's affective response during each distress episode (i.e., overhearing the infant cry, watching the adult wrench her back). Emotional responses were subsequently categorized from videotapes by two coders as negative (tension or fear) or neutral (an apparent lack of affective arousal). Interobserver reliabilities for these ratings were 72% (negative) and 82% (neutral). Empathy (looking upset or worried for the victim) was scored but was not reliably coded. Self-reports of emotional arousal were also obtained in a different setting. A tape-recording of an infant cry was played in the child's presence and the child was asked to rate his or her response as to degree of empathy, anger, and fear on a 3-point scale.

The Peabody Picture Vocabulary Test was administered to assess verbal intelligence. Two standard perspective-taking tasks were used: Chandler's Bystander Task (1973) and Flavell's Seven Picture Story (1968). We also devised our own measure of social cognition. These stories were based on situations that had been established as being within the life experiences of even the youngest children studied. Children were told eight stories, accompanied by photographs, in which one story character was confronted with the distress of another. The eight stories are presented in Table 6-2. In some stories the child made a prosocial response, in others the child stood back in the face of distress, while in still other stories the behavior toward the victim contained some ambiguity. In certain stories the child was the cause of the distress. The questions following each story were intended to elicit the child's perception of the feelings and motives of the story character. Coding categories are described in Table 6-3, along with examples and the interobserver reliabilities. All disagreements were adjudicated, with a third person serving as the tie breaker when necessary. Cumulative scores across stories were used for each category in the analyses. Multiple coding was used when a child's responses were represented in more than one category.

Does prosocial behavior toward peers involve different affective and cognitive processes than prosocial behavior toward adults? The first column in Table 6-4 contains the partial correlations (controlled for age) between the affective and cognitive variables and a composite score for behavior directed toward infant peer and adult victims combined. Examination of just these data would lead to identification of attributions of guilt, verbal intelligence, and empathy as positive correlates of prosocial behavior, and of negative emotional responses to adults and peers as negative correlates of prosocial behavior. When the targets of prosocial behaviors were analyzed independently, however, there were some indications that children's prosocial responses to adults and to the infant peers could not be treated interchangeably (Table 6-4). The attribution of guilt to a story character was a positive predictor of altruism to an adult; negative affect toward the distressed adult, and fear in response to an infant cry were related negatively to prosocial responses to the adult. In contrast, the variables of empathy and anger in response to a hypothetical infant peer were positive and negative correlates, respectively, of prosocial responses to infant peers. Perhaps the clearest indication that different motivational processes may be implicated in prosocial behavior to peers versus adults is that two mediators, prosocial attributions in the stories and lack of affect in response to observed peer distress, were significantly and positively

Table 6-2. Stories for Assessing Children's Prosocial Reasoning About Hypothetical Distresses

1. Here comes little Bobby, just beginning to walk. He holds on to the chair so he can stand up steady. Across the room, baby Suzy is lying in her crib. Suddenly she begins to cry. Bobby stops. Listens. He looks at Suzy. Then Bobby sits on the floor and starts to cry. Now what do you think is going on inside Bobby? What is he feeling? Who does he feel sorry for, Suzy or himself?

2. Mother and her child Mary are in the kitchen. Mary is sitting at the counter watching while mother cuts apples for apple pie. While mother is slicing the apples, the knife slips and mother cuts her finger and says "ouch." Mary turns to her mother, throws her arms around mother's waist, and hugs her tightly. What do you think is going on in Mary's head? How is she feeling?

3. Priscilla and Jane are watching TV. They're watching *The Brady Bunch*. Priscilla is sitting on a cushion and Jane is in the red rocking chair. Jane is rocking, rocking. She rocks too far. The chair falls over. She falls and the chair hits her head. She cries. Priscilla keeps right on watching TV. Then she looks over at Jane. And again now, what is going on inside Priscilla? What is she feeling?

4. Aaron and Jane are playing in the backyard with the bicycle. Aaron wants a turn. He starts to get on the bicycle but Jane screams, "No." She pushes Aaron away. Aaron's foot gets caught in the wheel of the bike and he falls down. He gets really upset and he starts to cry. Jane looks at him. "Okay, Aaron, you can ride the bike. Here, you want a piece of bubble gum?" What do you think was going on inside of Jane?

5. Mother and her child, Cindy, are in the kitchen. Cindy is sitting at the counter while mother fixes dinner. Mother leans over to get a bowl and bumps her head. "Ouch, ouch, that really hurts." Cindy turns to her mother, throws her arms around mother's waist and hugs her tightly. Once more, can you tell us what is going on in Cindy's head? What is she feeling?

6. Peter's mother has brought him to the babysitter. It's time for Peter's mother to leave. He's so sad. You can almost see the tears rolling down his cheeks. He blinks them back. Wendy watches and then she brings him a teddy bear and says, "Don't cry, Peter." What do you think was going on inside Wendy? What is she feeling?

7. Mike and David are playing on the balance beam. They are trying to see if they can walk from one end to the other without losing their balance. Whoops, Mike loses his balance and falls to the floor. He's so ashamed. He wishes he had done better. David looks at him and laughs. He grins and points at Mike lying on the floor, "Dummy, dummy." What do you think was going on inside of David? What is he feeling?

8. Wendy drops a big heavy toy and it falls right on her foot. Henry sees it all happen. He looks at Wendy's foot and starts to rub his own foot all the time looking at Wendy. Can you tell me what is going on inside Henry's head and what he is feeling?

Table 6-3. Scoring Categories for Responses to Distress Stories

Category	Description	Examples	Relia-bility (%)
Empathy	Story character expresses feelings similar to those of victim	"He's sad because she's sad." "Feels sorry that the other person is hurt."	80
Prosocial Intervention	Story character attempts to comfort, aid, or assist the victim	"She's trying to cheer her up." "He wants to show her how to make her foot feel better."	94
Guilt	Story character feels remorse, personal blame, or responsibility	"She's sorry she pushed him down."	98
Self-concern	Story character is concerned with him/herself rather than the victim's distress	"He thinks he's great cause he didn't fall off." "She wants her turn."	90
Aggression	Story character is described as aggressive, hostile, or uncaring	"He's glad that he fell." "She just wanted to ignore her."	95
Complexity	Story character displays more than one meaning, motive, or affect in response to the situation	"First she felt she hadn't had enough of her turn, then she felt upset that she had pushed him."	94
Generation of hypotheses	Child describes rule or theories to explain the circumstances of the story	"He looks to young to feel sorry for her." "She believes that it's her turn."	85

related to altruistic concern for infant peers but negatively related to concern for adults. These relations would have been concealed by the exclusive use of combined scores for prosocial behavior. The consistent negative relations between negative emotions and prosocial acts suggests that too much emotion may interfere with prosocial intervention. The variance accounted for in any of the correlations, however, is not impressive, and neither affective nor cognitive variables appeared to predominate as predictors of altruism. Again, as with the younger children, we are reminded of the real difficulty in obtaining reliable and valid indices of empathy and in understanding the complex nature of the different forms of affective arousal that may facilitate or inhibit prosocial acts.

Table 6-4. Cognitive and Affective Processes as Predictors of Prosocial Behavior Toward Infant Peers Versus Adults

Process measures	Combined[a]	Infant Peer[a]	Adult[b]
Themes or attributions in distress stories			
Empathy	-.01	-.15	-.12
Prosocial intervention	-.02	.26**	-.18*
Guilt	.25**	.06	.24**
Self-concern	.12	.15	.04
Aggression	.06	-.09	.04
Complexity	.13	.20*	.05
Generation of hypotheses	.07	.07	.03
Cognitive measures			
Peabody Picture Vocabulary Test	.33***	.28**	.19*
Chandler's role-taking measures	-.01	.09	-.05
Flavell's role-taking measure	.08	-.03	.15
Affect observed during simulated distress			
Negative affect to adult hurt	-.24**	.00	-.22**
Lack of affect to adult hurt	-.11	-.11	-.07
Negative affect to infant cry	-.16	-.13	-.08
Lack of affect to infant cry	.01	.29**	-.19*
Self-report of affect to an infant cry			
Fear	-.29**	-.07	-.26**
Anger	-.24**	-.34***	-.05
Empathy	.18*	.22*	.03

[a] Partial correlations controlled for age, based on 55 children 4-11 years old.
[b] Partial correlations controlled for age, based on 60 children 4-11 years old.
*$p < .10$
**$p < .05$
***$p < .01$

The principal purpose of these analyses has been to illustrate the point that antecedents and correlates of altruism may differ depending on whether the recipient of altruism is an infant peer or an adult. Refinements and extensions of methodology are necessary. Prosocial responses to same-age peers, as well as different-age peers, should be studied; multiple assessments of prosocial responding would provide better samples of behavior. It is also necessary to distinguish, in the cognitive and affective measures, whether the role being taken or the empathy expressed is toward a peer or nonpeer. Finally, naturalistic as well as laboratory measures of altruism would increase our knowledge about mediators of prosocial acts. A laboratory setting may itself generate a problem-solving orientation that does not typify everyday acts of helping and sympathy.

Peers and Socialization

Prosocial behavior describes a type of social interchange between individuals. This interchange does not take place in a vacuum, but rather is part of a process that is influenced by the characteristics of the individuals involved, their personal and family histories, the structure of the interactions and groups, institutional and cultural determinants of that structure, and the other members of the groups as contributors to the dialectical process. Important issues to be explored in conceptualizations of prosocial behavior are (a) interrelations of peer processes with family and culture, and (b) the role of the peer as a socializer of prosocial behavior.

Influence of Family and Culture on Peer Processes

Parents and Parental Style

Parents influence prosocial behavior through their capacity as models, as tutors, and as caregivers. Parental caregiving and discipline practices are associated with individual differences in children's prosocial dispositions (reviewed in Radke-Yarrow et al., in press). Prosocial interactions between peers may reflect early patterns established within the family. For example, although causal influences are difficult to disentangle, there are indications that parental nurturance may mediate the nature and structure of prosocial behaviors between peers (Bryant & Crockenberg, 1980). As another example, in a laboratory setting children's responses to inductive versus power assertive appeals for generosity to peers were found to follow a pattern that was consistent with the parental style the children perceived as present at home (Dlugokinski & Firestone, 1974). Parental influences on children's prosocial patterns also may be perpetuated by parent's and children's selection of friends (particularly if children's friends reflect the values of the parents).

The interaction of parental and peer influences on prosocial behavior is a relatively unexplored but potentially exciting research domain. Peers may use many of the same techniques for control as do parents. Casual observations of peer interactions will produce examples of power assertion, bargaining, love withdrawal, physical control, and induction. What techniques do peers use at different ages? Do changes in these techniques reflect parallel changes in parental techniques? What are the effects of peer control techniques on children's prosocial behavior? How does the composition of the peer group affect the child's prosocial learning? Do patterns of peer interaction influence prosocial behavior in the family environment in a manner similar to the influence of parents on peer interactions? The answers to these questions await further research. Here, we examine how adults have structured the peer environment in attempting to enhance prosocial behavior.

Cooperative versus Competitive Learning Environments

Much of the research on the effect of cooperative and competitive goal structures on prosocial behavior focuses on differences in classroom structure and on experimental manipulations of cooperative and competitive peer groups. *Cooperative goal structures* occur when the goals of the peer group take precedence over the goals of the individual and reward of the individual is dependent on the successful performance of the group. In *competitive goal structures* reward is based on the success of the individual relative to the other group members. Competitive structures can take two forms: the winner receives all the rewards, or the rewards are proportional to the individual's relative performance. Another goal structure, *individualistic*, involves rewards based on absolute performance, independent of other members (Deutsch, 1949). The cooperative structure generally allows for more interaction between peer members than the other conditions.

Stendler, Damarin, and Haines (1951) investigated the effect of cooperative and competitive environments on positive and negative behaviors in 7-year-olds. A greater frequency of positive behaviors (i.e., sharing, helping, and friendly conversation) was observed in the cooperative conditions than in the competitive conditions. Subsequent research has continued to demonstrate the facilitation of prosocial behaviors through the use of a cooperative goal structure in which peers work together. The classic demonstration of this finding is the "Robber's Cave" study (Sherif, Harvey, White, Hood, & Sherif, 1961). Agonistic, noncooperative behaviors between two groups were established with intergroup competition. Although other attempts to promote harmony between the two groups failed, the provision of situations which required cooperative effort for the attainment of individual goals substantially increased cooperative interaction and decreased aggressive behavior between the groups. Cooperative interaction has been shown also to increase concern for peers (e.g., Crockenberg & Bryant, 1978).

There have been few systematic attempts to examine cooperative interactions in order to determine the relative importance of reinforcement contingencies, interaction with peers, and other elements that may influence cooperation. In Piaget's (1965) argument that moral development is enhanced through cooperative exchanges between peers, it is implied that social exchange rather than the goal structure is the crucial element. Children's cooperative interactions have been shown to enhance performance on measures of perspective taking and lead to better peer relations (e.g., Aronson, Bridgeman, & Geffner, 1979). These processes may account for the effect of cooperative peer interactions on prosocial behaviors since perspective-taking processes sometimes have been linked to increased prosocial behavior (e.g., Iannotti, 1978).

Families and cultures may encourage a particular goal structure in sibling and peer interactions outside of the educational setting. It is reasonable to assume that the average child experiences a variety of cooperative, competitive, and individualistic patterns of exchange as he or she moves from family, to school, to recreational settings. There is both experimental (Mithaug & Wolfe, 1980) and field research (Avgar, Bronfenbrenner, & Henderson, 1977) demonstrating that exposure to a cooperative environment may produce stable patterns of cooperative exchange which are maintained even when the goal contingencies are no longer cooperative, or when competitive contingencies are experienced in other settings such as the family.

Cultural differences in cooperative behavior toward peers suggest a pattern of greater cooperation in those cultures that emphasize cooperative goal structures (Avgar et al., 1977) or which are rural (Madsen & Yi, 1975). One pattern in these findings is that cultural norms emphasizing group goals result in cooperative peer behaviors even when cooperative behavior is not adaptive to the particular goal structure in force. The separate elements of the culture which may contribute to this cooperative behavior are not examined in these studies. Extensive peer interaction, cooperative adult models, parental styles, responsibility for family and group needs, and cooperative economic systems may all contribute to the establishment of a cooperative disposition. Peer interaction and socialization processes may be a necessary element since those cultures in which peers are characteristically cooperative tend to emphasize peer group activities.

Peers as Socializers

Peers as models. The observation of models can influence a child's behavior in several ways. Direct learning may occur, in which a child learns how to perform a particular act in a particular setting. Generalization of imitation to other settings may also occur if children learn the norms or principles governing a particular category of behavior. Finally, exposure to a model may alter the emotional response to that behavior, such that children may learn to perceive that behavior as positive and acceptable or as unacceptable.

Characteristics of the model, the context, and the consequences of the modeled behavior influence the extent of behavioral change produced. Generally, the greater the similarity between the model and the observer and between the situation depicted in the model stimulus and the observer's situation, the more substantial is the effect on the observer's behavior. It is surprising, then, that most studies of prosocial modeling involve adult models rather than age-mates.

Children do imitate their peers, and, depending on the characteristics of the model, the imitator, and the context, prosocial models foster prosocial behavior (Strain, Cooke, & Apolloni, 1976). For example, peers who are rewarded for prosocial behaviors serve as effective models for prosocial behavior. The extent to which positive peer models promote prosocial behavior is also dependent on whether the modeling is accompanied by additional training procedures, such as peer discussion of the prosocial content (DeVoe, Render, & Collins, 1979).

The function of peers as models merits further attention. Issues that need to be addressed include the following: What is the relative effect of prosocial peer models versus prosocial adults models? What is the relative effects of a prosocial versus a deviant peer model? What is the role of model characteristics such as friendship and familiarity? Is the effectiveness of peers as models dependent on the particular category of prosocial behavior? Can peers be used to model the motivational processes mediating prosocial behavior (e.g., empathy) in addition to the prosocial content?

Peers as teachers. In the section on age-heterogeneous peer groupings, we implicated peers as teachers of altruism. Furman, Rahe, and Hartup (1979) applied the intervention paradigm of Suomi and Harlow (1972) to peer interactions of socially withdrawn children. Exposure to play sessions with a peer increased the social activity of isolates, particularly when the peer was younger by 15 months. In other experimental work, being assisted by a peer helper produced greater sharing with peers (Bryant & Hansen, 1978). These studies illustrate the value of peer "therapists" for children who exhibit antisocial or asocial behaviors and suggest the use of this procedure as a means for promoting prosocial behavior.

Peers have also been used as agents of reinforcement for prosocial behavior (Strain et al., 1976). One procedure is to have peers report prosocial behaviors that occur in the classroom (Grieger, Kauffman, & Grieger, 1976). This behavior may be explicitly rewarded with a small token (e.g., a gold star) from the teacher, or the attention received from the peers may be sufficient reward. Prosocial behaviors of the entire classroom are sometimes enhanced by such procedures. An operant explanation for this increase is that the tokens received from the teacher serve as a reinforcer. It is also possible, however, that the responsibility for attending to and reporting prosocial behaviors affects the behavior of the observer. By making the behaviors salient to the children and their peers, the investigators have taught them that prosocial behaviors are a significant component of social interaction. Support for this interpretation comes from Rogers-Warren and Baer (1976), who found that simply rewarding true (i.e., honest) reporting of sharing by peers increased both reporting and actual prosocial behaviors.

The use of influence attempts (verbal attempts to persuade a child to behave prosocially or deviantly in a hypothetical situation) by peers versus adults was studied by Berndt (1979). For younger children, parent-induced prosocial conformity was greater than peer induced, but for older children peers and adults were equal in their ability to produce prosocial conformity.

Influences of peer groups. Peer groups are frequently used as a vehicle for training prosocial behaviors. Not only is group training more convenient but the dynamics of the interaction between members of the group may also provide particular opportunities for learning that cannot be derived from dyadic interaction. In one study of relations between role taking, altruism, and aggression in 6- and 9-year-old boys (Iannotti, 1978), groups of five peers were used to train awareness of the feelings and motives of others through role-taking procedures. The two experimental peer groups differed as to whether they were taught to play a single role during the training session or to regularly change roles. Spontaneity of peer exchanges and real interpersonal problems were frequently present in these group training sessions that would have been less likely in interactions with a single peer or adult. It was not unusual for a peer to correct the role enactment of another child or to suggest the implications of a change of perspective. Since these were familiar peers the procedure was more likely to have significant value to the participants. Both of the training conditions produced increased awareness of the feelings and motives of others when compared to control procedures. Some corresponding changes in sharing behaviors also occurred.

Natural and selected peer groups have been used to increase prosocial behavior in aggressive adolescents (Goldstein, Sherman, Gershaw, Sprafkin, & Glick, 1978), and to increase prosocial behavior in young children (Ahammer & Murray, 1979). In a study of preschool children (Radke-Yarrow, Scott, & Zahn-Waxler, 1973) individual and group training conditions in combination with high and low adult nurturance were used to develop prosocial behaviors. Under conditions of high nurturance, children sensitized in group training conditions to the distresses of "real" others were especially likely to show generalized prosocial behaviors during simulations of distress of an adult and of a young child; this is another indication of the possible importance of learning altruism in a group setting.

Conclusions

Cumulative research findings have yielded insights into the multiple ways in which peers serve as stimulators, elicitors, and recipients of altruism. Peers, as well as parents, are significant socializers of altruism. This fact merits greater recognition in existing theoretical accounts of the origins of altruism; it also has practical implications for the prosocial rearing of children. However, we are still some distance, methodologically and conceptually, from understanding the processes underlying altruism in relation to peers and nonpeers. Thus, many interesting questions await investigation. One recurrent theme in this chapter is the different antecedents, mediators, and motivators of prosocial behaviors in children. There are indications that empathic arousal is a component of some acts of altruism at different stages of development. However, the question of how to distinguish affective empathic arousal from other forms of affective arousal remains a challenge for research.

Although children's prosocial influences on their companions are less dramatically conveyed than negative influences (and are less publicized as well), this does not render positive learning between peers any less significant. Children (and adults) carry with them the potential for influencing others through acts of cruelty *and* acts of kindness. There is a need to study the conditions that shape both types of interactions. If the early and middle years of childhood are critical times for the establishment and maintenance of prosocial peer interactions, there are corresponding implications for research strategies and intervention designs. It would be important to study whether early prosocial experiences with peers help children through the strains of adolescence and make them less vulnerable to later negative peer influences.

Acknowledgments

We would like to express our deep appreciation to our collaborators Marian Radke-Yarrow and E. Mark Cummings for their many contributions to the research work presented in this chapter. We are also very grateful to Maris Udey and Rita Dettmers for their assistance in the preparation of this manuscript.

Reference Notes

1. Radke-Yarrow, M., Zahn-Waxler, C., & Cummings, M. *Continuities and change in the prosocial and aggressive behavior of young children.* Paper presented at the biennial meeting of the Society for Research in Child Development, Boston, 1981.
2. Berndt, T. *Prosocial behavior between friends and the development of social interaction patterns.* In *The influence of friendships on social behavior and development.* Symposium at the Biennial Meeting of the Society for Research in Child Development, Boston, 1981.
3. Dodge, K., Behavioral antecedents of peer social rejection and isolation. In *Methodological and substantive issues in the observation of peer interaction.* Symposium at the biennial meeting of the Society for Research in Child Development, Boston, 1981.

References

Abramovitch, R., Corter, C., & Lando, B. Sibling interaction in the home. *Child Development*, 1979, *50*, 997-1003.

Ahammer, I. M., & Murray, J. P. Kindness in the kindergarten: The relative influence of role playing and prosocial television in facilitating altruism. *International Journal of Behavioral Development*, 1979, *2*, 133-157.

Aronson, E., Bridgeman, D., & Geffner, R. Interdependent interactions and prosocial behavior. *Journal of Research and Development in Education*, 1979, *12*, 16-27.

Avgar, A., Bronfenbrenner, U., & Henderson, C. R. Jr. Socialization practices of parents, teachers, and peers in Israel: Kibbutz, moshav, and city. *Child Development*, 1977, *48*, 1219-1227.

Berndt, T. Developmental changes in conformity to peers and parents. *Developmental Psychology*, 1979, *15*, 608-616.

Bizman, A., Yinon, Y., Mivtzari, E., & Shavit, R. Effects of the age structure of the kindergarten on altruistic behavior. *Journal of School Psychology*, 1978, *16*, 154-160.

Bryant, B. K., & Crockenberg, S. B. Correlates and dimensions of prosocial behavior: A study of female siblings with their mothers. *Child Development*, 1980, *51*, 529-544.

Bryant, B. K., & Hansen, B. K. The interpersonal context of success: Differing consequences of independent and dependent success on sharing behavior among boys and girls. *Representative Research in Social Psychology*, 1978, *9*, 103-113.

Bühler, C. *The first year of life.* New York: Day, 1930.

Bühler, C., & Hetzer, H. Das erste Verstandnis fur Ausdruck im ersten Lebensjahr. *Zeitschrift fur Psychologie*, 1928, *107*, 50-61.

Chandler, M. Egocentrism and antisocial behavior: The assessment and training of social perspective-taking skills. *Developmental Psychology*, 1973, *9*, 326-332.

Cicirelli, V. Effects of sibling structure and interaction on children's categorization style. *Developmental Psychology*, 1973, *9*, 132-139.

Crockenberg, S., & Bryant, B. Socialization: The "implicit curriculum" of learning environments. *Journal of Research and Development in Education*, 1978, *12*, 69-78.

Cummings, M., Zahn-Waxler, C., & Radke-Yarrow, M. Young children's responses to expressions of anger and affection by others in the family. *Child Development*, 1981, *52*, 1274-1282.

Deutsch, M. Theory of cooperation and competition. *Human Relations*, 1949, *2*, 129-152.

DeVoe, M., Render, G., & Collins, J. Microtechnology processes and cooperative behavior of third grade children. *Journal of Experimental Education*, 1979, *47*, 296-301.

Dlugokinski, E. L., & Firestone, I. J. Congruence among four methods of measuring other-centeredness. *Child Development*, 1974, *44*, 304-308.

Dunn, J., & Kendrick, C. Interaction between young siblings in the context of family relationships. In M. Lewis & L. A. Rosenblum (Eds.), *The child and its family.* New York: Plenum Press, 1979.

Eckerman, C. O., Whatley, J. L., & Kutz, S. L. Growth of social play with peers during the second year of life. *Developmental Psychology*, 1975, *11*, 42-49.

Eisenberg-Berg, N., & Hand, M. The relationship of preschoolers' reasoning about prosocial moral conflicts to prosocial behavior. *Child Development*, 1979, *50*, 356-363.

Feshbach, N., & Roe, K., Empathy in six- and seven-year-olds. *Child Development*, 1968, *39*, 133-145.

Fincham, F. Recipient characteristics and sharing behavior in the learning disabled. *The Journal of Genetic Psychology*, 1978, *133*, 143-144.

Flavell, J. H. *The development of role-taking and communication skills in children.* New York: Wiley, 1968.

Freud, A., & Dunn, S. An experiment in group upbringing. *Psychoanalytic Study of the Child*, 1951, *6*, 127-168.

Furman, W., Rahe, D. F., & Hartup, W. W. Rehabilitation of socially-withdrawn children through mixed-aged and same-age socialization. *Child Development*, 1979, *50*, 915-922.

Ginsberg, H. Altruism in children: The significance of nonverbal behavior. *Journal of Communication*, 1977, 82-86.

Goldstein, A., Sherman, M., Gershaw, N. J., Sprafkin, R., & Glick, B. Training aggressive adolescents in social behavior. *Journal of Youth and Adolescence*, 1978, *7*, 73-92.

Gottman, J. M., & Parkhurst, J. T. A developmental theory of friendship and acquaintanceship processes. In A. Collins (Ed.), *Minnesota Symposia on Child Psychology* (Vol. 13). Norwich, N. J.: Erlbaum, 1980.

Grieger, T., Kauffman, J., & Grieger, R. Effects of peer reporting on cooperative play and aggression of kindergarten children. *Journal of School Psychology*, 1976, *14*, 307-313.

Hartup, W. W. Two social worlds: Family relations and peer relations. In M. Rutter (Ed.), *Scientific foundations of developmental psychiatry*, London: Heinemann, 1980.

Hay, D. F. Cooperative interactions and sharing between very young children and their parents. *Developmental Psychology*, 1979, *15*, 647-653.

Hay, D. F., Nash, A., & Pederson, J. Responses of six-month-olds to the distress of their peers. *Child Development*, 1981, *52*, 1071-1075.

Hoffman, M. L. Developmental synthesis of affect and cognition and its implications for altruistic motivation. *Developmental Psychology*, 1975, *11*, 605-622.

Iannotti, R. J. Effect of role-taking experiences on role taking, empathy, altruism, and aggression. *Developmental Psychology*, 1978, *14*, 119-124.

Iannotti, R. J. Prosocial behavior, perspective taking, and empathy in preschool children: An evaluation of naturalistic and structured settings. Paper presented at the meeting of the Society for Research in Child Development, Boston, April 1981. In *Abstracts of Individual Papers*, SRCD, 1981, *3*, 140.

Keasey, C. B., Social participation as a factor in the moral development of pre-adolescents. *Developmental Psychology*, 1971, *5*, 216-220.

Kurdek, L. A. Perspective taking as the cognitive basis of children's moral development: A review of the literature. *Merrill-Palmer Quarterly*, 1978, *24*, 3-28.

Lambroso, D., Tyano, S., & Apter, A. Attitudes of the Israeli adolescent to the mentally ill and their treatment. *Israel Annals of Psychiatry and Related Disciplines*, 1976, *14*, 120-131.

Madsen, M. C., & Yi, S. Cooperation and competition of urban and rural children in the Republic of South Korea. *International Journal of Psychology*, 1975, *10*, 269-274.

Mann, S. A. Sharing in kindergarten children as a function of friendship status and socio-economic status. *Dissertation Abstracts International*, 1974, *34*, 4050.

Mannarino, A. P. Friendship patterns and altruistic behavior in preadolescent males. *Developmental Psychology*, 1976, *12*, 555-556.

Marcus, R. F., & Jenny, B. A naturalistic study of reciprocity in the helping behavior of young children. *The Alberta Journal of Educational Research*, 1977, *23*, 195-206.

Mithaug, D., & Wolfe, M. Reciprocal cooperation in dyads. *Journal of Experimental Child Psychology*, 1980, *29*, 481-501.

Mueller, E., & Rich, A. Clustering and socially-directed behaviors in a play group of 1-year-old boys. *Journal of Child Psychology and Psychiatry*, 1976, *17*, 315-322.

Murphy, L. B. *Social behavior and child personality*. New York: Columbia University Press, 1937.

Peterson, G. Factors related to the attitudes of nonretarded children toward their EMR peers. *American Journal of Mental Deficiency*, 1974, *9*, 412-416.

Piaget, J. *The moral judgment of the child*. Glencoe, Ill.: Free Press, 1965. (Originally published, 1932.)

Radke-Yarrow, M., Scott, P. M., & Zahn-Waxler, C. Learning concern for others. *Developmental Psychology*, 1973, *8*, 240-260.

Radke-Yarrow, M., & Zahn-Waxler, C. Dimensions and correlates of prosocial behavior in young children. *Child Development*, 1976, *47*, 118-125.

Radke-Yarrow, M., & Zahn-Waxler, C. The emergence and functions of prosocial behavior in young children. In M. S. Smart & R. C. Smart (Eds.), *Infants, development and relationships* (2nd ed.). New York: Macmillan, 1978.

Radke-Yarrow, M., Zahn-Waxler, C., & Chapman, M. Children's prosocial dispositions and behavior. In M. Hetherington (Ed.), *Handbook of child psychology* (Vol. 3): *Social development*. New York: Wiley, in press.

Rheingold, H. L., Hay, D. F., & West, M. J. Sharing in the second year of life. *Child Development*, 1976, *47*, 1148-1158.

Rogers-Warren, A., & Baer, D. M. Correspondence between saying and doing: Teaching children to share and praise. *Journal of Applied Behavior Analysis*, 1976, *9*, 335-354.

Ross, H. S., & Goldman, B. D. Establishing new social relations in infancy. In T. Alloway, L. Kramer, & P. Pliner (Eds.), *Advances in the study of communication and affect* (Vol. 3): *Attachment behavior*. New York: Planum Press, 1977.

Rubin, K. H., & Everett, B. Social perspective-taking in young children. In S. Moore & C. Cooper (Eds.), *The young child*. Washington, D.C.: National Association for the Education of Young Children Publications, 1982.

Sharabany, R., Gershoni, R., & Hoffman, J. Girlfriend, Boyfriend: Age and sex differences in intimate-friendship. *Developmental Psychology*, 1981, *17*, 800-808.

Sharabany, R., & Hertz-Lazarowitz, R. Do friends share and communicate more than nonfriends? *International Journal of Behavior and Development*, 1981, *4*, 45-59.

Sherif, M., Harvey, O. J., White, B. J., Hood, W. R., & Sherif, C. W. *Intergroup conflict and cooperation: The robbers cave experiment*. Norman Institute of Group Relations, University of Oklahoma, 1961.

Simner, M. L. Newborn's response to the cry of another infant. *Developmental Psychology*, 1971, *5*, 136-150.

Stanjek, K. Das Uberreichen von Gaben: Funktion und Entwicklung in den ersten Lebensjahren. *Zeitschrift fur Entwicklungspsychologie und Padagogische Psychologie*, 1978, *10*, 103-113.

Staub, E. A child in distress: The influence of age and number of witnesses on children's attempts to help. *Journal of Personality and Social Psychology*, 1970, *14*, 130-140.

Staub, E., & Sherk, L. Need for approval, children's sharing behavior, and reciprocity in sharing. *Child Development*, 1970, *41*, 243-252.

Stendler, C., Damarin, D., & Haines, A. Studies in cooperation and competition: I. The effects of working for group and individual rewards on the social climate of children's groups. *The Journal of Genetic Psychology*, 1951, *79*, 173-197.

Stith, M., & Connor, R. Dependency and helpfulness in young children. *Child Development*, 1962, *33*, 15-20.

Strain, P., Cooke, T., & Apolloni, T. The role of peers in modifying classmates' social behavior: A review. *Journal of Special Education*, 1976, *10*, 351-356.

Strayer, J. A naturalistic study of empathic behaviors and their relation to affective states and perspective-taking skills in preschool children. *Child Development*, 1980, *51*, 815-822.

Strayer, F. F., Wareing, S., & Rushton, J. P. Social constraints on naturally occurring preschool altruism. *Ethology and Sociobiology*, 1979, *1*, 3-11.

Sullivan, H. S. *The interpersonal theory of psychiatry.* New York: Norton, 1953.

Suomi, S. J., & Harlow, H. F. Social rehabilitation of isolate-reared monkeys. *Developmental Psychology*, 1972, *6*, 487-496.

Whiting, J. W. M., & Whiting, B. B. Altruistic and egoistic behavior in six cultures. In L. Nader & T. W. Maretzki (Eds.), *Cultural illness and health: Essays in human adaptation.* Washington, D.C.: American Anthropological Association, 1973.

Willis, J. B., Feldman, N. S., & Ruble, D. N. Children's generosity as influenced by deservedness of reward and type of recipient. *Journal of Educational Psychology*, 1977, *69*, 33-35.

Wright, B. A. Altruism in children and the perceived conduct of others. *Journal of Abnormal Social Psychology*, 1942, *37*, 218-233.

Zahn-Waxler, C., & Radke-Yarrow, M. The development of altruism: Alternative research strategies. In N. Eisenberg-Berg (Ed.), *The development of prosocial behavior.* New York: Academic Press, in press.

Zahn-Waxler, C., Radke-Yarrow, M., & King, R. A. Child-rearing and children's prosocial initiations toward victims of distress. *Child Development*, 1979, *50*, 319-330.

Chapter 7

A Structural Approach to Research on the Development of Interpersonal Behavior Among Grade School Children

Carolyn R. Stone and Robert L. Selman

As we introduce our work we ask the reader to imagine a group of grade school girls building and decorating a puppet stage. Jane is painting a clown on the side of the stage. When Lee joins her and begins to paint on the clown, Jane exclaims, "This is *my* clown. I got here first." But Lee replies that this is a group project and they are all working on it. Lee and Jane begin to push and shove at each other, and Diane steps in to stop them, saying, "Look, this is Jane's clown. You can make a clown on the other side, Lee." In our work we have sought to make developmental distinctions among children's attempts to negotiate with one another. We studied interactions such as the one just described to distinguish the many ways that grade school children try to influence each other. Could we say that Jane used a one-way strategy which expressed only her point of view? Was Lee's strategy somehow more complex or mature because she tried to present a group perspective? Or was she simply using group interest as a guise for her own self-interest? Was Diane standing up for her friend against Lee or was she trying to coordinate the interest of the two girls?

Over the past 4 years we have worked on the general problem of studying development in children's interpersonal behavior. In this chapter we present the aspects of our work that we find most interesting and suggestive for further research. At the beginning of our work we used structural-developmental theory and pilot observations of children at play to generate hypotheses about the development of interpersonal behavior. Our next step was to conduct a quasi-naturalistic study with two objectives: to produce data that we could use to design our coding system and to allow a more systematic look at developmental differences in behavior and their possible relationship to interpersonal understanding. Experience taught us that data on the qualitative aspects of behavior are often as useful as quantitative results. Although statistics are important to validate the coding system, case studies are often fruitful sources of information about the subtleties of development and directions for further research. In this chapter we present a brief theoretical orientation followed by a description of the coding system itself with illustrations drawn from the field study. In the second half of the chapter we will present qualitative and quantitative results of the field study. We will conclude with a brief discussion of research implications of our work thus far and possible directions for further work.

A Model for the Development of Interpersonal Behavior

Social perspective taking is an individual's capacity to coordinate psychological perspectives of self and other. In his recent work, Selman (1980) has shown that one can use the developmental levels of perspective taking to analyze children's conceptions of interpersonal understanding (e.g., conceptions of friendship and peer group relations). We supposed that the same differences in levels of perspective taking could be used to make developmental distinctions in interpersonal behavior. The levels of social perspective taking are a sequence of qualitative levels that begin in early childhood, when the child moves from sensorimotor to symbolic-representational forms of thought and action. Very young children do not verbally distinguish between their own understanding of interpersonal situations and others' understanding. Somewhere between the ages of 3 and 6 years, children begin to express verbally the distinction between their own intentional and unintentional actions. At this first level they also understand that two people may have subjectively different understandings of the same objective situation. Roughly between the ages of 6 and 10 years, children's reflective understanding proceeds to a second level. At this point children understand that they can reflect upon their own subjective experience (feelings, thoughts, and motives) and that they can reflect upon the perspective of another in a social situation. A third level emerges in early adolescence, when children begin to articulate a third-person perspective, that is, the possibility that one can step outside a dyadic relationship to reflect upon the self and the other in relationship. In our observations we we looked for the interpersonal logic, or level of social perspective-taking behaviors, and we used this logic to make developmental distinctions.

We also used the model of structural-developmental stages to guide our hypotheses about ways to describe the development of social behavior (Selman, 1980). We hypothesized that the stages of interpersonal understanding occur in an invariant sequence. Individual children may proceed at different rates, but they do not skip stages or proceed out of order. Second, the logic of each stage is qualitatively different from the logic of the stage before. Third, the logic of each stage is similar across social contents because the logical structure of social perspective taking is assumed to underlie the stages of interpersonal understanding. Fourth, the logic of each stage is a hierarchical integration of the logic in the stage before. For instance, in the stages of understanding of peer group relations, at Stage 1 (unilateral relations) a child knows that a leader can tell others what to do and that group members may overthrow a grossly unfair leader. The child can see the perspective of the leader or that of the group but does not coordinate the two. At Stage 2 (bilateral partnerships) a new concept, the cooperative leader who coordinates the interest of group members, is the result of the integration and differentiation of Stage 1 logic (Selman, 1980). At the outset, we assumed this model for the development of interpersonal behavior.

There were theoretical considerations that led us to use the development of interpersonal understanding to plan our study of the development of interpersonal behavior. The work of Piaget on the relationship of thought and action provides some context for our work. It is useful to refer to Piaget's conception of stages and his assumptions about how cognitive development occurs. Piaget and Inhelder (1969) described each stage of reasoning as a "state of mobile equilibrium," the product of interaction between the child and the world around. In theoretical and empirical work on the relation between thought and action, Piaget (1976) observed that children often perform a task, such as walking on all fours, before they can describe their own actions accurately. In fact, they are not aware of the discrepancy between their behavior and their description of it. Generalizing from these observations, Piaget proposed that the process of becoming aware of one's own actions is a constructive process which results in reflective understanding. For instance, as children become aware of their own social interactions, they construct concepts of social interaction.

According to Piaget, children begin with consciousness of two elements, a goal pursued by an action and the result obtained. The action or means to the goal is not consciously perceived as separate from the goal. Imagine a kindergartner in an arts and crafts program who wants the tape when another child is using it. Her automatic, unexamined means toward this goal might be physical force. If she is successful in getting the tape, she could assimilate this action scheme (i.e., grabbing) to her logical structure. If she is unsuccessful, she might have to accommodate the scheme by noticing that people get mad when she grabs, but they don't when she asks. By repeated observation of the goal and her actions, the child comes to differentiate her actions from her goals.

With development the child uses his or her current logic to infer coordinations between goals and actions and choose a plan of action. Such coordination can be done on the basis of direct observation (i.e., trial and error) or by inference from the characteristics of the situation at hand. Abstraction from the features of the social situation need not be conscious (i.e., reasoned). Much automatic social interaction goes on quite successfully. Piaget proposed that since coordinations can occur without conscious reasoning, a child can use strategies that he or she would not be able to describe accurately, for instance, in a reflective interview. Through the growing cognizance of action schemes, the child elaborates conceptual schemes which can then be used to consciously organize subsequent behavior. In summary, the organization of action is the forerunner of conceptual organization. Thus, in the study of the development of social interaction, it made theoretical sense to begin with a general abstract aspect of conceptual development, the levels of social perspective taking, and work backward to the development of interpersonal behavior. In this way the levels of social perspective taking are heuristic tools for the study of the relation between reasoning and behavior.

It was clear that we had to study an aspect of interpersonal behavior in which we could observe developmental differences. We observed that the ways in which children tried to influence each other told us something about their understanding of relationships in the moment of action. In order to influence successfully, one must infer something about the other and choose a strategy. Such inference draws upon one's interpersonal understanding, among other variables such as context and history of the interaction. A similar observation was made by Garvey (1975) in her study of children's requests and responses. She observed that the form, or linguistic modality, of a child's request informs the observer of that child's social understanding and linguistic competence. Thus, we decided to study social negotiation strategies, the ways in which children attempt to change each other's behavior or attitudes.

Using the levels of perspective taking, Stone (Note 1) hypothesized levels of social negotiation strategies. Each level is more reflective, more interactive, and more complex than the preceding level. The strategies are described in detail below. Briefly, Level 0 includes impulsive strategies such as grabbing or hitting. Level 1 includes one-way strategies such as commanding. Level 2 strategies are two-way in that they acknowledge the reality of reciprocity between the self's and the other's points of view; these strategies include persuading, suggesting, and voting. Level 3 strategies are collaborative; often they have a joshing, joking quality that allows the speaker to communicate multiple meanings.

We hypothesized that the development of social negotiation strategies would be hierarchical, that the lower level strategies would remain in a child's behavioral repertoire as higher level strategies came into use. This assumption is particularly important in the analysis of behavior because the context of behavior heavily influences the choice of strategy. Thus, a person does not always perform at the height of his or her competence. At times lower levels are more appropriate than the higher levels.

Clearly, the levels of social negotiation strategies are somewhat different from the perspective-taking levels (Selman, 1981). Since levels of perspective taking are forms of understanding, they are ontogenetic, i.e., they develop sequentially with rare instances of regression. In contrast, depending on the context and the affective quality of a situation, an individual who has developed through the sequence of social negotiation strategies may use any of the previous levels, and it might be appropriate to do so, as such, the levels of social negotiation strategies can stand on their own as descriptions of qualitatively different ways to influence another person.

One may wonder how such levels can be considered developmental. One way to understand this is through comparison of a person's behavioral repertoire across different ages. Children aged 4-11 years might all use Level 0 strategies at one time or another; however, the hierarchical model predicts that the younger children would not use the higher level strategies because those strategies would not yet be in their behavioral repertoires. Preschoolers may have a repertoire consisting only of Levels 0 and 1 because they have only proceeded through Level 1 in the developmental sequence. They use these two levels according to contextual cues, but they do not have more complex and subtle strategies available to them. Similarly, children who use Level 3 strategies should also use Levels 0, 1, and 2 at times. There are no gaps in development. With age, children add higher levels to their behavioral repertoires. Thus, developmental differences are manifested in the range of strategy levels in the behavioral repertoire.

This theoretical model has several implications for empirical work. We decided that in order to understand how children's strategies for negotiation change with age we must define strategies in the stream of naturalistic behavior. The beginning and end of a strategy could not be defined by arbitrary criteria, such as 10-second time samples; rather, strategies were defined by a child's initiation of a negotiation and the eventual resolution in the interaction. The analysis of developmental differences in strategies required that the observer infer the child's intent in the negotiation. A valid inference of intent must take into consideration the context of the interaction and its history. Thus, we needed to observe children in rather lengthy segments of behavior in order to preserve the context, and we had to observe the same children repeatedly in order to understand their relationships. The type of observation chosen was focal child sampling (Altmann, 1974), in which we observed a child and her interactions for 10 minutes at a time before moving on to another child. Using this method, we allowed children of different ages to actually show us the developmental differences in their interpersonal behavior.

The hierarchical model of development and the concept of behavior repertoire also influenced the research strategy. Frequent use of a particular level in a certain context is indicative of an interactional competence at *at least* that level; a child might have higher level strategies in his or her repertoire that would not be observed in the contexts sampled. For this reason the extent of a child's repertoire is best ascertained by observations over time in a variety of contexts. Through repeated observations the observer is most likely to obtain a representative sample of the child's social negotiation strategies.

Field Study

In our work we have used both theory and behavior observations to define the various categories of social negotiation strategies. Before presenting the strategies in detail, we will present briefly the field study in which we gathered data used to define the strategies. This study was undertaken in a quasi-naturalistic setting, and it was designed to allow examination of the relation between children's use of social negotiation strategy levels, their level of interpersonal understanding, and their age (Abrahami, Selman, & Stone, 1981; Selman, Schorin, Stone, & Phelps, in press; Stone, 1981).

A 2 by 2 factorial design was used in which the two factors were grade (second and third vs. fourth and fifth) and level of interpersonal understanding (Level 1 vs. Level 2) as assessed by an individual reflective interview (Selman, Jaquette, & Bruss-Saunders, Note 2). In the data analysis these factors were related to differences in children's interaction strategies. Because previous research indicates that the relative numbers of boys and girls can powerfully affect group dynamics among grade school children (Hartup, 1970; Schofield, 1981), we decided to observe same-sex groups.

Four groups of six middle-class girls, homogeneous with respect to grade and interpersonal understanding level, met weekly for adult-supervised, after-school arts and crafts activities for 12 weeks from mid-October through January of one school year. Each meeting lasted 1½-2 hours, and each group completed the same three large projects. The projects were designed to encourage peer interaction (e.g., making puppets and putting on an original puppet show). A planned shortage of materials further elicited negotiation among subjects. The activities were facilitated by an adult group leader who was familiar with the research goals but blind to the interpersonal understanding levels of the subjects.

In each meeting an observer, also blind to interpersonal understanding levels, tape-recorded a live, 10-minute observation of each subject. Observation order was rotated weekly. Observations were transcribed promptly and filled out by the observers themselves. The narratives included as nearly as possible a verbatim account of all the target child's interactions with other children.

In the transcribed narratives on-task activity was identified and divided into discrete episodes. These episodes were further categorized by the function of the interaction: material distribution (i.e., transfer of goods needed for the project), helping (i.e., asking or offering assistance), and implementation (i.e., attempts to carry out a portion of the project). The next step of analysis, defining and coding the levels of social negotiation strategies, was eased by comparison of strategies used to carry out similar functions. A social negotiation strategy coding manual was written for each of the three functions (Stone, Robinson, & Taylor, Note 3), and the narratives were coded accordingly. Cohen's (1960) kappa values for intercoder reliability were as follows: implementation .70; helping .87; and material distribution .90.

Table 7-1 shows the four levels of social negotiation strategies which were coded under implementation. A similar listing could be shown for material distribution and helping. Social negotiation strategies were coded by inference from the process of the interaction, the syntax used, and the content of subjects' statements. In the next section the reader will note that our category definitions are highly related to syntax and the verbal form of strategies. In general, we have not tried to code properties of strategies such as intent or affect, although we acknowledge their importance. Although the levels are organized in a logical, hierarchical sequence, the question as to whether they actually form a developmental sequence must be resolved empirically. This field study analyzed the same data used to define the strategy levels, and thus its findings are not definitive.

Social Negotiation Strategies

The levels of social negotiation strategies are presented in this section. The discussion of each level begins with a summary of the aspects of social perspective taking and interpersonal understanding that were used to help organize strategies into levels. Each of the levels is then explained with numerous examples taken from the data. The levels were used to identify differences in the process of interaction, rather than differences in subjects. Because children use a range of strategies, we cannot point to children whose strategies fall all at one level. It is important to reiterate that although each level is roughly defined from a corresponding level of perspective taking, a person who uses a Level 1 social negotiation strategy, for instance, is not limited to understanding at that level. Each person uses a range of strategies.

Although we claim that these levels form a logical, hierarchical sequence, we also acknowledge that higher is not necessarily better, where better is defined by other than developmental criteria. For instance, Level 3 strategies are not expected to be more successful in general. Context, interactional norms, and affect generally have as much to do with strategy choice as developmental level. Among un-

Table 7-1. Levels of Social Negotiation Strategies for Implementation

Level 0
   Verbal grabbing: *"Michelle!"* (shouted)
   Physical force: pushing, hitting
   Insult: "You turkey!"

Level 1
   Command, threat, demand: "Stop drawing a minute."
   Complaint: "Everybody doesn't do it good."
   Seeking adult's permission: "Can I do my own?"
   Tattle: "She keeps pushing me."
   Justification on the basis of authority: "She (adult) said I was gonna do this side."
   Justification: me, "I was here first."
   Competition: self, "Betcha mine's better than yours."
   Exclude other: "Forget it. I don't want your name on it." (the stage)
   Mock compromise: "Let's try it my way, and if not, we'll do it your way" (when
      there's no going back)
   Assertion: "I'm drawing a tree."
   Negation: "Well, the heck with Liz."
   Level 1 process: "I think we should all do our own play."
   Sarcasm: a put-down, "Meg, you mind just leaving things alone?"
   Adult moderates:[a] "Couldn't you each use half?"
   Level 1 information question: "How do you spell you name?" (for individual
      work)

Level 2
   Suggestion: "You could be a witch." (in a Halloween play)
   Elaboration on other's ideas: building on another's suggestion
   Level 2 information question: "Where are we going to put it on?" (when work-
      ing together)
   Question request: "Could you stop drawing a minute?"
   Directive: "You color in the spots, and I'll hold it for you."
   Showing and explaining: elaborate explaining with supporting gestures
   Coalition: "Make sure she doesn't make anymore."
   Mediating and compromise: "She's drawing this clown. You can do one over
      here."
   Joint gesture: nonverbal working together
   Switch perspective: "I wouldn't do that to Liz if I were you."
   Request votes: "Okay, who likes this curtain?"
   Offer: "Okay, I'll take the tacks out for you." (without being directly asked)
   Level 2 process: "Three against one. We won." (majority rules)
   Feeling, motive: "Don't you trust her?"
   Check out other: "Do you know how to make a coyote?"

Level 3
   Joking: sarcastic, but mutual. "Get out. That stinks." (both parties laughing)
   Level 3 process: "It's not fair for you to go ahead and do it just because there
      are more." (rights of the minority)

[a] Not included in data analysis.

familiar people the directness of a Level 1 strategy might seem impolite (e.g., "Give me a glass."), while the more formal Level 2 strategy would be more appropriate (e.g., "Could you please hand me a glass?"). In contrast, in an emergency situation the directness of the Level 1 strategy would be more appropriate even among strangers (e.g., "Find an exit!"), while the Level 2 strategy would seem foolish (e.g., "Could you please find an exit?"). Thus, some contexts actually elicit higher or lower level strategies. People make such choices within the constraints of their behavioral repertoire.

Level 0: Demand

At Level 0 perspective taking the child does not distinguish between his or her own and others' points of view in a situation. The child does not reflect on either the self's perspective or the other's. Thus children's understanding of relationships at this level is nonpsychological. Relationships, such as they are, are based on physical qualities or the self's material needs.

Behavior strategies that we generated from this level of understanding indicate no reflection on what the self does or says, nor do they express reflection upon others' needs or desires in a situation. Often they are impulsive behaviors. For instance, one Level 0 category is verbal grabbing, in which a child forcefully repeats the name of another child, perhaps with an expletive. This strategy is often used after a higher level strategy has been used to no avail. (All subjects used levels higher than Level 0 at some time during the study.) In this way the actor calls attention to another's infraction without expressing what he or she would like done. Another such category is the use of physical force to make someone do what the actor wants without using any verbal marker to explain intent. In addition, a child may use insults to tell others what to do. For example, one group of subjects was planning decorations for a puppet stage. Mary said, "Let's do all flowers on it." Carolyn answered, "No, that's stupid." Carolyn used only an insult to tell Mary that she did not want flowers. There was no verbal elaboration.

Some Level 0 strategies have a quality of magical thinking because they demand actions of others without engaging any person in dialogue. We often observed quite young children call out for materials that they needed, such as scissors, without first trying to find out where the scissors were and asking the person who had them. Instead, as soon as they realized the need for scissors, they simply called out, "Scissors!" and expected a response.

Strategies for conflict resolution are quite infrequent at this level of negotiation because the child does not reflect upon the self's or the other's point of view. However, one way to resolve a conflict is to leave the scene impulsively. If the child does not express what he or she wants, and does not appear to be leaving in a manipulative manner (e.g., looking over her shoulder to see what response she has triggered), coding is limited to Level 0.

To conclude, Level 0 strategies are nonpsychological behaviors; they are the beginning of the sequence.[1] If a child uses only a Level 0 strategy, his or her negotiation is limited in that it does not express an understanding of two agents (self and other) acting with different intentions. Thus the strategies often have a cryptic, unelaborated, and impulsive quality.

Level 1: Command

Level 1 perspective taking is sometimes called unilateral, one-way understanding. Children who are reasoning at this level understand that self and other can have different perspectives in a given situation, but they consider only one perspective at a time. At this level of interpersonal understanding children also express the belief that conventions of externally perceived authorities (e.g., parent, teacher, God) provide immutable (unilateral) standards of behavior. One can see the one-way quality of this thinking: "They say, therefore you do."

Our behavioral analogues to this level of reasoning are one-way strategies that focus only on the self in an interpersonal situation. Using these strategies, children express only the self's needs or wishes in a situation. They do not refer to or inquire about the other's needs or wishes. Syntactical markers such as imperatives (e.g., "Put a tree there.") are used in coding some Level 1 strategies. Another Level 1 strategy is "getting back," on the plane of action. This is an immediate eye-for-eye type of strategy. For instance, Terry takes the glue Carolyn is using, so Carolyn takes Terry's magic marker. Carolyn says, "She did it to me, so I did it to her." Justification on the basis of the self's perspective is another Level 1 strategy (e.g., "I'm doing this. I got here first."). When using Level 1 strategies, it is difficult for children to coordinate with each other. For instance, in a discussion of a theme for their puppet show, some children gave only their own ideas and did not respond to others' ideas (e.g., "Let's do Star Wars." "Donnie and Marie." "Snow White and the Seven Dwarfs."). Each child sent her own idea out to drop in the middle of the table. No one responded to or built upon others' ideas.

---

[1] It is important to clarify that although Level 0 social negotiation strategies are the beginning of our sequence, they do not represent the earliest strategies used by children. For instance, crying is a type of strategy used by infants to get their basic needs met. It drops out as a strategy as mothers learn their babies' cues, and as infants learn to crawl and talk. Crying is a preverbal and perhaps preintentional strategy of the sensorimotor stage. Our sequence of social negotiation strategies encompasses the preoperational and operational stages. It assumes development of the symbolic function and verbal communication.

When using Level 1 strategies children also depend upon adults or conventional manners to define participants' rights and obligations in interactions. These strategies are unilateral in that only the authority's point of view is expressed. Thus, children can censure each other by referring to the other's bad behavior (e.g., "Every time I try to do it, she pushes me."). One can also invoke the adult's authority (e.g., "She said I could do this one."). Finally, one can appeal to the adult to use his or her authority to control another child (e.g., tattling, "She's hoggin' the stapler," addressed to an adult).

Using one-way strategies for conflict resolution, children also concentrate on one perspective or an external authority. They do not consider the relationship between disagreeing parties. When one girl cried because another had teased her, a third child advised the girl crying to just forget about it. Her strategy did not focus on the relationship. A decision-making device which fits at Level 1 is drawing choices from a hat. In this way chance becomes the external authority that makes the decision.

Level 1 strategies are logically one step more complex than Level 0 strategies in that children who use such strategies express one point of view, usually their own. Their motivation appears to come either from their own perspective or from that of an external authority. The limitation of these strategies is that children who use them do not express coordination of points of view, and they do not verbally acknowledge the other person's point of view. Of course, a person using a Level 1 strategy may understand the other's point of view and be willing to compromise, but nothing in the strategy itself would tell an observer of that awareness.

Level 2: Pragmatic Coordination

The child capable of using Level 2 perspective taking has a two-way understanding of interactions. The child understands that not only do self and other have perspectives on a situation which may differ, but they can also try to coordinate their perspectives or compromise. Thus, it is important to find out what the other wants to do because the exchange of viewpoints serves a function toward achieving one's own ends. This coordination of perspectives is pragmatic rather than entirely mental. It might consist of saying, "Well, if you want to use the only pair of scissors and I do too, we'll have to take turns." Along with coordination comes a concept of equality in interpersonal relations. Everyone has equal rights and should be equally satisfied with any decision. Associated with the idea of equality is a strong sanction against being bossy or stuck-up; bullies and big shots do not fit into a situation where everyone has equal rights and fairness is important. Equality and pragmatic coordination of perspectives both mold behavior strategies.

Using Level 2 strategies children express an awareness of other people as thinking individuals whose opinions and behaviors influence their own behavior. In order to coordinate with other people, children need to be able to express their intents in a nonbinding manner. Among friends a suggestion or opinion offered in the form of a question (rather than a command) invites a response (e.g., "Why don't we do a play on Peanuts?"). Questions are also used to indicate awareness of the other's point of view when making requests (e.g., "Can I have the scissors after you finish?"). Compare this with the Level 1 request, "I need the scissors," which does not verbally acknowledge the other's needs (point of view). Tag questions and words such as *maybe* and *probably* also indicate that the other person can contribute or disagree. Another way to keep a working partnership effective is to request information about one's own actions (e.g., "Tell me when it's tight enough," when one child is tying a knot for another). Finally, certain types of mutual physical coordination may be indicative of nonverbal Level 2 strategies. For example, this could occur when a child wants to do something that requires three or four hands. One comes to the aid of another and together they coordinate their actions, for instance, to mount a panel on one side of a puppet stage. All of the above strategies involve coordination of needs or intentions in a dyad.

Use of some strategies indicates a mental coordination in the process of interaction. One such strategy is elaboration on another's suggestion in the context of a discussion. For instance, one child might suggest that the group do a play about animals in the woods, and another child would say, "Yeah, we could call it *The Lost Kitten*." In this case, the second child heard the first one's suggestion, took it, and contributed an idea of her own. Compare this with the Level 1 discussion illustrated above, in which the children did not respond to each other. The elaboration indicates that the children are aware of each other's perspectives.

In the area of conflict resolution and decision making one sees the use of compromise. Using Level 2 strategies a child can accommodate his or her behavior slightly to agree with another but still serve his or her own needs. For instance, in one group some children wanted to do a puppet show using the Peanuts characters. Others wanted to use a Halloween theme. One child pointed out that they could do a play about the Peanuts characters on Halloween. In this way the children accommodated each other to arrive at a solution.

Use of some strategies also shows concern about equal opportunity and satisfaction. Voting is a prototypical Level 2 decision-making strategy. In this way every child's suggestion has equal chance for consideration by all involved, and each child can express his or her own opinion. Other pragmatic and egalitarian methods of settling disputes are turn taking and dividing the goods. In these ways people are assured equal, yet individual satisfaction.

Level 2 social negotiation strategies are slightly more complex than Level 1 strategies in that their form allows and invites response from others. These strategies are suited to the cultivation and maintenance of working partnerships. Level 1 strategies, on the other hand, are limited to overt expression of only one perspective. However, Level 2 strategies have their limitations. They are quite straightforward. Such strategies cannot encompass many behaviors used among close friends—the types of strategies which work because of shared knowledge based in the history of a relationship which is not explicitly stated in dialogue. Such strategies are used to act out a more complex type of interaction than is possible using Level 2 strategies.

Level 3: Collaboration

Children capable of Level 3 perspective taking can step outside of a dyadic relationship and examine it from a third-person perspective. With this somewhat detached view, children become aware of inter-actional norms and use them in pursuit of their immediate concerns and goals. They also develop an understanding of group interaction which is more complex than the dyadic understanding used at Level 2.

To a greater extent than other levels, Level 3 social negotiation strategies are defined in the interaction. Children use intonation, facial expression, and posture, as well as words, to communicate multiple, often ironic, meanings. At times this is done to accomplish an "in joke" between two children. Ervin-Tripp (1976) noted that sarcastic directives are behavioral acknowledgments of norms for interaction. When an older sister says to a younger brother, "Could I trouble you to take out the garbage, Joe?" the request is biting because such formal requests are not the norm for interaction among siblings (Ervin-Tripp, 1976, p. 60). We observed this type of implicit reference to norms in a strategy we called "mutual sarcasm." Using this strategy children contrast the verbal form of an utterance with their tone of voice or the interpersonal context to communicate multiple meanings. Both speaker and hearer appreciate the resulting humor. Such strategies allow children to register dissatisfaction without getting others angry. For example, in one group Nora had been asking for help on something for some time. She had especially asked Liz, who was busy washing her hands. When Nora saw that Liz was done, she said, "Will you please come help me, *now that you're all washed up?*" By using such a formal request be-tween peers, along with the extra emphasis, she was effectively saying, "Get the heck over here and help me." Both Nora and Liz giggled, and Liz complied. In such usage children employ a contrast between the form they use and the form generally used in peer interaction. This contrast combined with paralinguistic cues is employed to communicate contrasting messages in the service of maintaining a mutual interaction. Note that this definition excludes insulting, angry sarcasm, such as saying, "Oh, that's good!" with a sneer; such insults do not serve to maintain interaction.

Another more specific type of Level 3 strategy is observed in decision making. The recognition that voting always leaves someone dissatisfied is a Level 3 understanding of group interaction. Thus, children who try to meet the needs of the minority in a vote or who try to move toward a consensus are often using Level 3 strategies. However, such talk can be deceiving, as the reader will see below. The articulation of high-level understanding does not necessarily indicate a high-level strategy.

The contrast between Level 2 and Level 3 strategies has a different quality than the distinctions among the first three levels. Each of the first three levels adds one more logical step to the dyadic relationship. Using Level 0, the child acts, apparently without reflection upon perspectives. Using Level 1, the child expresses his or her own point of view. Using Level 2, the child uses strategies that acknowledge and invite the other's point of view. Each level is slightly more dyadic and slightly more supportive of an ongoing relationship. By coordinating multiple channels of communication, the child using Level 3 strategies expresses greater complexity in his or her own perspectives. In addition, implicit recognition of interactional norms often involved in these strategies is also a reference to the history and context of a relationship. The expression of a complex understanding of group interaction, for instance by rejecting voting because someone must lose, also indicates an increased awareness of subtlety in interaction.

Qualitative Results: The Contrast Between High Understanding and Demonstrated Interactional Competence

The observation that a child with high interpersonal understanding does not necessarily use high-level social negotiation strategies can be illustrated with material from the high-understanding (Level 2), low-grade (second and third graders) sample in our field study. Unknown to the observers and the group leader, Lee had the highest interpersonal understanding level in the entire sample. We did notice, however, that she was highly verbal, and she articulated a Level 3 understanding of group interaction during the group meetings. The other children in her group, however, were noticeably unimpressed and often irritated by her complex ideas. She lacked the behavioral strategies to implement her ideas, and often she acted in a bossy, pseudoadult manner. Although the adults saw her as a bright, articulate child, her peers saw her as a bossy, poor sport.[2]

---

[2] At three times (after each major activity) during the 12 weeks of after-school activities, each subject ranked herself and the other members of her group on five different attributes. These attributes were attractiveness, gets others to do what she wants them to, gets pushed around a lot, helps the group get organized, and does

In the following episode this group of six girls is well along on a puppetry project. They have each made their own puppets, and they are beginning to make a portable stage for their puppet show. After nailing the frame together, they have to cover the stage with brown paper and decorate the paper. This is the occasion for group decisions in which Lee clearly articulates her Level 3 understanding of the situation but simply cannot implement her ideas. The left column gives the observer's narrative of the events. The right column gives our interpretation of the events and their meaning for the participants. As this episode begins, the adult leader is getting out the brown paper for covering the stage.

Narrative	Interpretation
Jane (looking at the stage): "Everybody doesn't do it good. I don't like that."	Jane doesn't want to have everyone participate in working on the stage because some people won't do a good job.
Lee (in a supportive tone): "Well, so say what you want."	Here Lee is trying to facilitate give and take in the planning, a Level 2 strategy.
Jane: "I think we should do it like this. All the way down to here." *(She takes the brown paper and holds it up in front of the stage. Lee watches.)*	

At this point the adult steps in and asks for suggestions for decorating the puppet stage. Diane has an idea and tells the group.

Lee: "Why couldn't we have the paper on the side, and then have the material on the front and strings to pull it so it could open?"	This is an idea for the stage curtain given in a Level 2 strategy. It is thrown to the group in the form of a suggestion to which others are offered the opportunity to respond.

The adult commends this idea, but the other girls do not pick up on it. Feeling rejected, Lee walks away angrily from the group. She sits at a desk holding her puppet while the others continue to discuss how to make the stage. (Retreat was a fairly common strategy for Lee. In our coding system this is a Level 0 strategy when it seems impulsive and unreflective. If

---

good work on the project. The adults (group leader and observer) also ranked the girls in each group on these attributes. In this way self-rankings could be compared with peer rankings and adult rankings. These rankings are the source of our contention that the other children saw Lee as bossy.

the observer had judged that Lee left in a manipulative manner, to make the others feel badly or give in, the strategy would have been Level 2.)

The adult tells the girls that they have to decide whether to color the paper before it's up on the stage or after. Sandra wants to color it first, but Diane and Jane don't.

Lee (walks back to the group): "I think we should put *something* on it." *(No response.)*	Lee sounds angry, as though she thinks she is being left out. This is a Level 1 strategy, because Lee expresses only her own feelings and opinion.

The adult reflects the positions that have been stated and tries to encourage everyone in the group to participate.

Lee (to adult): It's too complicated. I don't want to do it. Some people want to do it one way, and some people want to do it another way, and if we do it one way, the people that wanted to do it the other way are going to get mad at us."	Here Lee quite clearly articulates the problem at hand to the adult. Her understanding of the situation is at Level 3—she can see that a vote would always leave some people unsatisfied.

The adult commends Lee and directs her back to the group.

Lee (to group, in a bossy tone): "I'd like to tell you something. What are you doing, Diane?"	Lee sounds like a teacher calling on someone who has not been paying attention. She is using a Level 1 strategy.
Diane (dryly): "Cutting."	Diane and Jane are not very receptive because, in addition to disliking Lee's manner, they know that she wants to do the stage in a different way from their idea.
Lee: "Jane, can I tell you something? Everybody wants to do it a different way."	

Jane is impatient and angry, and she interrupts.

Lee (still sounding bossy): "Don't interrupt me. It's not nice. Everybody wants to do it a different way, and if we do it one way, then the other people are going to be upset.	Lee catches Jane up for her manners, and then she proceeds to deliver her Level 3 understanding in a Level 1, bossy tone of voice. This *tone* makes the statement a Level 1 strategy.
Jane: "Be quiet. Be quiet. Be quiet."	Jane responds at Level 1.

Lee tries to stop Jane by forcefully putting her fingers over her mouth. This is Level 0, physical force.

At least two factors were at work in this episode. One was that Lee appeared to have a more complex understanding of the decision-making process than the other girls did, and the other girls probably did not understand Lee's interpretations of the group process. In addition, Lee's motivation for considering the rights of the minority was quite high—she knew that she would lose a vote. However, the others observed that she came forth with her opinions when she was likely to lose, and that she did so in a bossy manner. Although Lee had a high-level understanding of group dynamics, in this context she did not present high-level strategies to bring her ideas to fruition. In her efforts she used mainly Level 1 and Level 0 strategies. The result was that the other girls considered her pushy. In their eyes she would not accept the consummate justice of voting because she would lose the vote; and we must agree that part of Lee's motive for expressing her Level 3 point of view was her desire to have her own way. She used a low-level strategy and justified it with high-level understanding. On two later occasions, when the girls voted and Lee was on the winning side, she did not insist on considering all points of view including the losing one.

Affective and interpersonal factors were also important in understanding Lee's behavior. Lee always came up against Diane and Jane in group decisions. They were close friends, and whenever Diane took a position, Jane staunchly defended her against all comers. Lee's most likely ally in the group was Ann, but Ann was often not very involved in the group activities. The remaining two girls were often unwilling to take a stand in tense moments. Thus, Lee could not count on supporters, and this must have made the situation upsetting for her. Perhaps this is why she used the lower end of her behavioral repertoire in these episodes. She was observed on other occasions to make greater use of Level 2 strategies.

Quantitative Results

In this section some of the results from the field study which we consider most important are presented. They address the accuracy of the hierarchical model as a description of development of social negotiation strategies and the relationship between the development of interpersonal behavior and interpersonal understanding. As stated above, the data analyzed were the same as those used to define the social negotiation strategies. Therefore, these results are best considered as the basis for further research.

To investigate the hierarchical model, the number and percentage of each group's strategies which were high level (i.e., Levels 2 and 3) and low level (i.e., Levels 0 and 1) were compared. The levels were collapsed into high and low to show differences more clearly. Levels 0 and 3 were used quite infrequently; although the number of times they were used represents competence at those levels, the differences between the groups' usage of those levels alone cannot be considered meaningful. An examination of Table 7-2 shows a steady increase in the number of high-level strategies with an increase in interpersonal understanding within grades and across grades. The number of low-level strategies did not decline with grade and level, except that the low-grade, low-interpersonal understanding group used the most low-level strategies.

Another approach to the data was to ask whether a child's level of interpersonal understanding predicted the level of social negotiation strategies which she used in group interaction. This was investigated with two correlational comparisons. First, a mean social negotiation strategy level was computed for each subject based on all the strategies she used during the course of the 12 group meetings. These means were correlated with the interpersonal understanding scores for each subject, and a nonsignificant positive relationship was found ($r = .16$). Examination of the distribution of mean social negotiation strategy levels showed very little variation. The subjects used mainly Levels 1 and 2 in their interactions, and this was reflected in the means. The infrequent fluctuation in the use of Level 3 and Level 0 strategies did not affect the means; but this fluctuation is important because it indicates the range of each subject's repertoire. Table 7-2 shows that the number of high-level (Levels 2 and 3) social negotiation strategies varied substantially between groups. According to the hierarchical model, one would expect the relation between behavior strategies and interpersonal understanding to be stronger with the high-level strategies only than with all strategies; that is, development should be evident at the growing edge of the behavior repertoire. Another correlation was calculated on the interpersonal understanding scores and the number of

Table 7-2. Number and Percentage of High- and Low-Level Social Negotiation Strategies Used by Each Group

| Group | Social negotiation strategy level | | Total |
	Low	High	
Grades 2-3			
Low[a]	560 (72)[b]	222 (28)	782
High	384 (59)	265 (41)	649
Grades 4-5			
Low	366 (54)	310 (46)	676
High	459 (60)	319 (40)	778
Total	1,769	1,116	2,885

[a] Level of interpersonal understanding.
[b] Percentages are shown in parentheses.

high-level strategies for each subject. This was significant ($r = .45$, $p \leqslant$ .05). Together, these correlations support the hypothesis that interpersonal understanding is related to the growth and differentiation of a child's behavioral repertoire. Since low-level strategies remain in the repretoire of older children, the mean social negotiation strategy level is not strongly related to the interpersonal understanding level.

Conclusions

The results of the field study illustrate the usefulness of our structural approach to research on the development of interpersonal behavior. It seems possible to use the levels of social perspective taking to define behavioral analogues in the interactions of growing children. The hierarchical model of development is particularly well suited to the development of social behavior because it allows for the diversity of behavior which individuals display due to contextual and affective variation. The theory can accommodate the fact that a child may engage in insults and physical force in one context and use collaborative strategies in another context. Because developmental comparisons are made by examination of children's entire behavioral repertoires, the theory frees the researcher from the rigid assertion that Level 1 is somehow less adaptive or successful than Level 2. However, we do assume that Level 1 strategies appear ontogenetically in a child's repertoire before Level 2 strategies do. Clearly, we are at the beginning of this research, and the social negotiation strategy coding system should be verified on another, similar sample. Longitudinal studies also will be needed to confirm our initial evidence for the hierarchical development of behavior repertoires.

While there are strengths in our theoretical position, it poses methodological constraints that some researchers might consider difficult to meet. Our coding system necessitates that the observer be quite familiar with the interactional setting and the participants, and gaining such familiarity takes time. In addition, such coding requires attention to all channels of communication, especially for coding Level 3 strategies. Thus, either narratives should be coded immediately, or the coding should be done from videotape. The former choice is somewhat attractive for two reasons. First, it is less expensive. Second, an observer who knows the setting uses all the cues in the interaction and relies on his or her own naive psychology to make sense of and code the interaction. Researchers who have used videotape know that it does not record the context and history of an interaction. Coding from videotape would still have to be done by someone familiar with the original situation. Our theoretical position also necessitates the observation of each subject in a variety of settings over time in order to assess the child's behavioral repertoire. Such research cannot be done quickly, but we have found that the resulting data are remarkably rich and informative.

In extending our work there are a number of obvious avenues of basic research. First, how would grade school boys' behavior look when coded in this manner? How would mixed groups look? Would we find new behaviors at each level? In moving to a new population we could take the basic logical framework of the social negotiation strategy coding system, but pilot work would be needed to define the specific behaviors that each population uses for each level strategy. Some people speculate that boys are more physical in their interactions, whereas girls are more verbal; however, that does not mean that boys would be coded more often at Level 0. In the existing code, well-coordinated nonverbal communication is coded at Level 2. Perhaps more examples would be observed. In moving to other socioeconomic or ethnic groups the use of an observer who is familiar with the setting and the theory would become extremely important. The verbal and nonverbal cues used within ethnic groups have been documented as the cause for misunderstandings in cross-ethnic communication. It would be irresponsible to make developmental comparisons without attention to these subtle details.

In terms of further refinement of our coding system, two possible avenues present themselves. The social negotiation strategies as they stand now focus heavily on syntax and form of strategy. To some extent intent and affect were less emphasized, although certainly not disregarded, in the definition of strategies and assignment to levels. To continue with this coding system as it stands now would probably lead to the study of social skills and the structure of social interaction. However, if the social negotiation strategies were enriched to take into account more fully the intent and affect of the actor, the research and theory might take a somewhat different direction (Selman, 1981). The inclusion of intent and affect would bring aspects of personality into the study of interaction, and such research could draw upon the field of ego development. It might be possible to study personality characteristics through patterns of behavior strategies. Although a coding system that emphasizes syntax and form can describe developmental differences in usage, it would not describe differences of character. These are some of the choices that face us in further research.

Acknowledgments

The research presented in this chapter was supported by a grant from the Foundation for Child Development to the Harvard-Judge Baker Social Reasoning Project.

Reference Notes

1. Stone, C. *Recommendations for observation research on the development of peer group behavior.* Qualifying Paper, Harvard Graduate School of Education, September 1977.

2. Selman, R. L., Jaquette, D. S., & Bruss-Saunders, E. *Assessing interpersonal understanding: An interview and scoring manual in five parts constructed by the Harvard-Judge Baker Social Reasoning Project.* Unpublished manual, 1979. Available from Harvard-Judge Baker Social Reasoning Project, 613 Larsen Hall, Harvard Graduate School of Education, Cambridge, Mass. 02138
3. Stone, C., Robinson, S., & Taylor, S. *Manual for coding negotiation of task completion.* Unpublished manual, 1980. Available from the Harvard-Judge Baker Social Reasoning Project, 613 Larsen Hall, Harvard Graduate School of Education, Cambridge, Mass. 02138

References

Abrahami, A., Selman, R. L., & Stone, C. A developmental assessment of children's verbal strategies for social action resolution. *Journal of Applied Developmental Psychology*, 1981, *2*, 145-163.

Altmann, J. Observational study of behavior: Sampling methods. *Behaviour*, 1974, *19*, 227-267.

Cohen, J. A coefficient of agreement for nominal scales. *Educational and Psychological Measurement*, 1960, *20*(1), 37-46.

Ervin-Tripp, S. Is Sybil there? The structure of some American English directives. *Language in Society*, 1976, *5*, 25-66.

Garvey, C. Requests and responses in children's speech. *Journal of Child Language*, 1975, *2*, 41-63.

Hartup, W. Peer interaction and social organization. In P. Mussen (Ed.), *Carmichael's manual of child psychology* (Vol. 2, 3rd ed.). New York: Wiley, 1970.

Piaget, J. *The grasp of consciousness, action and concept in the young child.* (S. Wedgwood, trans.), Cambridge, Mass.: Harvard University Press, 1976.

Piaget, J., & Inhelder, B. *The psychology of the child.* (H. Weaver, trans.), New York: Basic Books, 1969.

Schofield, J. W. Complimentary and conflicting identities: Image and interactions in an interracial school. In S. Asher & J. Gottman (Eds.), *The development of friendship*. New York: Cambridge University Press, 1981.

Selman, R. L. *The growth of interpersonal understanding: Developmental and clinical analyses.* New York: Academic Press, 1980.

Selman, R. L. The development of interpersonal competence: The role of understanding in conduct. *Developmental Review*, 1981, *1*, 401-422.

Selman, R. L., Schorin, M., Stone, C., & Phelps, E. A field study of social understanding as expressed in reflective interviews, group discussions, and group task negotiations. *Developmental Psychology*, in press.

Stone, C. *A structural-developmental approach to the study of peer interaction.* Unpublished doctoral dissertation, Harvard Graduate School of Education, 1981.

Part II
Peer Relationships

Chapter 8

Social Interaction in the First Year: Infants' Social Skills with Peers versus Mother

Deborah Lowe Vandell and Kathy Shores Wilson

In recent years, considerable attention has been paid to the nature of toddlers' social encounters with peers (Bronson, 1975; Eckerman, Whatley, & Kutz, 1975; Goldman & Ross, 1977; Mueller & Brenner, 1977; Mueller & Lucas, 1975). From these studies, a preliminary catalogue of toddler social skills may be derived. For example, it appears that toddlers are able both to initiate and maintain encounters with peers. In addition, they are able to combine social acts into complex social messages and to coordinate those messages with a partner into fairly sophisticated games. In contrast to the numerous studies of toddler social skills, however, we know relatively little about infants' interactions with peers. One purpose of this chapter is to describe in more detail some social skills that are apparent in infant-peer interaction. As part of this discussion, some limitations of infant social abilities are also discussed.

A second issue to be explored is the characteristics of infant social interaction with two different partners, the peer and the mother. While other researchers (Lamb, 1977; Parke, 1979) have contrasted infants' interactions with mother and father, we know little about the ways in which mother-infant and infant-infant interactions are similar or different. Several researchers (Ross, 1982; Mueller, 1978; Eckerman & Stein, Note 1) have speculated that the infant-peer system may represent a better measure of infant social skill than the mother-infant system because highly competent and involved mothers may make infants look more skilled than they are, but we have little data to document this hypothesis. We also know little about what social skills infants may demonstrate equally with mother and peer.

A third issue to be examined is the interrelationship between infants' interactions with mother and peer. A central issue underlying much of the early peer interaction research has been the origins of peer relations. Do infants' interactions with peers grow out of infants' interactions with the mother, or are peer interactions and mother-infant interactions basically autonomous? A number of factors (the large amount of time the infant spends with the mother, the high emotional involvement between mother and infant, the mother's considerable social competence relative to the infant) would argue for the generalization hypothesis, but some peer researchers (Mueller, 1978; Mueller & Vandell, 1979) have argued that peer interaction may not grow out of mother-infant interaction; rather, they have contended that toddler-toddler interaction grows out of encounters around toys and other children. We have, however, few direct tests to aid in evaluating these two hypotheses and the limited studies that are available (Easterbrooks & Lamb, 1979; Lieberman, 1977; Vandell, 1977) have looked at toddlers or preschoolers. Because we were interested in the origins of peer relations and social skills, we have extended this examination of intersystem relationships to the first year.

Early Social Development Project

The Early Social Development Project began in 1977. First-born (32) and second-born (32) infants were observed repeatedly as they interacted with a variety of partners. Equal numbers of boys and girls were observed. All infants were from middle- to upper-middle-class families. All infants were videotaped at 6½ (± 15 days) months and at 9½ (± 15 days) months as they interacted (a) with an unfamiliar, same-sex, same-age peer and (b) with the mother. Second-born infants were also videotaped with their 3- to 5-year-old siblings, and first-borns with mother and peer at 12½ months. In this chapter, the infant-infant and mother-infant interactions are described.

Each infant-infant session was 15 minutes in duration, with toys present for 10 minutes and absent for 5 minutes. Toys were primarily small manipulative objects such as plastic keys, pop beads, etc. The mothers were present during the infant-infant sessions, but were asked not to initiate or sustain interactions with their children. Each mother-infant session was about 10 minutes long, and toys comparable to those in the infant-infant session were present throughout. We told the mothers that we wanted to compare what babies would do when another infant was available and not available. During this "peer absent" period, the mother was asked to pretend that she and the infant were in their own home with a few free minutes.

Both the mother-infant and infant-infant sessions were conducted in a carpeted laboratory playroom with one-way glass on the upper half of two opposite walls. A special effects generator provided a split-screen composite picture from two videocameras hidden behind the one-way mirrors. (With this videotape arrangement, the faces of both infants and mothers were almost always available and a detailed coding scheme could be used.) Date and time to the nearest second were superimposed at the bottom of the videotaped picture. A microphone was suspended from the ceiling to provide auditory access to the room.

Catalogue of Infant Social Skills

The study of toddler social skills has been multifaceted and has reflected somewhat divergent ideas about what a social skill is and how it should best be studied. According to *Webster's New Collegiate Dictionary* (1973), a skill may be defined as an "ability," as a "technique," and as "proficiency." Interestingly, as reflected in several recent studies, each of these definitions has been used to tap somewhat different aspects of infant social skill. In some cases, social skill has been seen as behaviors (or techniques) that lead to more and longer intreactions (e.g., Eckerman, Note 2). In other cases, skill has been defined as the ability to engage in particular types of advanced interactions such as games or role play (e.g., Goldman & Ross, 1977; Mueller & Lucas, 1975). Still others have emphasized interaction proficiency with the assumption that some children are more skilled than others and that one can study individual differences in social skill (Brenner & Mueller, in press; Lee, Note 3). These definitions of social skill will now be examined in more detail.

Behaviors Leading to Interaction

Eckerman (Note 2) argued that interactive skill may be seen as any way of behaving that increases the likelihood of children interacting. Consequently, she examined behaviors that appeared to facilitate interaction between toddler peers. One such behavior was mutual visual regard. Eckerman reasoned that, because social interaction requires a coordination of actions between participants, mutual looking should help toddlers to orchestrate their exchanges. There are some data to support this argument. Eckerman and Stein (Note 1), for example, reported that 70% of 2-year-olds' social signals occurred when a peer partner was looking and 60% of 18-month-olds' signals occurred when the partner was looking. Similarly, Goldman and Ross (1977) found that toddler social games with peers were typically marked by mutual visual regard.

Mutual looking also appears to be an interactive skill during the first year. In observations of our 6- to 12-month-old, first-born infants, we found that 85% of their social interactions involved mutual visual regard. (We did not complete this analysis on second-born infants.) If infants were interacting, they were typically looking at one another simultaneously. However, mutual visual regard did not inevitably lead the infants to interact with one another. While mutual regard occurred in one-third of the 10-second frames of a time sample code, mutual regard accompanied by social interaction occurred in only about 12% of the 10-second frames; the infants appeared to capitalize on their joint looking only about one-third of the time.

A second set of behaviors seen as leading to interaction is the ability to manipulate the same toy simultaneously. From numerous observations (Eckerman & Stein, Note 1; Mueller & Brenner, 1977, Mueller & Rich, 1976), it appears that toys or objects draw toddlers together; the argument is that from these mutual object encounters interactions can emerge. In some cases, one child may see another child with a desired toy and the children are forced to interact to resolve the toy conflict. In other cases, toddlers have been observed to use toys as a more positive fulcrum around which to interact; as, for example, when one child peeks from behind a curtain and the second child laughs at the spectacle. Eckerman and Stein (Note 1) found object contacts of these types to be very common between toddler peers (50% of a 20-minute play session for 2-year-olds and 25% of the play sessions for 18-month-olds). More important from the standpoint of interactive skill, however, all dialogues (defined as at least two acts per child) observed by Eckerman and Stein occurred during mutual object contacts. Mueller and Brenner (1977) reported a similar high proportion of interactions around objects: fully 83% of the interactions they observed in toddler boys were embedded in object contacts.

The importance of joint object manipulation as an interactive skill appears to be less central in the first year, primarily because infants rarely interact with the same toy at the same time. We observed the 6- to 12-month-old infants to manipulate toys nonsocially in over 50% of the 10-second frames of a time sample, but they played with the same toys simultaneously in less than 8% of the 10-second frames; they played with the same toys socially in only about 1% of the 10-second frames. Thus, in contrast to the toddlers described by Mueller or Eckerman, the infants appeared to spend considerably less time in joint object activity.

Nevertheless, there was evidence of the growing role of joint object activity, especially toward the end of the first year: 91% of the infants' mutual social use of objects grew out of their mutual nonsocial object contacts. A similar pattern was reflected in other social behaviors. For example, looking at the partner was regularly associated with mutual object contacts. At 6 months, in 78% of the 10-second frames in which mutual object contacts occurred, looking at the partner also occurred. At 9 months, in 81% of the 10-second frames in which mutual object contact occurred, looking at the partner occurred. At 12 months, the figure was 82%. In addition, there was a linear increase in the proportion of 10-second frames with mutual object use and social behaviors other than looking. At 6 months, these other social behaviors (smile, touch, vocalize, social object use) occurred in 27% of the 10-second frames that included mutual object use. At 9 months, they occurred in 47% of the frames in which there was mutual object use. At 12 months, the figure was 62%. Thus, although mutual object manipulations were relatively uncommon events between infants, they appeared to have the potential to elicit social behaviors.

Imitation has been described as a third skill that facilitates interaction between toddlers. Eckerman (Note 2) argued that imitation encourages interaction by freeing toddlers from having continually to develop novel social responses. In fact, data from some toddler studies support these arguments. Eckerman and Stein (Note 1) found that 2-year-olds engaged in imitations about 20 times within a 20-minute observation; 18-month-olds engaged in imitation about 7 times within the same period. Even more important in the context of interactive skill, all but two of the dialogues observed by Eckerman and Stein involved imitation. It appeared that imitation did free the toddlers for more sustained encounters. Similarly, Goldman and Ross (1977) found that about one-third of the toddler games they observed (interactions marked by positive affect and nonliterality) were imitative. Imitation, however, does not appear to play as central a role in infant-infant interactions. In our observations of the 6- to 12-month-old first-born infants, 32 long interactions (four units or greater) were observed, but only 8 of these interactions involved imitation.

Ability to Engage in More Complex Social Encounters

In addition to viewing skills as behaviors leading to or facilitating interaction, social skills may be seen as the ability to engage in various complex social encounters. One such skill, reported by Brenner and Mueller (in press), is the ability of toddlers to engage in interactions around a common topic. Brenner and Mueller found that toddler boys who were participating in playgroups were able to interact around 12 topics (peek-a-boo, run-chase, object exchange, object possession struggle, vocal copy, motor copy, aggression, shared reference, rough and tumble, curtain running, positive affect, vocal prosocial) on which both children appeared to agree.

There were several pieces of evidence that these "shared-meaning" interactions were more advanced (or skilled) than non shared-meaning interactions. Shared meanings were found in 75% of the interactions longer than three units and in only 22% of the shorter interactions. In addition, shared meanings were more common in older toddlers than in younger toddlers. Finally, toddlers who were more involved in shared-meaning interactions were more skilled in other areas, such as the complexity of their social messages.

Interaction skill in toddlers has also been seen as the ability to engage in social games (Goldman & Ross, 1977; Hay, Ross, & Goldman, 1979; Ross, 1982). Toddler social games, as described by Ross and her colleagues, are difficult accomplishments involving four features: turn taking through at least four turns, mutual involvement, positive affect, and evidence that the exchange is nonliteral. Ross (1982) examined 48 dyads of 15- to 24-month-old toddlers and reported over 66 instances of social games. Imitative games in which there was a response matching were most common in the 18-month-olds; reciprocal games in which there were role reversals were more common at 21 and 24 months.

Ross found additional evidence of toddler skill in the types of themes developed. Many themes used by toddlers were "new" ones that had not been previously observed in the toddlers' games with adults, suggesting that the toddlers were generating the games within the peer context. This ability to engage in games appears, however, to be less characteristic of infant-infant interaction. We found no examples of infant games in the 720 minutes of observation of first born infants between 6 and 12 months of age.

A third example of skill defined as the ability to engage in complex encounters may be seen in infants' and toddlers' friendship formations. Howes (Note 4) conducted a comprehensive study of early friendships among children attending community day care programs. Infants (5-14 months of age), toddlers (16-23 months), and preschoolers (35-49 months) were observed at 2-month intervals over a 1-year period as they played in their classrooms. Three criteria were used to determine friendship: (a) friends were expected to respond to one another's initiations at least 50% of the time, (b) friends were expected to have at least one reciprocal interaction during an observation, and (c) friends were expected to have at least one affectively positive exchange per observation. Using these rather strict criteria, Howes found considerable evidence of friendship pairings: 14% of the infant dyads observed were friends, and 41% of the toddler dyads formed friendships. In addition, all toddlers had at least one friend, and over 70% of the infants had at least one friend. She found, however, that there were some differences in infants' and toddlers' friendships. Once they were established, infant friendships were maintained over all subsequent observations, while toddlers showed a pattern of both maintained and sporadic friendships. Unfortunately for the purposes of this chapter, it is not clear from Howes' analysis how many of the infant friendship pairs were found between children younger than 12 months.

Social Skills Examined in this Project

Socially Directed Behaviors

Consistent with the approach adopted by Howes, Ross, and Mueller, we also viewed social skill as the ability to engage in certain social encounters; but the skills we studied in the first year were less complex than friendship or games (Vandell, Wilson, & Buchanan, 1980). At the heart of our examination was a decision to study socially directed behaviors (SDBs). These SDBs were defined as discrete acts directed to another person, usually accompanied by visual regard of the partner.[1] The assumption was that SDBs give evidence of rudimentary social ability. Two types of SDBs, simple and coordinated, were coded. A simple SDB was defined as a single social act (e.g., a smile) accompanied by visual regard of the partner, while a coordinated SDB was defined as two or more acts (e.g., a smile and vocalization) accompanied by visual regard.

The distinction between simple and coordinated SDBs was seen as important. Following a Piagetian orientation, one would assume that a coordinated SDB would indicate a more advanced performance than a simple SDB because the child is doing more than one thing at a time. In some of our earlier work with toddlers, this assumption appeared to be justified. For example, parents used a higher proportion of coordinated SDBs than their toddler sons, and the boys showed systematic increases over time in the frequency and proportion of their coordinated SDBs. Consequently, in our current examination, we once again examined the relative usage of simple and coordinated SDBs.

A time demarcation of 3 seconds was used to determine whether two acts represented two separate SDBs or a single coordinated SDB. This relatively brief time period seemed representative of the rapidity of infant responses: 28 seconds typically separated acts that were not part of the same SDB, while 1.1 seconds typically separated acts that were part of the same SDB. It appeared, then, that these fairly young infants had considerable social ability or skill in terms of sending complex social messages rapidly. In addition, we saw these SDBs as the building blocks for social interaction, a second basic social ability. Within our analysis, social interaction was defined as an exchange in which the SDB of one person was responded to by a second person's SDB. Thus, social interactions were seen as constructed of chains of SDBs. In previous observations, we had allowed toddlers 3 seconds to respond socially to a social behavior, and we found this period to be more than adequate. In fact, if a response was going to occur, it typically came in 1.8 seconds. The division between the end of one interaction and the

---

[1] A coding manual that outlines all the rules used for analyzing the videotapes is available upon request.

beginning of the next interaction was more on the order of 28.7 seconds. In the current study, because we thought that infants might not be able to respond as readily as toddlers, 5 seconds was alloted for a response to create an interaction. In fact, however, the rapidity of the infants' responses rivaled the toddlers: actor changes within interactions typically occurred every 2.6 seconds, while the division between the end of one interaction and the beginning of the next interaction was 40.6 seconds.

From the study of the social interactions, a number of social skill indices were derived. The most basic indications of social ability were seen as interaction frequency and interaction duration. It was assumed that more interactions of a longer duration were indicative of greater social interest and ability than were fewer and briefer interactions. Using a similar rationale, we examined the number of actor units in the longest interaction, assuming the longer the longest chain, the more skilled the performance. We also examined the proportion of interactions greater than two turns as an indication of how often infants could engage in longer exchanges.

Sequences

While social interactions (SDB/SDB chains) were viewed as requiring social involvement from both participants, we thought that infants might also engage in other types of exchanges. While these exchanges might, on the surface, resemble social interactions in that a pattern of contingent responses occurred, they were expected to differ from interactions in that one or both participants would lack a clearly social focus. These encounters were designated under the global category, *sequence.*

Four types of sequence were analyzed. First, it was considered possible that person A could direct a social behavior to person B (e.g., A looks at and shows B a toy) that could elicit a response from B (B looks at and grabs the toy). This type of sequence was conceptualized as "A social behavior (SDB)/B elicited response (ER)." Likewise, it was considered possible that person A could do some nonsocial behavior (e.g., A plays with a toy nonsocially) which could elicit a social response from person B (e.g., B looks at A and says "mine"). This sequence could be conceptualized as "A nonsocial behavior (BEH)/B social behavior (SDB)." Using the same reasoning, a third type of sequence was anticipated. Person A could do some behavior (e.g., A rolls a ball) without any clear social intent which might elicit a response from person B that also has no clear social intent (e.g., B picks up the rolling ball). This type of sequence was seen as "A nonsocial behavior (BEH)/B elicited response (ER)." A final sequence type included a mixture of SDBs, ERs, and BEHs, as when A does a nonsocial behavior (BEH) that B responds to socially (SDB), which elicits a nonsocial response from A (ER). These sequences were designated as "mixed."

It was hypothesized that some exchanges would be more characteristic of infant-infant interaction, while other exchanges were expected to characterize mother-infant interaction. In particular, SDB/ER sequences were expected to occur more frequently in mother-infant encounters because we expected mothers' activities (especially object-related demonstrations) to be very good elicitors of infant responses. Furthermore, we hypothesized that BEH/SDB sequences would be more characteristic of mother-infant encounters because we expected mothers to be more responsive to their infants' activities than infant peers would be. BEH/ER sequences, on the other hand, were expected to be more common in infant-infant interaction because in these contingencies neither partner would take the predominant social role. A priori, we were less certain whether infants would engage in more social interactions (SDB/SDB) with the mother or with the peer, although one might expect the mothers' greater social competence to result in more social interactions occurring in the mother-infant system.

Individuals Interactive Abilities

In addition to the examination of the features of dyadic exchanges, we analyzed individual social abilities (or skills) within interactions and sequences. For example, we looked at who initiated exchanges. (An initiation was defined as the first act in an exchange.) We also examined individual responsiveness to a partner's initiation as measured by the proportion of successful initiations. We expected each of these variables to be indicative of the infants' sociability. The more skilled individuals were expected to be more responsive to the other's initiations (as measured by their partner's proportion of successful initiations) and also to be more successful initiators themselves (as measured by initiation frequency and proportion of their own successful initiations). Finally, while perhaps less indicative of skill and more indicative of the flavor of the encounters, we recorded the content of the infants' and mothers' social behaviors. In particular, the frequencies of vocalizations, touches, motor acts, object-related social acts, cries, and smiles were tallied.

This coding scheme was used in the analysis of both mother-infant and infant-infant sessions. Consequently, we were able to describe (in comparable terms) infants' encounters with two different partners.

Social Skills Demonstrated in Infant-Infant and Infant-Mother Interactions

Infant-Infant Interaction

Within the 15-minute play sessions, the first- and second-born infants directed, on the average, 13 SDBs to the peer; 43% of the SDBs were complex, coordinated SDBs involving multiple social acts.[2] In all, on the average, over 25 social acts per child per 15-minute session were observed; 40% of the infants' attempts to initiate exchanges were successful. Somewhat surprisingly, given the age of the children, the most common exchanges observed between the infants were social interactions in which one infant directed a social behavior to the peer, who then responded socially ($M = 3.49$). Even more surprising, every dyad engaged in at least one of these social interactions per observation. In contrast, social behaviors were less likely to elicit nonsocial responses (frequency of SDB/ER, $M = .65$). Other types of sequences were also less common than social interactions during the peer sessions (mixed sequences, $M = 1.20$; BEH/SDB, $M = 1.20$). Completely nonsocial sequences were the least common exchange (BEH/ER, $M = .85$). As another indication of the children's awareness of one another, only 1 infant out of the 64 did not initiate any sequences or interactions.

One hesitates, however, to overemphasize the infants' social interest and ability. Many interactions and sequences were very brief and fleeting: about 56% were simply two-unit chains. The amount of time spent in interactions or sequences was also limited: only about 23 seconds were spent in social interactions and about 16 seconds were spent in sequences. The length of the longest interaction was typically three units and the longest exchange observed during an infant-peer session was six units.

In regard to the content of the infant-peer interactions, the infants predominantly vocalized to one another ($M = 8.92$). Smiles ($M = 4.71$), touches ($M = 3.79$), and motor acts such as gestures and arm flaps ($M = 3.71$) were relatively common. Cries ($M = 1.28$), agonism ($M = .46$), and object-related social acts ($M = 1.17$) were less common. The relatively infrequent social use of objects and agonism was in marked contrast to observations made of toddler-peer interaction. As noted earlier, Eckerman (Note 2) and Mueller (1978) discussed toddlers' reliance on objects during social interactions; and Bronson (1975) and Ross and Hay (Note 5) noted that agonistic encounters between toddler peers are frequent.

The social encounters were also examined for evidence of reciprocity between the infant pairs. Cairns (1979) noted that interactions between

---

[2] This and all subsequent analyses of the first- and second-born infants are based on the 6- and 9-month observations because the second-born infants were not observed at 12 months.

older children are characterized by response matching such that one can reliably predict the activity of one child by observing the second child; and Sherman (1975) found a matching in 4-year-olds' activity levels and types of toys played with. We found some reciprocity, although not as pronounced, among the infant dyads. While the 6- and 9-month-old infants reciprocated in their use of simple SDBs and object-related social acts, no significant relationships (i.e., correlations) were found between the dyad members' behaviors for most variables: frequency of initiations, coordinated SDBs, vocalizations, cries, agonism, smiles, touches, etc. The behaviors of the infant dyad members appeared to be more independent than was found in the older peer dyads reported by Cairns and Sherman.

Mother-Infant Interaction

During the 10-minute mother-infant sessions, infants spent over one-half of the time (341 seconds) involved in either interactions or sequences. These exchanges were almost always sequences (frequency, M = 11.2; duration, M = 329 seconds) and were typically marked by the mother acting socially and the infant acting nonsocially. For example, SDB/ER sequences occurred regularly, with the mother typically demonstrating a toy for the infant and the infant then responding in an object-centered way (SDB/ER frequency, M = 3.4). In these sequences, mothers appeared to establish chains of responses with infants under their complete control. While some of these exchanges resembled social interactions, a closer examination revealed the infants' lack of social involvement.

Another type of sequence, BEH/SDB, was also relatively common (M = 2.7) during mother-infant sessions. In these sequences, infants typically did something that mothers then treated as a social act. For example, infants regularly manipulated toys, with mothers then commenting on the manipulations. Once again, mothers created a pattern that superficially looked like mutual dyadic involvement, but in fact was not.

Even more common than BEH/SDB and SDB/ER sequences were mixed sequences, in which nonsocial behaviors, elicited responses, and social behaviors were combined in ongoing chains of actions (M = 5.3). By definition, these mixed sequences involved mother and infant in at least three turns. Typically, an infant's nonsocial behavior elicited a social response from the mother that then elicited a nonsocial response from the infant. The average sequence length per dyad was about 8 units, and the average dyad had sequences up to 24 turns. The longest sequence observed in any mother-infant dyad was 135 turns.

In contrast to the considerable amount of time spent in sequences, infants spent surprisingly little time interacting socially with their mothers (interaction frequency, $M = 1.0$; interaction duration, $M = 11.9$ seconds). Even when "modified" interactions were examined (cases in which SDB/SDB exchanges were incorporated into ongoing sequences), only limited numbers of interactions were observed (frequency of modified interactions, $M = 3.5$). Thus, it appeared that the level of the infants' social involvement with their mothers, as measured by social participation in interactions, was minimal.

This impression of the infants' minimal social involvement relative to the mother was further supported by examining the infants' and mothers' individual performances within the dyad. Mothers initiated significantly more exchanges than did infants (mother, $M = 8.0$; infant, $M = 4.2$). Moreover, this comparison still exaggerates the infants' social initiations. Over one-half of the initiations attributed to infants were actually nonsocial behaviors to which mothers responded socially. The proportion of successful social initiations was further evidence of differences between mothers and infants. Mothers responded to almost 86% of the infants' initiations, whereas infants responded to about 64% of the mothers' initiations (i.e., the proportion of successful initiations for the infants was .86; the proportion of successful initiations for the mothers was .64). In regard to the complexity of the social behaviors, 80% of the mothers' SDBs were coordinated (i.e., involved multiple social acts), whereas 50% of the infants' social behaviors were coordinated.

Differences between mother and infant were also found in the types of social acts used. Not surprisingly, given the mothers' greater social involvement, mothers used significantly more vocalizations, touches, smiles, motor acts, and object-related social acts than did infants. Of more interest to us, however, was the relative likelihood of the different social acts used by mother and infant. Mothers were relatively more likely to vocalize, use objects socially, and touch the infants, while infants were more likely to smile and use motor acts such as flapping their arms.

Even with the apparent differences in mother and infant behavior, there was evidence of considerable match or reciprocity between mother and infant at 6 and 9 months. For example, significant positive correlations were found between the frequency of the mothers' SDBs to the infant and the frequency of the infants' SDBs to the mother. This reciprocity was also apparent at both 6 and 9 months for the frequencies of mothers' and infants' coordinated SDBs, motor acts, object-related social acts, and smiles.[3]

---

[3] Although the number of pairs for the mother-infant correlations was 64 and the number of pairs for the infant-infant correlations was 32, it did not appear that the greater reciprocity in the mother-infant as opposed to infant-infant system was a statistical artifact. The magnitude of the infant-infant correlations would not have been significant even with the larger degrees of freedom. The mother-infant correlations would have been significant even with reduced degrees of freedom.

Comparison of Infants' Interactions with Mothers and with Peers

From our observations of infants' interactions with their mothers and with peers, it became apparent that infants were doing different things with the two partners. To determine whether these differences were "significant," the infants' performance during the toys-present portion of the peer session was contrasted with the infants' performance during the 10-minute mother-infant sessions when toys were also present. As shown in Table 8-1, numerous differences were found in the infants' encounters with the mother and with a peer. First sequences were much more characteristic of mother-infant encounters. The overall statistical difference was primarily the result of much greater frequencies of SDB/ER, BEH/SDB, and mixed sequences with the mothers. Mothers were more likely than peers to treat infants' nonsocial activities as if they were social and to direct social behaviors that elicited nonsocial responses from the infant. Likewise, the proportion of infants' initiations that were responded to was significantly greater with the mother than with a peer. Finally, the proportion of exchanges longer than two

Table 8-1. Comparison of Infants' Social Behaviors with Mother and with Peer During 10-Minute Observations

Variables	With mother	With peer
Interaction frequency	1.01	1.62*
Interaction duration (seconds)	11.91	9.74
Sequence frequency	11.21	2.71***
Sequence duration (seconds)	329.46	8.58***
BEH/ER frequency	.12	.80***
BEH/SDB frequency	2.69	1.05***
SDB/ER frequency	3.41	.29***
Mixed-sequence frequency	5.31	.58***
Modified interaction frequency	3.49	.29***
Proportion longer interactions	36.87	24.92*
Initiation frequency	4.17	2.20***
Isolated SDB frequency	.08	3.35***
Proportion successful initiations	85.83	39.75***
Simple SDB frequency	3.79	4.06
Coordinated SDB frequency	3.76	2.74
Proportion coordinated SDBs	49.80	40.29
Vocalization frequency	5.33	4.38
Social cries frequency	.25	.42
Social motor acts frequency	1.33	1.61
Object-related social acts frequency	.56	1.02*
Social smiles frequency	4.25	2.19**
Social touches frequency	.83	1.36

$*p < .05.$
$**p < .01.$
$***p < .001.$

units was greater in mother-infant than in infant-infant exchanges. For each of these variables, it appeared that the mother was assuming the brunt of the responsibility for the superficially "social" encounters. In many ways, infants' encounters with the mother were less indicative of the infants' social abilities and more indicative of maternal interest and skill. (This is not to say that the infants were completely unaware of their mothers; their behavior and play may well have been influenced and/or prolonged by their sequences with their mothers, but these sequences appeared to be primarily the result of maternal involvement and social skill.)

Other differences between mother-infant and infant-infant exchanges were found with larger values being registered with peers. As predicted, infant-peer dyads had significantly more BEH/ER sequences, in which both partners engaged in apparently contingent responses that were not social. We also found infants to have more isolated SDBs (SDBs that were not part of ongoing sequences) with a peer than with the mother. For both of these variables, the infant peer did not make the baby "look good" in the way the mother did. One difference favoring the infant-peer dyads was unexpected, however. Strictly social interactions—those exchanges that required social involvement from both partners throughout—were more frequent with peers than with mothers.

For other variables, infants' encounters with mother and peer were remarkably similar. For example, no difference was found in the proportions of coordinated versus simple SDBs with mother and peer. These similar proportions support Mueller and Vandell's (1979) argument that the ability to coordinate social behaviors is an underlying cognitive skill as well as social skill. What was even more surprising, given the vastly different social behaviors of mother and peer, the frequencies of the infants' simple and coordinated social behaviors were roughly equivalent with the two partners. Infants also used roughly equivalent numbers of vocalizations and motor acts to the two partners.

Social Skill Defined as Differential Social Ability

Thus far in this chapter, social skills in infancy have been treated as abilities leading to or characterizing interaction. A different approach to skill has been to examine differential manifestations of skill. Lee's (Note 3) frequently cited observation of a popular and unpopular infant is a case in point. Lee found that one "popular" infant, Jenny, was less likely than other infants to initiate interactions and that her initiations were more likely to be inobtrusive "looks," whereas an unpopular infant, Patrick, made initiations that were more typically intrusive "grabs." In regard to responsiveness, Patrick engaged in interactions only when he initiated exchanges, while Jenny was equally responsive in interactions initiated by others as in those interactions she initiated herself. This early study is most notable for suggesting that even young children may differ in their social proficiencies.

Brenner and Mueller (in press) outlined other individual differences in toddler social skills with peers. One child, designated the "superstar," participated in a disproportionate share of interactions around a shared topic, while another child never participated in a shared meaning. Brenner and Mueller also found that some children were shared-meaning "specialists": Their shared meanings were inevitably around particular themes, such as vocal imitation, and they never used other themes.

Toddlers also appear to differ in their proficiency (or skill) in engaging in social games. In observations of 18-month-olds paired with either a 12-month-old or 24-month-old partner, Goldman and Ross (1977) noted a range of social games participation. Of 32 dyads observed, 21 never played a game, 9 played only 1 or 2 games each, and 1 dyad played 3 games; most notable in terms of individual differences was 1 dyad who played 13 games!

In still another approach to individual differences in social skill, Vandell and Mueller (Note 6) looked at stability over time and situation in toddlers' sociability. A group of toddlers was observed at 16, 19, and 22 months in a dyadic play situation and in a group play situation. Consistent with the studies reported above, considerable variability was found in the toddlers' social skills. Even more interesting, however, was the stability in the toddlers' performance across time and situation. The relative frequencies of the toddlers' vocalizations, motor acts, and interactions were significantly correlated between the dyadic and group situations. In addition, there was stability in the toddlers' performance over time. We found positive correlations among the data of 16, 19, and 22 months for the proportion of social acts that were a particular child's and the frequencies of interactions, vocalizations, and motor acts.

We also completed a similar examination of individual differences in the 6- and 9-month-olds' social abilities. As was the case with toddlers, we found considerable variability in the infants' apparent ability to interact with peers. The frequency of social behaviors toward peers, for example, ranged from 2 to 53 per 15-minute session and the frequency of social behaviors toward peers, for example, ranged from 2 to 53 per 15-minute session and the frequency of social acts constituting the SDBs ranged from 1 to 115. Other variables, such as frequency of vocalizations, motor acts, and smiles, showed a similar variability. Variability was also found in the infants' apparent social skills with their mothers. Some infants, for example, never initiated an interaction or sequence with their mothers, while other infants initiated as many as 16 exchanges.

From this variability, several questions emerge: Are these differences stable across time? Are these individual differences stable across partners? How do these differential skills develop? Do infants who are more skilled with one partner generalize these skills to another partner over time? Are some maternal styles (high vs. low interactive; more vs. less responsive) more conducive to infants' subsequent development of social skills with peers?

Stability in Infant Social Skill over Time

We found significant positive correlations between the data of 6 and 9 months for several of the infants' behaviors with peers: the frequencies of social interactions, initiations of interactions, vocalizations, and simple SDBs. If social skill is defined as the ability to engage in social interactions or to use social behaviors, then these skills were stable over the 3-month period.

Considerable stability was also apparent in infants' social behaviors to their mothers at 6 and at 9 months. For example, it appeared that those infants who frequently initiated exchanges with their mothers at 6 months were more likely to initiate exchanges at 9 months as well ($r = .368$). In addition, the frequency of SDBs ($r = .286$), social motor acts ($r = .309$), and object-related social acts ($r = .374$) were positively correlated between 6 and 9 months. Finally, the proportion of the infants' successful initiations was positively correlated between 6 and 9 months ($r = .464$).

Stability in Infant Social Skills Across Partners

To examine the stability of social interactions across social partners, the frequencies of infants' behaviors to their mothers at 6 months were correlated with the frequencies of the infants' behaviors to their peers at 6 months; and the same correlations were examined at 9 months.

From these analyses, some similarities were found in infants' encounters with the two partners. At 6 months, for example, a significant positive correlation was found in the proportion of longer exchanges (more than two units), such that 6-month-olds who were more frequently part of longer exchanges with their mothers were also more likely to engage in longer sequences with their peers ($r = .463$). In addition, positive correlations were found for interaction frequency ($r = .308$), sequence frequency ($r = .323$), and modified interaction (social interactions that were part of ongoing sequences) frequency ($r = .331$). At 9 months, significant positive correlations were found in the frequencies of the infants' modified interactions with mother and peer ($r = .661$) and in the length of the longest interaction with mother and peer ($r = .450$).

As notable as the positive correlations found, however, were the variables in which no relationship occurred. The frequencies with which infants vocalized, smiled, touched, or used objects with the two

partners were unrelated. Thus, it appeared that, while there were similarities in infants' social skills with mother and with peer, similarities
were less apparent on stylistic variables such as smiling and vocalizing.
Infants did not generalize the content of their social acts in the same
way as they did the ability to participate in interactions.

Relationship Between Mother-Infant and Infant-Infant Interactions
over Time

A third set of questions concerned how the individual differences in
skill develop. Is there a sequential relationship between infants' skills
with mother and peer over time such that infants first develop a skill
with their mothers and later demonstrate the same skill with their
peers? In order to examine this issue infant behavior to the mothers
at 6 months was correlated to infant behavior to peers at 9 months,
and infant behavior to peers at 6 months was correlated to infant
behavior to the mothers at 9 months. Examination of these correlation
matrices revealed no significant sequential relationships. For all variables the infants' behaviors with one partner at 6 months did not predict
their behaviors with the other partner at 9 months.

Another possible relationship between mother-infant and infant-
infant interaction was explored. We examined the relationship between
maternal behaviors and infants' interactions with peers. In particular,
we sought to determine if the mothers' behaviors at the 6- or 9-month
observations influenced the infants' peer-directed behaviors either
synchronously or over time. It might be, for example, that mothers
who frequently vocalized or used SDBs with their infants would have
infants who would then frequently use the same behaviors with their
peers. Accordingly, the mother's behavior to the infant at both 6
months and 9 months was correlated to the infant's behavior to a peer
at both ages, resulting in four sets of correlations. From these analyses,
we found *no* relationship between maternal behavior and infant behavior
either at the same point in time or over the 3-month interval. What
the mothers did with their infants in the laboratory situation had very
little to do with their infants' performance with peers.

Intersystem Relationships During the First Year

What do these analyses mean for an overall discussion of the relationship between mother-infant and infant-infant interactions? Not surprisingly, no simple answer is forthcoming, because the relationship is
a complex one. At one level, infants' encounters with their mothers
and with peers appeared to be basically different and autonomous.
The mothers, much more than peers, responded to the infants' social

and nonsocial actions, thereby creating sequences that occupied the majority of the play sessions and made their infants "look good." We should not give the infants too much credit for these exchanges; the mothers were definitely in charge. With peers, the infants had more unsuccessful initiations, but they also had more exchanges that were strictly social interactions in which both partners were actively involved. Stylistically, we found other evidence that the two systems were basically different. A significantly higher proportion of the infants' social acts with their mothers were vocalizations and smiles, while touches, cries, and motor acts were relatively more common with peers.

Other data supported the notion of autonomy between the mother-infant and infant-infant systems. From the cross-lag correlations, we found no evidence of social skills emerging first with one partner and then appearing with the second partner. Infants who frequently interacted with their mothers at 6 months were no more likely to interact with their peers at 9 months than were other infants. Furthermore, we did not find any evidence that infants generalized a style of interacting from one partner to the other over time. Infants who frequently vocalized to one partner at 6 months were no more or less likely to vocalize to the other partner at either 6 or 9 months.

At the same time, one should not overstate the case for the autonomy of the mother-infant and infant-infant systems. Other evidence points to the underlying stability in infants' social skills with their mothers and with peers. At both 6 and 9 months, those infants who interacted more with their mothers also interacted more with their peers; and those infants who engaged in longer interactions with their peers engaged in longer interactions with their mothers. In other words, those infants who were "more social" at a given point with one partner were also "more social" with the other partner in the same period.

How should these results be interpreted? Given the lack of significant cross-lag correlations, it does not appear that infants developed skills with one partner and subsequently applied those skills to the other partner; rather, interaction skills were reflected simultaneously with both mother and peer. Perhaps, then, infants' social skills may be better conceptualized as a larger organizational unit of underlying infant sociability. While this sociability may vary stylistically in interaction with mother and peer, the underlying skill is there.

Experiences with Peers and Siblings as a Source of Individual Differences in Infant Social Skills

Given the richness of the infants' social world, it seems probable that interaction experiences other than those with the mother can affect infants' peer interactions. Two potential sources of influence are interactive experiences with infant peers and with preschool-age siblings.

A number of researchers have found peer experience to have a positive effect on older children's social skills. Lieberman (1977), for example, reported that peer experience in preschoolers was positively related to responsiveness to an unfamiliar playmate and to the number of chains in children's interactions. Mueller and Brenner (1977) found greater social skill, as measured by sustained interaction and complex social behaviors, in toddlers who were more peer experienced. Moreover, we found a relationship between peer experience and parent-child interaction (Vandell, 1979); while there were no significant differences prior to a playgroup experience, toddlers who attended a playgroup came over time to display significantly more social skill with parents than home-reared toddlers.

In our investigations of social skills during the first year, we included an analysis to determine whether infants were also positively affected by age mate experience. Mothers were asked at the beginning of each peer session to specify how much contact their infants had had with a peer during the preceding 3 months. We found significant differences in the infants' social skills with peers associated with the level of peer experience (Vandell, Wilson, & Whalen, 1981). Infants who were around age mates once a week or more were more likely to initiate exchanges (M = 4.10) than were infants who were around age mates less than once a week (initiations M = 2.62). The proportion of successful initiations with peers was also greater in peer experienced (M = 42.8%) versus less experienced (M = 24.8%) infants. Thus, we found some suggestive evidence that peer social skills may develop from previous peer interactions.

We found other experiences to have negative effects on the infants' interactions with peers. The second-born infants (all of whom had a preschool-age sibling) were significantly less skilled with peers than were the first-born infants. Second-born infants engaged in fewer social interactions (M = 4.37 and 2.60 for first- and second-born infants respectively) for a briefer duration (M = 28.8 and 17.5 seconds) and initiated significantly fewer interactions and sequences (M = 4.60 and 2.93) than first-born infants. The proportion of interactions longer than two units (55.9% vs. 32.5%) and the number of units in the longest interaction (3.56 vs. 2.56) were also smaller in the second-born infants. Finally, specific social acts, such as gestures (M = 1.44 and .87 for first- and second-born infants, respectively) agonism (M = .46 and .08), social object use (M = 1.59 and .75), and approaches (M = .59 and .24) were less frequent in the second-born infants. From these data, it appears that some experiences did not have a positive effect on infant-infant interaction but rather depressed the infants' apparent social skills with peers.

One wonders why the second-born infants were less socially involved with peers. One possibility is that the infants' experience with preschoolers negatively affected the infants' encounters with peers. Some data support this hypothesis. From the questionnaire, we were able to divide the first-born infants according to frequent (defined as once a week or more) and rare (defined as less than once a week) experience with preschoolers. Three-way analyses of variance were then calculated comparing second-born infants who had a preschool-age sibling, first-born infants who were frequently around preschoolers, and first-born infants who were rarely around preschoolers. We found significant differences among the three groups ($p < .05$). First-born infants who were rarely around preschoolers initiated more interactions ($M = 5.30$) than did first-born infants who were frequently around preschoolers ($M = 4.58$) or second-born infants ($M = 3.15$). They also used significantly more simple SDBs ($M = 9.07, 8.28, 4.81$, respectively), coordinated SDBs ($M = 8.36, 6.49, 4.68$), and gestures ($M = 2.27, .88, .66$). In each case, it appeared that the less the exposure to preschoolers, the greater the interest in and skill with peers.

We are currently analyzing the second-born infants' interactions with their preschool-age siblings to determine what aspects of those encounters may be negatively affecting the infants. A cursory examination of these data indicates that the infants may have had relatively little opportunity to practice social skills with the preschoolers because the preschoolers typically ignored the infants. If the development of social skill requires active involvement in social interactions, infant-preschooler encounters may not regularly afford this opportunity.

Acknowledgments

This research was supported by a grant from the Hogg Foundation for Mental Health and by an Organized Research Grant from the University of Texas at Dallas. We are indebted to Lorrie Anderson, Ginger Ehrhardt, William Whalen, and Nola Buchanan, who were instrumental in completing work on various stages of the project. Medical City Hospital, Dallas, and the following physicians were very helpful in supplying the names of interested families: Robert Kramer, Doyle Stacy, Larry Patton, Claude Prestidge, and Ross Finkelman.

Reference Notes

1. Eckerman, C. O., & Stein, M. R. *Using peer encounters to discover the infant's developing social skills.* Paper presented at the Southeastern Conference on Human Development, Alexandria, Va., April 1980.
2. Eckerman, C. O. *The attainment of interactive skills: A major task of infancy.* Colloquium address delivered at the University of Virginia, Charlottesville, October 1978.
3. Lee, L. C. *Social encounters of infants: The beginnings of popularity.* Paper presented at the International Society for the Study of Behavioural Development, Ann Arbor, Mich., August 1973.
4. Howes, C. *Patterns of friendship in young children.* Paper presented at the

biennial meeting of the Society for Research in Child Development, Boston, April 1981.
5. Ross, H. S., & Hay, D. F. *Conflict and conflict resolution between 21-month-old peers.* Paper presented at the biennial meeting of the Society for Research in Child Development, New Orleans, March 1977.
6. Vandell, D. L., & Mueller, E. *Individual differences in early social interactions with peers.* Paper presented at the biennial meeting of the Southwestern Society for Research in Human Development, Dallas, April 1978.

References

Brenner, J., & Mueller, E. Shared meaning in boy toddlers' peer relations. *Child Development*, in press.
Bronson, W. Peer-peer interaction in the second year of life. In M. Lewis & L. Rosenblum (Eds.), *Friendship and peer relations.* New York: Wiley, 1975.
Cairns, R. *Social development: The origins and plasticity of interchanges.* San Francisco: Freeman, 1979.
Easterbrooks, M. A., & Lamb, M. E. The relationship between quality of infant-mother attachment and infant competence in initial encounters with peers. *Child Development*, 1979, *50*, 380-387.
Eckerman, C. O., Whatley, J., & Kutz, S. Growth of social play with peers during the second year of life. *Developmental Psychology*, 1975, *11*, 42-49.
Goldman, B. D., & Ross, H. S. Social skills in action: An analysis of early peer games. In J. Glick & K. A. Clarke-Stewart (Eds.), *Social and cognitive development: The development of social understanding* (Vol. 1). New York: Gardner Press, 1977.
Hay, D. F., Ross, H. S., & Goldman, B. D. Social games in infancy. In B. Sutton-Smith (Ed.), *Play and learning.* New York: Gardner Press. 1979.
Lamb, M. Father-child and mother-child interaction in the first year of life. *Child Development*, 1977, *48*, 167-181.
Lieberman, A. F. Preschoolers' competence with a peer: Relations with attachment and peer experience. *Child Development*, 1977, *48*, 1277-1287.
Mueller, E. Toddlers + toys = An autonomous social system. In M. Lewis & L. Rosenblum (Eds.), *The child and its family.* New York: Plenum Press, 1978.
Mueller, E., & Brenner, J. The origins of social skill and interaction among play-group toddlers. *Child Development*, 1977, *48*, 854-861.
Mueller, E., & Lucas, T. A. A developmental analysis of peer interaction among toddlers. In M. Lewis & L. Rosenblum (Eds.), *Friendship and peer relations.* New York: Wiley, 1975.
Mueller, E., & Rich, A. Clustering and socially-directed behaviours in a playgroup of 1-year-olds. *Journal of Child Psychology and Psychiatry*, 1976, *17*, 315-322.
Mueller, E., & Vandell, D. Infant-infant interaction. In J. D. Osofsky (Ed.), *Handbook of infant development.* New York: Wiley-Interscience, 1979.
Parke, R. D. Perspectives on father-infant interaction. In J. D. Osofsky (Ed.), *Handbook of infant development.* New York: Wiley-Interscience, 1979.
Ross, H. S. The establishment of social games among toddlers. *Developmental Psychology*, 1982, *18*, 509-518.
Sherman, S. J. *Social interchanges in children: Formation, stability, and contextual constraint.* Unpublished doctoral dissertation. University of North Carolina at Chapel Hill, 1975.

Vandell, D. L. Boy toddlers' social interaction with mothers, fathers, and peers. (Doctoral dissertation, Boston University, 1977). *Dissertation Abstracts International*, 1977, *37*, 6309B-6310B. (University Microfilms No. 77-11, 428)

Vandell, D. L. Effects of a playgroup experience on mother-son and father-son interaction. *Developmental Psychology*, 1979, *15*, 379-385.

Vandell, D. L., Wilson, K. S., & Buchanan, N. R. Peer interaction in the first year of life: An examination of its structure, content and sensitivity to toys. *Child Development*, 1980, *51*, 481-488.

Vandell, D. L., Wilson, K. S., & Whalen, W. T. Birth order and social experience differences in infant-peer interaction. *Developmental Psychology*, 1981, *17*, 438-445.

Chapter 9

Social Relations Among Children: Comparison of Sibling and Peer Interaction

Debra Pepler, Carl Corter, and Rona Abramovitch

Of all the relationships in which young children are involved, perhaps the least understood is that between siblings. Until recently, the mother and child were the focus of most studies of social development. Over the past decade there has been an increasing interest in the role of peers (e.g., Ross & Goldman, 1976) and a growing awareness that the child's early social development should be viewed in terms of broader social contexts (Bronfenbrenner, 1979). Although family relations in general are seen as primary in the socialization process, research has been restricted to competencies that develop in the parent-child relationship and their extension to and supplementation by peer relations; very little attention has been paid to the role played by siblings in the development of social skills.

The child's social world is clearly an interwoven network of relations (Bronfenbrenner, 1979); however, it may be described in terms of several social systems. Among these are the child-parent system, the child-sibling system, and the child-peer system. Each system may be characterized by a unique style of interaction, although there is bound to be overlap and interrelationships among them. For example, Whiting and Whiting (1975) found that the interactions between children and their parents comprised intimacy, dependence, nurturance, and caretaking, and interactions among peers comprised prosocial and agonistic behaviors. Sibling interaction was a blend of the behaviors comprising the adult and peer systems: it was characterized by nurturance and caretaking as well as by prosocial and agonistic behaviors. In this chapter, we examine the special nature of sibling interaction and the role played by sibling interaction in the development of social skills. Three main questions will be explored: First, what is the nature of sibling interaction in the preschool years? Second, what are the similarities and differences between sibling and peer interactions? Finally, what influence does sibling interaction have on subsequent peer interactions?

Sibling Interaction

Although there is a good deal of speculation about the role of sibling interaction in birth order effects on intellectual and personality characteristics (Sutton-Smith & Rosenberg, 1970), there has been little examination of the nature of sibling interaction and its relation to the development of social skills in both older and younger siblings. This is an important area of inquiry since sibling interaction may differ from parent-child or peer interaction in its socializing function. It seems likely that siblings play unique roles in each other's lives. They are in the same household, are involved in continual interactions with each other and with the same set of parents, and typically share space, toys, clothes, and other material objects as well as the love and attention of their parents.

In examining sibling interaction we will discuss the extent, frequency, and qualitative aspects of sibling interaction and focus on the more specific factors that may contribute to the patterning of interactions, such as the different ages of the children, the sex of the individual children, the sex composition of the dyad, and the age interval between siblings. Our discussion will refer to our own longitudinal home observations (Abramovitch, Corter, & Lando, 1979; Abramovitch, Corter, & Pepler, 1980; Pepler, Abramovitch, & Corter, 1981), the home observations of Dunn and Kendrick (1979, 1981), and the laboratory observations by Lamb (1978a, 1978b). Our sample comprised same- and mixed-sex dyads in which the children were separated by either a small age interval (1-2 years) or a large age interval (2½-4 years). Our first set of observations was conducted when the younger sibling was 1½ years old and the second set of observations was conducted when the younger child was 3 years of age; the older siblings' ages ranged from 2½ to 4½ and 4 to 7 years for the first and second observations, respectively. Dunn and Kendrick observed 14-month-old children and their older siblings, who ranged in age from 32 to 57 months. Lamb conducted two laboratory studies. In the first he observed 18-month-old children and their older siblings, who ranged in age from 38 to 70 months. The second was a short-term longitudinal study starting with 12-month-old children and their 30- to 58-month-old siblings who were observed again 6 months later.

Nature of Sibling Interaction

The siblings in our studies interacted a great deal in both sets of our home observations. The mean number of initiations per dyad over the 2 hours of observations was 83.3 in the initial observations and 99.8 in the follow-up observations. The mean number of responses per dyad was 41.9 and 64.1 for the initial and follow-up observations, respectively. This high level of interaction was similar across the various types of dyads: sex of the individual child, sex composition, and age interval had little effect on the rate of interaction. In addition, there were many behaviors that occurred relatively frequently but were not recorded (e.g., looking at, vocalizing, responding to imitation, or simply playing together). Thus the extent of interaction was even greater than we have reported. It is likely, therefore, that sibling interaction may have a particularly salient role in social development during the preschool years since children spend a large part of their time in the company of their siblings and, as our observations indicate, interact frequently when they are together.

As a result of the time siblings spend together and the frequency of their interactions, they are likely to become very intimate and familiar (Bossard & Boll, 1960) and to develop empathy and communication patterns with each other (Circirelli, 1976). Although there has been no systematic study of the affective nature of sibling interaction, Dunn and Kendrick (1979) reported that in 16 of the 20 families they observed there were interactions which reflected altruism and empathy between siblings of a very young age. Older children frequently demonstrated concern for their younger siblings. These incidents of empathy included such acts as helping the younger sibling when he or she was frustrated and offering objects when the younger child was distressed. In contrast to hypothetical measures of empathy in a laboratory situation, in which empathy is seldom demonstrated prior to age 3, Dunn and Kendrick observed a few examples of empathy by children as young as 14 months of age, in which the children showed concern over the distress of others and some degree of understanding for the wishes of others. This early emergence of empathy in sibling interaction could reflect the high degree of intimacy and familiarity between siblings.

The wide range of social experiences, both positive and negative, that characterize sibling interaction may also contribute to the development of social skills. Dunn and Kendrick (1979) reported that interactions between the siblings were marked by a strong affective component ranging from warm and affectionate to hostile. Similarly, our home observations of siblings revealed many instances of prosocial behavior, such as helping, cooperation, and affection, but there was also a variety of agonistic behaviors, including object struggles, verbal insults, and physical aggression. In contrast to psychoanalytic and popularized accounts of sibling interaction, portraying it as being primarily rivalrous (Levy, 1937; White, 1975), we observed a high proportion of positive social exchanges between siblings. In the initial observations, 44% of all behavior initiated was prosocial, whereas 29% was agonistic and 27% was imitative. Similarly, in the follow-up observations, 61% of the behavior was prosocial, 25% agonistic, and 13% imitative. These proportions were not markedly different for large- and small-interval dyads or for same- versus mixed-sex dyads. The ratio of prosocial to agonistic behaviors in the initial study was 3:2 and in the follow-up study it was 2:1, suggesting that sibling interaction is generally more positive than agonistic. On the other hand, whereas some laboratory studies of sibling interaction indicate very low levels of agonism (Lamb, 1978a, 1978b), our data indicate that the siblings did engage in a considerable amount of aggressive behavior; nevertheless, the sibling interaction clearly was not based predominantly on rivalry.

Birth Order

The different ages of siblings is one salient factor influencing sibling interaction. In both phases of our research, there were marked differences between the older and younger children's behavior that were consistent across all groups. Older siblings initiated more prosocial behavior: 65% and 58% of all prosocial behaviors in the initial and follow-up studies, respectively. The older siblings engaged in significantly more cooperation, help, comfort, and praise, whereas younger children approached their older siblings more frequently. Younger siblings also responded positively to prosocial behavior more frequently than their older siblings, except in the case of same-sex siblings in the initial observations, in which responses to prosocial behavior were equivalent for older and younger siblings.

There was also an age difference in agonism: older siblings initiated 79% and 71% of all agonistic behavior in the initial and follow-up studies, respectively. Whereas the younger children initiated very little agonism in the initial observations, they became more equal partners in the follow-up observations. There were no age differences in physical agonism or object struggles in the follow-up phases, and the greater overall agonism of the older children was primarily due to their greater verbal agonism. On the few occasions that the younger siblings initiated aggression, their older brothers and sisters often retaliated, whereas younger siblings were more likely to submit to agonism.

The pattern of age differences was reversed for imitation. The majority of imitation was exhibited by the younger children; they imitated an average of 17 times in the initial observations. The older children, however, also engaged in a considerable amount of imitation, averaging 6 imitations in the initial observations. This high level of imitation is consistent with Dunn and Kendrick's (1979) observations. They suggested that it indicates the rapport and mutual interest between siblings and the salience of the older sibling as a model for the younger. Lamb (1978a, 1978b) also noted a high frequency of imitation in the laboratory and suggested that the older sibling may play an important role in the infant's "mastery of the object environment."

The pattern of differences in the older and younger siblings' behavior indicates that their roles are more distinct than they might be in peer interaction. As expected, older siblings assume a leadership role in initiating and directing the interaction, which is most likely a function of their larger repertoire of social skills. The younger siblings, however, may have an important role in maintaining the interaction by reciprocating positively to prosocial behavior, submitting to aggressive behavior, or imitating their older siblings.

Sex of the Individual

The sex of the individual children was an important factor in the patterning of sibling interaction in the initial phase of the study; however, in the follow-up phase, the sex of the children had little effect. In the first observations of both same- and mixed-sex pairs, older sisters initiated more prosocial behavior than older brothers. In addition, older boys in same-sex pairs initiated significantly more physical aggression than older girls in same-sex pairs. In mixed-sex dyads, there were no sex differences on any measure of aggression and in both phases there were no effects of sex on imitation. In the follow-up observations no sex differences were found. The lack of an effect of sex was also found by Dunn and Kendrick (1981) in their home observations.

Sex Composition of the Dyad

Sibling interaction may also be affected by the sex composition of the dyad. Dunn and Kendrick (1979) reported that same-sex sibling pairs in their sample had a higher proportion of positive interactions than mixed-sex pairs, whereas mixed-sex pairs had a higher proportion of negative interactions than same-sex siblings. In contrast, we found few effects of the sex composition of the dyad. The frequencies of prosocial and agonistic behaviors in same- versus mixed-sex dyads were very similar in both phases of our research. Although the same- and mixed-sex dyads did not differ in the frequency of imitation during the initial observations, they did differ in the follow-up observations. Same-sex siblings, both older and younger, imitated more frequently than mixed-sex siblings. This difference may be related to the importance of same-sex models in the sex-role identification process. Both older and younger children in same-sex dyads may perceive their siblings as more similar to themselves or the activities and toys of their siblings as more appropriate for themselves than do mixed-sex sibling dyads. Therefore, same-sex siblings may be more inclined to engage in imitation than mixed-sex siblings who, at 3-7 years of age, may be starting to perceive their siblings as different.

Age Interval

Age spacing or interval, unlike age, had almost no effect on the patterning of interactions. Despite the many theories and advice about the importance of spacing siblings in particular ways (e.g., White, 1975), both our work and that of Dunn and Kendrick (1981) found no appreciable effect of differences in spacing. The lack of an interval effect should be considered tentatively, however; Dunn and Kendrick did not have clearly differentiated intervals and our largest age spacing was 4 years. In addition, in our studies age and interval were confounded: that is, the oldest children were always in the large-interval groups. In the future, researchers should examine similar age intervals with different aged children and larger intervals in order to assess the effects of interval more precisely.

Summary

This description of the nature of sibling interaction serves as a framework for considering the potentially unique features of sibling relations in later sections. Siblings direct a great deal of behavior to one another when they are together. They exhibit a wide range of behaviors from very positive to considerably hostile, and, contrary to psychoanalytic accounts, sibling interaction is generally more positive than rivalrous. The roles of the older and younger siblings seem to be clearly differentiated, with the older siblings assuming leadership in initiating more prosocial and agonistic behaviors. The younger siblings, however, may have an important role in maintaining the interaction by responding positively to prosocial behaviors or submitting to aggressive ones. Finally, interaction between preschool- or early school-age siblings does not appear to be affected to any great extent by the sex of the individual child, sex composition of the dyad, or age interval between the two children. There is little doubt, however, that siblings provide a wide variety of social experiences for each other and play a significant role in each other's social lives. In order to examine the potentially unique experiences that sibling interaction may provide, the similarities and differences between sibling and peer interaction will be considered in more detail in the next section.

Sibling Versus Peer Interaction

Familiarity

During the preschool years siblings are likely to spend considerably more time in each other's company than with peers. Consequently, siblings are likely to be more intimate and familiar, and develop a much stronger rapport and understanding of the other as compared to peers. The high degree of familiarity within the sibling relationship, in addition to promoting earlier expressions of altruism, as discussed above, may also affect other qualitative aspects of interaction such as sociability or complexity of play. Research comparing familiar and unfamiliar 3-year-old peers indicates that interaction with a familiar peer is more frequent and is characterized by social overtures and a higher cognitive level of play (Doyle, Connolly, & Rivest, 1980). With somewhat younger children, more proximity, imitation, and positive interaction have been found with a familiar playmate than with an unfamiliar playmate (Lewis, Young, Brooks, & Michalson, 1975). Lewis et al. (1975) suggested that the common play experiences of familiar peers gradually lead to similar response repertoires, which may, in turn, facilitate higher levels of social interaction. They also suggested that the common play experiences and shared response repertoires may contribute to perceptions of similarity and thus to the development of friendship.

If familiarity and its attendant processes relate to more sociable and complex interactions between peers who have been together at least twice a week (Lewis et al., 1975) or in the same day care class (Doyle et al., 1980), we might expect a greater effect of familiarity on interaction between siblings who are together many hours each day. To date, no observational data are available comparing interaction with a sibling and with a peer, although Vandell and Wilson (Chapter 8, this volume) conducted such observations in a laboratory setting. Dunn and Kendrick compared the nature of play they observed between the siblings and that reported in other studies of peer interaction. Some studies of early social interaction between peers indicated that play appears to revolve around objects (e.g., Mueller & Lucas, 1975), although other research indicated that objects are much less important in sustaining early peer interaction (Eckerman & Whatley, 1977; Vandell & Wilson, Chapter 8, this volume). Objects were also found to be less important in sustaining positive social interactions between siblings (Dunn & Kendrick, 1979); many more positive interaction sequences occurred in the absence of objects than with objects. In addition, sibling interactions were found to be quite complex: Dunn and Kendrick observed several interactions between 14-month-olds and their older siblings in which each child did different, but complementary acts. Simple complementary interactions have also been observed between 12- and 18-month-old peers (Ross & Goldman, 1976). This type of interaction was described by Mueller and Lucas (1975) as the third and most advanced stage of social contact between toddlers. It appears, therefore, that the extensive contact, intimacy, and familiarity between siblings may promote a high level or early acquisition of complex and successful, sustained social interactions. In this respect, sibling interaction may provide an important opportunity for social learning.

The sibling system may differ from the peer system on the dimension of equality of roles of the interactants. Since siblings are ordinarily of different ages, the sibling system is likely to be less egalitarian than the peer system, in which the children are most often of the same age or at least of comparable levels of competence (Lewis & Rosenblum, 1975).

In contrast to the peer system, the behaviors of the partners in the sibling system are likely to be more differentiated. The older sibling may have the opportunity to be assertive and assume a leadership role in initiating and directing sibling interaction, whereas these functions are generally shared by peers. As discussed earlier, observations of siblings do indicate marked birth-order differences: older siblings are more likely to initiate both prosocial and agonistic behaviors, whereas younger children's responses may serve to maintain the interaction.

Age Composition of the Dyad

A comparison between siblings and peers on the basis of age composition of the dyads is limited, since research on peers has emphasized interaction between agemates; however, a few recent studies compared same-age with mixed-age peer interaction. Given that siblings are generally of different ages, interaction between siblings is likely to be similar to interaction between mixed-age peers. Despite the limited research base, there has been considerable speculation about the socializing function of mixed-age interactions. Konner (1975), for example, suggested that multiage groups protect younger chidren and provide them with broader social experiences. In mixed-age groupings older children may have the opportunity to develop leadership skills and cooperative behavior. Mixed-age interactions may also have potential in rehabilitating social isolates (Furman, Rahe, & Hartup, 1979; Suomi & Harlow, 1972) and in peer tutoring (Graziano, French, Brownell, & Hartup, 1976).

Naturalistic observations of same- and mixed-age interactions among children in six different cultures (Whiting & Whiting, 1975) indicated that with age-mates children were likely to be more verbally and physically aggressive and more sociable than with much younger children. Interestingly, laboratory studies do not indicate higher levels of aggression or social interaction with same-age as compared to mixed-age peers. Although more social behavior between same-age versus mixed-age peers was reported (Langlois, Gottfried, Barnes, & Hendricks, 1978), the only differences were in nonverbal vocalizations and playing with a truck, which do not appear to be clear socially oriented activities. Differences in the frequency of vocalizations between same- and mixed-age peers were also reported (Graziano et al., 1976; Langlois et al., 1978; Lougee, Grueneich, & Hartup, 1977); however, the results were inconsistent and may be related more closely to the ages of the partners than to the age composition of the dyad. There are clear differences, however, in the roles of the partners in mixed-age peer dyads. Older children are more likely to take a leadership role by initiating, eliciting, and maintaining activity (Furman et al., 1979; Graziano et al., 1976), whereas younger children are more likely to imitate their older partners (Lewis et al., 1975).

To some extent a comparison of sibling interaction with same- and mixed-age peer interaction will be speculative since there are no data on same-age sibling interactions. Rough comparisons are still possible, however. First, in contrast to Whiting and Whiting's (1975) naturalistic observations of lower levels of prosocial and aggressive interaction among mixed-age groupings, our naturalistic research of sibling interaction and that of Dunn and Kendrick (1979) indicate relatively high rates of both prosocial and agonistic behaviors. The frequency of interaction between siblings brings into question the generality of Hartup's (1980) contention that same-age peer groupings might be more beneficial in promoting social skills because of greater positive reinforcement. Furthermore, in one study positive reinforcement among peer dyads did not differ between pairs consisting of a social isolate and an age-mate and those of a social isolate and a younger peer (Furman et al., 1979). Hartup (1980) also suggested that aggression in mixed-age situations would lead to mutual withdrawal rather than continued social interaction, especially in the case of the younger partner. Although our initial observations might be interpreted in this way, the younger siblings in our follow-up observations were equally likely to counterattack and submit to agonism: the means were 5.6 and 5.5, respectively. These data suggest that sibling interaction may provide a unique opportunity for engaging in both prosocial and agonistic interactions within a mixed-age context.

A second point of comparison based on age composition is the object-oriented nature of play. As indicated above, laboratory studies have found that there is more object-directed activity between same-age than mixed-age peers (Langlois et al., 1978; Lewis et al., 1975). A similar finding was suggested by Dunn and Kendrick (1979); their observations of siblings indicated that objects were less important in social interaction between siblings than has been reported by some studies of age-mates. Rather than indicating less sociability in mixed-age interaction, as Langlois et al. (1978) inferred, the lack of object orientation may reflect more socially directed and complex interactions between mixed-age siblings. As mentioned above, however, there is some doubt in the peer literature as to the role of objects in play. The sibling research tends to support the notion that objects may be less important in sustaining early interaction.

Finally, observations of the differential experiences of older and younger siblings coincide with those of peer interactions. Older siblings have been found to initiate a large proportion of the interactions (Abramovitch et al., 1979, 1980; Dunn & Kendrick, 1979; Pepler et al., 1981). Thus, as in mixed-age peer interactions, the older partner takes a leadership role. In both home (Abramovitch et al., 1979) and laboratory studies (Lamb, 1978a, 1978b), younger siblings have been found to imitate their older siblings a great deal. This is consistent with the higher incidence of imitation in interactions with older peers as compared to age-mates (Lewis et al., 1975). The mixed-age context of sibling interaction may provide the opportunity for younger children to acquire object mastery (Lamb, 1978a) and social skills by modeling their older siblings.

In summary, sibling interaction is similar to mixed-age peer interaction as it provides opportunities for older children to direct social activity and for younger children to imitate more competent partners. On the other hand, sibling interaction may be unique in that it provides the opportunity for both prosocial and agonistic interactions in a mixed-age context and may provide the younger child, at least, with the opportunity to engage in more complex social exchanges than are possible with age-mates.

Sex of the Individual

In addition to age composition, the sex of the individual child may be an important factor affecting the nature of sibling or peer interaction. Data on sex differences in peer interaction (e.g., Maccoby & Jacklin, 1974) indicate that boys are often more aggressive and girls more cooperative and nurturant. Similar patterns have been found in some sibling studies. For example, Circirelli (1976) found that older sisters were better "teachers" for their younger siblings in laboratory problem-solving tasks; they were more likely to give help and be accepted as teachers than older brothers. Older sisters were also found to be more prosocial in our initial observations, whereas boys in same-sex pairs were more physically aggressive than girls in same-sex pairs. This pattern was not evident, however, in our follow-up observations or those of Dunn and Kendrick (1981), in which there were no sex differences. Therefore, although there is some evidence of similarity in the behavior patterns of boys and girls when sibling and peer interactions are compared, sex differences in sibling interactions are not as consistent and may depend, to some extent, on the sex composition of the dyad.

Sex Composition of the Dyad

Sex composition has been found to affect the nature of peer interaction. Observing the interaction of previously unacquainted 33-month-old children, Jacklin and Maccoby (1978) found that more social behavior was directed to same-sex playmates than to mixed-sex playmates. Similarly, previously acquainted 5-year-olds showed more social behavior in same-sex rather than mixed-sex dyads (Langlois, Gottfried, & Seay, 1973).

Dunn and Kendrick (1979) reported differences in sibling interaction that are consistent with the sex composition differences found in peer interaction: same-sex pairs had a higher percentage of positive interactions and a lower percentage of negative interactions than mixed-sex pairs. Imitation was also more frequent in same-sex dyads. Dunn and Kendrick suggested that these differences may be due to perceptions of similarity and consequently greater interest in social interaction in same-sex dyads. They also tested the notion that same-sex pairs have more common activities, but the type of play did not reflect such a difference. Differences were found, however, in the frequencies of activities: same-sex siblings engaged in significantly more joint physical play and gross motor activities than mixed-sex siblings.

Other data on the effects of sex composition on sibling interaction are somewhat inconsistent with the patterns for peer interaction. In his laboratory studies, Lamb (1978a, 1978b) found no effect of sex composition on sibling interaction. Our home observations yielded similar findings: in both the initial and follow-up studies there were no differences in the amount of prosocial or agonistic behavior between same- and mixed-sex dyads. The only main effect of sex composition was in the frequency of imitation in the follow-up study: the older and younger children in same-sex dyads imitated more frequently than their counterparts in mixed-sex dyads. Another effect was suggested by longitudinal changes: for mixed-sex dyads the frequency of aggression increased and the frequency of imitation decreased, whereas the frequencies for same-sex dyads were relatively stable over time. These changes for mixed-sex dyads may reflect their fewer common interests, which become more salient as the children get older. On the whole, although there were some differences, sex composition had relatively little effect in our data.

The discrepancies between our naturalistic data and Dunn and Kendrick's data with respect to sex composition may be partially attributable to differences in the samples. Their subjects were from British working-class families and the younger siblings were 14 months of age. Our studies were conducted with Canadian middle-class families in which the younger children were 20 and 36 months of age.

Our results and Lamb's (1978a, 1978b) laboratory studies suggest that findings from studies of same- versus mixed-sex peer interaction do not extend easily to sibling interaction. One explanation for the differences between sibling and peer interactions may be that the familiarity between siblings creates perceptions of similarity which, in turn, may contribute to a higher level of social interaction. In their comparison of interactions with friends versus stranger peers, Lewis et al. (1975) suggested that with increasing familiarity and common play experiences, children may learn similar response repertoires which, in turn, facilitate social interaction. Since our observations of siblings in their homes indicate that they interact frequently, it is likely that they would develop similar response repertoires and hence perceptions of similarity that might contribute to higher levels of interactions, even between mixed-sex siblings. Perceptions of similarity are also suggested as contributing to the greater sociability found with same-sex peers (Jacklin & Maccoby, 1978). The familiarity and potential perceptions of similarity developed between siblings in day-to-day interactions may outweigh the effects of sex composition found in peer interaction. In fact, when we asked mixed-sex siblings, "How are you different from your brother/sister?" in a wide-ranging interview 1 year after the second home observations, only 5% mentioned sex as a point of difference!

Summary

In summary, comparisons of sibling and peer interactions reveal both similarities and differences. The distribution of roles according to age composition is similar: older children tend to imitate and direct the interactions and younger children tend to initiate in both sibling and mixed-age peer interactions. Other comparisons, however, indicate differences in the qualitative nature of sibling versus mixed-age peer interactions. There is also less consistency between sibling and peer relations on the factors of sex and sex composition. The differences between sibling and peer relations may, in part, account for the inconsistent patterns. Unlike peer friends, siblings have not chosen each other as partners; they have an intimate relationship by virtue of their status. The sibling relationship is also different in that it is constantly affected by parents and others. Therefore, the differences in peer interaction according to age and sex composition may not be evident in sibling interaction because of the familiarity and special nature of the relationship as well as the influence of others on the development of the sibling bond. The differences between sibling and peer interactions reinforce the suggestion that sibling interaction during the preschool years may provide unique social opportunities and experiences.

Influence of Sibling Interaction on Peer Interaction

In the previous sections we have attempted to document how sibling interaction constitutes a major and unique source of social experience during the preschool years. For younger siblings interactions with brothers and sisters usually precede interactions outside the family and thus may serve as a bridge between the family and peer systems. If, in fact, sibling interaction contributes to the development of social skills, one might expect that children with siblings would be more socially competent with peers than only children. In addition, given that the roles of older and younger children from two-child families seem to be clearly differentiated in sibling interaction, one might also expect birth-order differences in their subsequent social interactions with peers. Two issues are examined in this section: whether children with siblings are more socially competent than only children, and whether the patterns of interaction of first and later born siblings transfer to peer interactions.

Effects on Social Competence

As an extension of our naturalistic observations of sibling interaction, we were interested in examining the effects of sibling experience on peer interaction. We observed 40 3- and 4-year-old children during free-play sessions in four day care centers in a Toronto suburb; 20 children with older siblings were matched with 20 only children from the same centers. Between 8 and 12 children were observed at each center and each child was observed for 2-3 hours per week for 12 weeks. The observer used a behavior checklist to record a variety of prosocial, agonistic, and play behaviors that were similar to the behaviors we observed in the home. Each time a behavior on the checklist occurred, the behavior, the initiator, and the recipient were recorded.

In general, there were very few differences in the interaction patterns of children with siblings and only children. There were no differences in the frequencies of prosocial and agonistic behaviors and no differences in their play behaviors (i.e., whether they engaged in solitary, parallel, or cooperative play). The only differences were in the types of behaviors directed to siblings and nonsiblings. Significantly more agonistic behaviors were directed to only children and there was a slight indication of more prosocial behavior being directed to children with siblings. It is difficult to understand why there were no observable differences between the behaviors of siblings and only children, although there were differences in the behaviors directed to them. Since we did not collect data on the quality of prosocial and agonistic behavior, we may have missed the behaviors that characterize effective social interaction, for example, initiation skills, positive reinforcement, and communication skills. Therefore, based on these data we can only make the tentative suggestion that children who have had experience with siblings may have developed more effective social responses than those without siblings to account for the differences in the behaviors directed at siblings and only children. On the whole, however, this study provides no clear evidence of an advantage in peer interactions in favor of children who have had 3-4 years of experience interacting with older siblings at home compared to children who have had no experience interacting with siblings.

The evidence on the benefits of sibling interaction from other observational research is inconsistent. There are a few naturalistic studies of children in a preschool setting indicating that children with siblings are different than only children in their interactions with peers.

Blurton Jones (1972) reported tendencies for only children to exhibit less aggressive behavior and more rough-and-tumble play, whereas 3-year-old children with siblings were more likely to engage in more nonverbal social behavior. DiBona (cited by Vandell & Mueller, 1980) also found that children with older siblings were more likely to engage in more aggressive behavior and more behaviors overall than children without siblings. Finally, Kelly (cited by Vandell & Mueller, 1980) observed that children with older siblings initiated more peer interactions than only children. These preschool observations suggest that experience with siblings may contribute both to the development of prosocial behavior and to the socialization of aggression.

In contrast to the preschool observations, there are several laboratory studies with unfamiliar peers that demonstrate no differences between children with siblings and only children. Observations of children 10-36 months old revealed no differences between children with siblings and only children in the frequencies of initiating peer interactions, peer-directed behaviors, or playing games with peers (Bronson, 1975; Eckerman, Whatley, & Kutz, 1975; Goldman & Ross, 1978; Lewis et al., 1975; Lieberman, 1977).

In summary, there is no clear verdict on whether having a sibling facilitates peer relationships. While our observations of children in a preschool setting revealed few differences, other naturalistic studies did find that children with siblings displayed more social behavior than only children. In contrast, laboratory studies of interaction with an unfamiliar peer consistently indicate no effects of having a sibling. In considering these discrepancies, it seems obvious to suggest that an advantage of having siblings, if there is one, emerges with familiar peers in a familiar setting. Future research ought to examine this possibility, paying special attention to birth-order effects.

Transfer of Sibling Interaction Patterns to Peer Interaction

The second issue, of whether certain features of sibling interaction transfer to peer interaction, has been examined both indirectly and directly. Koch (1957) asked children about the characteristics of their playmates and found that, in general, children preferred playmates of the same age and sex as themselves, but the choices of playmates of different ages and sex reflected characteristics of the sibling. In other words, older siblings were more likely to say they preferred younger playmates and younger siblings were more likely to choose older playmates. In addition, siblings from mixed-sex dyads were more likely to say that they preferred opposite-sex playmates.

Sutton-Smith (1966) postulated a relationship between sibling and peer interactions by examining the different roles within the sibling system. He asked school-age children questions regarding their roles in play with siblings as compared to friends. First-born children reported that they took high-power roles when playing with siblings, but relatively low-power roles with friends. Sutton-Smith suggested that first-borns' friendship play behavior reflects their position within the parent-child system. In contrast, later born children reported a low-power role with the sibling, but a high-power role with friends. According to Sutton-Smith, this suggests that later born children model the powerful role taken by their older siblings and transfer these dominating tactics to the peer situation, in which they can successfully assert themselves. These findings suggest that for younger siblings, at least, there is a relationship between the social experiences in sibling interaction and peer interaction. There is both supporting and conflicting evidence for this viewpoint.

Recent observational research supports the suggestion that first-borns may take a less dominant role and be more accommodating with peers. Snow (Note 1) observed 33-month-old children interacting with a same-sex peer and reported that first-born children were more sociable with the peer than later born children. Although the higher sociability of the first-born may be accounted for by a variety of factors (e.g., more opportunity for social interaction with parents), these findings, in conjunction with those of Sutton-Smith, suggest that birth order may relate to social interaction with peers and that first-born children may be more socially responsive. These patterns must be considered tentative, however, since other research relating birth order to peer interaction suggests opposite patterns in the roles taken by older and younger siblings when playing with peers (e.g., Miller & Maruyama, 1976; see below).

Comparative research suggests that later born offspring have the advantage in social interaction. Suomi and Harlow (1975) reported that third-born monkeys show more rapid and complete social development than second-borns, who, in turn, are superior to first-borns. They attributed this advantage to the availability of older siblings as additional social partners for later born offspring.

Miller and Maruyama (1976) found a similar advantage in favor of later born children in an examination of the relationship between birth order and popularity. Later born children were rated by peers as more popular than middle or first-born children. Later born children were also rated by teachers as being more sociable and friendly and less demanding and jealous than earlier born children. These authors suggested that the different roles within the sibling system may shape different social skills according to birth order. Whereas older siblings learn to be assertive and dominant during sibling interaction, younger siblings must develop social skills such as "powers of negotiation, accommodation, tolerance, and a capacity to accept less favorable outcomes" (p. 123). Miller and Maruyama explained the birth-order differences by suggesting that older children may transfer their behavior patterns from sibling to peer interactions and attempt to be dominant and arbitrary with peers, leading to their less popular ratings. In contrast, younger siblings may be more prosocial and accommodating with peers, who, in turn, rate them more positively. It should be noted that the studies cited above were not based on observations of naturalistic sibling interaction but relied on questionnaires (Koch, 1957; Sutton-Smith, 1966), ratings of peer interactions (Miller & Maruyama, 1976), or laboratory observations (Suomi & Harlow, 1975; Snow, Note 1), which may account for the inconsistencies in the results.

Summary

The above differences suggest that features of sibling interaction do, in fact, transfer to peer interaction; however, the effect of birth order on sociability with peers is unclear. Some research suggests that first-borns are more accommodating and sociable with peers, and other research suggests that first-borns are dominant, arbitrary, and less socially mature than later borns, who have presumably learned to be more socially responsive through sibling interaction. Unfortunately, as noted above, observational studies of peer interaction comparing children with siblings to those without siblings have not demonstrated birth-order effects and have presented an inconsistent picture of the relations between sibling and peer interactions.

Conclusions

The speculation about differences in peer interaction between first and later born children illustrates some of the potential complexities in relating the peer and sibling systems. On the one hand, there are arguments suggesting a fairly direct transfer from the style of sibling interaction to the style of peer interaction. Thus the bossy first-born should be the bossy playmate. On the other hand, there are arguments suggesting a compensatory relation between the sibling and peer systems. Thus the trod-upon later born becomes the assertive playmate. As noted earlier, the data concerning these arguments are equivocal and, in fact, it is not too difficult to imagine that the transfer could in some cases be direct and in other cases involve the kind of compensation described above. Taking things further, it is possible that transfer can also work in the other direction—from peer experience to sibling interaction, although we have argued that early in life the generally more extensive nature of sibling experience is likely to lead to more transfer from sibling to peer systems.

Further complexities in the relation between sibling and peer experience are suggested by examinations of the relation between the mother-child system and the peer system (Hartup, 1979). One possibility is that skills learned by the infant's interaction with the mother transfer directly to peer interaction. On the other hand, the quality of the relationship may facilitate or impede peer experience and attendant learning of social skills. Thus the securely attached child has a more secure base from which to explore his or her social world. It may be stretching the concept of attachment quality to suggest that the affective quality of sibling relations influences peer interaction very directly. However, the point is that there may be more to the relations between systems than the transfer of social skills. For example, the later born child could make use of compromise skills learned in interacting with a more powerful older sibling but not need them in a playground showdown with a classmate because the older sibling is looming nearby ready to protect the younger sibling.

In conclusion, the available data do not yet allow us to understand the relations among social systems with any certainty. More than additional data is needed. Research which is designed to examine the social ecology of the child is needed to answer firmly the types of questions posed in this chapter; examining one of the systems and then speculating about the possible relation with other systems is not enough.

Acknowledgments

We would like to thank Rosemary Bell, Fiona Jeffrey, Sheila McClarty, Susan Ranson, Sandra Reiman, Susan Ruscher, Jane Summers, and Gail Waytowych for their help in carrying out the project examining the effects of sibling experience on peer interaction in the preschool.

Reference Notes

1. Snow, M. E. *Birth order differences in young children's interactions with mother, father and peer.* Paper presented at the biennial meeting of the Society for Research in Child Development, Boston, April 1981.

References

Abramovitch, R., Corter, C., & Lando, B. Sibling interaction in the home. *Child Development*, 1979, *50*, 997-1003.

Abramovitch, R., Corter, C., & Pepler, D. Observations of mixed-sex sibling dyads. *Child Development*, 1980, *51*, 1268-1271.

Blurton Jones, N. Categories of child-child interaction. In N. Blurton Jones (Ed.), *Ethological studies of child behaviour.* Cambridge: Cambridge University Press, 1972.

Bossard, J. H. S., & Boll, E. *The sociology of child development.* New York: Harper & Row, 1960.

Bronfenbrenner, U. *The ecology of human development.* Cambridge, Mass.: Harvard University Press, 1979.

Bronson, W. C. Developments in behavior with age mates during the second year of life. In M. Lewis & L. A. Rosenblum (Eds.), *Friendship and peer relations.* New York: Wiley, 1975.

Cicirelli, V. G. Siblings teaching siblings. In V. L. Allen (Ed.), *Children as teachers*. New York: Academic Press, 1976.

Doyle, A. B., Connolly, J., & Rivest, L. P. The effect of playmate familiarity on the social interactions of young children. *Child Development*, 1980, *51*, 217-223.

Dunn, J., & Kendrick, C. Interaction between young siblings in the context of family relationships. In M. Lewis & L. Rosenblum (Eds.), *The social network of the developing infant*. New York: Plenum Press, 1979.

Dunn, J., & Kendrick, C. Social behavior of young siblings in the family context: Differences between same sex and different sex dyads. *Child Development*, 1981, *52*, 1265-1273.

Eckerman, C. O., Whatley, J. L., & Kutz, S. L. Growth of social play with peers during the second year of life. *Developmental Psychology*, 1975, *11*, 42-49.

Eckerman, C., & Whatley, J. Toys and social interaction between infant peers. *Child Development*, 1977, *48*, 1645-1656.

Furman, W., Rahe, D. F., & Hartup, W. W. Rehabilitation of socially withdrawn preschool children through mixed-age and same-age socialization. *Child Development*, 1979, *50*, 915-922.

Goldman, B. D., & Ross, H. S. Social skills in action: An analysis of early peer games. In J. A. Glick & K. A. Clarke-Stewart (Eds.), *Studies in social and cognitive development* (Vol. 1). New York: Gardner Press, 1978.

Graziano, W., French, D., Brownell, C. A., & Hartup, W. W. Peer interaction in same- and mixed-sex triads in relation to chronological age and incentive condition. *Child Development*, 1976, *47*, 707-714.

Hartup, W. W. Two social worlds of childhood. *American Psychologist*, 1979, *34*, 944-950.

Hartup, W. W. Two social worlds: Family relations and peer relations. In M. Rutter (Ed.), *Scientific foundations of developmental psychiatry*. London: Heinemann, 1980.

Jacklin, C. N., & Maccoby, E. E. Social behavior at thirty-three months in same-sex and mixed-sex dyads. *Child Development*, 1978, *49*, 557-569.

Koch, H. L. The relation in young children between characteristics of their playmates and certain attributes of their siblings. *Child Development*, 1957, *28*, 175-202.

Konner, M. Relations among infants and juveniles in comparative perspective. In M. Lewis & L. A. Rosenblum (Eds.), *Friendship and peer relations*. New York: Wiley, 1975.

Lamb, M. Interactions between 18-month-olds and their preschool-aged siblings. *Child Development*, 1978, *49*, 51-59. (a)

Lamb, M. The development of sibling relationships in infancy: A short-term longitudinal study. *Child Development*, 1978, *49*, 1189-1196. (b)

Langlois, J. H., Gottfried, N. W., Barnes, B. M., & Hendricks, D. E. The effect of peer age on the social behavior of preschool children. *The Journal of Genetic Psychology*, 1978, *132*, 11-19.

Langlois, J. H., Gottfried, N. W., & Seay, B. The influence of sex of peer on the social behavior of preschool children. *Developmental Psychology*, 1973, *8*, 93-98.

Levy, D. M. Sibling rivalry. *American Orthopsychiatric Association, Research Monograph No. 2*, 1937.

Lewis, M., & Rosenblum, L. A. Introduction. In M. Lewis & L. A. Rosenblum (Eds.), *Friendship and peer relations*. New York: Wiley, 1975.

Lewis, M., Young, G., Brooks, J., & Michalson, L. The beginning of friendship. In M. Lewis & L. A. Rosenblum (Eds.), *Friendship and peer relations.* New York: Wiley, 1975.

Lieberman, A. F. Preschoolers' competence with a peer: Relations with attachment and peer experience. *Child Development*, 1977, *48*, 1277-1287.

Lougee, M. D., Grueneich, R., & Hartup, W. W. Social interaction in same- and mixed-age dyads of preschool children. *Child Development*, 1977, *48*, 1353-1361.

Maccoby, E., & Jacklin, C. *The psychology of sex differences.* Stanford, Calif.: Stanford University Press, 1974.

Miller, N., & Maruyama, G. Ordinal position and peer popularity. *Journal of Personality and Social Psychology*, 1976, *33*, 123-131.

Mueller, E., & Lucas, T. A developmental analysis of peer interaction among toddlers. In M. Lewis & L. A. Rosenblum (Eds.), *Friendship and peer relations.* New York: Wiley, 1975.

Pepler, D. J., Abramovitch, R., & Corter, C. Sibling interaction in the home: A longitudinal study. *Child Development*, 1981, *52*, 1344-1347.

Ross, H. S., & Goldman, B. D. Establishing new social relations in infancy. In T. Alloway, L. Krames, & P. Pliner (Eds.), *Advances in communication and affect* (Vol. 4). New York: Plenum Press, 1976.

Suomi, S. J., & Harlow, H. F. Social rehabilitation of isolate-reared monkeys. *Developmental Psychology*, 1972, *6*, 487-496.

Suomi, S. J., & Harlow, H. F. The role and reason of peer relationships in rhesus monkeys. In M. Lewis & L. A. Rosenblum (Eds.), *Friendship and peer relations.* New York: Wiley, 1975.

Sutton-Smith, B. Role replication and reversal in play. *Merrill-Palmer Quarterly*, 1966, *12*, 285-298.

Sutton-Smith, B., & Rosenberg, B. *The sibling.* New York: Holt, Rinehart & Winston, 1970.

Vandell, D. L., & Mueller, E. C. Peer play and friendships during the first two years. In H. C. Foot, A. J. Chapman, & J. R. Smith (Eds.), *Friendship and social relations in children.* Chichester, England: Wiley, 1980.

White, B. Critical influences in the origins of competence. *Merrill-Palmer Quarterly*, 1975, *21*, 243-266.

Whiting, B. B., & Whiting, J. W. M. *Children of six cultures.* Cambridge, Mass.: Harvard University Press, 1975.

Chapter 10

Friends, Acquaintances, and Strangers: The Influence of Familiarity and Ethnolinguistic Background on Social Interaction

Anna-Beth Doyle

"Because The Hooded Fang is childish," cried Jacob Two-Two twice. "He's one of us."

"Oh, I never! I most certainly am not!" shouted The Hooded Fang, peeking at them between his fingers.

"The proof is," cried Jacob Two-Two, "The proof is, whenever he struts across the prison yard, grunting and growling, *he is careful not to step on cracks.*"

"I'm not childish," protested The Hooded Fang.

"Empty his pockets," said Jacob Two-Two.

"No, please! Not that!"

But, even as he protested, The Hooded Fang was seized by the intrepid Shapiro and the fearless O'Toole. One of The Hooded Fang's pockets yielded a handful of jelly beans and the other, a ball of string, eight rubber bands, three pieces of beach glass, five pebbles, a fountain pen top, and three packages of bubblegum . . .

"You see," said Jacob Two-Two, "You see" . . . The Hooded Fang burst into tears. "I want my mommy," he wailed.

Everybody laughed. Jacob Two-Two hugged The Hooded Fang. (Richler, 1975, pp. 84-85)

The above quote illustrates an important aspect of children's friendships. Children, like adults, are attracted to those they perceive as similar (Berscheid & Walster, 1978). Moreover, the similarity may apply not only to stable visible features such as skin color, sex, and age, but also to such idiosyncratic behavior as avoiding cracks. Children with similar behavioral repertoires may be attracted to each other, become friends, and seek each other out for further interaction.

In this chapter, it is suggested that the degree to which preschool children perceive a peer as similar strongly influences their social experiences, that is, their choice of playmates and the quantity and quality of their social interaction with these playmates. Since interaction with peers may contribute to the child's social development

(Lieberman, 1977; Mueller & Brenner, 1977), it is important to understand the factors affecting it. At this point, there are few data concerning the effects of perceived similarity to use in generating hypotheses about its influence. In the present chapter two studies are described in which perceived similarity is presumed to be important. They concern (a) patterns of interaction between acquainted and unacquainted children, and (b) the influence of similarity in ethnolinguistic background on friendship choices and patterns of social interaction.

Studies of Social Interaction in Acquainted vs. Unacquainted Peers

The importance of prior acquaintance with playmates is apparent in studies of early social interactions. Mueller (1972) and Garvey and Hogan (1973) each videotaped dyads of preschool children at play in similar settings. In Mueller's study the children were unacquainted; in Garvey and Hogan's investigation the children were classmates. In the latter study, where the children were acquainted, they spoke twice as often as the unacquainted children did in the former study. Focusing directly on the effect of peer acquaintance, Schwarz (1972) videotaped 4-year-olds in a novel environment with a friend, with a stranger, or alone. Children were happier, more mobile, and more talkative with friends than with strangers or when alone. Schwarz interprets his findings in terms of Berlyne's (1967) arousal-reinforcement theory, suggesting that in an unfamiliar context the child is aroused to a nonoptimal level for interaction or exploration. The presence of a familiar peer is thought to reduce the child's distress (arousal) to a more optimal level.

Of course, even young friendships are characterized by more than just acquaintance. Young friends typically live near one another, are similar in sex, social class, and preferred activities, and share an emotional bond (Bigelow & LaGaipa, 1980; Hartup, 1975; Furman & Bierman, Note 1). At the most basic level, however, friends are familiar and the differences in behavior between friends and strangers may be due to that familiarity. Schwarz's findings, for example, were replicated with 2-year-old children whose acquainted partners were not close friends (Ispa, Note 2). Subsequently, Gottman and Parkhurst (1980) studied the verbal interactions of children 2-10 years old with friends and with strangers. They found that preschool-age friend dyads engaged in more connected discourse and more fantasy play of an extended nature than strangers did. Preschool friends were also more responsive to each other than strangers were; that is, they were more compliant and responsive to questions.

In studies in which play with friends and with nonfriend acquaintances is compared the results are remarkably consistent. Friend and nonfriend acquaintances may also differ in degree of familiarity. Phinney and Rotherham (Note 3) examined preschoolers' play initiations in a naturalistic classroom setting. Initiations to friends were more successful than initiations to acquaintances, and this successfulness was particularly pronounced for nonverbal joining in, physical aggression, and invitations to play. In a particularly creative study, Howes (Note 4) contrasted pairs of children who were friends over the course of her study with pairs between whom friendship was unstable (i.e., short-lived or nonexistent). In a longitudinal investigation of classes of infants, toddlers, and preschoolers, she defined friendship primarily in terms of frequency of successful social overtures. Play in maintained or stable friend pairs was at all ages longer in duration, more complex, more positive, and more vocal. Unstable friend dyads were intermediate between maintained and nonfriend dyads on most of these measures. These behaviors also increased over time in the maintained friends but not in the other groups. It is noteworthy that play with friends was not only more frequent but also more complex. Additional evidence comes from Rubenstein and Howes (1976), who observed 8-month-old infants at play with a familiar peer or alone with their mothers. Object play was more complex in the presence of the peer.

Howes' study (Note 4) is one of the few that contrasts the behaviors of friends and nonfriends developmentally. However, the results of studies of children both younger and older than the preschool age are remarkably consistent. Lewis, Young, Brooks, and Michaelson (1975) observed that proximity, imitation, and positive interaction over toys were greater in acquainted compared with unacquainted 1-year-olds. Lewis et al. suggested that with growing familiarity children learn similar response repertoires. Since behaviors similar to the child's own are positively evaluated, the infants are attracted to each other and engage in further interaction. Foot, Chapman, and Smith (1977) also found 7- and 8-year-old friends to be more socially responsive to each other than to strangers. Foot et al. paired children either with strangers or with friends (as defined by mutual sociometric choice) and showed them cartoons. Friends laughed, smiled, looked, and talked more than strangers did. Foot et al. suggested that interaction behaviors by one peer lead to increased arousal in the other because of increased intimacy. If the initiating child is a friend, these arousal changes are positively labeled and the behaviors are reciprocated. If the initiating child is a stranger, the arousal is negatively labeled and the behaviors are not reciprocated. This model seems to require the child to know norms of intimacy; while this is reasonable for 7- and 8-year olds, it may not be fully applicable to preschool children. These results may also be restricted to pleasant, noncompetitive situations. When children were given task-oriented or competitive instructions, friends of this age talked and shared less and were generally less responsive than nonfriends were (Berndt, 1981; Gottman & Parkhurst, 1980; Sharabany & Hertz-Lazarowitz, 1981). It may be that for older friends friendly behavior can be subordinated to the task demands.

On the assumption that many of these differences in interaction between friends and nonfriends were due to the degree of familiarity between the children, my colleagues and I made some specific predictions about the behavior of children who primarily differed in familiarity (Doyle, Connolly, & Rivest, 1980). On the basis of the similarity-attraction hypothesis, familiarity was expected to decrease inactive, unoccupied behaviors and increase positive affect. Moreover, an increase was also predicted in the frequency of social play relative to nonsocial play, and in the frequency of specific behaviors designed to maintain social interaction. Finally, on the basis of arousal theory (Berlyne, 1967), the presence of a familiar peer was expected to promote more complex object play.

Description of the Study of Acquainted and Unacquainted Children

The study involved 16 3½-year-old children who were observed twice each in pairs in a laboratory playroom. On one occasion the peer was a familiar classmate from the preschool class, and on the other the child was an unfamiliar peer from a different preschool, with order of sessions counterbalanced. The children were brought to the playroom by undergraduate assistants and had paid a preliminary familiarization visit to the playroom prior to the first session. The large playroom was equipped with a variety of toys and equipment, such as riding cars, dolls, trucks, dress-up clothes, and paints. A female assistant acted as supervisor in the playroom. She responded to the children's requests and needs warmly but otherwise took a nondirective role.

Both children in a dyad served as subjects and were concurrently observed for 1 hour from behind a one-way mirror, each by a different observer. Social participation, complexity of object play, and affective tone were recorded during two 10-minute periods in the middle of the session. Discrete socially directed behaviors were recorded during two 15-minute periods at the beginning and end of the sessions.

Since we were interested in whether play with familiar peers was more mature or sophisticated than with unfamiliar peers, we examined measures previously found to distinguish competent from less competent children. Competence of play, however, is a difficult concept to operationalize (Anderson & Messick, 1974). We included traditional measures of both the maturity of social participation (Parten, 1932) and the cognitive complexity of play (Smilansky, 1968), adapting from Rubin, Maoni, and Hornung (1976) a coding system combining both measures. In addition, in an attempt to elucidate the manner in which global changes in play were achieved, changes in specific social behaviors were examined. In 1976, when we began this study, there were few data on discrete social behaviors indicative of competence. The Social Behavior Checklist (White & Watts, 1973) was adapted.

Level of social participation, cognitive play, and affective tone. The level of social participation was assessed during 30-second time samples. Categories included unoccupied behavior, onlooker behavior, solitary play, parallel play, associative play, and cooperative play. The cognitive complexity of the child's object play was simultaneously assessed with the categories oral, functional, constructive, creative, and dramatic play. Finally, the affective tone of the child's behavior was described as positive, negative, or neutral. More detailed descriptions of the categories are available in Doyle, Connolly, and Rivest (1980).

Discrete socially directed behaviors. The Social Behavior Checklist (White & Watts, 1973) was used to record 19 behavioral events directed to peers. These included attention seeking, question asking, leading, following, and the expression of affection and hostility. Most categories were further scored as successful or unsuccessful and as positive or negative. The behaviors were noted each time they occurred and were summed across the two 15-minute periods.

In addition to category scores, two summary scores were computed: the total number of peer-directed behaviors, and a peer-interaction quality-effectiveness score (PIQES) derived from Wright (1980). The PIQES was the sum of four variables: gains-attention-peer-successful, uses-peer-as-resource-successful, leads-peer-positive-successful, and shows-affection-to-peer.[1] Wright found these variables were most indicative of social competence in preschoolers; they loaded heavily on a peer-inter-action factor, increased with preschool experience, and related more than other peer-directed behaviors to standardized measures of pre-school competence, such as the Circus tests and the Preschool Inventory.

Methodological Issues: Observer Reliability and the Problem of Dyadic Dependencies

Four undergraduates, blind to the hypotheses of the study, and the authors served as observers. For assessment of interrater agreement, two observers, one undergraduate and one author, simultaneously but independently coded each child's behavior. Observer reliability based on the percentage of agreement averaged 75% for the social participation categories, 65% for the cognitive play categories, and 80% for

---

[1] In prepublication work available at the time of this study, Wright included shows affection to peer in the PI,Q-ES. However, because correlations with competence were only significant at assessment time 2, it was later dropped.

the affective tone categories. For the discrete social behaviors, observer reliability averaged .78 for the 19 categories. (Pearson r was used because the data for each category were frequencies per 15 minute sample.) Preliminary analyses indicated no systematic tendency for the sophisticated observers (authors) to be biased differentially in the two conditions. Therefore, the two observers' scores were averaged.

In this study each child was observed twice, each time with a different partner who also served as a subject. As in any study of dyads, the statistical dependency between subject and partner was an issue. Other studies have handled this problem by including data from only one member of the dyad (Lieberman, 1977), by averaging across individuals and analyzing dyad scores (Eckerman, Whatley, & Kutz, 1975), or by computing the intraclass correlation coefficient to show nonsignificant associations within dyads across subjects (Garvey & Bendebba, 1974). The situation was more complex in our study since repeated observations were made of each subject, each time with a different partner. Thus there were two kinds of correlations between measures: first, correlations owing to each child serving in both conditions, and second, correlations owing to the children being observed simultaneously. In order to take these into account, children were grouped prior to observation in same-sex sets of four children each, with two children in a set selected at random from each of the two participating preschools. In each session a child's partner was a peer from the child's set of four. For statistical analyses a reduced degrees-of-freedom model was used which made no assumptions about the variance structure within each set of children; that is, the error terms for these analyses were based on the variance between sets rather than the variance between subjects. In addition to handling the interdependencies, this model is also robust with respect to potential heterogeneity of variance across conditions. (Dr. Louis-Paul Rivest derived this model and conducted the analyses.)

Results

Social participation, cognitive level of play, and affective tone. Low frequencies among the nested social-cognitive play categories and statistical dependencies among the categories of each type of play precluded a factorial analysis. Social and cognitive play categories were therefore first analyzed separately and then several summary scores were computed.

The social participation categories were strongly affected by playmate familiarity, as shown in Table 10-1. The nonsocial activities of onlooker and solitary play occurred more frequently in the unfamiliar than in the familiar condition; social interaction (associative and cooperative play) occurred more frequently in the familiar condition. To summarize these data the proportion of peer intervals which in-

Table 10-1. Mean Social and Cognitive Play Scores for Acquainted Versus Unacquainted Peers

Category	Acquainted	Unacquainted	Test statistics[a]		
Social play					
Unoccupied	.01[b]	.02	z (8)	=	.91
Onlooker	.05	.14	F (1, 2) =		26.72*
Solitary	.26	.49	F (1, 2) =		22.84*
Parallel	.15	.14	F (1, 2) =		.07
Associative	.43	.21	F (1, 2) =		121.95**
Cooperative	.10	.01	z (10)	=	2.34**
Cognitive level of play					
Oral	.07	.13	F (1, 2) =		1.61
Functional	.45	.53	F (1, 2) =		.51
Constructive	.31	.29	F (1, 2) =		.02
Creative	.02	.02	z (11)	=	.42
Dramatic	.14	.02	z (13)	=	2.44**

[a] Wilcoxan tests (z) were used where low frequencies precluded parametric techniques.
[b] Values represent proportions of scorable intervals.
*$p < .05$.
**$p < .01$.

volved social orientation (parallel, associative, or cooperative play) was computed. Parallel play was included in the category of social play on an a priori basis because social orientation was inherent in its definition although it did not differentiate the conditions. Social orientation was significantly higher in the familiar ($M = .68$) than in the unfamiliar ($M = .36$) condition, F (1, 2) = 172.31, $p < .01$. The interaction of sex and condition was also significant, F (1, 2) = 19.27, $p < .05$. Post hoc Scheffé tests revealed that the increase in social play in the familiar condition was greater for girls ($M = .76$ and .34 for familiar and unfamiliar conditions, respectively) than for boys ($M = .59$ and .36).

In contrast to social participation, the cognitive level of play initially appeared less affected by the familiarity of the playmate. Only dramatic play changed significantly; it occurred almost exclusively with a familiar peer. We suspected that familiarity might only affect the cognitive level of play when the two children interact socially. Therefore, following the rationale of Rubin, Maioni, and Hornung (1976), we computed complexity scores separately for social and for nonsocial play. Each score was the proportion of object play that was high in cognitive level (constructive, creative, or dramatic). When two children were in socially oriented play, their play was more complex if the peer was familiar rather than unfamiliar, $M = .50$ and .29, respectively, F (1, 2) = 17.26, $p < .05$. When children were not in socially oriented play, the familiar and unfamiliar conditions did not differ significantly, M = .34 and .32, F (1, 2) = .38, not significant. Peer familiarity affected cognitive level of object play but only in the context of social interaction. Affective tone of interaction did not differ for familiar and unfamiliar peers. However, regardless of the familiarity of the playmate, girls showed more friendly affect than boys M = .23 and .06, respectively, F (1, 2) = 40.56, $p <$ .025.

Discrete socially directed behaviors. To assess the effect of peer familiarity on the frequency of specific behaviors, each of the 19 peer behaviors of the Social Behavior Checklist was examined. As shown in Table 10-2, 4 of these events differed significantly across conditions and 3 events were of borderline significance; 6 of these 7 events were more frequent in the familiar than in the unfamiliar condition. As predicted, these events were predominantly those which could be categorized as positive and/or successful.

To summarize these results, both the total number of peer-directed behaviors and the proportion that was positive and successful were examined. Children showed more social behaviors with a familiar than with an unfamiliar peer, M = 73.8 and 47.8, respectively, F (1, 2) = 24.55, $p <$ .05. These results reinforce the social play findings stated previously. In fact, the total peer-directed scores correlated positively with the proportion of play that was social, r (14) = .64, $p <$ .01, and r (14) = .31, not significant, for familiar and unfamiliar conditions, respectively.

The PIQES was used to summarize those behaviors that were positive and successful. Included in this score were three behaviors which significantly differentiated the conditions: gains-attention-peer-successful, leads-peer-positive-successful, and shows-affection-to-peer. Uses-peer-as-resource-successful was also included. The proportion of total behaviors that were positive and effective was greater with familiar than with unfamiliar peers, M = .36 and .26, respectively, F (1, 2) = 82.25, $p <$ .025. Thus familiarity not only increased social participation but also positive and effective behaviors.

In an attempt to ascertain the relation of these behaviors to the global categories previously discussed, the correlations of the PIQES proportion with the social participation, cognitive level, and affect categories were examined. The correlations were generally nonsignificant. With the active social play categories, however, these coefficients were uniformly positive, ranging from r (14) = .09 to r (14) = .44, not significant.

Table 10-2. Mean Behavioral Event Frequency for Acquainted Versus Unacquainted Peers

Event	Acquainted	Unacquainted	Test statistics
Seeks-attention-peer-successful	5.7	2.5	$F(1, 2) = 13.41*$
Seeks-attention-peer-unsuccessful	1.6	1.6	$F(1, 2) = 0.00$
Uses-peer-resource-instrumental-successful	2.9	1.5	$F(1, 2) = 6.50$
Uses-peer-resource-instrumental-unsuccessful	.4	1.1	$z(11) = .62$
Leads-peer-activities-positive-successful	11.2	3.6	$F(1, 2) = 82.66***$
Leads-peer-activities-positive-unsuccessful	4.1	2.1	$F(1, 2) = 24.20**$
Leads-peer-activities-negative-successful	.7	1.4	$z(13) = 1.47$
Leads-peer-activities-negative-unsuccessful	1.0	.5	$z(11) = .84$
Serves-as-model	7.6	4.5	$F(1, 2) = 1.38$
Follow-peer's-lead-verbal	7.6	3.4	$F(1, 2) = 193.60***$
Follows-peer's-lead-nonverbal	7.2	9.2	$F(1, 2) = 1.16$
Refuses-to-follow-peer	5.5	2.7	$F(1, 2) = 10.22*$
Imitates-peer	7.1	3.9	$F(1, 2) = 1.90$
Shows-affection-to-peer	8.3	5.1	$F(1, 2) = 10.21*$
Shows-hostility-to-peer	1.6	2.5	$F(1, 2) = 1.51$
Competes-for-adult-attention-successful	.0	.5	$z(6) = 2.20$
Competes-for-adult-attention-unsuccessful	.0	.2	$z(4) = 1.83$
Competes-for-equipment-successful	.7	.7	$z(9) = .36$
Competes-for-equipment-unsuccessful	.5	1.1	$z(11) = .40$
Total peer-directed behaviors	73.8	47.8	$F(1, 2) = 24.55**$
PIQES ratio	.36	.26	$F(1, 2) = 82.25**$

*$.05 < p < .10$.
**$p < .05$.
***$p < .01$.

Discussion

The results of this study show that peer familiarity is a salient variable in children's play. The presence of a familiar peer increased the frequency of social overtures, the amount of social interaction, and the complexity of toy play during this social interaction.

Given the magnitude of these effects, it is surprising that peer familiarity has been so neglected in studies of the development of social skills (Allen & Masling, 1957; McGrew, 1972; Mueller & Brenner, 1977; Mueller & Lucas, 1975; Schwarz, Krolick, & Strickland, 1973). Since familiarity with peers often covaries with age or social experience, some results that have been attributed to other factors, such as cognitive maturation or social skill learning, may in fact be attributable to peer familiarity. Its significance as a mediating variables deserves further investigation.

These results permit some speculation about the process by which the presence of a familiar playmate affects the quality of social interaction. With a familiar peer, there was a significant increase in those play categories involving active verbal and/or physical exchange between children, that is, in associative and cooperative play. There were also increases in discrete peer-directed social bids, particularly in the positive and successful behaviors of seeking attention, asking questions, leading, and showing affection. We suggest that these social bids mediate the increases in observed associative and cooperative play. While appealing, such a conclusion cannot be unambiguously supported by the present study; limitations on observational capacity existed and therefore specific peer-directed behaviors and social participation were not simultaneously assessed.

Passive watching and solitary play were also lower in the presence of a familiar peer. This shift from noninvolvement to active participation might be mediated by arousal change, as postulated by Schwarz (1972). However, changes in arousal cannot easily account for the fact that familiarity affected only social participation and not the overall frequency of play with toys, or the cognitive level of nonsocial object play, or the affective tone of the children (although collecting the tone measures in the middle of the session may have failed to capture early differences in affect). An interpretation in terms of Lewis et al.'s (1975) similar repertoire analysis is more consistent with the data. Prior to the playroom sessions, the familiar peers had experienced daily exposure to each other in the day care center. We assume that this exposure fostered interaction and the learning of common play repertoires. These shared behavioral repertoires were mutually understood and served to highlight the similarity of the playmates to each other. Therefore, the familiar children were attracted to each other in the play session and their attempts to interact were likely to be reciprocated (Leiter, 1977), in part because the attraction was mutual. In theories of interpersonal attraction it has been suggested that this attraction is based on reduced uncertainty (Zajonc, 1968), social validation of the self (Festinger, 1954), or anticipation of rewarding interaction (Bersheid & Walster, 1978; Byrne, 1969). Arousal level may also be involved; that is, interactions with similar peers may for any or all of the above reasons establish optimal levels of arousal (Berlyne, 1967).

In contrast to the striking effect of familiarity on social interaction, the effects on cognitive level of play initially seemed minimal. Only dramatic play occurred more frequently with a familiar peer. However, further analyses revealed that the effect on cognitive level of play was tied intrinsically to peer involvement. When two children interacted, familiar peers were more likely to exploit the unique properties of objects and less likely to engage in manipulation than were unfamiliar peers. There was no comparable effect of familiarity when children were not interacting. The process by which such an effect might result is unknown. Rubenstein and Howes (1976) suggest that the peer models for the target child new functional possibilities with toys. When in the presence of a familiar peer, the child is, because of similarity and attraction, more likely to imitate that peer's object play. Thus the child is more likely to learn new ways of exploiting the unique properties of the object. In the present study, some very tentative support for this hypothesis may be found. The mean frequency of imitation was higher in the familiar than in the unfamiliar condition, but the difference did not approach significance (Table 10-2).

In summary, in play with a familiar peer, the child performs in a more socially active, competent, and cognitively mature fashion. These effects are possibly elicited and mediated by the previous learning of positive and successful social behaviors in the context of mutually shared and mutually understood interaction sequences; that is, prior interaction leads to common behavioral repertoires, which then increase perceived similarity. This perceived similarity in behavioral capacity is hypothesized to increase interpersonal attraction and subsequent mature, positive interaction.

After completing this study, we wondered whether other forms of similarity, that is, ethnicity and language, might affect social interaction patterns in similar ways. It seemed reasonable that even unfamiliar peers who speak the same language would be treated as similar in comparison to peers who speak a different language.

Friends and Acquaintances: The Influence of Ethnolinguistic Status on Social Behaviors

In this section, we assess the possibility that perceived similarity in ethnicity and language influences children's patterns of interactions and also their initial choice of play partners. Children as young as 4 years old choose predominantly same-sex playmates (Serbin, Tonick, & Sternglanz, 1977). In the same vein, behavioral preference for peers of the same race has been found as early as the preschool years (Lambert & Taguchi, 1956; McCandless & Hoyt, 1961). In a recent study (Doyle, Rappard, & Connolly, 1980) we examined the role of ethnolinguistic background. Interactions between children who were of different language backgrounds (French vs. English) were compared to those between children of the same language background. Children were observed at free play in their nursery classrooms, rather than in dyads as in the previous study. We were able, therefore, not only to determine the quality of the children's interactions but also their choice of play partner.

Our premise in this study was that in any bilingual community, whether a classroom or a country, effective social functioning requires communication with members of the other linguistic group. Simard and Taylor (1973) pointed out that cross-cultural social interaction among adults in Montreal is at best minimal, with 99.9% of social interactions of French and English Canadians confined to their own language group. Taylor and Simard (1975) summarized evidence that one or both groups are sufficiently fluent to communicate cross-culturally but are not motivated to do so. Classes containing children from diverse language backgrounds are often the norm in Canada and in the United States, where many children do not speak English at home (Chandler, 1980). Linguistically segregated patterns of interaction in these classes may have negative consequences ranging from restricted opportunities to acquire competence in the school language, to polarized attitudes toward and lack of cooperation between cultural groups. It seemed imperative to assess whether such segregation exists in early childhood and to identify the controlling factors.

Primary school Montreal children have been found to segregate themselves by language groups. MacNamara, Svarc, and Horner (1976) assessed friendships of English-speaking and French-speaking children attending French- and English-language schools. Pupils of both language backgrounds who attended French-language schools chose friends primarily from their own ethnic group. This tendency was particularly strong for the English-speaking children. Segregation was not found in children attending English-language schools.

Additional evidence of early sensitivity to ethnic differences comes from studies of children differing in race. Ethnic identification and attitudinal preference appear to develop by 3-5 years of age, but behavioral evidence of these preferences (sociometric or observational) is not usually found before 9 or 10 years of age (Brand, Ruiz, & Padilla, 1974). However, two studies of preschool classes reported behavioral preferences. McCandless and Hoyt (1961) found that white and oriental Hawaiian children, all native speakers of English, interacted significantly less often across than within ethnic groups. Lambert and Taguchi (1956) also found that oriental children in Montreal made more within-group friendship choices than expected, but that the same was not true for their white classmates. In this case, however, the white children came from varied ethnolinguistic backgrounds.

These studies suggest that there may be a significant degree of segregation along racial lines at the preschool level. However, the degree of racial segregation at this age does not appear great; other factors such as gender appear more salient. For example, in the McCandless and Hoyt (1961) study described above, play occurred between racial groups at about 90% of the expected rate, whereas play with the opposite sex occurred only 58% as often as expected. Therefore, we questioned whether ethnolinguistic status is a salient factor in the play patterns and friendship choices of preschool children. It is possible that even less segregation might exist between groups of young children distinguished on the basis of an auditory feature such as language than on the basis of a visual feature such as race. On the other hand, ability to communicate verbally may be a very salient factor in the play choices of young children. To address this issue, we studied preschool children's tendency to interact with and be accepted by children of another ethnolinguistic background.

The Two Solitudes Study: Design and Procedure

The study was conducted over 2 years on two samples. In each sample the frequencies of social interaction and sociometric friendship choices within versus across ethnolinguistic lines were compared. In addition, as in the previous study, qualitative comparisons of the patterns of inter-action (duration, affective tone, use of language, successfulness of influence attempts, and engagement in fantasy play) were made. Finally, the children's tendency to interact with linguistically dissimilar peers was examined in relation to individual differences in fluency in the school language. This analysis permitted an assessment of the possible role of fluency versus motivational factors, such as perceived similarity, as determinants.

In Sample 1, 31 children attending preschool in their second language (French or English) and 16 native-speaker controls participated. For the second-language or bilingual children the majority of their class-mates and teachers were native speakers of the school language. There-fore, the second-language children formed a minority group. There were 13 children from English-language homes attending two French-language day care centers and 18 children from French-language homes attending two English-language day care centers. The majority-language or native-speaker children were selected proportionally from the same centers and equated with the minority group in age, sex, social class, time per week at the center, and nonverbal IQ (WPPSI picture completion subtest in home language). In Sample 2, 31 minority-language children and 31 majority-language controls were selected as in Sample 1.

The degree to which social behavior was segregated along language lines was assessed in two ways: first, by time sampling social interaction during free play, and second, by eliciting sociometric friendship choices. In Sample 1, social interaction was time sampled for each child during two 10-minute periods using a 7-second "observe," 3-second "record" cycle. The observer noted whether the child was engaged in social interaction and whether the interaction was new or continuing. If the interaction was new, the observer noted the identity of the partner, whether the child played an initiatory role, and whether he or she used language.

In Sample 2, each child was observed for 40 1-minute observation intervals. During each interval, the number of seconds the child spent in social interaction with peers was recorded. An observer also noted each occurrence of discrete peer-directed social behaviors using a refinement of the Social Behavior Checklist (White & Watts, 1973) described in the familiarity study (see Table 10-2). Several changes were made on the basis of the frequencies and patterns of correlations obtained in that study in an attempt to eliminate infrequent categories and to improve reliability. The 12 retained categories are shown in Table 10-3. In addition, at the end of each 1-minute interval social interaction was rated for predominant affective tone (positive, neutral, or negative), predominant partner (same or different ethnic background), and use of language. The occurrence of shared pretend or fantasy play was also noted again because of its hypothesized importance in the development of social and cognitive skills (Smilansky, 1968) and friendship (Gottman & Parkhurst, 1980).

From these observations in both samples, the frequency of interaction, the mean duration of interaction, and the proportion of intervals in which language was used were derived separately for partners of same and different ethnic backgrounds. In Sample 1 the proportion of interactions initiated by the child was also calculated. In Sample 2, the proportions of positive and negative intervals, the total frequency of discrete social behaviors, and the proportions that were successful were also computed (Table 10-3).

Friendship choices were measured by a peer-nomination picture sociometric test derived from Marshall and McCandless (1957). Individual photographs of each child in a class (minority, matched majority control, and other majority children) were mounted on a board. Children, tested individually, were asked to name each child pictured, and then were told, "Let's pretend there is a new game at school that only two can play. Show me who you would like to play it with." The chosen picture was removed from the board, and the child was told, "Let's pretend he/she's not here today. Now who would you pick to play the special new game?" In this way, each child selected three preferred playmates. The number of nominations received by each child from his or her own language group and from the other language group were computed.

Table 10-3. Mean Behavioral Event Frequency for Peers of Same and Different Ethnic Background

Measure	Same background	Different background
Seeks-attention-successful	.10[a](.08)[b]	.09 (.11)
Seeks-attention-unsuccessful	.04 (.04)	.07 (.10)
Uses-peer-as-resource-total	.05 (.05)	.03 (.06)
Leads-peer-neutral-successful	.11 (.09)	.12 (.13)
Leads-peer-positive-successful	.10 (.10)	.08 (.09)
Leads-peer-unsuccessful	.07 (.05)	.08 (.08)
Follows-peer's-lead	.31 (.13)	.29 (.17)
Refuses-to-follow-peer	.06 (.05)	.05 (.14)
Shows-affection-to-peer	.14 (.09)	.14 (.12)
Competes-total	.02 (.02)	.02 (.04)
Total social behaviors	61.55 (39.2)	32.15 (35.3)

[a] Proportion of total behaviors.
[b] SD is shown in parentheses.

In addition to measures of social behavior, measures of second-language fluency were utilized. Minority-language children and majority-language controls were assessed in the school language on receptive vocabulary, receptive grammar, and verbal expression. Since equivalent measures were needed in English and French centers, French translations of the tests were employed. Although norms were not available for these translations, there is some evidence of equivalence: raw scores on the French and the English form of the Peabody Picture Vocabulary Test correlated similarly with chronological age (Doyle, Champagne, & Segalowitz, 1977). In addition to these standard measures of fluency, as noted above, we also assessed the child's tendency to use language in play.

Reliability and the Issue of the Relative Size of the Language Groups

Reliability of observation was computed for a random subset of the observation periods as the percentage agreement between two independent observers. For the time-sampled events, the average agreement on 12% of Sample 1 was 89%, and on 7% of Sample 2 it was 84%. For the discrete social behaviors, Sample 2 agreement based on 7% of the observations averaged 78% for occurrence only. For friendship choices, the test-retest reliabilities over a 2-week interval for total nominations received in two separate classes were .77 ($n = 16$) and .71 ($n = 28$).

In both samples, the proportion of minority children in a class varied considerably, from a high of .50 to a low of .18. We thought it possible that because the majority group was larger, children might be more likely just by chance to interact with and be chosen as friends by its members. The operation of such chance factors would appear as an own-group preference for the majority children and an other-group preference for the minority children. Howver, if chance were operating in this way, interaction rate and friendship choices would also vary with the ratio of minority to majority children. The obtained proportion of friendship choices received from the other ethnolinguistic group did vary with the minority/majority ratio in the class; however, the proportion of social interactions with the other group did not. Therefore, the numbers of sociometric in-group and out-group choices received were prorated to compensate for differences in the relative size of the minority and majority groups. These adjustments differ somewhat from those previously described in Doyle, Rappard, and Connolly (1980); therefore, the following results represent a new look at that data with operative chance factors eliminated.

An additional statistical adjustment to the sociometric scores was made. Class sizes varied from 8 to 35. In Sample 1, therefore, we divided each child's score by Willingham's (1959a, 1959b) correction for variations in nominating group size; this statistical correction is based on the size of the nominating group (class size) and also on the computed internal consistency of scores in that group. However, in Sample 2, as recommended by Willingham (1959b), the number of nominations made by each child was proportional to class size, with 3 nominations in classes of 30, and 2 nominations in classes of 20.

Results

Segregation in social interaction and friendship choices. The first hypothesis was that interaction and friendship choices would be less frequent across than within ethnolinguistic groups. With respect to social interaction, in Sample 1 there was significantly more interaction with children of the same ethnolinguistic group, $F (1, 43) = 9.89; p < .01$ (Table 10-4). In fact, two-thirds of interaction time was with children of the same background. Choice of partner, however, also interacted with language status (minority, majority) and language of day care center (English, French), $F (1, 43) = 5.13, p < .05$; that is, only children from English-speaking homes, whether minority or majority language in their centers, were significantly more likely to select partners on the basis of similar ethnolinguistic group. Children from French-speaking homes also showed a slight but nonsignificant preference for similar partners. In Sample 2, the tendency to select on the basis of ethnolinguistic background was also interactive, in this case with language group, $F (1, 58) = 94.49, p < .001$. Preference for children of the same background was confined to the majority children, $M = 26.9$ vs. 2.6. In fact, the minority children significantly preferred children of the majority group, $M = 15.6$ vs. 9.2, $p < .01$. Moreover, two minority and four majority children never played with minority peers, whereas all children played with majority peers. These results were replicated identically in analysis of the total discrete social behaviors, which correlated .97 with the num-

Table 10-4. Differences in Social Behavior with Peers of Similar Versus Different Ethnolinguistic Background

Measure	Similar background	Different background	F score
Interaction frequency			
Sample 1	22.0	11.3	$F(1, 43) = 9.89$**
Sample 2			
Minority	9.2	15.6	$F(1, 58) = 94.49$**
Majority	26.9	2.6	
Friendship nominations			
Sample 1	3.54	1.22	$F(1, 43) = 25.26$**
Sample 2	.17	.06	$F(1, 58) = 25.82$**
Quality of interaction			
Sample 1			
Duration (sec)	32.11	24.94	$F(1, 37)^a = .86$
Initiations	.55	.54	$F(1, 37) = .00$
Use of language	.67	.61	$F(1, 37) = .53$
Sample 2			
Duration (sec)	30.17	27.92	$F(1, 52)^a = 5.35$*
Use of language	.79	.66	$F(1, 52) = 10.12$**
Pretend play	.27	.21	$F(1, 52) = 5.62$*

[a] Degrees of freedom are reduced because cases were eliminated if no interaction occurred with one group.
*$p < .025$.
**$p < .01$.

ber of interaction intervals. It seems clear that at least majority-language children's interactions are based on ethnolinguistic group, but that minority children's may not be.

With respect to sociometric friendship choices, there were also significantly more nominations received in each sample from children of the same ethnolinguistic background, $F(1, 43) = 25.26, p < .001$ and $F(1, 58) = 25.82, p < .001$. As before, over two-thirds of choices were from the child's own group. This was true for both minority and majority children; no interactions were significant.

In summary, in Sample 1 we found a striking degree of segregation between ethnolinguistic groups in the interaction and friendship choices of preschool children. At least two-thirds of interaction time and sociometric friendship choices were within a child's own ethnic group. In Sample 2, this was again true for friendship choices, but for frequency of social interaction it was only true for the majority children.

Patterns of cross-cultural interaction. Since frequency of social interaction and sociometric preference differed with respect to the partner's ethnic similarity, we asked whether the quality of children's interactions might also vary. In Sample 1 the duration of interaction, the initiation rate, and the degree to which language was used did not differ significantly. In Sample 2, a larger set of qualitative features were examined: namely, duration, rate, and successfulness of social behavior; proportions of negative and positive intervals; use of language; and amount of pretend play. Differences were found for partner (similar vs. dissimilar), multivariate F (7, 46) = 3.01, $p < .01$. Univariate analyses indicated that children talked and engaged in pretend play significantly more when interacting with partners from the same ethnolinguistic background. Their play was also of longer duration. Interactions with group and center were not significant (Table 10-4). It appears that in addition to preferring partners from the same ethnolinguistic group, children also differ in the quality of their interactions with the preferred versus nonpreferred playmates.

Communication Difficulty as a Determinant of Segregated Play

It seemed plausible that these segregated patterns of play might be a result of the minority child's lack of fluency in the school language. On the school-language measures minority children scored far below the majority. Conversation and joint fantasy between ethnolinguistic groups may therefore have been less frequent because the minority children were not sufficiently fluent in the school language to carry out these linguistically demanding tasks. Individual differences in the minority children's interaction and popularity with majority peers were compared to their fluency in the school language. In Sample 1 no relationships were significant; r (26) ranged from -.03 to .22. In Sample 2, relationships with standardized language measures were generally positive but accounted for no more than 10% of the variance, r (23) ranged from -.13 to .39. However, the best predictor of cross-cultural interaction was the minority child's tendency to speak the school language when interacting with majority-language children, r (29) = .57, $p < .01$. This strong association was unrelated to standardized measures of fluency in the school language; that is, the correlation remained unchanged when standardized measures were partialed out. It seems that minority children's interactions with members of the opposite language group are a product not of fluency but of some motivational factors which also encourage the child to use the school language in such interactions.

Interpretation of Cross-Cultural Play Patterns

In summary, preschool children showed clear tendencies to prefer children from the same ethnolinguistic background. These data reflect the importance of the relationship between the children's ethnolinguistic statuses; that is, partners from similar ethnic backgrounds were preferred in four of five analyses. Both the minority- and the majority-group children showed this preference in their friendship choices. In observed social interaction, however, this was primarily true of the majority group. Nevertheless, for both groups, interactions with dissimilar children tended to be shorter and less likely to include fantasy play and conversation. In Sample 2, with respect to social interaction, in addition to the similarity between the child and the partner's ethnolinguistic group, the child's status in the class (minority, majority) was also important. Both groups sought speakers of the majority language as partners. The child's ethnolinguistic status in the community (English or French background) was less important. In Sample 1, children from English-speaking homes showed more preference for interaction with similar peers. This finding, however, is based on small samples ($n = 13$ and 10) and was not replicated in Sample 2. To summarize, in comparison with studies of segregation between different races or sexes (Lambert & Taguchi, 1956; McCandless & Hoyt, 1961; Serbin et al., 1977; Singleton & Asher, 1979), it appears that language spoken is a particularly salient ethnic marker.

Play with ethnolinguistically similar children was of longer duration and involved more conversation and fantasy than play with dissimilar children. From these findings it seems that interactions between ethnolinguistic groups in the preschool do not foster cross-cultural friendships. Gottman and Parkhurst (1980) hypothesized that engagement in joint fantasy is one of the necessary factors in the development of preschool friendships. In particular, extended fantasy play, which is of longer duration and involves language (Connolly, 1980), is identified as important. It seems that there may be a cyclical cause-and-effect pattern in operation, where children play less actively with dissimilar partners and thus do not develop common repertoires to the same extent. These peers are therefore not often selected as friends, and, at least for the majority children, as partners for subsequent interactions. Because of the lack of attraction, subsequent encounters are also less intimate.

Our final analysis demonstrated that individual differences in play with peers from another ethnolinguistic background were not strongly related to fluency in the other language. On the contrary, the tendency to play with dissimilar peers was associated with individual differences in the use of the other language irrespective of fluency. It is possible that factors are at work which motivate the minority child both to interact with majority peers and to use the majority language in such interaction. Variations in perceived similarity may be the salient factor. The language spoken in the home has been shown to be an important dimension of perceived similarity for children as young as 6 years (Aboud, 1976). Lambert and Klineberg (1967) postulated that the young child is trained by parents and other socializing agents to notice dissimilarities among social groups, and during such training emotional tone about cultural differences is also transmitted to the child. The possibility that child cognitions and parental attitudes may be important determinants of segregated behavior is a fruitful area for further research.

From the results of this study it appears that lack of cross-cultural interaction exists very early in life and that when interaction does occur it differs from communication within a culture. It is also possible that these qualitative differences may perpetuate the lack of interaction. Moreover, the lack of a strong relation between cross-cultural interaction and fluency in the second language implies that the controlling factors may involve complex motivational as well as cognitive components.

Implications for Future Research and Educational Policy

Both the study of prior acquaintance and the study of ethnolinguistic background demonstrate the effect of perceived similarity of peers on the nature of social interaction. Both familiar and ethnolinguistically similar peers engage in more social interaction, including more discrete peer-directed social behaviors. In addition, peers who are familiar or of the same ethnic background engage in more dramatic or fantasy play. Familiar peers also interact more positively and effectively, whereas ethnically similar peers use language more frequently.

If we accept that different forms of play have different functional significance (Rubin & Pepler, 1980), then such effects merit more investigation. For example, a relationship has been identified between fantasy play and growth in social skills and social cognition (Connolly, 1980; Rubin, 1980). It is possible that the greater frequency of fantasy play by familiar and ethnolinguistically similar peers leads these children to develop more advanced social skills. Moreover, the greater frequency of positive, effective behaviors between familiar peers may indicate additional opportunity for the practice and consolidation of these socially appropriate behaviors. There is some evidence that such prosocial skills transfer to new situations. Goldberg and Maccoby (1965) gave some second-grade children practice on a competitive task with a group of peers of constant membership, and others practice with groups of constantly changing membership. When all children were given the task with new partners, those who had worked with familiar peers did better. It is also possible that the greater frequency of social interaction with familiar peers itself contributes to growth; that is, familiar children may be more likely to teach each other new behaviors acquired outside the play setting. In addition, in the course of their interaction new "shared meanings" are likely to be evolved (Brenner & Mueller, 1982).

It may be more conducive to the growth of social skill, therefore, to provide children with extended contact with familiar peers than to provide equal opportunities for play with a constantly changing peer group. The park or "drop-in" playgroup may not provide optimal peer experiences for the preschool child.

Differences in frequency and style of play with ethnically dissimilar peers do not seem likely to affect the child's overall social growth given a context where similar partners are also available. Such segregated play patterns may, however, restrict opportunities to learn more about the other ethnolinguistic group and to develop experiences and skills in common. To the extent that ethnolinguistically different peers have different play repertoires, segregation in play will maintain or even enhance these differences. These play patterns may thus detract from the development of perceived similarity, interpersonal attraction, and friendship. For the minority-language child the perception of dissimilarity may also result in reduced motivation to learn the school language and, at older ages, to achieve in school settings. For the majority child, for whom differences in play seem more pronounced, they may be the beginnings of prejudice.

We are continuing to investigate the determinants of segregated play patterns. At present we are developing a measure of individual differences in the degree to which ethnolinguistic background is a salient factor in children's social judgment. It is important also to study how these play patterns change over time, and how they can be modified by adult intervention. Teacher reinforcement of cooperative play between boys and girls is temporarily effective in modifying sex-typed play (Serbin et al., 1977). Similar encouragement of cross-cultural interaction would be expected to increase the perceived similarity of the children through increased familiarity and shared experiences. Moreover, fantasy play can be increased by adult intervention (Smilansky, 1968). Given the hypothesized relation between fantasy play and friendship (Gottman & Parkhurst, 1980), the teacher's encouragement of cross-cultural fantasy play might be particularly effective in reducing segregated play patterns.

Acknowledgments

I am indebted to Jeff Brenner, Barbara Alexander Pan, Dorothy Haccoun and, of course, Kenneth Rubin and Hildy Ross, for their helpful comments on preliminary versions of this chapter.

Reference Notes

1. Furman, N., & Bierman, K. *A features model theory of children's conceptions of friendship.* Paper presented at the biennial meeting of the Society for Research in Child Development, Boston, April 1981.
2. Ispa, J. *Familiar and unfamiliar peers as "havens of security" for Soviet nursery children.* Paper presented at the biennial meeting of the Society for Research in Child Development, New Orleans, March 1977.
3. Phinney, J., & Rotherham, M. *The influence of friendship on type and outcome of social overtures in a preschool setting.* Paper presented at the biennial meeting of the Society for Research in Child Development, Boston, April 1981.

4. Howes, C. *Patterns of friendship.* Paper presented at the biennial meeting of the Society for Research in Child Development, Boston, April 1981.

References

Aboud, F. E. Social development aspects of language. *Papers in Linguistics*, 1976, *9*, 15-37.

Allen, G. B., & Masling, J. M. An evaluation of the effects of nursery school training on children in the kindergarten, first, and second grades. *Journal of Educational Research*, 1957, *81*, 285-296.

Anderson, S. & Messick, S. Social competency in young children. *Developmental Psychology*, 1974, *10*, 282-293.

Berlyne, D. E. Arousal and reinforcement. *Nebraska Symposium on Motivation* (Vol. 15). Lincoln, Nebr.: University of Nebraska Press, 1967.

Berndt, T. J. The effects of friendship on prosocial intentions and behavior. *Child Development*, 1981, *52*, 636-643.

Berscheid, E., & Walster, E. H. *Interpersonal attraction.* Reading, Mass.: Addison-Wesley, 1978.

Bigelow, B., & LaGaipa, J. The development of friendship values and choice. In H. C. Foot, A. Chapman, & J. R. Smith (Eds.), *Friendship and social relations in children.* New York: Wiley, 1980.

Brand, E., Ruiz, R., & Padilla, A. Ethnic identification and preference. *Psychological Bulletin*, 1974, *81*, 860-890.

Brenner, J., & Mueller, E. Shared meaning in boy toddler's peer relations. *Child Development*, 1982, *53*, 380-391.

Byrne, D. Attitudes and attraction. In L. Berkowitz (Ed.), *Advances in experimental social psychology* (Vol. 4). New York: Academic Press, 1969.

Chandler, B. J. (Ed.). *Standard education almanac 1980-81.* Chicago: Marquis Academic Media, 1980.

Connolly, J. *The relationship between social pretend play and social competence in preschoolers: Correlational and experimental studies.* Unpublished doctoral dissertation, Concordia University, 1980.

Doyle, A. B., Champagne, M., & Segalowitz, N. Some issues in the assessment of linguistic consequences of early bilingualism. *Working Papers in Bilingualism*, 1977, *14*, 21-30.

Doyle, A. B., Connolly, J., & Rivest, L. P. The effect of playmate familiarity on the social interactions of young children. *Child Development*, 1980, *51*, 217-223.

Doyle, A. B., Rappard, P., & Connolly, J. Two solitudes in the preschool classroom. *Canadian Journal of Behavioral Science*, 1980, *12*, 221-232.

Eckerman, C. O., Whatley, J. L., & Kutz, S. L. Growth of social play with peers during the second year of life. *Developmental Psychology*, 1975, *11*, 42-49.

Festinger, L. A theory of social comparison processes. *Human Relations*, 1954, 7, 117-140.

Foot, H. C., Chapman, A. J., & Smith, J. R. Friendship and social responsiveness in boys and girls. *Journal of Personality and Social Psychology*, 1977, *35*, 401-411.

Garvey, K., & Bendebba, M. Effects of age, sex and partner on children's dyadic speech. *Child Development*, 1974, *45*, 1159-1161.

Garvey, C., & Hogan, R. Social speech and social interaction: Egocentrism revisited. *Child Development*, 1973, *44*, 562-568.

Goldberg, M., & Maccoby, E. Children's acquisition of skill in performing a group task under two conditions of group formation. *Journal of Personality and Social Psychology*, 1965, *2*, 898-902.

Gottman, J., & Parkhurst, J. A developmental theory of friendship. In W. A. Collins (Ed.), *The development of cognition, affect and social relations*. New York: Erlbaum, 1980, pp. 198-253.

Hartup, W. W. The origins of friendship. In M. Lewis & L. A. Rosenblum (Eds.), *Friendship and peer relations*. New York: Wiley, 1975.

Lambert, W. E., & Klineberg, O. *Children's views of foreign peoples: A cross-national study*. New York: Appleton-Century, 1967.

Lambert, W. E., & Taguchi, Y. Ethnic cleavage among young children. *Journal of Abnormal and Social Psychology*, 1956, *53*, 380-382.

Leiter, M. P. A study of reciprocity in preschool play groups. *Child Development*, 1977, *48*, 1288-1295.

Lewis, M., Young, G., Brooks, J., & Michaelson, L. The beginning of friendship. In M. Lewis & L. A. Rosenblum (Eds.), *Friendship and peer relations*. New York: Wiley, 1975.

Lieberman, A. F. Preschoolers' competence with a peer: Influence of attachment and social experience. *Child Development*, 1977, *47*, 1277-1287.

MacNamara, J., Svarc, J., & Horner, S. Attending a primary school of the other language in Montreal. In A. Simeos (Ed.), *The bilingual child*. New York: Academic Press, 1976.

Marshall, H. R., & McCandless, B. R. A study in prediction of social behavior of preschool children. *Child Development*, 1957, *28*, 149-159.

McCandless, B., & Hoyt, J. Sex, ethnicity and play preferences of preschool children. *Journal of Abnormal and Social Psychology*, 1961, *62*, 683-685.

McGrew, W. C. Aspects of social development in nursery school children, with emphasis on introduction to the group. In N. Blurton-Jones (Ed.), *Ethological studies of child behavior*. London: Cambridge University Press, 1972.

Mueller, E. The maintenance of verbal exchanges between young children, *Child Development*, 1972, *43*, 930-938.

Mueller, E., & Brenner, J. The origins of social skills and interaction among play group toddlers. *Child Development*, 1977, *48*, 854-861.

Mueller, M., & Lucas, T. A developmental analysis of peer interaction among toddlers. In M. Lewis & L. A. Rosenblum (Eds.), *Friendship and peer relations*. New York: Wiley, 1975.

Parten, M. Social participation among preschool children. *Journal of Abnormal Psychology*, 1932, *24*, 243-269.

Richler, M. *Jacob Two-Two Meets the Hooded Fang*, New York: Bantam, 1975.

Rubenstein, J., & Howes, C. The effects of peers on toddler interaction with mother and toys. *Child Development*, 1976, *47*, 597-605.

Rubin, K. H. Fantasy play. Its role in the development of social skills and social cognition. In K. H. Rubin (Ed.), *Children's play: New Directions for Child Development*. San Francisco: Jossey-Bass, 1980.

Rubin, K., Maioni, T., & Hornung, M. Free-play behaviors in middle- and lower-class preschoolers: Parten & Piaget revisited. *Child Development*, 1976, *47*, 414-419.

Rubin, K., & Pepler, D. The relationship of child's play to social-cognitive growth and development. In H. Foot, A. Chapman, & J. Smith (Eds.), *Friendship and social relations in children*. New York: Wiley, 1980.

Schwarz, J. C. Effect of peer familiarity on the behavior of preschoolers in novel situations. *Journal of Personality and Social Psychology*, 1972, *24*, 276-284.

Schwarz, J. C., Krolick, G., & Strickland, R. G. The effects of early day care experience on adjustment to a new environment. *American Journal of Orthopsychiatry*, 1973, *43*, 340-346.

Serbin, L. A., Tonick, I. J., & Sternglanz, S. H. Shaping cooperative cross-sex play. *Child Development*, 1977, *48*, 924-929.

Sharabany, R., & Hertz-Lazarowitz, R. Do friends share and communicate more than non-friends. *International Journal of Behavioral Development*, 1981, *4*, 45-59.

Simard, L., & Taylor, D. M. The potential for bicultural communication in dyadic situations. *Canadian Journal of Behavioral Science*, 1973, *5*, 211-225.

Singleton, L. C., & Asher, S. R. Racial integration and children's peer preferences: An investigation of developmental and cohort differences. *Child Development*, 1979, *50*, 936-941.

Smilansky, S. *The effects of sociodramatic play on disadvantaged children.* New York: Wiley, 1968.

Taylor, D. M., & Simard, L. Social interaction in a bilingual setting. *Canadian Psychological Review*, 1975, *16*, 240-254.

White, B. L., & Watts, J. C. *Experience and environment* (Vol. 1). Englewood Cliffs, N.J.: Prentice-Hall, 1973.

Willingham, W. W. Estimating the internal consistency of mutual peer nominations. *Psychological Reports*, 1959, *5*, 163-167. (a)

Willingham, W. W. On the deriving of standard scores for peer nominations with subgroups of unequal size. *Psychological Reports*, 1959, *5*, 397-403. (b)

Wright, M. J. Measuring the social competence of preschool children. *Canadian Journal of Behavioral Science*, 1980, *12*, 17-32.

Zajonc, R. B. Attitudinal effects of mere exposure. *Journal of Personality and Social Psychology Monograph Supplement*, 1968, *9* (2,Pt. 2), 1-27.

Chapter 11

Fairness and Friendship

Thomas J. Berndt

Disputes concerning the fair distribution of rewards or other resources arise frequently in the interactions of children with their peers. Conflicts between preschool children often revolve around favorite toys. For example, if one girl wants to play with a specific doll by herself, other children are likely to object when the girl refuses to share the doll with them. They would probably feel that they all should take turns with the doll, so that each one has an equal amount of time to play with it. Among older children and adolescents, both the sources of conflicts and the decisions about a fair resolution may differ. In a basketball game, one player may claim that another one is "hogging" the ball and taking too many shots. On some occasions, the other players may not agree that equal access to the ball is most fair; instead, they may reply that the child accused of being a ball hog deserves to take more shots because he or she usually gets a basket. In the other players' view, the basketball is allocated fairly when the best players get it most of the time.

These examples suggest that the principles used in judging a particular distribution of resources as fair or unfair may change with age. The preschool children were assumed to favor the principle of equality, which would require that all children get the same amount of time with the doll. The older basketball players were assumed to favor allocations based on merit, which would mean that players with more ability get more time with the ball. In a large number of studies, developmental psychologists have attempted to identify and to explain the changes with age in children's judgments about the fairness of different principles for distributing resources. In addition to investigating children's judgments, these psychologists have examined the distributions that children actually make at different ages. The major themes in the developmental research are reviewed in the first section of this chapter.

Social psychologists have approached the problem of distributive justice from a different perspective. They argue that the principles for a

fair distribution vary in different situations. The variations are attributed to differences in the social roles and relationships of the persons in
each situation. In the previous examples, the preschool children view
each other as separate individuals with equal rights to the desired toy.
In contrast, the basketball players may be members of a team trying to
win a game or practicing plays for a future game. These variations in
social roles and relationships may influence the distribution principle
that is chosen. A number of specific hypotheses about the connections
between social relationships and principles of fairness have been presented in the social-psychological literature. These hypotheses are discussed in the second section of this chapter.

Attempts to integrate the developmental and social-psychological
perspectives on fairness are rare. Integration of the two perspectives
could be especially valuable in illuminating the developmental changes
in children's social world. Developmental changes in children's judgments of fairness and in their actual distributions of rewards could be
related to changes in their social roles and relationships. Conversely,
hypotheses about developments in social relationships could be tested
with adaptations of previous methods for studying fairness principles.
In the third section of this chapter, one example of this research strategy is described. The connections between developments in friendship
and in fairness are examined in detail. Age changes in the principles of
fairness that children apply in interactions with friends are used as
evidence of changes in friendships themselves.

Developmental Research on Distributive Justice

Piaget's Theory of Distributive Justice in Peer Relationshps

The first major theory of the development of distributive justice was
proposed by Piaget (1932/1965) in his early book on moral judgment.
Piaget presented a general theory of moral development; his research on
distributive justice was one of many sources of evidence for the general
theory. Subsequent researchers have devoted less attention to the theory than to Piaget's description of developmental trends for specific
types of moral judgments. Nevertheless, Piaget's interpretation of
these trends can only be understood in terms of the theory.

Structure of adult-child and peer relationships. Piaget's central assumption was that children's orientation toward moral issues mirrors the
structure of their most important social relationships (see Youniss,
1980). He further assumed that the most important relationships for
the young child are those with adults. Adults provide rules for the
child's behavior and demand obedience to the rules. Although children

normally accept adults' rules, the relationship between adults and children is asymmetrical. Piaget defined the relationship as one of unilateral respect: the children's respect for adults is unilateral because it is not based on a full understanding of the reasons for the adults' rules; furthermore, the rules are made by adults for children and never vice versa.

As children grow older and spend more time with peers, they discover a different model for social relationships. In a group of peers, no child can claim the authority to make rules for the other children. Any rules made by the group must be a product of mutual agreement. Agreement can only be achieved, according to Piaget, when children discuss their opinions with each other in a spirit of cooperation. In the company of peers, children experience a true exchange of ideas and start to understand the reasons for other children's opinions. Relationships between peers are characterized by reciprocity: each child expects to have an equal part in making all decisions and each grants the same rights to other children. Piaget defined this relationship as one of mutual respect.

Piaget was careful to point out that not all relationships between children fit his ideal picture. Mutual respect is difficult for young children to achieve because they lack the ability to understand other children's perspectives. They are egocentric—locked in their own view and unable to appreciate other people's views. As a result, they cannot engage in true discussions of ideas nor achieve consensus through mutual agreement. Piaget argued that the decline in egocentrism and the accompanying rise in mutual respect as children grow older are a joint function of cognitive development and social experience. He suggested that the transition in the structure of peer relationships occurs around 8-10 years of age, although he cautioned that it is a gradual rather than a sharp transition.

Why should changes in the structure of children's social relationships affect their judgments of fairness? Piaget gave slightly different answers to this question for adult-child and for peer relationships. Children who interact primarily with adults and older children regard these authorities' rules as defining what is fair. In particular, young children accept unequal treatment as fair if it is sanctioned by an authority. Children who interact primarily with peers do not accept the judgments of external authorities about what is fair. Instead, they judge what is fair by analogy to the procedures they use in making group decisions. The practice of free and open discussions where everyone's opinions have an equal chance to be heard leads naturally to a belief that fairness demands equality in treatment and in outcomes; that is, the principles that underly interactions between peers determine the principles for the fair distribution of resources. As children gradually develop peer relationships characterized by discussion, reciprocity, and mutual respect, they gradually shift toward a conviction that equality is the most critical element of fairness.

Piaget's research. To investigate the development of children's judgments about fairness, Piaget told children stories about situations involving the distribution of materials and then asked them various questions. One strength of Piaget's method was the use of several types of stories and the reporting of results for each type separately. This characteristic of his method can be described more formally as the sampling of different stimulus situations. The sampling is especially illuminating in the research on distributive justice between peers. For three types of stories, Piaget found three different patterns of results. One example of each type follows, along with a summary of the age changes in children's responses to the story.

> Some children are playing ball in a courtyard. When the ball goes out of bounds and rolls down the road one of the boys goes of his own free will to fetch it several times. After that he is the only one they ask to go and fetch it. What do you think of that? (Piaget, 1932, p. 309)

Responses to this story did not change between 6 and 12 years of age. All children agreed that it was unfair to ask one boy to run for the ball each time. All children said the boys should have taken turns retrieving the ball. These results are inconsistent with Piaget's hypothesis that the belief in equality between peers increases with age. On the other hand, the story does not involve either an adult authority or older children. When an authority figure or the specter of authority is present, young children's acceptance of unequal treatment may be more obvious. Nevertheless, the findings for this story indicate that children across a wide age range believe fairness among same-age peers requires equal treatment.

> Two boys, a little one and a big one, once went for a long walk in the mountains. When lunch-time came they were very hungry and took their food out of their bags. But they found that there was not enough food for both of them. What should have been done? Give all the food to the big boy or to the little one, or the same to both? (Piaget, 1932, p. 310)

Most 6- and 7-year-olds said the bigger boy should have had the most food, not because he was more hungry but because he was older. These responses demonstrate the unilateral respect for elders that Piaget attributed to young children. Most 9- and 10-year-olds said the younger child should have more food. Piaget attributed these responses to the older children's understanding of a higher form of equality;[1] that is, the children took account of differences between the two boys when judging what would be fair, rather than considering equality in outcomes alone. Perhaps they assumed the younger boy would be less able to complete

---

[1] Piaget described the older children who gave these responses as following the principle of "equity." This term is not used here because it has a different meaning in the social-psychological literature.

the walk without a good lunch. The two boys then would be more equal in the most important sense, if the younger one received a more than equal share of the food (cf. Youniss, 1980).

> Two boys were playing marbles. One was big, the other little. Should they both have started from the same place [i.e., shot their marbles from behind the same line], or should the little one have started nearer [closer to the other marbles]? (Piaget, 1932, p. 311)

The oldest children said the little boy should have started nearer. Their responses suggest the higher form of equality that was evident for the second story. The marbles game would only be fair if the younger child was given special treatment: he needed a handicap. Young children said both boys should shoot from the same place. According to Piaget, these responses do not represent a true preference for equality, because the children justified their answers by saying that the rules require everyone to shoot from the same place. The responses thus indicate the unthinking respect for rules that is a fundamental feature of unilateral respect.

Connections between Piaget's theory and research. The age changes in responses to Piaget's stories provide qualified support for his theory about the development of fairness judgments. Young children accepted unequal treatment as fair if the inequality resulted from giving more to a bigger and older child. Older children seemed more concerned with achieving a final state of equality, but they frequently proposed that resources be distributed unequally in order to compensate for preexisting differences between children. Moreover, in same-age peer groups, equality apparently was the norm for both younger and older children.

Piaget did not attempt to investigate directly the antecedents of developmental changes in fairness judgments. He did not empirically examine the structure of adult-child and peer relationships; he did not explore the relation between the amount of interaction children had with adults or peers and their preference for equality. Subsequent investigators showed the same bias. They studied age changes in specific types of moral judgments far more often than they examined Piaget's theory about the connections between the structure of children's social relationships and their moral judgments. In addition, research attention was directed toward certain types of judgments to the relative exclusion of others (Keasey, 1978; Lickona, 1976). To a large extent, Piaget's description of developmental trends in reasoning about distributive justice between peers was ignored.

Recent Research on Distributive Justice: Two Piaget Revisionists

During the 1970s, there was a revival of interest in children's judgments about fair distributions of rewards. The new interest in distributive justice had two sources. First, Kohlberg's (1969) theory of stages in moral reasoning provoked a general concern with qualitative changes in thinking about justice. Second, social psychologists investigated principles of justice in business, close relationships, and society at large. Occasionally, the principles first investigated in research with adults were later studied with children. The models for the development of distributive justice that emerged from these two traditions are extremely different, but, taken together, they include the bulk of recent research. The two traditions can be summarized in terms of the research programs of Damon and of Hook.

Damon's Stages of Positive Justice

Theoretical framework. Damon (1975, 1977, 1980) suggested that young children's moral dilemmas often concern what he called *positive justice*. The domain of positive justice includes all moral questions regarding prosocial interactions. However, the dilemmas that Damon studied most extensively involve distributive justice. Damon's model of the development of reasoning about distributive justice is similar to Kohlberg's general model of moral development. Damon assumed first that developmental changes can be described most adequately in terms of qualitative changes in children's reasoning about moral dilemmas. The qualitative changes mark children's progress through a distinct series of stages. Second, he assumed that children pass through the stages in an invariant sequence; they neither skip stages nor return to stages that they had abandoned earlier. Third, he assumed that the maturity of children's reasoning about moral dilemmas is closely related to their cognitive development; more specifically, children's reasoning about distributive justice is related to their status on Piaget's (1970) stages of concrete and formal operations. The relation is expected because children must use the same cognitive operations in reasoning about physical objects and about justice. For example, when distributing rewards they must classify people into groups, deciding which individuals should and should not be treated similarly.

Assessment of developmental levels. Like Piaget, Damon told children hypothetical stories involving distributions of rewards and then asked them a number of questions. Damon's stories and questions were more complicated than those of Piaget, however. One story involved a class of school children who made drawings that they later sold at a fair. The children then had to decide how to divide the money that they made from selling the drawings. Some children wanted the most money to go to the children who drew the most pictures; others wanted the most money to go to the children who drew the best pictures; others suggested that the children who were best behaved at school should get more money. Damon also asked about children who were lazy and didn't draw many pictures. He further mentioned that there were some children who were poorer than their classmates. Through their answers to these questions, Damon determined how children weighed various criteria when deciding how the money should be distributed.

From responses to this story and others, Damon devised six levels of reasoning about distributive justice. Children at the lowest level, labeled 0-A, do not give a clear reason for their decision. When a story involves the subject's own candy or toys, children at this stage give self-interested responses: "I should get it because I want it." At the next level, 0-B, children justify their decisions by referring to external and observable characteristics of the people involved, such as their size or sex. Piaget's findings that young children favor a bigger and older child are consistent with this description. Damon, however, stressed that these justifications tend to be selfishly motivated when children's own resources are at stake. For example, a boy may claim that boys should get more.

At Level 1-A, children insist on equal distributions of rewards in all situations. At Level 1-B, children consider relative performance: children who do the largest share of the work (e.g., draw the most pictures) are given the largest share of the rewards.

At Level 2-A, children recognize that several principles can be used for distributing rewards. Unlike children at the lower levels, they believe it is fair to take into account each child's needs. Therefore, they may decide to give more rewards to those who seem most deprived, for example, the poor children in the class. Children at this stage do not have a procedure for deciding between different criteria. Consequently, when faced with the conflict between distributing rewards on the basis of performance and distributing them on the basis of need, they seek a quantitative compromise. They give a little more to children who did more than average and a little more to children who seem most deprived.

At Level 2-B, children avoid compromising between different criteria by focusing on the function of the distribution of rewards. For example, they may say that the children who drew the most pictures should get the most money so that all the children will try their hardest the next time. Alternatively, they may consider the sale of drawings as a class project and assume that it should be shared equally among the children in the class. Children at this level may refuse to give more money to poor children because the children's poverty has no direct bearing on their status as class members or the number of pictures they could have drawn.

Damon commented that there are levels for distributive justice higher than his Level 2-B, but he stated that the higher levels normally are found in children above age 9 years, the age of the oldest children in his research.

Evidence and explanations. In a cross-sectional study (Damon, 1975), levels of distributive justice reasoning were strongly related to age (r = .85). In a longitudinal study (Damon, 1980), very few children showed

any regression in levels of positive justice reasoning over a 2-year period. Most children advanced to higher levels of reasoning, as expected.
The hypothesis that distributive justice reasoning is related to cognitive
development also was supported (Damon, 1975). Levels of justice
reasoning were highly correlated ($r = .76$ to $.88$) with measures of
stages in classification, seriation, and perspective taking.

Damon has made only a few statements about the explanation for
age changes in children's reasoning. He clearly regards the development
of cognitive operations as essential for mature reasoning about justice.
He also assumes that social experience may influence conceptions of
fairness. For example, experiences in peer groups may provide examples
of conflicts over fairness and their resolution (Damon, 1977). On the
other hand, it is not clear whether he expects experiences with peers to
affect only the rate of development through the stages of positive justice, or the content of the stages themselves. As noted earlier, Piaget
(1932/1965) assumed that the structure of peer relationships determines the content of principles of fairness. Greater attention to the
explanation of age changes, and not just to their description, will be
necessary to resolve this issue.

Hook's Model of the Development of Equitable Distributions

The standard equity problem. Social psychologists interested in the
study of distributive justice began by examining the principle of equity.
In an equitable distribution individuals receive rewards or other outputs
in proportion to their inputs (Walster, Berscheid, & Walster, 1973).
Although most of the research on equity has been done with adults, a
few social psychologists have tried to determine the earliest age at
which children understand and use the principle of equity.

In the typical experimental paradigm, children are asked to perform
a simple task, for example, completing a dot-to-dot picture. The children are told that another child is also working on the task. When the
experimenter asks the children to stop working, he or she tells them
how much they finished on the task and how much the other child finished. Children are then given a number of rewards and asked to divide
them between themselves and the other child in any way they want. In
a few studies, children were not asked to work on a task themselves,
but were asked to help the experimenter divide rewards among two
other children who had worked on it.

Hook and Cook (1979) reviewed the research that used the standard
paradigm with children and adults. Although most studies included children at one age or in a small age range, the tabulation of results for all
studies revealed a regular developmental trend. From 4 to 6 years of age,
children usually distributed the rewards equally or kept most of the
rewards for themselves. Between 7 and 12 years of age, children usually

gave more rewards to the child who had completed more of the task, but the ratio of work accomplished by the two children did not correspond exactly to the ratio of rewards for the two of them. One child might do 75% of the work but get only 60% of the rewards or vice versa. After age 13, children usually distributed rewards in direct proportion to work accomplished.

Hook and Cook (1979) showed that the developmental trend for distributions closely matched the trend established in previous research on children's understanding of proportions. In experiments on many different topics, Piaget (e.g., Inhelder & Piaget, 1958) discovered that preschool children were completely unable to compare differences on two different dimensions. If they saw a train travel faster than another one, for example, they could not judge whether it would go a longer distance than the other train. The inability to deal with two dimensions simultaneously is one feature of the preoperational stage of cognitive development. At the next stage, concrete operations, children recognized that the faster train would go farther, but they could not judge how much farther it would go even if they were told the relative speed of the two trains. With the development of formal operations, children mastered this final hurdle and achieved the ability to use proportions correctly.

Developmental study. Hook (1978) attempted to demonstrate the relation of equitable distributions to proportional thinking in a study of 5-, 9-, and 13-year-olds. These ages were chosen to represent the three stages in understanding of proportions. Each child first was asked to solve several cognitive problems, including one set that measured the children's ability to deal with proportions. Then the experimenter indicated how much "work" the child had done on all the problems by pointing to a board showing a number of checkmarks. The child also was told that another child did the same amount of work, three times as much work, or one-third as much work. Then the child was asked to divide 20 pennies so that he or she and the other child both got what they should get.

As expected, the 5-year-olds took more pennies for themselves, regardless of their performance relative to the other child. The 9-year-olds gave more pennies to the child who seemed to have done more work, but the ratios for work accomplished by the two children and pennies distributed to each of them were not identical. Only the 13-year-olds distributed pennies in exact proportion to the amount of work accomplished.

These findings suggest a precise but narrow interpretation of age changes in children's distributions of rewards. Children only gradually develop the ability to perform the mental calculations required for an exactly equitable distribution, so they only gradually make such distributions. The development of equity judgments and behavior is related not to cognitive development in general, but to proportional thinking in particular.

An Appraisal of the Developmental Research

Piaget, Damon, and Hook have presented sharply contrasting descriptions of the development of distributive justice in reasoning and in action. Although Piaget and Damon used the same general method for investigating children's reasoning, their descriptions differ as much from each other as either description differs from that of Hook. Thus the contrasts between the three researchers cannot be attributed directly to variations in experimental procedure. In a broader sense, however, the differences do appear to be methodological in nature. Each researcher presented children with a distinctive set of stimulus situations, that is, a distinctive pattern of information about the social context in which the distribution of rewards took place. Children seemed to employ different principles of fairness in different social contexts.

The effects of the social context can be illustrated by considering three of the apparent discrepancies in findings across studies. First, Damon and Hook reported that 4- to 5-year-old children made self-interested distributions of rewards: they took most of the rewards for themselves and said that their behavior was fair. Piaget did not find self-interested responses in slightly older children, but with his stories children had no opportunity to favor themselves. In Hook's (1978) study, children were asked to decide on a fair distribution of rewards to two other children after they had divided rewards between themselves and another child. The same 5-year-olds who took most of the rewards for themselves said that the other two children should divide the rewards equally. These responses indicate that young children understand the principles of equality and use it when they have nothing to lose by doing so.

Second, Damon and Hook reported that some children distributed rewards in an approximately equitable manner, giving more rewards to individuals who did more work. Piaget did not find any children who made distributions of this type, but he did not present stories in which children were rewarded for the amount of work they accomplished. Damon found that equitable distributions were regularly made only by one group of children around 7 years of age, at Level 1-B. Hook found that equity was the primary principle used by children from middle childhood through adolescence. On the other hand, Damon presented information about the needs of different children that was not included in Hook's stories. Consequently, it appears that children can use the principle of equity, at least by 7 years of age, but they do not accept equity as the only principle for all contexts.

Third, Piaget and Damon drew different conclusions about the degree to which children at different ages consider another child's needs when distributing rewards. Piaget suggested that consideration of needs marked the highest development of principles of fairness. In Damon's model, emphasis on the needs of other children is greatest at Level 2-A. At the next level, 2-B, children evaluate whether or not the information about others' needs is relevant to the decision being made. The discrepancy seems to reflect differences in the situations presented to children. In Damon's stories, but not in Piaget's, children sometimes were "needy" in ways that had no effect on their performance relative to their peers.

A recent series of experiments by Anderson and Butzin (1978) suggested the more startling conclusion that even preschool children consider both the relative performance of other people and their relative need when allocating rewards to them. For example, preschool children said that other children who helped their mothers for a longer time should receive more toys from Santa Claus. The children also said that Santa Claus should give more rewards to children who were more needy, that is, children with fewer toys initially. Anderson and Butzin argued that previous studies underestimated children's knowledge of fairness principles because the studies used between- rather than within-subject designs, because their procedures were more complex or less interesting to children, or because the children's fairness judgments depended heavily on their understanding of number.

Taken together, the results of previous research suggest that children across a wide age range utilize several principles of fairness, including equality, equity, and distributions based on need. There are age changes in children's ability to distribute rewards in exact proportion to the amount of work accomplished. Children's ability to consciously and systematically choose between different fairness principles also seems to increase with age. Nevertheless, age changes appear to reflect primarily children's selection of fairness principles for different contexts, rather than their ability to understand or use different principles.

A Social-Psychological Perspective on Fairness

Not surprisingly, social psychologists have emphasized the influence of the social context on fairness judgments and behavior. The most extensive treatment of the effects of social roles and relationships on actual distributions is found in a series of papers by Lerner (Lerner, 1977; Lerner, Miller, & Holmes, 1976; Lerner & Whitehead, 1980). Like Piaget, Lerner assumed that different conceptions of justice are evoked by different social relationships. Rather than focusing on only two types of relationships, however, Lerner described a variety of situational roles or transsituational relationships that are linked to a variety of forms of justice. The following description of five types of relationships between peers is adapted from Lerner's model.

First, children or adults may consider themselves as *co-workers*. They are part of the same social system or institution, but they react to each other as occupants of specific roles rather than as unique personalities. For example, they may work in the same office or on the same assembly line. Individuals who perceive themselves as co-workers, in this sense of the term, are expected to regard equitable distributions of rewards as fair. Individuals are rewarded for their relative contribution to the final objective of the entire group.

Children or adults may also consider themselves as *teammates or as comrades*. They may be partners in a law practice; they may play touch football together. Teammates or comrades are expected to regard equal distributions of resources as most fair. They are working together and therefore believe they should share equally in the fruits of their work.

In contrast, children or adults may consider themselves as *competitors or opponents*. They are not really enemies because their competition simply reflects their particular social roles. In a social system or institutional structure, they are expected to compete with each other, but there is nothing "personal" about it. Of course, they are required to compete fairly, following the accepted rules and acting honestly toward their opponent. Lerner (1977) defined the fairness principle that holds in competitive encounters as "justified self-interest."

Even children or adults who view each other as *enemies* accept a rudimentary principle of fairness. It may be called the "law of the jungle." Lerner called it "Darwinian justice." Relations between enemies are personal ones: enemies do regard their antagonism as going beyond their social roles or institutional responsibilities. Nevertheless, these relations can be considered fair because both parties accept the terms of their conflict. It may be governed by certain rules (e.g., "no hitting below the belt") or completely unrestrained ("no holds barred"), but enemies recognize and agree on the behavior that is allowed.

At the opposite extreme, children and adults may consider another person as a *close friend*. They become deeply concerned about the friend's joy and suffering, reacting to them as they do to their own. They view the friend as so like themselves that they cannot draw a line between their wants or needs and those of the friend. Consequently, fairness between friends goes beyond equality; friends respond in a completely unselfish way to each other's needs.

The effects of variation in social roles and relationships on distributions of rewards have been investigated in many studies with children and adults (Berkowitz & Walster, 1976; Mikula, 1980). Most studies have focused on the distinction between the equality and equity principles and, in most cases, subjects' perceptions of their relationship to each other have been experimentally manipulated. Less research has been done on relationships formed outside the laboratory—relationships between lovers, spouses, enemies, and friends (Kelley, 1979).

Developments in Friendship and in Fairness

Hypotheses about the association between fairness principles and types of social relationships are especially intriguing to a developmental psychologist because they suggest a paradigm for studying age changes in relationships. Relations between friends are of particular interest because friendships constitute the most significant of children's peer relationships. Previous theories of the development of friendship can be used to generate hypotheses about the way in which friends distribute resources among themselves, that is, the principles of fairness that they accept for their interactions.

Although Piaget (1932/1965) discussed peer relationships at length, he did not distinguish between friendships and other peer relationships. The best known theoretical statement on the development of friendship was presented by Sullivan (1953). He argued that children in the early school years are insensitive to their peers, whether or not the peers are friends. Children at these ages may compromise with peers in order to get what they want, but they are more likely to compete than to cooperate with peers. As they approach adolescence, however, children develop a strong and intimate same-sex friendship. They try to satisfy their friend's desires and try to choose activities that will be mutually satisfying. In short, during early adolescence children stop competing with friends and start to show special concern with their friends' needs.

The literature on children's friendships has increased dramatically in a very short time (Asher & Gottman, 1981; Foot, Chapman, & Smith, 1980; Hartup, 1978; Rubin, 1980). Nevertheless, interactions between friends have been investigated in relatively few studies. Most of these studies were not designed primarily as tests of Sullivan's and Piaget's theories, but their results provide a substantial degree of support for the theories. The following research review is organized around a series of studies in an ongoing research program by the present author.

Study 1: Sharing and Competition Between Friends

The major goal of the first study (Berndt, 1981b) was to compare the amount of sharing by friends and by nonfriends under conditions in which sharing required self-sacrifice. Pairs of close friends or pairs of classmates who neither strongly liked nor strongly disliked each other were asked to work on a task together. Each child in the pair was given a model of a geometric design to color. To complete their designs, the children had to share a single set of crayons. They were told that they could use only one crayon at a time, so they had to pass it back and forth between them. They also were told that each of them would get a prize that depended on how much of their own design they completed. To show them how well they were doing, the experimenter gave out rewards (nickels) after each trial. The child who colored more on each trial received two nickels; the child who colored less received one nickel. Children who let their partner use the crayon for a long time were likely to get less done on their design and get fewer rewards than their partner. In addition, children who viewed the task competitively might regard themselves as losing trials on which they received fewer nickels than their partner.

There were 116 children in the study, fairly evenly divided between kindergarten, second, and fourth grades. The children first were asked to name their best friends and rate their liking for all of their same-sex classmates on a 5-point scale. Children then were randomly assigned to the friend or classmate condition and paired with a specific friend or classmate. Children were considered friends if their ratings on the 5-point scale averaged 4.0 or more and at least one of the children had nominated the other as a best friend. Pairs were considered merely as classmates if neither one had nominated the other and their ratings of each other averaged less than 4.0, but neither one had rated the other at the lowest point on the liking scale (1, meaning "don't like").

Then each pair was observed as they worked on the coloring task. For the first two trials, the same child was given the crayon at the start. Then two more trials were administered in which the other child was given the crayon at the start. On all trials, the experimenter recorded how long the child who initially had the crayon shared it with the other child, how often each child requested the crayon, and how often a request was unsuccessful because the other child ignored it or refused to pass the crayon.

The results indicated that sharing was not significantly greater for friends than for other classmates. Girls shared the crayon fairly equally with friends and with other classmates. Second- and fourth-grade boys sometimes shared significantly less with friends than with other classmates, although their responses varied for the first and second halves of the task. Boys' requests for the crayon also tended to be less successful if they were paired with a friend rather than another classmate. Girls usually received the crayon shortly after they requested it, regardless of their relationship to the partner. Finally, the discrepancy between the amounts colored by the two children in a pair was significantly greater for boys paired with friends than for boys paired with other classmates. The discrepancy was low for girls in both cases.

The girls' responses on the task illustrate the preference for equality that has been found in previous research (e.g., Skarin & Moely, 1976). The boys' responses are more surprising. Apparently, boys sometimes shared less with friends and refused to grant a friend's requests because they wanted to complete more of the design than their friend. In other words, they preferred to compete with the friend rather than share equally with him. These results support Sullivan's hypothesis that competition is a salient feature of friendships in middle childhood, at least for boys. Comparable results were reported by Staub and Noerenberg (1981) for third- and fourth-grade boys (cf. Gottman & Parkhurst, 1980).

The more puzzling question is why boys competed more with friends than with other classmates. Children probably view themselves as similar to their friends and often compare their own performance with that of their close friends (Rubin, 1980; Tesser, Note 1). Social comparison may provoke competition, as children try to demonstrate that they are equal to their friends rather than inferior to them. Competition between friends is especially likely when they view their performance on a task as a reflection of their overall ability (Tesser & Smith, 1980).

Several other studies suggested that friends' interactions are more harmonious and mutually regulated than the interactions of nonfriends (Foot, Chapman, & Smith, 1977; Newcomb & Brady, 1982; Newcomb, Brady, & Hartup, 1979). In these studies, however, children either were not observed in competitive situations or the tasks were not as competitively structured as those in Study 1. For example, the relative performance of the two friends was not compared on a series of trials. Of course, the task of sharing the crayon could be altered so that it would be less likely to elicit competition. Then close friends would be expected to share more than children who were not close friends. One purpose of the second study was to test this hypothesis.

Study 2: Age Changes in Sharing and Helping Between Friends

Children in the second study (Berndt, 1981a) were asked again to share crayons while coloring a design, but the reward structure of the task was changed. Children received more nickels than their partner if they colored more than the partner; they received the same number of nickels if they colored the same amount; and they received fewer nickels if they colored less than their partner. (In Study 1, children rarely colored exactly the same amount on a trial, and in those cases the experimenter gave more nickels to the child who had colored more neatly). Consequently, children had a third option besides "winning" and "losing": they could try for equality in rewards.

The pairs of children were then observed as they did a second task that provided opportunities for one child to help his or her partner. One child was asked to complete a large block design. The second child was given the alternatives of helping to complete the block design or working on a different activity by himself or herself. There was a disadvantage to helping, however. If children helped their partner for an entire trial, they received one nickel and the partner received three nickels. If they did not help the partner at all, they received three nickels and the partner received one nickel. As in the sharing task, equality was a third option. If children divided their time between helping and working on their own activity, both they and the partner received two nickels. The roles of the two children, potential helper and one in need of help, were reversed halfway through the task so that both children had an opportunity to help their partner.

The design of the study differed from that of Study 1 in two major respects. First, pairs of children were observed in both the fall and the spring of the school year. Second, at the beginning of the year all children were paired with a close friend. Children kept the same partners, whether or not they were still friends, when observed in the spring. Because of the longitudinal design, it was possible to link changes in friendship to changes in friends' sharing and helping; that is, it was possible to evaluate whether the behavior of children who were still friends differed from that of children who were no longer friends. In addition, the study included children from first grade and fourth grade. Therefore, age changes in friends' behavior toward each other could be assessed.

The sample originally included 88 children. One pair of friends was lost from the sample due to one child's moving out of the school district, so the final sample included 86 children. In addition to the measures of sharing and helping, the frequency of refusals to share the crayon and refusals to help the partner were recorded.

The results for the four dependent measures showed two distinct patterns. First, the amount of helping and the frequency of refusals to share differed for first and fourth graders but did not change between the fall and the spring. Fourth graders more often helped their partner and less often refused to share with their partner than first graders did. The age changes are consistent with Sullivan's hypothesis that sensitivity to a friend's needs and desires increases around 9 or 10 years of age, the age of the fourth graders in the study. The age changes also are consistent with Piaget's data on the development of a higher form of equality defined by responsiveness to the needs of another child. Unless children helped their partner, the partner could not get the same number of rewards as they did. Thus, by helping the partner, children could produce equality in outcomes. It is interesting although not unusual that in this case the need and equality principles for fairness converge (cf. Youniss, 1980).

Second, the amount of sharing and the frequency of refusals to help did not vary between the fall and the spring for fourth graders, but first graders shared less with their partners and more often refused to help their partners in the spring than in the fall. At first glance, the findings seemed unrelated to changes in friendships from the fall to the spring, because most children at both ages still appeared to be close friends with their partner in the study. On the other hand, the apparent stability of friendship could have been increased by a specific type of response bias. Children might have been primed to name their partner in the study as a best friend because they had participated in an experimental session with the partner.

Other evidence suggested that the first graders probably had not maintained friendships with their partner that were as strong as the fourth graders' friendships. First, the stability of friendships in the sample as a whole was significantly greater for fourth graders than for first graders. Fourth graders retained 78% of their friendships from the fall to the spring; first graders retained only 57%. Second, in the spring a significantly larger proportion of fourth graders than first graders named their partner in the study as one of their two or three very best friends (55% vs. 26%). It seems safe to conclude, therefore, that the changes in the first graders' behavior between the fall and the spring were due to a weakening in their friendships that did not occur as often in the fourth graders' friendships. The conclusion is particularly significant because it suggests that even first graders who are good friends are more responsive to each other's needs and requests than first graders who are not good friends (cf. Newcomb et al., 1979).

No main effect of sex was found for any variables and interactions with sex were rare. The absence of sex differences implies that the change in the reward structure of the task from Study 1 to Study 2 did reduce children's competitiveness and increase their preference for equality, as expected. Unfortunately, this explanation cannot be confirmed directly because children's motives for their behavior were not assessed. In the next study, children were asked to report their motives after they were given opportunities to behave in generous and helpful ways toward a partner.

Study 3: Generosity and Helpfulness in Children's and Adolescent's Friendships

The central purpose of the third study (Berndt, Note 2) was to determine if the difference between friends' and nonfriends' interactions increases from childhood to adolescence. Sullivan (1953) assumed that the development of intimate friendships in the years shortly before adolescence leads to the emergence of a distinctive pattern of interactions between children and their friends. According to Sullivan, behavior toward a friend becomes very different from behavior toward other classmates when children develop an intimate friendship. Therefore, the contrast between friends' interactions and other classmates' interactions should increase with age. This hypothesis was tested in Study 3.

The study included 118 children from the fourth, sixth, and eighth grades. The children were paired either with a close friend or with another classmate, as in Study 1. In another session, the pairs of children were observed as they performed two tasks. The first task was an adaptation of the Kagan and Madsen (1972) measure of generous behavior. Children were shown cards that depicted two alternative ways of distributing rewards (pennies) to themselves and to their partner.

The alternatives varied on different cards, but one alternative was always more generous to the partner than the other. In addition, one alternative usually provided an equal number of rewards for the child and his or her partner. Each child was asked to make several distributions of rewards by picking one alternative from each of a set of cards. Although the two children in a pair made their choices simultaneously, they used separate decks of cards and were given no information about their partner's choices.

For the second task, the two children were asked to make a flag by pasting small colored triangles on a large cardboard sheet. Each child was given one section of the flag to color, but one child's section was twice as large as the other child's section. The experimenter mentioned the inequality to the children and said that the child with a smaller section could help the other child if he or she wanted to help. The experimenter added that children would get rewards that depended on how much they completed on their assigned section. The instructions made it clear that children would not be rewarded for helping the partner. As usual the roles of the two children were reversed halfway through the task.

After finishing both tasks, the children were asked to indicate their motives when doing them. They independently completed questionnaires in which they ranked four motives for behavior: (1) equality (i.e., "I tried to get the same amount of money as my partner"); (2) competition ("I tried to get more money than my partner"); (3) their own gain ("I tried to get as much money for myself as I could"); and (4) altruism ("I tried to let my partner get a lot of money"). Children also made attributions about their partner's motives when doing each task.

The results for the measures of generous and helpful behavior were similar. The number of choices of the generous alternative on the cards and the number of triangles children placed on the flag for their partner did not vary significantly for friends and other classmates for fourth or sixth graders. Eighth graders, however, made more generous choices and helped their partner more if the partner was a close friend rather than another classmate. Girls were more generous to both friends and other classmates than boys were, but helping did not vary with sex.

Comparable results were found for children's reports on their own motives and their attributions about their partner's motives. For fourth and sixth graders, attributions about the most important motive for the partner's behavior did not vary for friends and other classmates. The eighth-grade children usually said their friends tried for equality; they usually said other classmates competed with them. Boys said their partners (friends and classmates) competed with them more than girls did. The same effects were not found for children's reports on their own motives, probably because children were unwilling to attribute competitiveness to themselves even if they believed their partner was competing with them.

The results support Sullivan's hypothesis that the differences between children's behavior toward friends and toward other classmates increase with age. Nevertheless, it is surprising that significant friend-classmate differences were not found before eighth grade. The results of Study 2 suggest that children who are good friends behave more prosocially toward each other than children who are not good friends even in first grade. The findings from the two studies are not contradictory, however, because they involved different procedures and tasks. The apparent inconsistency can be resolved by assuming, first, that friends' preferences for equality over competition do increase with age and, second, that better friends have a stronger preference for equality even in the early school years. Because friends could attain equal outcomes only by responding to each other's needs and desires, the results also are consistent with the general hypothesis from social-psychological research that good friends define responsiveness to each other's needs as fair.

Sharing and Helping Between Friends in Everyday Life

The findings for friends' behavior in Studies 1-3 are limited because they were obtained in a particular social context, one in which friends or classmates were interacting with each other and had to decide whether to aim for equality, compete, or try to maximize their own gains. Social contexts similar to those studied in the research are found in children's daily lives—individual or team sports and other games provide good examples. Nevertheless, different results might be expected in different social contexts. For example, in everyday life children who are not already playing or working together may begin an interaction when one child asks the other for help. How does friendship affect behavior in these situations? An indirect answer to this question can be obtained from results for another measure used in all three studies of friendship.

Children were interviewed individually and asked to describe how much they would help or share with their partner in the study in several situations typical of children's own lives. For example, one situation involved the partner's request to try out a new bike that the child had just received. Another situation involved the partner's request for a loan of money so that he or she could go on rides at a school carnival. After each situation was described, children were asked if they would share or help their partner and, if so, how long. Their responses were defined as measures of prosocial intentions (Fishbein & Ajzen, 1975).

In Study 1, girls said they would help and share with a friend more than with another classmate. Boys said they would treat friends and classmates alike. Responses did not vary between kindergarten and fourth grade. The same pattern was found in Study 3. Girls said they would show more prosocial behavior toward a friend than toward another classmate. Boys said they would act similarly toward friends and toward other classmates. No changes in responses between fourth and eighth grade were found.[2] In Study 2, the situations included in the measure of prosocial intentions were different from those in other studies because some of them were modeled on the tasks used to measure sharing and helping. In this case, the findings for prosocial intentions were similar to those for actual behavior: Effects of age and time (fall or spring) were significant and effects of sex were not.

The sex differences for Studies 1 and 3 seem to reflect a stronger preference in girls than boys for small and exclusive friendship networks characterized by intimate self-disclosure and extremely prosocial interactions. Girls tend to have fewer friends than boys; they tend to make friends less rapidly than boys (Eder & Hallinan, 1978). Girls also show more intimate self-disclosure toward a same-sex peer than boys (Maccoby & Jacklin, 1974). These features of girls' friendships may be related to their prosocial intentions. Because they have a relatively small number of friends, girls may find it easier than boys to treat their friends in an especially positive way. Boys may be concerned that all their friends will demand the same treatment, so they limit the amount that they help any particular friend. The sex differences in the exclusiveness of friendship occasionally have been attributed to differences in parents' treatment of sons and daughters (Waldrop & Halverson, 1975) or differences in boys' and girls' participation in team sports (Lever, 1978). Although these hypotheses are plausible, they have not been carefully tested.

The results for prosocial intentions also suggest that prosocial behavior is used to mark the boundary between "insiders" (friends) and "outsiders" (nonfriends). Girls encourage interactions with friends by responding positively to their requests to share or help; they discourage interactions with nonfriends by responding less positively to their requests. The insider-outsider distinction is an addition to the typology for social relationships presented earlier in this chapter, although there is a long tradition of research on differences in behavior toward members of one's own group and those outside the group (e.g., Feldman, 1968). Girls differentiate between friends and nonfriends more clearly than boys, but the same distinction probably would appear if boys' responses toward friends and strangers were compared.

---

[2] The correlations between prosocial intentions and the behavioral measures in Study 1 were low and seldom significant. The comparable correlations in Study 3 were also low, although there was a significant correlation between children's prosocial intentions and their generosity on the card task. The low correlations are not surprising because the two types of measures showed different patterns of effects for age, sex, and friendship.

Conclusions

Developments in Social Relationships and Social Justice

Recent research has demonstrated convincingly that children and adults consider several principles when deciding how to distribute resources fairly. They may distribute the resources equally, give more to individuals who seem to have earned more, or give more to those in greater need. Young children often give themselves most of the resources available and, in some cases, they apparently regard their behavior as fair. Social psychologists have pointed out that adults accept distributions based on self-interest as fair under certain conditions, so children are not unique in this respect. Social psychologists also have noted that people view competitive behavior as fair in certain situations; that is, people consider it fair for individuals to compete and fair for the outcome of the competition to determine the distribution of rewards.

By the time children enter elementary school, if not earlier, they appear to understand all of the principles of fairness that adults use frequently. There are age changes in children's application of fairness principles in specific social contexts. These changes seem due primarily to developments in children's conceptions of social relationships. For example, the shift with age from self-interested to equal distributions of rewards that occurs for friends and nonfriends alike (Berndt, 1981a; Damon, 1977) can be explained by a shift in children's orientation toward peers. Piaget (1932/1965) described it as an increase in mutual respect. If children take the concept of mutual respect as the foundation for their peer interactions, they cannot accept self-interested behavior. When everyone wants most of the resources for themselves, no agreement on their distribution can be reached. The lack of agreement could provoke a serious conflict. Conflict is much less likely if children try for equality.

This general perspective on children's application of fairness principles is of greatest value, however, when it is linked to a theory of the development of specific types of social relationships. This approach is illustrated by the research on children's friendships reviewed in this chapter. The hypotheses of Sullivan (1953) and Piaget (1932/1965) concerning the development of peer relationships, and friendships in particular, were tested with data on the prosocial behavior of children at different ages toward friends and other classmates. The results were consistent with the hypotheses to a large degree, although not in all details. More specifically, there was evidence for competition between children who were friends during middle childhood, but a shift away from competition toward equality during adolescence. On the other hand, recent research by different investigators has suggested that competition does not disappear completely from friendships. When situations strongly elicit competition, even adults may compete more with a friend than a stranger. The ways friends handle competition, or avoid it, are likely to influence strongly the quality and duration of their relationship.

The recent studies also revealed features of friendship that affect children's distributions of resources but do not change with age. Across the age range from kindergarten to eighth grade, girls said that they would help and share with a close friend more than with another classmate. Boys said that they would treat friends and other classmates similarly. The sex difference in responses may be related to a consistent difference in boys' and girls' patterns of interactions with friends. Although the evidence is not conclusive, girls seem to prefer interactions with a single other girl and boys seem to prefer interactions with a group of other boys throughout middle childhood and adolescence (Berndt, 1981c).

The evidence on age changes and sex differences in friends' behavior and intentions acquires additional meaning when linked to current conceptions of fairness principles. The data on friends' competition suggests that children, particularly boys, may have an ambivalent view of close friendships. In Lerner's (1977) terms, children want to identify with a close friend as "another self," but they also recognize that a friend may be an opponent or rival. Both features of friendship are consequences of the similarity between friends; similarity promotes identification and the social comparison that can lead to competition. In Lerner's original model, as in most of the popular literature of friendship, this source of ambivalence in the relationship between friends has been overlooked. Nevertheless, the explanation for competition between friends can be clearly and precisely stated in terms of the model.

The sex difference in intentions to help and share with a friend appears to call for an extension of the initial typology for social relationships. Relationships between children who are neither friends nor enemies, but who are not members of the same group, must be considered as a distinct type. What counts as fair between outgroup members needs to be better determined. This example indicates that the conceptual framework used to explore fairness principles in social relationships is flexible and open. It can be corrected and modified on the basis of research findings. Furthermore, it seems to be fruitful in generating hypotheses about age changes in children's conceptions of different types of social relationships. It may be considered, therefore, as a useful theoretical paradigm for further investigations of social development.

Explanations of Developments in Fairness Principles

As already indicated, social experience is an important factor in children's application of fairness principles to different social contexts. For example, the sex difference in girls' and boys' intentions to help and share with friends and nonfriends in everyday situations has been tentatively attributed to a sex difference in experiences with parents and peers. Similarly, the decrease in competition between friends in early adolescence has been linked to the emergence of especially close and intimate friendships.

Attributing variations in the selection of fairness principles to social experience does not rule out a contribution of cognitive development. As Piaget (1932/1965) noted, cognitive development and social experience are closely related. The increase during adolescence in the intimacy of friendships, for example, may be related to the development of a greater understanding of other people's thoughts, feelings, and personality characteristics. In addition, intimacy between friends may be related to the friends' ability to take each other's perspective (Selman, 1980; Youniss, 1980). On the other hand, cognitive development cannot completely explain why one adolescent has an intimate friendship and another adolescent does not. By the same token, cognitive development cannot completely explain why one adolescent assumes that fairness demands responsiveness to a friend's needs and another adolescent assumes that fairness is compatible with competition between friends. To explain these differences, it may be most important to consider children's and adolescents' experiences with their own friends.

Experiences with friends may have a limited effect on children's social interactions; that is, they may affect interactions with other children who are regarded as friends but not affect interactions with other peers or adults. In contrast, experiences with friends may affect children's behavior toward all other people, regardless of the children's relationship to them. Although the more general effects of experiences with friends have been emphasized in previous theories (Sullivan, 1953), few writers have tried to define what types of experiences with friends have general effects on children's behavior. From the perspective presented in this chapter, the answer is fairly obvious. Experiences with friends can affect interactions with nonfriends in two major ways: First, because of their history of interactions with a specific friend, children may change their view of all social relationships. After sharing a friend's joys and sorrows, they may emphathize more with people to whom they are not closely related (Hoffman, 1975). Second, after using certain principles of fairness with friends, children may begin to regard these principles as generally applicable. Children who compete with friends may adopt a competitive orientation toward people at large because they assume that everyone else is as competitive as they are (Kelley & Stahelski, 1970). These hypotheses have not been directly tested in previous research and it may not be easy to measure the constructs to which they refer. Nevertheless, the hypotheses are worth testing because they are central to an understanding of social and moral development.

Acknowledgments

Preparation of this chapter was supported in part by Grant BNS78-24157 from the National Science Foundation and a grant from the Spencer Foundation.

Reference Notes

1. Tesser, A. *Self-evaluation maintenance processes and inter-personal relationships.* Paper presented at the Vanderbilt University conference on Boundary Areas in Psychology: Developmental and Social, Nashville, June 1981.
2. Berndt, T. J. *Generosity and helpfulness between friends in early adolescence.* Manuscript submitted for publication, 1981.

References

Anderson, N. H., & Butzin, C. A. Integration theory applied to children's judgments of equity. *Developmental Psychology*, 1978, *14*, 593-606.

Asher, S. R., & Gottman, J. M. (Eds.). *The development of children's friendships.* Cambridge, England: Cambridge University Press, 1981.

Berkowitz, L., & Walster, E. (Eds.), *Equity theory: Toward a general theory of social interaction (Advances in Experimental Social Psychology*, Vol. 9). New York: Academic Press, 1976.

Berndt, T. J. Age changes and changes over time in prosocial intentions and behavior between friends. *Developmental Psychology*, 1981, *17*, 408-416. (a)

Berndt, T. J. The effects of friendship on prosocial intentions and behavior. *Child Development*, 1981, *52*, 636-643. (b)

Berndt, T. J. Relations between social cognition, nonsocial cognition, and social behavior: The case of friendship. In J. H. Flavell & L. D. Ross (Eds.), *Social cognitive development: Frontiers and possible futures.* Cambridge, England: Cambridge University Press, 1981. (c)

Damon, W. Early conceptions of positive justice as related to the development of logical operations. *Child Development*, 1975, *46*, 301-312.

Damon, W. *The social world of the child.* San Francisco: Jossey-Bass, 1977.

Damon, W. Patterns of change in children's social reasoning: A two-year longitudinal study. *Child Development*, 1980, *51*, 1010-1017.

Eder, D., & Hallinan, M. T. Sex differences in children's friendships. *American Sociological Review*, 1978, *43*, 237-250.

Feldman, R. E. Response to compatriot and foreigner who seek assistance. *Journal of Personality and Social Psychology*, 1968, *10*, 202-214.

Fishbein, M., & Ajzen, I. *Beliefs, attitudes, intentions, and behavior; An introduction to theory and research.* Reading, Mass.: Addison-Wesley, 1975.

Foot, H. C., Chapman, A. J., & Smith, J. R. Friendship and social responsivness in boys and girls. *Journal of Personality and Social Psychology*, 1977, *35*, 401-411.

Foot, H. C., Chapman, A. J., & Smith, J. R. (Eds.). *Friendship and social relations in children.* New York: Wiley, 1980.

Gottman, J. M. & Parkhurst, J. T. A developmental theory of friendship and acquaintanceship processes. In W. A. Collins (Ed.), *Minnesota symposia on child psychology* (Vol. 13). Hillsdale, N.J.: Erlbaum, 1980.

Hartup, W. W. Children and their friends. In H. McGurk (Ed.), *Issues in childhood social development.* London: Methuen, 1978.

Hoffman, M. L. Developmental synthesis of affect and cognition and its implications for altruistic motivation. *Developmental Psychology*, 1975, *11*, 607-622.

Hook, J. The development of equity and logico-mathematical thinking. *Child Development*, 1978, *49*, 1035-1044.

Hook, J. G., & Cook, T. D. Equity theory and the cognitive ability of children. *Psychological Bulletin*, 1979, *86*, 429-445.

Inhelder, B., & Piaget, J. *The growth of logical thinking from childhood to adolescence.* New York: Basic Books, 1958.

Kagan, S., & Madsen, M. C. Rivalry in Anglo-American and Mexican-American children of two ages. *Journal of Personality and Social Psychology*, 1972, *24*, 214-220.

Keasey, C. B. Children's developing awareness and usage of intentionality and motives. In C. B. Keasey (Ed.), *Nebraska Symposium on Motivation 1977* (Vol. 25). Lincoln, Nebr.: University of Nebraska Press, 1978.

Kelley, H. H. *Personal relationships: Their structure and processes.* New York: Halsted Press, 1979.

Kelley, H. H., & Stahelski, A. J. Social interaction basis of cooperators' and competitors' beliefs about others. *Journal of Personality and Social Psychology*, 1970, *16*, 66-91.

Kohlberg, L. Stage and sequence: The cognitive-developmental approach to socialization. In D. A. Goslin (Ed.), *Handbook of socialization theory and research.* New York: Rand-McNally, 1969.

Lerner, M. J. The justice motive: Some hypotheses as to its origins and forms. *Journal of Personality*, 1977, *45*, 1-52.

Lerner, M. J., Miller, D. T., & Holmes, J. G. Deserving and the emergence of forms of justice. In L. Berkowitz & E. Walster (Eds.), *Equity theory: Toward a general theory of social interaction (Advances in Experimental Social Psychology*, Vol. 9). New York: Academic Press, 1976.

Lerner, M. J., & Whitehead, L. A. Procedural justice viewed in the context of justice motive theory. In G. Mikula (Ed.), *Justice and social interaction.* New York: Springer, 1980.

Lever, J. Sex differences in the complexity of children's play and games. *American Sociological Review*, 1978, *43*, 471-483.

Lickona, T. (Ed.), *Moral development and behavior: Theory, research, and social issues.* New York: Holt, Rinehart & Winston, 1976.

Maccoby, E. E., & Jacklin, C. N. *The psychology of sex differences.* Stanford, Calif.: Stanford University Press, 1974.

Mikula, G. (Ed.). *Justice and social interaction.* New York: Springer, 1980.

Newcomb, A. F., & Brady, J. E. Mutuality in boys' friendship relations. *Child Development*, 1982, *53*, 392-395.

Newcomb, A. F., Brady, J. E., & Hartup, W. W. Friendship and incentive condition as determinants of children's task-oriented social behavior. *Child Development*, 1979, *50*, 878-881.

Piaget, J. *The moral judgment of the child.* New York: Free Press, 1965. (Originally published, 1932.)

Piaget, J. Piaget's theory. In P. H. Mussen (Ed.), *Carmichael's manual of child psychology* (3rd ed., Vol. 1). New York: Wiley, 1970.

Rubin, Z. *Children's friendships.* Cambridge, Mass.: Harvard University Press, 1980.

Selman, R. L. *The development of interpersonal understanding: Developmental and clinical analyses.* New York: Academic Press, 1980.

Skarin, K., & Moely, B. E. Altruistic behavior: An analysis of age and sex differences. *Child Development*, 1976, *47*, 1159-1165.

Staub, E., & Noerenberg, H. Property rights, deservingness, reciprocity, friendship: The transactional character of children's sharing behavior. *Journal of Personality and Social Psychology*, 1981, *40*, 271-289.

Sullivan, H. S. *The interpersonal theory of psychiatry*. New York: Norton, 1953.

Tesser, A., & Smith, J. Some effects of task relevance and friendship on helping: You don't always help the one you like. *Journal of Experimental Social Psychology*, 1980, *16*, 582-590.

Waldrop, M. F., & Halverson, C. F., Jr. Intensive and extensive peer behavior: Longitudinal and cross-sectional analyses. *Child Development*, 1975, *46*, 19-28.

Walster, E., Berscheid, E., & Walster, G. W. New directions in equity research. *Journal of Personality and Social Psychology*, 1973, *25*, 151-176.

Youniss, J. *Parents and peers in social development*. Chicago: University of Chicago Press, 1980.

Chapter 12

Social Development Through Friendship

Jacqueline Smollar and James Youniss

During the past decade there has been a resurgence of interest in the study of friendship from a developmental perspective. The recent work, however, differs markedly from earlier research in that the focus now includes cognitions about friendship rather than merely the bases for friendship selections (Austin & Thompson, 1948; Cattell, 1934; Wellman, 1926). Investigations have concerned developmental trends in such areas as the expectations of friendship (Bigelow, 1977; Reisman & Shorr, 1978), the definitions of friendship (Bigelow & LaGaipa, 1975; Kon & Losenkov, 1978; Youniss & Volpe, 1978), and the meaning of friendship (LaGaipa, 1979; Selman & Jaquette, 1977). While the results of these studies have contributed to a broader understanding of friendship conceptions, little attention has been given to the implications these conceptions may have for social development in general (Hartup, 1978; Youniss, 1980). Friendship relations may foster the development of social concepts that may initially be features of friendship but are eventually extended to interpersonal functioning beyond the confines of the relation. The purpose of this chapter is to examine this proposition and to present data that support the thesis that friendship relations have important positive implications for social development in general.

This proposition has been presented as an aspect of the Sullivan-Piaget thesis (Youniss, 1980)—a theory of social development that integrates the perspectives of Piaget (1932, and 1965) and Sullivan (1953). According to this thesis, the objects of social knowing are not "selves" and "others" as beings, but the interpersonal relations which exist between selves and others. Children come to know these relations by focusing on the interactions that occur between persons and by cognitively abstracting from these interactions generalizable forms that serve to distinguish relations from one another. In his book on the development of moral thought, Piaget (1932/1965) depicted peer relations as characterized by an interactive form which he termed "mutual" or "reciprocal." This means simply that participants in peer relations are free to respond to an action taken by one member in any way they wish, including replication. If the peers are to maintain contact, they must cooperate to the extent that they must mutually construct the interaction "rules" they are to abide by. Piaget contrasts these relations with parent-child or authority relations which he describes as characterized by "unilateral" interactions. In parent-child relations the interaction "rules" are not mutually constructed but instead are set forth by one member of the relation (the parent) and conformed to or rebelled against by the other (the child). According to Piaget, these interactive forms (mutual and unilateral) have different consequences for social development. In particular, relations involving mutual interactions (peer relations) lead to the development of concepts of cooperation and mutual respect since they involve the mutual construction of a relation. Piaget saw the development of these concepts as critical for the development of moral thought.

For Sullivan, the foundations of mutual respect and understanding were also found in the context of peer relations. However, Sullivan specified the importance of *friendship*, and emphasized that these concepts may not emerge until a "friend" is differentiated from peers in general on the basis of personal qualities. This relation then represents for the child "...a perfectly novel relationship with the person concerned; he becomes of practically equal importance in all fields of value. Nothing remotely like this has ever happened before" (Sullivan, 1953, p. 245). From Sullivan's perspective, the recognition of the "personhood" of the participants in a friend relation leads not only to a validation of the personal worth of both self and other (i.e., mutual respect) but also fosters the development of interpersonal sensitivity and love.

Thus, according to the Sullivan-Piaget thesis, friendship provides a framework for the development of concepts of cooperation, mutual respect, and interpersonal sensitivity. Although these concepts may first appear as aspects of friendship conceptions, they may eventually be extended to other relations. In this chapter, data are presented that center on the emergance of these concepts in cognitions about friendship, and on the particular features of friendship that foster the development of these concepts. Where relevant, data pertaining to concepts of parent-child relations are introduced to emphasize particular points.

Results to be presented deal with various aspects of friendship. The first study (Volpe, 1976) pertains to the process of becoming friends: How are friends differentiated from classmates or other peers? The second study (Ryan & Smollar, Note 1) is focused on perceptions about the obligations of friendship: At what point are cooperation, mutual respect or interpersonal sensitivity seen as requirements of a friendship? The third study (Volpe, 1980) delineates some of the features of friendship that may foster social development. This study includes subjects' descriptions of the interactions that characterize friendships, their conceptions of changes in their own friendship relations over time, and, finally, their concepts of "self" within their own close friend relations. In all studies, except where noted, the friendship is described as "very close" or "very good" in order to control for possible variations in intensity of the relation (Button, 1979; LaGaipa, 1979).

Development of Concepts of Friendship

General Methodology

The data presented were collected through interviews with children and adolescents ranging in age from 6 to 24 years. All subjects were from middle- or upper-middle-class suburban households. Responses to interview questions were classified in the following manner: All response statements to each question were written out, with any information identifying age and sex removed. The statements were then classified on the basis of content similarity into categories that were not preestablished but developed from the responses themselves. Once categories were established, response statements were assigned category numbers by two independent raters. Reliability was established through a measure of interrater agreement on assignment of all response statements to specific categories.

Becoming Friends

To investigate conceptions about how people become friends, 84 subjects, 28 in each of 3 age levels — 6-7 years, 9-10 years, and 12-13 years (with males and females equally represented at each age level) —were presented with the following situation and questions.

> Mary and Susan (Bill and David for male subjects) are your age. They don't know each other. On their first day at a new school where no one knows each other very well, they are put into the same class and the teacher assigns them to seats which are right next to each other.
> 1. What do you think might happen to make Mary and Susan become friends?
> 2. What do you think might happen to make Mary and Susan not become friends?
> 3. What do you think might happen to make Mary and Susan become best friends?

Responses to these questions were classified on the basis of content similarity into the categories presented in Table 12-1 (interrater agreement was 91%). There were 8 idiosyncratic responses which were not included in the table. The distribution of categories across age levels and sex of subjects was analyzed by chi square tests of independence with the results for age shown in Table 12-1 (there were no sex differ-

Table 12-1. Ways Two Peers Become Friends, Do Not Become Friends, and Become Best Friends

Categories	Age (years)		
	6-7	9-10	12-13
Becoming friends[a]			
1. Perform an activity together ("play together," "talk to each other")	17	8	5
2. Share with or help each other ("share lunch if we forget it," "help with questions if one was late")	10	15	6
3. Get to know each other ("talk and talk and find out if they like the same things," "talk and get to know each other")	0	3	15
Not becoming friends[b]			
1. Do not interact or interact negatively ("purposely ignore," "fight," "call names")	21	19	9
2. Do not "act like" a friend ("don't share," "tell a secret," "take his pencil")	5	9	3
3. Discover they are different ("they find out they have different personalities," "don't have anything in common")	1	0	16
Becoming best friends[c]			
1. Increase amount of time together ("play together all the days," "really play together")	10	10	7
2. Do special things together ("sleep over at his house," "ride bikes together after school")	8	16	7
3. Be similar or exclusive ("like the same things," "have the same habits, like the same things," "be exactly the same and not like anyone else")	0	1	14

[a] χ^2 (4) = 32.73, $p < .001$.
[b] χ^2 (4) = 26.40, $p < .001$.
[c] χ^2 (4) = 35.33, $p < .001$.

ences). Responses of 12- to 13-year-olds differed significantly from those of 6- to 7- and 9- to 10-year-olds. In general, 9- to 10-year-olds did not respond differently from younger subjects except with regard to becoming best friends, χ^2 (1) = 5.45; $p < .05$.

For the most part, subjects in the two younger age levels indicated that two strangers would become friends if they simply "did something together" or did something special for one another (share or help). They would become best friends if the amount of time spent together was increased or extended to settings outside of school; they would not become friends if they did not interact at all or interacted in a negative fashion. In contrast, for the majority of 12- to 13-year-olds, becoming friends involved a process of "getting to know each other." Two people would become best friends if they discovered similarities between them and would fail to become friends if they discovered many differences.

The results of this study suggest that at ages 6-10 years, friendships are identified with interactive practices. Engaging in a positive inter-action constitutes the relation, while not interacting or engaging in a negative interaction negates the relation. As one 10-year-old boy explained: "Friends are easy to make. I can make a friend just like that [snaps fingers]. All you have to do is go up to a guy, say hello, and ask him if he wants to play ball; then he's a friend. If he don't want to play ball, then he's not a friend, unless you decide to play something else." By age 12, however, concepts of friendship include a recognition of the personal qualities of the people involved, particularly their likes, dis-likes, and abilities: "If they find out that they like the same things, they'll be friends." "If they don't have anything in common, one of them is kind of shy but the other is popular, then they won't be friends."

At age 10, the differentiation of peers into friends and "not" friends is based upon the qualities of actions rather than of persons. By age 12, however, differentiation on the basis of personal characteristics is fairly well established. Friends are now seen as people who are similar to one another with respect to their "personalities." This similarity appears to serve the function of maintaining or ensuring their equality; that is, the more similar they are, the more likely they will be to accord one another equal value in the relation. As one 13-year-old girl noted: "They've got to be alike, you know, if one is good at school or at sports and the other isn't, it won't work." A 12-year-old boy pointed out: "You don't want to be friends with someone who's not as good at sports as you, or who's better!"

Obligations of Friendship

Once friendship is conceptualized in terms of the perceived similarity and thus equality of the participants, the question remains as to what is then required of the participants in the relation: What are the "rules" that have been mutually constructed by the friends? Do these rules or obligations change systematically with age? To examine these questions, 125 subjects at ages 10-11 years (40), 13-14 years (38), and 16-17 years (47) (with males and females about equally represented at each age level) were individually asked the following questions:

> Mary and Susan (Bill and David) are your age and they are very
> close friends. What are some things that you think Mary should
> do for her close friend Susan?
> 1. Which one of these do you think is the *most* important?
> 2. Why do you think it is important for Mary to do this?
> 3. What do you think Susan might do if Mary did not do this
>   for her?

Responses to questions 1 (obligations), 2 (reasons), and 3 (reactions) were classified on the basis of content similarity into the categories shown in Table 12-2 (interrater agreement over all 3 questions was 89%). Frequencies across age and sex were analyzed by chi-square tests of independance with the results presented in Table 12-2. Frequencies are given in percentages because of the variation in the number of subjects at each age level and the exclusion of idiosyncratic (6 reasons and 4 reactions) and "don't know" (2 reasons and 7 reactions) responses.

As shown in Table 12-2 distributions of response categories varied significantly depending upon the age and sex of subjects. At age 10-11 years, the most frequently cited obligation of friendship was simply for one friend to behave in a positive manner toward the other. This behavior was described as important because it would benefit the actor either directly ("So he'll be nice to you, too.") or indirectly ("So the relation will keep going smooth."). In addition, failure to meet this obligation was thought most likely to result in a retaliation from the other person. At this age level, no sex differences in responses were apparent.

In contrast, for the majority of 16- to 17-year-olds, the most important obligation of friendship was the provision of emotional support (69% of females, 53% of males). This obligation was perceived as important because it would either benefit the other person (58% of females, 9% of males), or because it simply defined the relationship (17% of females, 57% of males). If one friend failed to meet this obligation, most 16- to 17-year-olds felt that the other persons' feelings would be hurt (56% of females, 33% of males). Subjects at the 13- to 14-year-old level provided the obligation of "protection" more often than did the other two age levels and focused on the "definition of the relation" as a reason for the importance of obligations. With respect to reactions, 13- to 14-year-olds gave primarily retaliation or confrontation responses.

Over all age levels, females were more likely than males to generate obligations dealing with emotional assistance and to give reasons based on the benefit to the other person. When the obligation was not met, females, more often than males, felt the reaction would be either hurt feelings or a confrontation. Males indicated that the reaction would be either retaliation or "nothing" (i.e., "They'd just let it pass.").

The correspondences over all age levels of the type of obligation with the reasons obligations were important are presented in Table 12-3. The significant Chi square analysis indicates that the type of reason given was dependent on the type of obligation. Being "nice" to the other corresponded most frequently with the benefit to the relation, being "protective" corresponded primarily with the definition of the relation, and providing emotional support occurred most frequently in conjunction with the benefit to the other person.

According to the data from this study, the major obligation of friendship for 10- to 11-year-olds is simply to get along with one another, to cooperate. Cooperation is seen as an advantage to the participants in the relations since it keeps the relation running smoothly and prohibits or at least limits instances of negative interactions. By age 13-14, this obligation is replaced by the obligations of protection and emotional support, and at age 16-17 the obligation of emotional support supercedes the other two. "Protection" in this study actually refers to the responsibility of friends to maintain one another's self-respect, that is, to "keep each other out of trouble," to "stick up for one another," to "be loyal to one another," to "not drop one for someone else," etc. At age 13-14, this rule is described as important because it defines the relation or *is* the relation. This is the "rule" that the participants have constructed in the context of their relation. A participant in a friendship is responsible for maintaining the other persons' self-respect because the other person is a *friend*. For most 13- to 14-year-olds, and 16- to 17-year-old males, the obligation to provide emotional assistance also corresponded to reasons based on the definition of the relation. Females at age 16-17, however, suggested that the obligation to provide emotional assistance was important because it contributed to the well-being of the other person. Failure to meet this obligation therefore, would not necessarily result in a retaliation, but would most certainly hurt the other person. Thus, for 16- to 17-year-old females, a participant in a friendship is responsible for providing emotional support to the other person not simply because the other person is a *friend*, but because the other person is a *person*. For these subjects, mutual respect is extended from the relation to the persons, and interpersonal sensitivity becomes an aspect of the relational concept.

In summary, the data from this study indicate that conceptions about the obligations of friendship and the reasons for these obligations incorporate concepts of cooperation, mutual respcet, and interpersonal sensitivity. In addition, the emergence of these concepts follows a developmental course. The latter two concepts do not emerge until concepts of friendship include qualities of persons as well as actions. In addition, interpersonal sensitivity appears after respect has been

Table 12-2. Obligations of Close Friend Relations, Reasons for Obligations, and Reactions to Failures to Meet Obligations

	Age (in years)			Sex	
Categories	10-11	13-14	16-17	F	M
Obligations[a]					
1. Be "nice to ("do things with her," help with school work," "don't fight with him")	80%	24%	11%	26%	48%
2. Be protective ("don't let him get into trouble," "don't leave her for another friend," "stick up for him")	15%	39%	28%	29%	5%
3. Provide emotional support ("listen to her problems," "be there when she needs you, to talk things out," "be understanding, don't laugh at her problems")	5%	37%	62%	45%	27%
Reasons[b]					
1. Benefits the relation ("keeps the relation going good," "so you don't fight")	31%	22%	13%	24%	19%
2. Benefits the actor ("then he'll do that for you," "so she'll like you better")	31%	22%	15%	17%	27%
3. Benefits the other person ("she'll be happier if you do," "because she needs it")	23%	16%	35.5%	42%	9%
4. Defines the relation ("that's what friends are supposed to do," "that's friendship")	14%	40%	35.5%	17%	45%
Reactions to violations[c]					
1. Retaliation ("pays her back," "don't talk to her anymore," "fight with him")	68%	42%	16%	27%	53%
2. Hurt ("she'll feel very sad," "he'd be upset," "she'll feel alone")	29%	12%	26%	42%	18%
3. Confrontation ("go up to her and say 'why did you do that?," "try to find out why")	0	24%	23%	25%	7%

Table 12-2 (*continued*)

Categories	Age (in years)			Sex	
	10-11	13-14	16-17	F	M
4. Acceptance ("he'd just let it pass," "she'd understand," "he'd forgive him")	3	21%	14%	5%	21%

[a]Age, χ^2 (4) = 54.39, $p < .001$; sex, χ^2 (2) = 7.17, $p < .05$.
[b]Age, χ^2 (6) = 12.92, $p < .05$; sex, χ^2 (3) = 22.16, $p < .001$.
[c]Age, χ^2 (6) = 32.45, $p < .001$; sex, χ^2 (3) = 22.38, $p < .001$.
Note. Values indicate the percentage of children whose responses fell into each category.

established and, for some reason, occurs at an earlier age for females than for males.

It is important to note that when subjects were asked these study questions with respect to parent-child relations (i.e., What should a person do for his or her mother [father]? Why? etc.) quite different categories and conceptions resulted (Ryan & Smollar, Note 1). Instead of cooperation, mutual respect, and interpersonal sensitivity, conceptions of parent-child relations were characterized by compliance and unilateral respect. The most frequent obligations given were obedience (10- to 11-year-olds) or meeting parental expectation (older subjects): the reason this obligation was important was most frequently becuase it benefited the child, and parental reactions to failures to meet obligations were usually punishments. This contrast serves to support the hypothesis that concepts of cooperation, mutual respect, and interpersonal sensitivity are fostered in the context of close friend relations.

Self-Concepts and the Interactions of Friendship

Although the data presented above shed some light on when concepts of cooperation, mutual respect, and interpersonal sensitivity emerge in cognitions about friendship, they do not deal with the question of why

Table 12-3. Correspondences Between Obligations and Reasons Obligations Are Important[a]

Obligations	Reasons			
	Benefits relation	Benefits self	Benefits other	Defines relation
Be nice	16	8	5	10
Be protective	4	6	5	15
Provide emotional support	6	4	20	12

[a]χ^2 (6) = 42.01, $p < .001$.

these concepts would be fostered in friendship relations; that is, what are the features of friendship that promote the development of these broader social concepts?

To explore this issue, 80 subjects, 20 in each of four age groups— 10-11, 14-16, 18-19, and 22-24 years (with equal numbers of males and females at each level)—were given the following tasks:

1. Please give three descriptions of the way you are when you are with your close friend, and explain why you are that way.
   When I am with my close friend I am _____ because _____.
2. Please give three descriptions of interactions that you feel characterize a close friend relation between two people who are the same age and sex as you are.
3. Which one of these do you think is most typical of your own relationship with a close friend?
4. Describe how your close friend relations have changed over the past 5 years (if they have).

Responses to the "self-concept" task (question 1) were classified as "descriptions of self" and "reasons" into the categories shown in Table 12-4 (interrater agreement was 92% for self-descriptions and 86% for reasons).

As shown in Table 12-4, the major age difference is that adolescents and young adults frequently described themselves as open and comfortable in close friend relations and gave reasons based on the mutual acceptance or non judgmental aspect of the relation, whereas these categories were rarely used by preadolescent subjects. A sex difference occurred in the frequency of descriptions of one's-self as "open" (67% of such self-descriptions were given by females), but no sex differences appeared with regard to reasons.

These self-concept data suggest that for adolescents and young adults close friendships provide a context of mutual acceptance in which participants are not only extroverted but also feel comfortable and act in open, honest, and spontaneous ways. Self-descriptions given in the context of parent-child relations (When I am with my mother [father] I am _____ because _____.) can be contrasted with these data. At all age levels descriptions of self as open and comfortable occurred infrequently in both the mother-child (19%) and father-child (10%) relational contexts. (Volpe, 1980). Within these relations self-descriptions such as "guarded," "uncomfortable," and "nervous" were given frequently. In addition, reasons based on mutual acceptance accounted for only 2% of those given in both parent-child contexts ($n = 240$ for each relation). Instead, the self's actions and feelings in parent-child contexts were most frequently seen as directed or guided by the parent's actions or feelings toward the child.

Descriptions of the three interactions of friendship were classified on the basis of content similarity into the four categories shown in Table 12-5 (interrater agreement was 94%). The distribution of most

Table 12-4. Descriptions of Self in Close Friend Relations and Reasons for Description

Categories	Age (years)				Sex	
	10-11	14-15	18-19	22-24	F	M
Self descriptions						
1. Happy (content, glad)	15	8	11	9	24	17
2. Comfortable (relaxed, unself-conscious, myself)	4	14	13	13	19	25
3. Open (honest, free, spontaneous)	4	8	13	14	26	13
4. Valued (worthwhile, affirmed, secure, confident)	1	3	5	3	8	4
5. Extroverted (joking, playing, active, talkative, outgoing)	22	17	12	13	31	33
6. Prosocial (considerate, attentive, helpful, friendly)	8	4	5	4	6	15
7. Serious (reflective, quiet, intellectual)	0	4	1	2	3	4
8. Antisocial (argumentative, bossy, manipulative)	4	1	0	0	1	3
9. Miscellaneous (jealous, creative)	2	1	1	1	1	3
Reasons						
1. Self's personality ("the way I am")	8	5	6	4	9	14
2. Feelings about other person ("I like her," "he deserves it")	20	11	16	17	32	32
3. Reactions to other person ("she does that for me")	5	5	3	3	13	3
4. Mutual activity or pleasure ("we're like that together," "we enjoy it," "that's the way we are")	17	16	10	11	26	28
5. Acceptance or understanding ("he doesn't judge me," "she accepts me the way I am")	3	21	25	21	37	33
6. Maintaining relation ("so we'll stay friends")	5	0	0	1	0	6
7. Miscellaneous	2	2	0	0	3	1

Table 12-5. Interactions Described as Characteristic and Most Typical of Close
Friend Relations

	Age (in years)				Sex	
Categories	10-11	14-16	18-19	22-24	F	M
Characteristic interactions						
1. Do something together ("play together," go out and have a few beers," "just sit around together")	42(30)[a]	20(12)	24(7)	11(7)	41	46
2. Talk about mutual interest ("talk about sports," "talk about girls," "have detailed discussions about people")	9(3)	16(13)	5(4)	8(5)	13	25
3. Do something special for ("do a favor for him you wouldn't do for anyone else," "lend each other your clothes")	4(4)	4(3)	6(4)	5(3)	5	14
4. Talk about personal problems and feelings ("talk about family problems," "tell each other everything, your most intimate details," "talk about your problems with your boyfriends")	5(3)	20(4)	35(15)	36(15)	59	37
Most typical interactions[b]						
1. Share interests or activities[c]	15	7	2	1	8	17
2. Share problems or feelings[d]	5	13	18	19	32	23

[a]Numbers of males is indicated in parentheses.
[b]Age χ^2 (3) = 28.43, $p < .001$, sex, χ^2 (1) = 4.72, $p < .05$.
[c]First two categories listed above combined.
[d]Fourth category listed above.

typical interactions was analyzed by the chi square test of independence
across age and sex with the first two categories combined to facilitate
analyses. The results presented in Table 12-5 indicate that the types
of interactions described as characteristic and most typical of ongoing
close friendships vary depending upon the age and sex of subjects. For
preadolescents (10-11 years), close friends simply do things together.
At age 14-16 years, males indicated that close friends not only do things
together, but also discuss topics of mutual interest; females said close
friends discuss personal problems and feelings. By late adolescence and
young adulthood, both males and females indicated that close friendships involve discussions of personal problems and feelings. Thus,
intimacy emerges as a feature of close friendships in early adolescence

and remains a dominant aspect throughout young adulthood. Intimate exchanges, however, occur earlier in female friendships than in male friendships.

Subjects' descriptions of changes in their own close friendships over the past 5 years (Table 12-6) lend further support to the age and sex differences presented in Tables 12-4 and 12-5 (interrater agreement was not calculated for these categories). For the most part, 10- to 11-year-olds suggested that their relations had changed because of a change in either the type of activities ("We used to play with dolls, now we do homework together." "We used to just play together, now we do homework and help each other.") or the level of cooperation ("We don't get into so many fights anymore, there's more cooperation.").

At age 14-16 years, the majority of females reported shifts in the level of intimacy of the relation ("When I was 11, I was hesitant about talking about myself to a friend. Now I can talk about anything, can tell her anything and I know she'll understand. I'm much more open."). Males at this age, however, continued to focus on changes in types of activities ("When you get older, there are more things to do. Stay over at his house, go to dances, you do a lot more than when you're younger.").

By age 18-19, males also described increases in intimacy in their close friendships ("My friendships have gone a lot deeper now. When I was 14, I shared interests but not feelings." "We talk about different things now. More about our problems and how we feel about things.") Females at this age no longer mentioned increases in intimacy but instead noted increases in their own sensitivity to the other person ("I'm more aware of a friend's feelings now, more sensitive to their needs."). By young adulthood, most females reported no changes in their friend relations since late adolescence, whereas 50% of the males continued to discuss changes in terms of increased intimacy or sensitivity to others.

In summary, close friend relations appear to be conceptualized in terms of three types of interactions—sharing activities, sharing interests, and sharing personal problems and feelings. The sharing of personal problems does not appear frequently in concepts of friendship interactions until early adolescence for females and late adolescence for males. In addition, the sharing of interests seems to characterize male friendships more often than female friendships.

The findings with regard to the three types of interactions and their corresponding ages of appearance are consistent with the results of the first study on becoming friends and also correspond to the findings of several other studies of friendship cognitions (Bigelow, 1977; Kon & Losenkov, 1978; LaGaipa, 1979). However, the sex difference found in this study was not apparent in Study 1, and the general research on friendship conceptions has produced conflicting results with respect to this factor.

Table 12-6. Descriptions of Changes in Friend Relations over 5 Years

Type of change	Age (in years)				Sex	
	10-11	14-16	18-19	22-24	F	M
Change in type of activity	12(6)[a]	4(4)	2(2)	0(0)	6	12
Increase in cooperation	5(2)	4(2)	0	0	5	4
Increase in intimacy	0	10(2)	7(5)	3(3)	10	10
Increase in interpersonal sensitivity	0	1(1)	7(1)	4(2)	8	4
No change in relation	3(2)	1(1)	4(2)	13(5)	11	10

[a]Number of males is indicated in parentheses.

When subjects were asked to describe parent-child interactions, quite different categories emerged. In particular, intimate exchanges with mothers were not mentioned with any frequency until age 22-24 years, and intimate exchanges with fathers were very rare at all age levels. In fact, of the 240 possible interactions in this relationship, only 5 involved intimate exchanges.

Implications for Social Development

When taken together, the data from the studies presented in this chapter provide a general picture of conceptions of friendship from age 6 years to young adulthood. In particular, three distinctly different "types" or "levels" of conceptions about friendship appear to emerge during this span, and they are reflected in the social concepts that emerge.

The first level characterizes the thinking of most of the preadolescents interviewed in these studies. At this level, friendship is conceptualized in terms of the quality of ongoing interactions, that is, positive or negative. Becoming a friend involves engaging in a positive activity together; friendships are characterized by the sharing of activities; and the self is seen as happy and extroverted because of the interactions that characterize the relation. In addition, friends are seen as having an obligation to keep interacting positively. Meeting this obligation ensures continuation of the relation. Failure to meet the obligation ensures retaliation and eventual dissolution of the relation. Thus friendship is understood as a relation in which all actions have similar or equal import regardless of actor. In order to maintain the relation, the friends must agree, either implicitly or explicitly, to continue interacting in a positive manner. Within this conceptual level, then, children perceive the major feature of friendship to be reciprocity and the governing "rule" of the relation (i.e., the form of interacting which maintains it) to be cooperation.

During preadolescence, the interactions of friendship seem to shift from a generalized "playing together," prevalent at age 6-7 years, to more specified activities (e.g., sports, dolls, homework, etc). This specification of activities suggests that the willingness of individuals to co-operate with one another in the maintenance of a friendship may depend upon how willing they are to engage in the same types of activities. Eventually, this willingness of an individual to engage in particular types of activities becomes conceptualized as an aspect or a characteristic of the person (his or her personality); it is at this point that a different type of friendship conception appears.

The second type of friendship conception emerges at the onset of adolescence and is characterized by a differentiation of peers into friends and "not friends," not on the basis of the qualities of actions, but rather on the qualities of persons. Becoming friends is seen as a process of discovering these qualities and establishing the similarity of the friends with respect to these qualities. Thus there is a recognition of the "personhood" of the participants, with particular emphasis on the similarity of personalities. This perceived similarity suggests that friendship is now seen as a relation in which persons as well as actions have similar or equal import. The equality status friends accord one another at this level is what appears to differentiate this relation from parent-child relations. Friends are aware that they approach inter-actions with one another on an equal footing; that is, the ideas, attitudes, or behaviors expressed by both members of the relation are assumed to have equal value and are considered from that perspective. This is reflected in the conception of friendship as a relation in which the self is accepted or not judged by the other: "She accepts me so I can let myself go." "I know he'll accept me no matter what I do." "He's my equal, he won't judge me." This sense of the importance of equality is also apparent in the conception of friendship as involving an obligation to maintain one another's self-respect: "Keep him out of trouble." "Stick up for her." "Be loyal to him." This obligation is seen as important because it is what the friends committed themselves to when they became friends.

At the second level, conceptions about friendship involve a recognition of the personal qualities and general equality of the participants. The dominant feature of the relation is acceptance, and mutual respect the governing rule. At this level, however, respect is accorded to the "other" because he or she is a *friend*, and equality is based on the perceived similarity of the friends. The concept of mutual respect is not yet extended beyond the limits of the relation. Such an extension of mutual respect to the other as a person and not merely as a friend is one of the features that characterizes the third type of friendship conceptions.

In the third type of conception, acceptance remains a major feature of the relation; however, here it fosters not only the feeling that a person can "let loose," but also that he or she can exchange personal information. Participants in a close friendship are now seen as free to reveal personal problems and feelings without fear of losing the other person's respect. At this level, not only is the revealing of personal information viewed as a dominant aspect of the relation, but the major obligation of the relation is to respond to such self-disclosures with support and assistance, This obligation is seen as important, not simply because it defines the relationship, but because it benefits the other person: "makes her feel better," "makes her happier," "meets some need" that he or she has. In addition, at this level, adolescents no longer stress the importance of similarity of personality: differences are tolerated with respect to interests, attitudes, and behavior, and the major "similarity" factor is that they are equals. Thus, the participants in the relation are no longer conceptualized as "actors" or as "similar in personality," but as individuals. There is, at this point, an appreciation of the individuality of the person and an acceptance of it as an aspect of both the other and the self.

An interesting finding with regard to these levels of friendship conceptions is that females reach the third level long before males do, and the conceptions of many males, even at young adulthood, do not incorporate interpersonal sensitivity as an aspect of the relation. One reason for this sex difference may lie in the finding that intimate exchanges—the feature of friendship that appears to foster interpersonal sensitivity—do not appear with any frequency in descriptions of male close friendships until late adolescence. Prior to this time in their friendships males reveal information about their feelings about things and their hopes and plans for life, but they do not discuss personal problems or get involved in intimate exchanges involving the admission of weaknesses or frailities. There are several possible explanations for this lag in the age of onset of intimacy in friendship. One is that self-disclosure among males is simply less culturally acceptable (Derlega & Chaikin, 1977), particularly at early to midadolescence when concern with masculinity appears to be high. Another possiblity is that male, unlike female friendships often involve group activities (e.g., sports) that are not conducive to intimate exchanges (Eder & Hallinan, 1978; Lever, 1978). Finally, a third reason may be that males prefer to discuss personal problems or feelings in the context of cross-sex rather than same-sex friend relations since they may perceive other males, even friends, as potential competitors (Komarovsky, 1974). Whatever the explanation, this sex difference in the development of friendship conceptions requires further investigation and has implications for understanding other relations, particularly marriage and parent-child relations, and the more general social functioning of males and females (Gilligan, 1977).

Another issue that requires further investigation is the apparent hierarchical nature of these levels of friendship conceptions. The results of these studies suggest that conceptions represent levels of thought and that earlier concepts, such as cooperation, equality, and respect, do not drop out, but are instead incorporated into later conceptualizations. Although this is implied by the results presented in this chapter, further study is needed to clarify both the characteristics of the levels and their hierarchical nature.

The three types of friendship conceptions discussed here have many similarities to the stages of friendship cognitions presented by Bigelow (1977) and Selman and Jaquette (1977), although a description of these types as "stages" is considered premature. In particular, Bigelow's description of friendship conceptions in terms of a reward-cost stage, a normative stage, and an empathetic stage corresponds to the concepts of cooperation, mutual respect, and interpersonal sensitivity. This work is intended to elaborate on the findings of Bigelow (1977) and others (Kon & Losenkov, 1978; Berndt, Note 2) by delineating some of the features of friendship that may foster the development of particular concepts, and by linking conceptions about friendship to a broader context of social development. In addition, the focus of this work is always the relationship; that is, conceptions about friendship are constructed from the types of interactions that take place within the relation and are aspects of the relation itself. This point is supported by the briefly mentioned findings that concepts of parent-child relations involve quite different elements.

It is also important to note that the descriptions of friendship conceptions presented here are not intended to suggest that adolescent friendships in actuality are idyllic relations in which participants live "happily ever after." Conflicts are frequent, friends can and do hurt each other, and friendships do end, often in very cruel and insensitive ways (Youniss, 1980). However, during their existence, friendships provide a context in which the development of concepts of cooperation, mutual respect, and interpersonal sensitivity are fostered. Although any given friend relation may end, the conceptual framework about the relation remains to be extended to other persons, to new relations, and to social functioning in general. It is precisely this broader implication of conceptions of friendship that makes them an important area of study for developmental psychologists.

Individuality and Social Cohesion

The present findings agree quite well with Sullivan's (1953) thesis regarding healthy psychological development. In particular, they bear out his argument concerning the value of friendship in self-acceptance. Sullivan viewed the individual in unilateral relations (such as parent-child) as figuring out "what to do to get what I want." This is based on the power differential wherein authority figures distribute approval and nonapproval for conformity and disobedience, respectively. In such an arrangement, seeking approval requires hiding faults and weaknesses. It may also foster exaggeration of one's talents and assets in order to gain approval. Given this situation, Sullivan wished that friends would get to know practically all they could about one another. He saw this as a remedy for repression and exaggeration and as a means of fending off the sense of feeling different than anyone else.

As was seen in the data, friends do in fact reveal themselves to one another, undoubtedly under the safeguards of trust and reciprocity. They go to each other with problems, seeking advice and validation. While they realize the risks of self-disclosure, they proceed under the guarantee that their friend will not judge them so much as try to understand them. As a consequence, friendship is conducive to realistic self-acceptance since it does not encourage defensive presentations of self. The self, with all its needs and weaknessess, as well as its capacities to help others, comes to be respected. Thus, within friendship, individuals feel that they can "really be themselves" and do not have to put on a false show.

The intriguing aspect of Sullivan's theory is that individuation progresses without the self's loss of need or of interest in the relationship; that is, late adolescents and young adults are sensitive to the other's personhood and keep in mind that their actions have an impact on the other's well-being. This will be recognized as an old problem in social science which concerns the "individual" and "social cohesion" (Becker, 1968). One of the standard solutions has been to posit rationality in the individual and then to call it the means by which individuals suppress self-interest for the sake of promoting the welfare of others. While this "enlightened self-interest" is a plausible hypothesis, Sullivan's relational approach is equally plausible and clearly supported by our data. Within the bond of friendship, the friends are able to maintain their individuality while they simultaneously see themselves as interdependent with others.

Thus one can see a further implication of friendship in the area of morality. It is almost futile to ask where individual interest leaves off and the interests of the relationship begin within the context of friendship. Apparently, once friends agree to cooperate, mutual needs and interests become as important as those of either individual. As was noted in the data, tit-for-tat reciprocity dropped out of friendship early and was replaced by a reciprocity of principle which freed the friends from time and amount restrictions. The economic idea of "I will do this for you, if you will do this for me" gave way to the moral thesis of *we will act for our common interest.*

While the concept of mutuality merits expansion, the present point is that psychological theorists in general have not given relational commitment its proper due. Instead, theorists have tended to focus on autonomy, wherein the individual is free from all relational constraints in a self-assured reliance on rational reasoning. In such a model, autonomy becomes competitive with relationships, the latter representing perhaps "lower stages" because they call for particularizations in adjustment rather than giving primacy to universal laws.

This is an unnecessary dichotomy. The *we* of friendship does not have to cancel either individuality or generality. Principles acquired through friendship may be transferrable to other relations; indeed they may serve as ideals for which individuals strive in their other relations (Piaget, 1932/1965). In regard to individuality itself, to view oneself as a member of relations does not imply loss of autonomy. The key notion is, of course, mutual respect, since once it is engendered through friendship, mutual and self-interest become two sides of one coin. Acts that promote the relationship simultaneously enhance the self and liberate the self from the distorting illusion that self-reliance on rationality is sufficient.

Acknowledgments

This work was supported in part by a grant from the W. T. Grant Foundation. Jacqueline Smollar's name also appears as "Volpe" in the text and references.

Reference Notes

1. Ryan, J., & Smollar, J. *A developmental analysis of obligations in parent-child and friend relations.* Unpublished manuscript, The Catholic University of America, 1978.
2. Berndt, T. J. *Children's conceptions of friendship and the behavior expected of friends.* Unpublished manuscript, Yale University, 1979.

References

Austin, M. C., & Thompson, E. E. Children's friendships: A study of the basis on which children select and reject their best friends. *The Journal of Educational Psychology*, 1948, *39*, 101-106.

Becker, E. *The structure of evil.* New York: Free Press, 1968.

Bigelow, B. J. Children's friendship expectations: A cognitive developmental study. *Child Development*, 1977, *48*, 246-253.

Bigelow, B. J., & LaGaipa, J. J. Children's written descriptions of friendship: A multi-dimensional analysis. *Developmental Psychology*, 1975, *11*, 857-888.

Button, L. Friendship patterns. *Journal of Adolescence*, 1979, *2*, 187-199.

Cattell, R. B. Friends and enemies: A psychological study of character. *Character and Personality*, 1934, *3*, 54-63.

Derlega, V. J., & Chaikin, A. L. Privacy and self-disclosure in social relationships. *Journal of Social Issues*, 1977, *33*, 102-114.

Eder, D., & Hallinan, M. T. Sex differences in children's friendships. *American Sociological Review*, 1978, *43*, 237-250.

Gilligan, C. In a different voice: Women's conceptions of self and of morality. *Harvard Educational Review*, 1977, *47*, 481-517.

Jacqueline Smollar and James Youniss

Hartup, W. Children and their friends. In H. McGurk (Ed.), *Issues in childhood social development*. London: Methuen, 1978.

Komarovsky, M. Patterns of self-disclosure of male undergraduates. *Journal of Marriage and the Family*, 1974, *36*, 677-686.

Kon, I. S., & Losenkov, V. A. Friendship in adolescence: Values and behavior. *Journal of Marriage and the Family*, 1978, *40*, 143-155.

LaGaipa, J. J. A developmental study of the meaning of friendship in adolescence. *Journal of Adolescence*, 1979, *2*, 201-213.

Lever, J. Sex difference in the complexity of children's play and games. *American Sociological Review*, 1978, *43*, 471-483.

Piaget, J. *The moral judgment of the child* (M. Gabain, trans.). New York: Free Press, 1965. (Originally published, 1932.)

Reisman, J. M., & Shorr, S. I. Friendship claims and expectations among children and adult. *Child Development*, 1978, *49*, 913-916.

Selman, R. L., & Jaquette, D. Stability and oscillation in itnerpersonal awareness: A clinical developmental analysis. In C. B. Keasey (Ed.), *The Nebraska Symposium on Motivation* (Vol. 25), Lincoln, Neb. University of Nebraska Press, 1977.

Sullivan, J. S. *The interpersonal theory of psychiatry*. New York: Norton, 1953.

Volpe, J. *The development of children's conceptions of friendship*. Unpublished master's thesis, The Catholic University of America, 1976.

Volpe, J. *The development of concepts of parent-child and friend relations and of self within these relations*. Unpublished doctoral dissertation, The Catholic University of America, 1980.

Wellman, R. The school child's choice of companions. *Journal of Educational Research*, 1926, *14*, 126-132.

Youniss, J. *Parents and peers in social development*. Chicago: University of Chiago Press, 1980.

Youniss, J., & Volpe, J. A relational analysis of children's friendship. In W. Damon (Ed.), *Social cognition*. San Francisco: Jossey-Bass, 1978, pp. 1-22.

Part III

Individual Differences in Peer Relationships and Social Skills

Chapter 13

Toward an Applied Social Ethology: A Case Study of Social Skills Among Blind Children

Henry Markovits and F. F. Strayer

One of the more important questions in developmental research concerns the effects of various forms of socializing experiences upon the acquisition of interactive skills among normal and atypical children. Programs of social integration for the atypical have been developed that focus upon particular aspects of the child's behavior which are thought to reflect an important part of general social competence. However, even assuming that we can define such general social competence, relatively little is known about the potential socialization processes that underlie social skill acquisition. Such knowledge is especially lacking for atypical children (Klein, 1977; Wynne, Ulfelder, & Dakoff, Note 1). In this respect, classical human ethology has already provided useful information concerning behavioral adaptations of atypical children (Hutt & Hutt, 1970; Tinbergen, 1974). Given its emphasis on direct observation of naturally occurring activity and its avoidance of premature theoretical constructs, social ethology promises to provide equally important normative information on the emergence of social skills among young children.

Ethology and Social Development

Ethology is often inappropriately defined as a discipline within the behavioral sciences which involves the direct observation of naturally occurring behavior. The problem with such a definition is apparent in the field of child psychology, where a strong emphasis upon the description of natural developmental phenomena has had a long and important history (Barker, 1930; Barker, 1965; Chittenden, 1942; Dawe, 1943; Emmerich, 1964; Gellert, 1961, 1962; Piaget, 1948, 1952; Shirley, 1933; Washburn, 1932). To distinguish between ethological and other approaches to behavior it is necessary to look beyond common interests in natural phenomena. The different approaches to descriptive analysis in ethological research and in developmental psychology reflect basic conceptual differences (Bateson & Hinde, 1976; Blurton-Jones, 1972; Kummer, 1971; Tinbergen, 1963).

Kummer ('1971) provides a thorough and concise summary of the explanatory network that constitutes the ethological framework for the analysis of behavior. Regardless of the explanatory perspective adopted within a particular research program, the initial questions necessarily concern the organization or structure of behavioral phenomena. A common focus in all ethological research is the commitment to provide a detailed description of behavioral patterns observed for a given species. Many of the important advances in child ethology during the past decade have dealt directly with specifying the diversity of behavioral patterns characterizing the activity of young children (Blurton-Jones, 1972; Blurton-Jones & Leach, 1972; Brannigan & Humphries, 1972; Grant, 1969; Leach, 1972; McGrew, 1970, 1972; Smith & Connolly, 1972). Although these descriptive studies were not intended to deal with the emergence of social relationships and group structure, they represent the necessary first step for a detailed ethological analysis of peer group social ecology. A basic assumption for such an analysis is that complex social phenomena cannot be understood without a detailed consideration of qualitative differences in the individual action patterns that constitute social exchanges between young children.

Although Kummer's discussion of the general framework for a biological analysis of behavior suggests a relatively unified conceptual orientation in ethological research, differences in emphasis have led to considerable diversity within the field. Crook (1970) has argued that there are two quite distinct theoretical approaches in modern ethology. The more traditional approach, classical ethology, focuses directly upon the detailed analysis of behavioral patterns, their immediate causation, and their development. The second approach, social ethology, deals more exclusively with patterns of social behavior, the coordination of activity between individuals, and the evolutionary history of social structures. Social ethology emerged as a separate branch of behavioral biology due to a marked increase in field information about social behavior among nonhuman primates. Given both the complexity and diversity of primate societies and their impact on individual development, the more classical approach to the analysis of individual differences proved inadequate. An adequate account of the contextual influences on social behavior forced primatologists to develop more elaborate methods for the analysis of group organization. According to Crook (1970), the concern in primatology with the social context of individual adaptation directly parallels the more traditional emphasis in classical ethology on the physical environment as the context for both species and individual development. However, social ethologists assume that influences of the physical environment upon the individual are most often mediated by the social ecology of the stable group. In this sense, social ethologists reformulate the traditional organism—environment dichotomy in terms of three continually interacting systems: the physical habitat, the social ecology of the group, and, finally, the organism itself. An adequate understanding of individual adaptation to the physical environment requires at least a preliminary consideration of the organization of the social unit in which the individual develops.

The stability and organization of any social unit depends upon a delicate balance between social activities promoting group cohesion and those leading to social dispersion (McGrew, 1972; Wilson, 1975). Dominance relations formalize dyadic roles during periods of aggressive conflict, and thus serve as a regulatory system that minimizes dispersive aggressive encounters between group members. In contrast, activities that promote group cohesion attract individuals to one another and maintain them in a coordinated social unit. Dominance relations have undoubtedly received the majority of research attention in both human and primate social ethology (Omark, Strayer, & Freedman, 1980). By comparison, comprehensive studies of cohesive activities have been both fewer in number and more limited in scope. Much of this limitation has resulted from a fragmentation of interest in different forms of cohesive activity. By using only certain behaviors in studies of social attraction, many researchers have provided arguments that are insufficient to account for observed patterns of social cohesion.

The central conceptual problem involves determining the relative utility of general descriptive concepts such as leadership, control roles, attention structures, attachment bonds, and kinship patterns as necessary and/or sufficient dimensions for the analysis of primate social organization (Chance & Jolly, 1970; DeVore, 1965; Jay, 1968; Jolly, 1972; Kummer, 1971). With the increasing awareness that standardized procedures for assessing primate social relations provided reliable information, but failed to predict social behavior within the group setting (Bernstein, 1970), researchers began to emphasize the descriptive analysis of spontaneously occurring behavior as the most appropriate means of identifying basic dimensions of social ecology for stable groups. This trend toward the use of direct observation culminated in a more systematic approach for the inductive analysis of social relationships and group structures (Hinde, 1974). This approach stresses clear distinctions among four levels of social description. The first level entails identification of social action patterns, defined as morphologically distinct motor movements directed toward or away from another group member (e.g., walk toward, smile at, run away, look away). Examination of recurrent sequential combinations of these patterns during the course of social participation between individuals permits the isolation of characteristic forms of social exchange for members of a stable group. The regularity and diversity of such forms of interaction for different dyads suggests larger categories of qualitatively different forms of social exchange that can be used as converging measures of specific dimensions of social relationships between peers. Finally, analysis of general principles that summarize the organization of observed relationships provides an empirical basis for the derivation of the social structures that comprise the social ecology of the stable group.

Given the relatively recent formulation of an inductive system for the investigation of social organization, it is not surprising that in most instances studies in child ethology have not offered detailed information about the social ecology of young children's peer groups. In fact, most studies have provided more classical analyses of individual behavioral units and the integration of these units into more extended individual action sequences (Blurton-Jones & Leach, 1972; McGrew, 1972). The few studies that have dealt more directly with questions about social relationships and group structures have adopted a unidimensional approach to social ecology by emphasizing agonistic interactions and group dominance hierarchies (Strayer & Strayer, 1976; Misshakian, Note 2) or have attempted to relate information about social dominance relations to measures of individual differences in rates of social activity (Abramovitch, 1976; Abramovitch & Strayer, 1978; Sluckin & Smith, 1977; Vaughn & Waters, 1978).

Research at our own laboratory has emphasized the development of analytical methods that can provide a more complete view of peer group social ecology. This work involves the concurrent use of observational procedures for the analysis of dispersive, or antisocial, exchanges, as well as cohesive, or positive, social interactions between preschool children during periods of free play. Our descriptive analyses emphasize the same functional distinction between forms of social behavior that was introduced by McGrew (1972). *Dispersive activities* are defined as those behavioral patterns that are generally followed by a separation of the children involved in interaction, while *cohesive activities* are those behaviors that are more often associated with the maintenance of social proximity and the continuation of social exchange.

Analysis of Social Dominance

From a comparative perspective, the resolution of social conflict within a stable group is seldom chaotic; rather, it is organized in terms of a system of dyadic prerogatives that we call the social dominance hierarchy. The concept of social dominance provides perhaps the best illustration of the difference between an ethological and more traditional psychological analysis of preschool social behavior. Social dominance is a descriptive concept that refers to an observable pattern for the resolution of social conflict among members of a stable social group. It is not a property of individuals, but rather reflects a relationship between them. While psychologists have tended to focus upon the frequency of aggressive acts as a measure of an individual disposition, ethologists have more characteristically concerned themselves with patterns of conflict resolution and the implications of such patterns for group stability. From an ethological perspective, the emergence of a stable dominance hierarchy helps to minimize the dispersive effect of social conflict and thus contributes directly to an increase in social cohesion for the group. Given a stable dominance hierarchy, each group member is able to anticipate and avoid the adverse consequences of severe social aggression.

Social dominance essentially involves asymmetrical social relationships. *Dyadic dominance* refers to the balance of social power between two individuals in a social group, while *group dominance structure* refers to the organizational system that summarizes the coordination of all such dyadic relationships. Among most nonhuman primates, the group dominance structure is hierarchically arranged and is governed by a linear transitivity rule. Thus, if individual A is dominant to B, and B is dominant to C, then A should also be dominant to C. Although such transitivity usually prevails among observed dyadic relationships, it is not uncommon to find exceptions where a circular structure better represents the relations between three group members. The appropriateness of the linear dominance model as a summary of the group dominance structure can be evaluated in terms of the proportion of observed relationships that correspond to a linear rule. In primate groups, more than 95% of the observed relations can usually be organized into a linear structure (Strayer, 1980).

Observational studies of normal preschool children have produced similar findings. In studies of 15 independent groups ranging in age from 12 to 62 months, between 88% and 97% of observed relations were found to be organized linearly (Strayer, 1980, Note 3; Gauthier, Note 4; Gauthier & Strayer, Note 5). These results indicate that throughout the preschool years, resolution of dyadic conflicts among normal children leads to a dominance hierarchy that closely resembles the linear transitive structure commonly evident among nonhuman primates.

Social Cohesion

Although a comparative perspective toward preschool social conflict has provided some insight into one structural aspect of peer group social ecology, corresponding methods for the analysis of cohesive social structures are not well developed. In fact, much of the comparative research on primate social organization, like the research on child social ethology, has placed primary importance upon dominance as an analytical concept. Theoretically, the relative neglect of more positive social bonds is curious, since the analysis of dominance structures assumes that there are strong cohesive factors that make group membership a viable option for all individuals. Only such cohesive factors would lead to the aggregation of individuals and the need to regulate dispersive social activity within a system of individual prerogatives that we call dominance.

Although elaborate methods for the analysis of naturally occurring cohesive structures have not been developed, considerable theoretical attention has been given to changes in the relative influence of different cohesive factors during the course of individual development (Hinde, 1974). The work of Bowlby (1969, 1973) and Harlow and Harlow (1965) provides an important conceptual framework for the comparative analysis of affectional ties between age-mates. From this perspective, such relationships should involve types of behavioral exchange that are similar in form or function to activities characteristically observed in mother-child attachment. Theoretically, such behaviors should be discriminately initiated toward specific figures in the stable peer group and have a high probability of being reciprocated by the selected peer.

Our current approach to the analysis of social bonds among preschool children entails a procedure that permits the identification of multiple preferences for each group member. Observations of normal groups indicate that the development of cohesive activities differs radically from that of social conflict (Strayer, 1980, 1981; Markovits & Strayer, Note 6). The number of affiliative gestures is much higher than the frequency of agonistic actions throughout the preschool years. In addition, the dyadic distribution of cohesive activity is not similar to that of aggression or competition. Levels of dyadic asymmetry are much lower and indicate that a hierarchical model cannot adequately represent the organization of affiliative relations within the preschool group. Nonetheless, individuals show definite affiliative preferences which can be determined by the relative frequency of cohesive gestures directed toward other members of the stable group. Such discriminative deployment of affiliative gestures permits the quantitative assessment of the strength of a preferential social choice, as well as qualitative judgments about whether it is reciprocated or remains unidirectional. Simultaneous consideration of all social choices reveals a social network which permits the identification of socially central and isolated individuals.

Research on older groups of preschool children shows a high level of reciprocated affiliative bonding providing the central cohesive core for the group, with relatively few social isolates (Strayer, 1980). Similar analyses with younger, 1- to 3-year-old children indicate a lack of such cohesive integration. In the latter groups, the relative proportion of reciprocal bonding was inversely related to age. This indicates that complex affiliative networks develop slowly over the preschool period, in sharp contrast to dominance structures, which appear to be quite stable throughout the preschool years (Strayer, 1981; Markovits & Strayer, Note 6).

Social Ethology and Atypical Children

Modern child ethology provides an analytical framework that accepts and accommodates the complexity of naturally occurring social interactions. It thus represents an excellent approach to the study of atypical development. However, there have not been many attempts to apply ethological methods in applied settings, despite Tinbergen's (1976) eloquent argument to this effect. Some work has been done in a psychiatric context, and certain studies have been made of handicapped children (Ispa & Matz, 1978; Porter, Ramsy, Tremblay, Iaccobo, & Crawley, 1980). A study has been recently completed in our laboratory that is interesting in this context. Delorme-Schoof looked at the social behavior of both physically handicapped and normal children in an integrated preschool setting. She found that there was no difference between these children in terms of both the quantity and the forms of affiliative behavior produced. However, the handicapped children had fewer preferential social partners and were involved in relatively fewer reciprocal bonds. These children were, on the whole, isolated in the context of the existing social network, despite their "normal" level of both production and reception of affiliative gestures (Delorme-Schoof & Precourt, in press; Delorme-Schoof, Strayer, & Precourt, Note 7).

The study by Delorme-Schoof provides a good example of the necessity of examining social behavior at various but precise analytical levels in order to obtain a truer image of social functioning in a given group. The present study extends both the techniques and the analytical framework of human ethology to the study of a group of blind preschool children. However, before discussing the results of this research it is important to indicate clearly both the limitations and the possible benefits of our approach.

The particular method which we have adopted has been characterized as a group case study in child ethology. This implies the analysis of a large base of data on the behavior patterns of a single group of individuals. It is clear that the particular group chosen is not necessarily characteristic of the population in question. In this respect, results of a given study cannot be generalized per se to other members of this population. Further studies must be performed in order to widen the data base available in terms of the number of individuals studied. In this respect, ethological methods appear less efficient than those involving large-sample techniques. However, large-scale studies in behavioral research are confronted with trade-offs between the sample size and the quality of information that can be collected. Typically, such studies involve testing procedures and/or sociometric assessments (Force, 1956; Richardson, Hastorf, Goodman, & Dombusch, 1961; Richardson, Ronald, & Kleck, 1974). These methods imply two methodological choices that have an important bearing on the validity of obtained results. First, both testing procedures and sociometric assessments rely on indirect measures of behavior. They are thus subject to what we call *symbolic stress*. Simply, this refers to the problem involved in correlating what children say they are doing with what they actually do. While studies of children's reports of their own social behavior, or performance on various test measures are of great interest, the exact relation between such studies and naturally occurring behavior is not clear (Krasnor & Rubin, 1981). Second, the use of large samples to analyze a phenomenon as complex as social behavior necessarily implies the selection of a limited subset of relevant variables for examination. Actual choices made in such studies vary greatly. In the context of concrete problems, these can determine the elaboration of long-term programs and the application of specific intervention strategies, yet there is no assurance that the specific factors examined in any given study are sufficiently descriptive of actual behavior to permit unequivocal choices. In fact, the plethora of existing intervention techniques for atypical children indicates the opposite.

With respect to these two factors, ethological group case studies present particular advantages. First, direct observation of actual behavior in a particular environment (home, school, institution, etc.) permits accurate descriptions of the specific social dynamic in question and eliminates problems posed by indirect assessment techniques. Second, using a restricted sample size enables a corresponding increase in the quality of the descriptive information that can be collected. It thus becomes possible to examine a larger array of parameters that are related to a particular problem. Such studies could in fact be used as bases for subsequent large-sample studies and could supply useful and important indications of the predictive value for actual behavior of a given subset of relevant factors.

In the present study, an attempt has been made to analyze social behavior of a group of blind preschool children. The results of this research are not intended to characterize the population of blind preschool children. Further studies must be conducted to assess the generalizability of our initial findings. On the other hand, this study has the advantage of considering a wide range of behaviors and several forms of organization of these behaviors. The problem of social skills among blind children is thus examined from a multileveled analytical perspective. In addition, although it cannot supply definite answers to the concrete problems facing special education teachers, the relative completeness of the ethological analysis presented should at least have the value of sensitizing educators to forms of behavior or structures of social interactions that are not always readily apparent.

Social Functioning of Blind Preschool Children

Subjects and Settings

The present study provides an ethological analysis of the social functioning of a group of blind preschool children brought together for an initial experience of peer socialization at the Institut Nazareth et Louis Braille in Montreal. Social functioning within two similar groups of sighted preschool children was examined in order to provide a comparative perspective for assessing potential social skill deficits among the blind subjects.

The first group consisted of six visually handicapped subjects whose average age was 48 months. All these children were legally blind (two had slight visual residues, the other four were totally blind). In all but one case the handicap was congenital. The two groups of sighted children were comprised of four and five children whose average age was 49 months.

The group of blind children met three mornings a week for 1 month. They met in a playroom at the institute under the supervision of three special education teachers. The two groups of sighted children met once a week for 2 hours of free play over a 3-week period. The sighted children were supervised by two adults who maintained a generally passive role. None of the children had any previous formal peer group experience.

Procedure

Social activities of the three groups were recorded on videotape. The blind children were filmed by means of a mobile camera using a 5-minute focal sampling method (Altmann, 1974). A total of 90 minutes of videotape per child was obtained. The two groups of sighted children were filmed by means of a fixed camera (McGrew, 1972). The camera was strategically placed to capture most of the available space in the room, and the children were encouraged to avoid the small corner that was not within the range of the camera. An average of 75 minutes of observation per child was obtained for these two groups.

Two observers trained in ethological analysis coded the videotapes using a social action inventory elaborated for preschool children (see Table 13-2). Social activity was coded using a dyadic syntax that explicitly describes the interactive aspect of social exchanges (Strayer, 1980).[1] For each dyadic interaction, the observer noted the initiator of the exchange, the behavior category observed, the social partner, and

---

[1] Copies of the coding scheme used in this study can be obtained by writing to the Laboratoire d'Ethologie Humaine, Université du Québec à Montréal, 1750 St. André, Montréal, Québec, Canada.

the behavior emitted in response to the initial social action. Lack of response was coded either as "ignores," which implied the absence of response to a clearly receivable message, or "doesn't perceive," which indicated that the social partner could not perceive the initial signal. When all aspects of an interaction sequence were not clearly observable, the code "not identifiable" was used to maintain the dyadic syntax. An uninterrupted series of dyadic exchanges was considered a sequence; it terminated when there was either a 5-second pause in activity or a change of social partner. A set of one or more sequences was labeled an interactive episode; it was terminated by either a 30-second pause or a change of social partner.

Levels of Analysis

Social behavior of the blind and sighted groups was examined at four distinct levels of analysis. The initial level involved examination of the relative frequency of observed social action patterns. The resulting measures provide direct indicators of the forms of social activity that characterize the blind and the sighted children and permit useful comparisons along this dimension. The second level examined the social consequences of the various interactive behaviors used by the children. The measures employed in this context reflect the extent to which given social action patterns encourage or inhibit the continuation of initiated social interactions. They provide an evaluation of the relative effectiveness of used behaviors that is independent of rates of emission. The first two levels of analysis deal essentially with group profiles and global interactive patterns. The final two levels concern the specific interactional patterns that characterize both dominance and affiliative relationships in each of the groups examined. The first of these levels involved an examination of the degree of asymmetry or reciprocity of the various dyadic relationships encountered in each of the groups. This permits examination of the overall directionality and stability of these relationships. Finally, dominance hierarchies and affiliative networks were constructed. These enable consideration of multiple relationships within a single group and permit comparisons of power structures and cohesive ties between groups.

Social Participation and Behavioral Profiles

Social participation. A general summary of social activity observed among our blind and sighted children is presented in Table 13-1. These measures reflect mean rates of various forms of social participation. The rate of total social behavior refers just to the emission of the specific categories of action included in our coding taxonomy. This measure shows that the rate of social activity was much higher among the seeing children than among the blind. A similar result was obtained in comparisons of rates of social exchanges. Social exchanges are emissions of action categories that result in directed responses by the social partner. These represent a minimal unit of social interaction and imply the continuation of social participation due to a successful bid by the child initiating the exchange. Sighted children showed a mean rate of social exchanges more than three times as high as that of the blind children. In other words, not only did they produce more social behaviors, but a much greater proportion of their behaviors provoked some sort of social response from their peers.

The final two measures in Table 13-1 concern the rate of participation in more complex units of interaction comprising several dyadic exchanges. An interactive sequence is a set of two or more exchanges that terminates with at least 5 seconds of inactivity or a change of social partner. These are more complex units of social participation in that they can represent a set of almost continuous social interactions between the same two partners. Mean rates of production of interactive sequences were remarkably similar for both blind and sighted children. This contrasts strongly with results obtained for behavioral rates and dyadic exchanges. It thus appears that the blind children produced fewer social acts, but these acts were distributed among a similar number of interactive sequences. Consequently, their social participation in interactive sequences was much shorter and comprised fewer social exchanges than those of their sighted peers. The final measure, interactive episodes, characterizes bouts between two social partners that may contain periods of inactivity yet somehow retain an essential continuity. Interactive episodes terminate with a period of at least 30 seconds of inactivity, or with the change of social partners. The 30-second interval is somewhat arbitrary but provides a satisfactory basis for distinguishing between basically continuous interactive bouts and adjacent sequences of discontinuous interactions involving the same social partners. The ratio between interactive sequence production and interactive episode production gives an indication of the number of times the same two children continued to interact despite the existence of a break that was longer than 5 seconds. These ratios are 1.11 and

Table 13-1. Measures of Social Participation

Form of participation	Blind		Sighted	
	Frequency	Hourly rate per individual	Frequency	Hourly rate per individual
Behaviors	633	70.3	1327	118.8
Exchanges	165	18.3	683	61.1
Sequences	224	24.9	281	25.2
Episodes	194	21.6	207	18.5

1.36 for the blind and sighted subjects, respectively. Although this difference is not very large, it provides additional support for the notion that the social participation of the sighted children was more complex than that of the blind children.

The differences in these preliminary measures of social functioning suggest potentially important differences in social skills of sighted and blind children. However, these measures do not provide sufficient insight into the nature of these divergent patterns of social participation. In order to arrive at a more complete description of the differences between the groups, a more detailed consideration of social behavior is required.

Behavioral profiles. The relative frequency of each form of social action included in our coding taxonomy is given in Table 13-2. Visual inspection of group profiles suggested qualitatively different modes of social functioning. A correlational analysis of the two profiles confirmed this initial impression (Pearson r (18) = -.01). The lack of correlation between group profiles indicates that blind and sighted children used relatively similar behavioral repertoires in quite different ways. Table 13-2 reveals several major differences in the use of social behaviors. The blind children initiated relatively fewer affiliative or cohesive behaviors than sighted children (48.6% compared to 68.4%). The lower proportion of affiliative behaviors among the blind children is coupled with a higher proportion of competitive and aggressive behaviors (12.1% for the blind and 4.0% for the sighted group). Not surprisingly, over one-half of the emitted affiliative behaviors in the blind group were concentrated in the category of physical contact. This result was expected, since physical contact is one of the privileged means of communication for the blind. In contrast, "speaks to" represented only 4.1% of emitted behaviors of the blind group, while this behavior comprised 8.0% of the repertoire of the sighted group. The relatively infrequent use of verbal communication to establish peer contact in the blind group was quite unexpected, since verbal contact is often considered to be a major form of compensatory interaction for blind children, even at very early ages (Fraiberg, 1977).

Two additional results merit attention. First, blind children responded with a relatively large proportion of "turns away" (9.3%) compared to their rather low level of "orients" (3.3%). This suggests that the blind children use turning away to signal an end to social interaction, but do not turn toward as a reaction to an initiated social signal. The second point involves the relatively high frequency of ignoring perceptible social actions in the blind group (in this case physical or verbal contact). This certainly reflects the lower level of social continuity within a single interactive context that was previously noted among the blind children.

That the behavioral profile of the blind children differs greatly from that of the sighted children was somewhat to be expected, since the

Table 13-2. Relative Frequency of Behavioral Activity

Class and Category	Blind	Sighted
Cohesion		
Orients	3.3	17.0
Maintains orientation	1.6	11.4
Signals	2.4	9.3
Approaches	2.2	9.4
Contact	28.2	2.4
Offers	3.3	3.2
Takes	2.2	6.0
Speaks to	4.1	8.0
Requests	0.8	0.8
Demands	0.5	0.9
Competition		
Competes with	3.0	1.0
Loses	0.9	0.5
Wins	1.3	0.5
Aggression		
Attacks	6.6	1.1
Threatens	0.3	0.9
Terminators		
Submits	5.5	0.5
Turns away from	9.3	15.3
Retreats	5.8	7.4
Other		
Ignores	13.9	1.7
Does not perceive	1.4	0.8
Not identifiable	2.7	1.8

sensory deficiency of the blind children renders at least some behaviors inappropriate and interferes with effective feedback for some others. Specifying the precise areas that distinguish blind from sighted subjects in terms of usage of social actions is an important first step in understanding the nature of the differences between them. However, the fact that blind children use behaviors with different frequencies than sighted children does not enable us to conclude that they are doing different things with these behaviors. The question of the social use of the behavioral repertoire of blind children is an important and complex one. Our approach to the functional importance of social behaviors is based upon the notion that the social value of a given act is directly related to the probability that its production will foster or inhibit social cohesion (Kummer, 1971; McGrew, 1972; Strayer, 1980).

Our first measure of such cohesion concerns the immediate consequence of a behavior and its direct contribution to the continuity of social participation. A behavior can be followed by a directed act that continues the social interaction, by an ending of the interaction (the behaviors "submit," "turns away," and "retreats"), or by a lack of reaction ("ignore," "does not perceive," or "not identifiable"). The proportions of continuations characterizing each behavior in the taxonomy are given in Table 13-3 for both blind and sighted children. The probability of a behavior leading to the direct continuation of interaction was generally lower for the blind than for the sighted children. This result reflects the already reported lower average length of interaction sequences among the blind children, and indicates that their social initiatives were generally less effective than those of their sighted counterparts. However, examination of the relative effectiveness of different actions within each group suggested a high degree of similarity. This was confirmed by a correlational analysis of the continuity indices of Table 13-3 (r (18)=.740, $p < .05$). In addition, corresponding analyses of probabilities of active termination or lack of response also indicated strong correlations between blind and sighted children (r (18)=.432 and r (18)=.783, $p < .05$, respectively). These results indicate that, despite considerable differences in individual

Table 13-3. Immediate Consequence of Social Activity

Behavior category	Observed responses leading to continuation of interaction (%)	
	Blind	Sighted
Orients	28	56
Maintains orientation	60	41
Signals	53	77
Approaches	28	60
Contacts	33	65
Offers	71	96
Takes	8	67
Speaks to	49	82
Requests	60	91
Demands	0	75
Competes with	84	99
Loses	0	33
Wins	36	66
Attacks	19	40
Threatens	50	92
Submits	6	29
Turns away	7	10
Retreats	3	29
Ignores	12	18
Does not perceive	11	37
Average	27	52

behavioral profiles and the generally lower effectiveness of initiated social actions among the blind, the immediate functional consequences of observed behavior showed a pattern that was similar for the blind and sighted children.

A second measure of the functional value of individual social behaviors is the average length of social interactions following their emission. This measure provides a different perspective of social function in that somewhat more long-term consequences are considered with respect to the continuity of social interaction. Two types of long-term social interactions were previously distinguished, and values were thus calculated for consequent interactive sequence length and for consequent interactive episode length (Table 13-4). Average interactive sequence lengths following the emission of given behaviors were uniformly lower for the blind children. However, as was the case for measures of immediate consequence, there was a strong correlation in relative effectiveness of different action patterns between the blind and sighted children (r (18) =.693, $p < .05$). Average interactive episode lengths following the emis-

Table 13-4. Average Number of Behaviors to End of Interaction (Sequence or Episode) After Emission of a Given Behavior Category

Behavior category	Behaviors to end of sequence		Behaviors to end of episode	
	Blind	Sighted	Blind	Sighted
Orients	2.4	3.7	3.0	6.1
Maintains orientation	3.1	3.6	3.7	5.7
Signals	3.2	4.5	3.9	8.3
Approaches	3.5	5.2	3.5	8.3
Contacts	2.7	5.1	3.0	6.5
Offers	2.9	4.7	3.5	8.3
Takes	2.2	4.4	2.2	7.6
Speaks to	3.2	4.1	3.9	6.0
Requests	3.0	6.6	3.0	9.1
Demands	2.0	5.5	2.0	5.9
Competes with	3.3	4.5	4.8	4.7
Loses	2.0	2.8	4.2	2.8
Wins	2.9	4.2	5.0	5.7
Attack	2.4	4.7	2.8	6.1
Threatens	3.0	6.4	3.0	6.9
Submits	1.2	2.9	1.7	3.3
Turns away	1.2	1.5	1.7	4.4
Retreats	1.2	2.4	1.2	4.6
Ignores	1.3	2.3	1.8	5.3
Does not perceive	1.3	3.7	1.3	5.7
Average	2.8	4.7	3.3	6.4

sion of given behaviors were also generally lower for the blind children. However, in contrast to previous results, tnere was a nonsignificant correlation between blind and sighted children in relative effectiveness of different action patterns in generating episodes.

Dyadic Relations and Group Structures

Measures of both direct continuity and longer term continuity of social interactions following emission of particular social actions provide an analytical framework that is more complex than our initial analysis of behavioral profiles. The latter measures reflect in a fairly clear way how social partners respond to given behavioral categories. However, they do not permit description of the nature and organization of relationships in the group. A more complete vision of social ecology requires meaningful measures of dyadic relations and group structures.

As mentioned in the introduction, both longitudinal and cross-sectional results in child social ethology demonstrate that preschool peer groups are organized according to two fundamentally different principles, derived from analyses of aggressive or competitive exchanges and cohesive behaviors. The latter are generally organized in an equilibrated manner that reflects interactive role reciprocity; that is, social partners tend to exchange peer attachment behaviors that function to promote group cohesion. In sharp contrast, aggressive and competitive activities involve high levels of interactive role differentiation; that is, social participants in these behavioral settings generally respond in a consistently assertive or submissive manner.

Dominance structures. Dyadic dominance relations describe behavioral asymmetries during aggressive and competitive social exchanges between members of a dyad. By examining behavioral outcomes that characterize such exchanges, we can derive measures of the balance of power between two peer group members. Recent developmental studies have shown that rigidity, a measure of dyadic asymmetry in first-order agonistic encounters in stable groups, increases systematically during the preschool years from .85 for 1-year-olds to .95 for 5-year-olds. This measure is the proportion of social episodes in which the assertive and submissive roles are assumed by the same members of given dyads (Strayer & Strayer, 1976). In the present study, this rigidity index was 100% and 91% for the two groups of sighted children and 86% for the blind group. Thus, even during this period of group formation, dyadic dominance roles in all three groups were similarly differentiated and were within the limits of previously observed variability.

A second descriptive index of social dominance reflects the relative importance of agonistic exchanges in interactive dyadic relationships that define the group structure (Strayer, 1981). This measure is simply the proportion of the dyads in a group that establish dominance relations. Among members of stable preschool groups, this index varies systematically from 84% among 1-year-olds to 35% among 5-year-olds. For the blind group, this index was 56%, while for the two sighted groups, it was 10% and 50%. These findings indicate that in one of the sighted groups dominance exchanges were concentrated in only 1 of 10 possible dyads. In contrast, in both the other sighted group and the blind group about 50% of all possible dyads maintained dominance differentials.

A final measure examines the hierarchical organization of established dyadic dominance relations. The linearity index reflects the proportion of established relationships that can be described by a linear transitive algorithm. This index remains relatively constant throughout the preschool years, with group variability ranging from 88% to 98% (Gauthier, Note 4; Gauthier & Strayer, Note 5). For the blind group the corresponding value was 80%, while for the two sighted groups it was 100% and 83%. Thus the organization of agonistic encounters in both the blind and sighted groups generally corresponded to that found in established normal preschool groups (Strayer, 1980; Gauthier, Note 4; Gauthier & Strayer, Note 5).

Cohesive networks. Current procedures for evaluating cohesive ties within stable groups involve examination of the differential deployment of peer attachment behaviors to specific members of the social unit. This procedure involves determining which partner receives more than the expected share of a given child's cohesive behavior. Developmental research shows a radical change in the degree to which peers are chosen as preferred social partners. Among younger children adults usually appear to be the preferred social partner, while among older children this pattern is replaced by a complex network of peer bonding (Strayer, 1981; Markovits & Strayer, Note 6).

In the groups we examined, the obtained networks were fairly elementary in structure and closely resembled those found among young preschool children. In each context, the adult supervisors served as the principle affiliative link among group members. This undoubtedly reflects the process of group formation for all three groups. Nonetheless, it is clear that certain common patterns emerged in both the blind and sighted groups. Definite preferential choices existed for at least some of the children in these groups. This indicates that the basic component for affiliative bonding is active. This bonding capacity is even more clearly shown by the existence of mutual preferences in three cases, one of which involved two of the blind children.

General Discussion

The results of this study represent some initial insights into the complex social environment which emerges in a group of blind preschool children. By contrasting their social behavior to that of similar groups of sighted children, we have attempted to clarify the similarities and differences that could possibly characterize this particular class of atypical children. It is important, however, to realize that this study must not be considered as more than an initial step in what must be a series of repeated analyses of various groups. The small number of children examined here precludes any inflated generalizations based solely on these data. Nonetheless, the patterns that have emerged from this analysis are important because they may add to educators' understanding and help determine future avenues of research.

Certain important trends are already apparent in the results of this applied ethological investigation. First, the organizational principles that governed the social structure of the blind children were qualitatively similar to those of the sighted groups. Both stable dominance relations and reciprocal affiliative bonds were found in all cases. In this respect, the lack of vision does not appear to affect group structure. In addition, the relative functional value (in terms of direct continuity and short-term continuity) of emitted social action patterns was comparable for the blind and sighted children. Thus the relative effectiveness of social actions within the overall behavioral repertoire and the organization of dyadic interactions determining social equilibrium were similar for both blind and sighted subjects. However, these similarities were coupled with important divergences in basic behavioral patterns. The relative frequencies of emission of different action patterns were found to vary between blind and sighted children. In addition, the overall social effectiveness of the blind children was markedly lower than that of the sighted children. The blind engaged in much shorter interactive sequences and had correspondingly fewer chances of successfully sustaining episodes of social contact.

Our results thus provide much needed information for a more profound understanding of the social functioning of young blind children. They also furnish an interesting example of the usefulness of the multi-leveled analytical model employed in social ethology. The central principle underlying this approach is that a single social act can have multiple meanings, which depend upon its relationship to other actions of both a given individual and social partners that shape the nature of dyadic social relationships. Understanding the organization of such relationships within a given group requires consideration of various conceptually distinct meanings. Analysis of a single level of behavioral organization provides at best an incomplete picture of social skills. In this study, for example, results concerning behavioral profiles indicate major differences between blind and sighted children. These differences are, of course, real and do have important implications. Nonetheless, the importance of such differences for general assessments of social competence cannot be properly evaluated without considering the fact that variations in relative emission of given behavior patterns coexist with strong similarities in the organizational principles governing the social functions and dyadic equilibrium of agonistic and cohesive activities among blind and sighted children.

It seems pertinent to contrast these general patterns of social functioning with the results reported by Delorme-Schoof, Strayer and Precourt (Note 7) in their study of mainstreamed handicapped preschoolers. In the latter case, no differences were found in the nature and function of observed social behaviors. However, in contrast to the present results, the handicapped children were less directly connected to the cohesive network of the peer group.

The attempt to consider the multiple layering of analytical concepts that are required to characterize naturally occurring social groups is one of the most important aspects of the social-ethological approach. This view of social adaptation provides indications of the relative importance of various sets of factors in understanding social development in atypical (and normal) children. Clearly, such differentiated analytical tools permit the elaboration of an important empirical base which could eliminate many of the controversies that have plagued more traditional educational research. This inductive approach suggests consistent and unambiguous directions for those concerned with the pressing problems of atypical social development.

Acknowledgments

The authors would like to express their gratitude to the staff of the Institut Nazareth et Louis Braille in Longeuil, Montreal, and to the children and parents who participated in this project. They would also like to thank Louis Gariepy, Michelle Dumont, Danielle Huet, Theresa Blicharsky, and Lise Petitclerc for their invaluable assistance in both data collection and analysis.

Reference Notes

1. Wynne, S., Ulfeder, L. S., & Dakoff, G. *Mainstreaming and early childhood education for handicapped children: Review and implications of research* (Final Rep., Contract OEC-74-9056). Washington, D.C.: Bureau of Education for the Handicapped, 1975.
2. Misshakian, E. A. *Aggression and dominance relation in peer groups of children six to forty-five months of age.* Paper presented at the annual conference of the Animal Behavior Society, Colorado, June 1976.
3. Strayer, F. F. *Attention, popularity and dominance: A cross-sectional study of preschool social organization.* Paper presented at the biennial meeting of the Society for Research in Child Development, Boston, April 1981.

4. Gauthier, R. *A cross-sectional study of agonistic interaction and peer dominance in the preschool.* Paper presented at the biennial meeting of the Society for Research in Child Development, Boston, April 1981.
5. Gauthier, R., & Strayer, F. F. *A cross-sectional study of asymmetrical status structures among preschool children.* Paper presented at the biennial conference of the International Society for the Study of Behavioral Development, Toronto, 1981.
6. Markovits, H., & Strayer, F. F. *A cross-sectional study of cohesive structures in the preschool peer group.* Paper presented at the biennial conference of the International Society for the Study of Behavioral Development, Toronto, 1981.
7. Delorme-Schoof, F., Strayer, F. F., & Precourt, P. *An ethological analysis of social behavior of handicapped children in mainstreamed preschools* (Research Memo). Montreal: University of Quebec, Laboratoire d'Ethologie Humaine, 1980.

References

Abramovitch, R. The relation of attention and proximity rank in preschool children. In M. Chance & R. Larsen (Eds.), *The social structure of attention.* London: Wiley, 1976.

Abramovitch, R., & Strayer, F. F. Preschool social organization. Agonistic spacing and attentional behaviors. In P. Pliner, T. Kramer, & T. Alloway (Eds.), *Recent advances in the study of communication and affect* (Vol. 6). New York: Plenum Press, 1978.

Altmann, J. Observational study of behavior: Sampling methods. *Behavior*, 1974, *49*, 227-267.

Barker, M. A. A technique for studying the social material activities of young children. *Monographs of the Society for Research in Child Development* (No. 3). New York: Columbia University Press, 1930.

Barker, R. G. Explorations in ecological psychology. *American Psychologist*, 1965, *20*, 1-14.

Bateson, P. P. G., & Hinde, R. A. *Growing points in ethology.* Cambridge, England: Cambridge University Press, 1976.

Bernstein, I. S. Primate status hierarchies. In L. Rosenblum (Ed.), *Primate behavior: Developments in field and laboratory research.* New York: Academic Press, 1970.

Blurton-Jones, N. Characteristics of ethological studies of human behavior. In N. Blurton-Jones (Ed.), *Ethological studies of child behavior.* Cambridge, England: Cambridge University Press, 1972.

Blurton-Jones, N., & Leach, G. M. Behavior of children and their mothers at separation and greeting. In N. Blurton-Jones (Ed.), *Ethological studies of child behavior.* Cambridge, England: Cambridge University Press, 1972.

Bowlby, J. *Attachment and loss* (Vol. I): *Attachment.* New York: Basic Books, 1969.

Bowlby, J. *Attachment and loss* (Vol. II): *Separation.* New York: Basic Books, 1973.

Brannigan, C. R., & Humphries, D. A. Human non-verbal behavior, a means of communication. In N. Blurton-Jones (Ed.), *Ethological studies of child behavior.* Cambridge, England: Cambridge University Press, 1972.

Chance, M. R., & Jolly, C. J. *Social groups of monkeys and men.* London: Cape, 1970.

Chittenden, G. E. An experimental study in measuring and modifying assertive behavior in young children. *Monographs of the Society for Research in Child Development*, 1942, 7(1).

Crook, J. H. Social organization and the environment: Aspects of contemporary social ethology. *Animal Behavior*, 1970, *18*, 197-209.

Dawe, H. C. Analysis of two hundred quarrels of preschool children. *Child Development*, 1943, *5*, 139-157.

Delorme-Schoof, F., & Precourt, P. Etude de l'adaptation sociale d'enfants handicappés et d'enfants normaux en milieux de garderie. *Apprentissage et Socialisation* (in press).

DeVore, I. *Primate behavior: Field studies of monkeys and apes.* New York: Holt, Rinehart & Winston, 1965.

Emmerich, W. Continuity and stability in early social development. *Child Development*, 1964, *35*, 311-332.

Force, D. J. Social status of physically handicapped children. *Exceptional Children*, 1956, *23*(3), 104.

Fraiberg, S. *Insights from the blind.* New York: Basic Books, 1977.

Gellert, E. Stability and fluctuation in the power relationships of young children. *Journal of Abnormal and Social Psychology*, 1961, *62*, 8-15.

Gellert, E. The effects of change in group composition on the dominant behavior of young children. *British Journal of Social and Clinical Psychology*, 1962, *1*, 168-181.

Grant, E. C. Human facial expression. *Man*, 1969, *4*, 525-536.

Harlow, H. F., & Harlow, M. K. The affectional systems. In A. Schrier, H. F. Harlow, & F. Stollnitz (Eds.), *Behavior of non-human primates* (Vol. 2). New York: Academic Press, 1965.

Hinde, R. R. *The biological bases of human social behavior.* New York: McGraw-Hill, 1974.

Hutt, S. J., & Hutt, C. *Behavior studies in psychiatry.* Oxford: Pergamon Press, 1970.

Ipas, J., & Matz, R. D. Integrating handicapped preschool children within a cognitive oriented program. In M. J. Guralnick (Ed.), *Early intervention and the integration of handicapped and nonhandicapped children.* Baltimore: University Park Press, 1978.

Jay, P. C. *Primates: Studies in adaptation and variability.* New York: Holt, Rinehart & Winston, 1968.

Jolly, A. *The evolution of primate behavior.* New York: Macmillan, 1972.

Klein, J. *Teaching the special child in regular classrooms.* Urbana, Ill.: ERIC Clearinghouse on Early Childhood Education, 1977.

Krasnor, L. R., & Rubin, K. H. The assessment of social problem-solving skills in young children. In T. Merluzzi, C. Glass, & M. Genest (Eds.), *Cognitive assessment.* New York: Guilford Press, 1981.

Kummer, H. *Primate societies: Group techniques in ecological adaptation.* Chicago: University of Chicago Press, 1971.

Leach, G. M. A comparison of the social behavior of some normal and problem children. In N. Blurton-Jones (Ed.), *Ethological studies of child behavior.* Cambridge, England: Cambridge University Press, 1972.

McGrew, W. C. Glossary of motor patterns of four-year-old school children. In S. Hutt & C. Hutt (Eds.), *Direct observation and measurement of behavior.* Springfield, Ill.: Thomas, 1970.

McGrew, W. C. *An ethological study of children's behavior*. New York: Academic Press, 1972.

Omark, D. A., Strayer, F. F., & Freedman, D. G. (Eds.). *Dominance relations: An ethological view of human conflict and social interaction*. New York: Garland Press, 1980.

Piaget, J. *The moral judgement of the child*. New York: Free Press, 1948.

Piaget, J. *The origins of intelligence in children*. New York: International Universities Press, 1952.

Porter, R. H., Ramsey, B., Tremblay, A., Iaccobo, M., & Crawley, S. Social interactions in heterogeneous groups of retarded and normally developing children: An observational study. In G. P. Sackett & H. C. Haywood (Eds.), *Observing behavior* (Vol. I): *Theory and applications in mental retardation*. Baltimore: University Park Press, 1980.

Richardson, S. A., Hastorf, A. H., Goodman, N., & Dombusch, S. M. Cultural uniformity in reaction to physical disabilities. *American Sociological Review*, 1961, *26*, 241-247.

Richardson, S. A., Ronald, L., & Kleck, R. E. The social status of handicapped and nonhandicapped boys in a camp meeting. *Journal of Special Education*, 1974, *8*(2), 143-152.

Shirley, M. M. The first two years: A study of twenty-five babies. *Institute of Child Welfare Monograph Series* (No. 7). Minneapolis: University of Minnesota Press, 1933.

Sluckin, A., & Smith, P. Two approaches to the concept of dominance in preschool children. *Child Development*, 1977, *48*, 917-923.

Smith, P., & Connolly, K. Patterns of play and social interaction in preschool children. In N. Blurton-Jones (Ed.), *Ethological studies of child behavior*. Cambridge, England: Cambridge University Press, 1972.

Strayer, F. F. Social ecology of the preschool peer group. In W. A. Collins (Ed.), *The Minnesota symposia on child psychology* (Vol. 13). Hillsdale, N.J.: Erlbaum, 1980.

Strayer, F. F. The organization and coordination of asymmetrical relations among young children: A biological view of social power. In M. D. Watts (Ed.), *New directions for methodology of social and behavioral science*. San Francisco: Jossey Bass, 1981.

Strayer, F. F., & Strayer, J. An ethological analysis of social agonism and dominance relations among preschool children. *Child Development*, 1976, *47*, 980-988.

Tinbergen, N. On the aims and methods of ethology. *Zeitschrift fur Tierpsychologie*, 1963, *20*, 410-433.

Tinbergen, N. Ethology and stress disease. *Science*, 1974, *185*, 20-27.

Tinbergen, N. Ethology in a changing world. In P. P. G. Bateson & R. A. Hinde (Eds.), *Growing points in ethology*. Cambridge, England: Cambridge University Press, 1976.

Vaughn, B., & Waters, E. Social organization among preschooler peers: Dominance, attention and sociometric correlates. In D. Omark, F. F. Strayer, & D. Freedman (Eds.), *Peer-group power relations: An ethological perspective on human dominance and submission*. New York: Garland Press, 1978.

Washburn, P. A scheme for grading the reaction of children in a new social situation. *Journal of Genetic Psychology*, 1932, *40*, 84-88.

Wilson, E. O. *Sociobiology: The new synthesis*. Cambridge, Mass.: Belknap, Harvard University Press, 1975.

Chapter 14

Peer Relationships of Young Children with Behavior Problems

Susan B. Campbell and Patricia Cluss

In this chapter we draw together constructs and research findings from child development which bear on the organization and course of social relations in young chilren with behavior problems. It is our contention that early identification and intervention are crucial from both clinical and theoretical perspectives and, furthermore, the identification and effective treatment of appropriate target groups requires the integration of developmental and clinical viewpoints. Deviant behavior in young children must be assessed within a developmental framework that considers both the age appropriateness of behavior and age changes in the behavioral manifestations of problems (Campbell, in press). Unfortunately, however, much clinical and research work in child psychopathology lacks a developmental focus. With this in mind, we review pertinent literature on the social development of young children that appears to be relevant to the development of peer relations in hyperactive children. Our literature review is necessarily selective, not exhaustive. We then present data from an ongoing early identification, intervention, and follow-up study which suggests that symptoms of hyperactivity and related behavior problems are apparent in very young children and interfere with functioning in a range of social and nonsocial situations.

Theoretical Perspectives: Peer Relations and Child Deviance

Recent research in social development has expanded from the focus on parents to an examination of young children as members of a peer group and wider social network (Hartup, 1976, 1979; Lewis & Feiring, 1979). Researchers have also begun to examine children's developing awareness of social relationships and social conventions (Damon, 1977). Much of this work derives from a perspective which incorporates ethological, ecological, and cognitive-developmental constructs and recognizes that children learn about themselves and the world from interactions with parents and siblings, as well as with other adults and children in their community.

Traditional theories of social development were based on the assumption that early experience with parents laid the groundwork for later friendships and that the mother-child relationship was the prototype of all later meaningful relationships (Bowlby, 1969; Freud, 1965; Kagan, 1958). More recently, Hartup (1976, 1979) has stressed the importance of peers in their own right and has noted that they serve as significant agents of socialization, influencing sex-role learning, moral development, and the control of aggression.

Despite these recent advances in developmental theory, social development in atypical children has been viewed in terms of the role the mother plays in either causing (Freud, 1965; Winnicott, 1957) or maintaining (e.g., Ross, 1974) problem behavior. This reflects the limited communication between developmentalists and child clinicians and the lack of a comprehensive theoretical model in the child psychopathology field. Psychoanalytical and behavioral approaches remain dominant, although neither has adequately addressed questions of the etiology or course of childhood disorders. Although psychoanalytical theorists have provided rich clinical descriptions, they have neglected empirical verification of their notions of etiology. In the behavioral framework, the focus has been primarily technique and sympton oriented with emphasis on the development and empirical evaluation of methods of behavior change. Psychoanalysts have thus focused on parents and parent-child interactions as causes of behavior disorders in children, while behaviorists have included parents in their roles as dispensers of reinforcement and punishment. Proponents of these models have not considered the qualitative changes children show in cognitive and social functioning with age, nor have they viewed the developing child as residing within an extended family, peer group, and wider social network.

While it may be acknowledged that peers are important, poor peer relations are assumed to be a common correlate of children's behavior problems (Campbell & Paulauskas, 1979; Serafica & Harway, 1979), and most child clinicians take for granted that children who have problems at home will also have difficulty at school and with peers. This follows logically from the hypothesis that peer relations evolve from relations within the nuclear family, but are, in themselves, of limited interest. Thus, research on the social development of problem children has been relatively neglected until recently.

Researchers in the field of child psychopathology have been forced, however, to attend more carefully to the importance of peers. Studies indicate that school-age children with a variety of symptoms that are expressed outward—including hyperactive and impulsive behavior, attentional problems, aggression, and discipline problems—are more likely to be rejected by peers than shy, withdrawn children or non-referred class-room controls (Bryan, 1974; Green, Beck, Forehand, & Vosk, 1980; Klein & Young, 1979). Similarly, children screened for primary prevention programs in the schools on the basis of teacher ratings and family interviews are also more likely to be perceived negatively by peers (Cowen, Trost, Izzo, Lorion, Dorr, & Isaacson, 1975). The evidence from studies of school-age samples, then, indicates that peers are relatively sensitive observers of deviance in classmates, although the specific cues to which they are responding and the mechanisms by which negative peer perceptions translate into behavior remain to be determined.

While it may not be too surprising that children designated as problems are perceived differently by peers at the time of screening or referral, follow-up studies indicate that early peer problems are among the most robust predictors of poor adult adjustment. Studies of former child guidance clinic attenders indicate that poor peer relations in childhood are associated with continued psychiatric disorder in adulthood (e.g., Robins, 1966, 1978), particularly antisocial behavior, alcoholism, and marital difficulties. Peer rejection may also predict later maladjustment. In a widely cited study, Cowen, Pederson, Babigian, Izzo, and Trost (1973) reported that children who were rejected by peers at age 8 years were more likely to show up on the psychiatric register in adulthood. Moreover, peer ratings were more sensitive predictors of later maladjustment than teacher ratings, measures of academic achievement, or self-report measures of personality. Thus, there appears to be an association between peer problems in elementary school and social maladjustment in adulthood. However, the mechanisms underlying this supposed continuity remain unexplored.

As Milich and Landau (1981) pointed out, these results cannot be interpreted to suggest that peer problems in childhood play a causal role in adult maladjustment; rather, borrowing from Sroufe's (1979) notion of continuity of adaptation, it is likely that early peer rejection reflects the child's deviance and that the difficulties underlying initial peer problems in elementary school also interfere with functioning in other areas. These difficulties probably continue to manifest themselves in one way or another, depending upon the age and life stage of the individual. Youngsters with limited social competence in childhood may be expected to have continuing experiences with social rejection and failure which will leave them ill equipped to deal with the increasingly complicated social demands of successive developmental stages. The youngster who is not readily accepted by the same-sex peer group in elementary school and has not learned important skills of social exchange may have an even more difficult time dealing with the intense heterosexual and same-sex peer pressures of adolescence and may attempt to gain notoriety by acts of aggression, bravado, and delinquency. In adulthood, such an individual may be expected to have difficulty establishing intimate relationships.

Evidence from studies of hyperactive children is consistent with this view. Children are usually referred for help in elementary school due to complaints about classroom behavior, school achievement, and discipline problems. These complaints reflect teacher and parent perceptions of the major "work" of childhood, that is, school achievement and adaptation to the specific expectations and mores of the nuclear family. Follow-up studies of hyperactive youngsters indicate that peer problems become an area of particular concern to parents and the children themselves in adolescence (Weiss, Minde, Werry, Douglas, & Nemeth, 1971) and that aggressive and delinquent behavior is often a concomitant (Milich & Loney, 1979). Whereas data indicate that younger hyperactive children also have peer problems (Klein & Young, 1979), complaints from parents and teachers initially focus on attentional and discipline problems. The peer pressures and expectations for greater peer involvement during adolescence seem to make peer problems more salient in older samples. It is likewise logical to argue that difficulty in getting along with peers should be among the major problems of toddlers and preschoolers who do not adapt optimally to the challenges of development (Sroufe, 1979), a topic to which we return shortly.

Hyperactivity

Nature and Symptoms

The focus in this chapter is on children with a cluster of high-rate, high-intensity symptoms about which adults complain: restlessness, inability to sustain attention, impulsivity, and discipline problems. Children showing this cluster of behaviors are typically referred to as "hyperactive" (Barkley, 1981; Douglas & Peters, 1979; Whalen & Henker, 1980) or as showing "attention deficit disorder" (American Psychiatric Association, 1980), although debates about terminology and differential diagnosis are often heated (Lahey, Green, & Forehand, 1980; Sandberg, Wieselberg, & Shaffer, 1980). In order to avoid confusing terminology and to side step diagnostic questions, we refer throughout this chapter to hyperactivity and/or behavior problems; the intent is to encompass youngsters with a range of symptoms that are expressed outward against the environment (i.e., externalizing as opposed to internalizing symptoms such as anxiety, withdrawal, or physical complaints; Edelbrock & Achenbach, 1980).

The nature of hyperactivity remains unclear despite hundreds of studies on cognitive functioning, psychophysiology, treatment effects, and family correlates (see reviews by Barkley, 1977; Douglas & Peters, 1979; Whalen & Henker, 1980). There is wide agreement that such youngsters are constitutionally more active and intense in reaction than average. The primary focus, however, is on the child's impulsive and inattentive behavior. Douglas (1980) recently proposed that deficits in three core self-regulatory processes underlie hyperactive symptomatology: (1) the inability to sustain attention; (2) a deficit in the inhibitory control of impulsive responding; and (3) a difficulty in the modulation of arousal level to meet environmental demands. This view is consistent with much of the data on cognitive functioning and treatment effects. If, indeed, this conceptualization is correct, deficits in social as well as cognitive functioning should be apparent and peer relations should be impaired. As we have argued elsewhere (Campbell & Paulauskas, 1979), an understanding of hyperactivity will require a broadening of our research strategies to include studies of social as well as cognitive functioning and to incorporate a developmental approach (Campbell, 1976).

Although these behavior problems have been studied almost exclusively in school-age samples, symptoms of hyperactivity appear to have their onset in infancy or toddlerhood (Barkley, 1981; Campbell, 1976). Thus, early identification and follow-up are crucial to an understanding of the nature and course of this disorder as well as to the delineation of factors that influence outcome. Follow-up studies and therapy outcome studies indicate that problems persist over time and that most treatments, instituted at school age, produce little more than a short-term amelioration of symptoms (Barkley, 1977; Douglas, 1980; Weiss, Kruger, Danielson, & Elman, 1975); these findings strengthen the argument for early identification and intervention.

Therefore, we have been studying a group of very young children (2-3½ years of age) whose parents complained of symptoms which fit comfortably under the rubric of hyperactivity. A diagnosis in this age group would be meaningless, given the state of our knowledge about disorders in very young children and the difficulty differentiating between children showing bona fide symptoms of persistent disorder and those going through a difficult developmental stage characterized by behaviors such as restlessness, short attention span, and tantrums. Furthermore, it would be virtually impossible to determine whether problems with activity and attention were more serious than problems with aggression and defiance given the age of the sample, the reliance on parental reports, and contextual influences on symptom expression. Children may appear more active and inattentive in some situations and more noncompliant or aggressive in others, depending upon situational demands (Whalen & Henker, 1980). Therefore, differential diagnostic questions cannot be resolved, although follow-up data should begin to shed some light on which initial symptoms predict good or poor adjustment later on.

Implications of Hyperactive Symptomatology for Social Development

When we follow the logic of Douglas (1980) and incorporate Sroufe's (1979) concept of continuity of adaptation, it seems reasonable to hypothesize that younsters with deficits in inhibitory control, sustained attention, and arousal regulation will have significant difficulties in social relationships since these deficits should interfere with the establishment of reciprocal interactions which are the basis of social exchange (Mannarino, 1980; Rubin, 1980). Anderson and Messick (1974), in their exhaustive list of the components of early social competence, included the appropriate regulation of disruptive and aggressive behavior and the control of attention as important elements in adaptive social functioning. Rubin (1980) suggested that the basic features of social interaction are sustained attention, turn taking, and mutual responsiveness. Indeed, these elements describe interactions between infants and caretakers (Brazelton, Koslowski, & Main, 1974; Stern, 1974), between very young children (Goldman & Ross, 1978; Mueller & Lucas, 1975), and between older children and adults, and therefore characterize most childhood dyadic interactions. It seems safe to speculate that the core features of hyperactivity, conceptualized as deficits in self-regulation, would tend to disrupt social reciprocity and might first be evident in infancy.

Infants who are poor at inhibiting responses, maintaining attention, and modulating arousal are likely to be easily overwhelmed by stimulation, both internal and external, and to be relatively ineffective at both shutting out even moderate amounts of stimulation (Brazelton, 1973; Korner, 1971) and adapting to changes in routine (Thomas, Chess, & Birck, 1968). Such infants would be expected to be relatively demanding, irritable, and difficult to soothe, necessitating considerable investment and effort from parents. They may also require that parents anticipate needs and engage in sensitive and well-timed interventions to prevent them from becoming excessively distressed, overaroused, and inconsolable. Reports from parents in our sample tend to confirm that, for many, their child's infancy was an extremely difficult time and they felt stressed and taxed by the demands of parenting an active, irritable, and highly excitable infant. Even highly responsive and sensitive parenting probably does not guarantee that such a youngster will become more manageable or begin to modulate his or her own impulses. On the other hand, parental insensitivity, intolerance, and negative control during infancy and toddlerhood are associated with increased irritability and noncompliance at ages 2 and 3 (Lytton, 1979; Thomas et al., 1968). Furthermore, maternal insensitivity is associated with the development of a relatively anxious and insecure infant-mother attachment which appears to set the stage for less competent interactions with peers in toddlerhood and the preschool years (Lieberman, 1977; Waters, Wippman, & Sroufe, 1979). The relationship between the quality of attachment and symptoms of hyperactivity remains unexplored.

As the child's social world widens to include peers, one would expect that the development of positive peer interactions would be particularly difficult for the intense, impulsive, and inattentive youngster. Peers are less likely than parents to respond to the hyperactive child's needs or to regulate their own behavior to accommodate the child's intensity of response or limited impulse control. Learning to share, to take turns and to wait, to attend to the cues of others, and not to grab, hit, or otherwise lash out would be especially difficult for youngsters with symptoms of hyperactivity.

Learning to control aggression may be particularly troublesome. Hartup (1974, 1976) suggested that young children learn to master aggressive impulses in the peer group, partly through experiences with rough-and-tumble play. Observations of preschool peer groups (Bronson, 1975; Smith & Green, 1975) also indicated that a substantial proportion of aggressive encounters begin as struggles over possessions, which Feshbach and Feshbach (1972) termed instrumental or object-oriented aggression. While studies have shown that aggressive initiations are more likely than friendly initiations to elicit an aggressive response (Leiter, 1977; Patterson, Littman, & Bricker, 1967), nonclinical samples of preschoolers have shown remarkable restraint. For example, Leiter (1977) recently reported that only 14% of social initiations observed during 40 hours of observations in two preschools were "demanding," a category which includes verbal commands, physical aggression, and taking objects; only 10.7% of these demanding initiations elicited a physically aggressive response. Similarly, Strayer and Strayer (1976) reported that only 21% of the agonistic initiations they observed elicited a counterattack. Thus it appears that nonproblem youngsters are likely to deescalate an aggressive encounter by a range of alternative responses including ignoring, submitting, arguing, leaving the situation, and seeking help from an adult (Leiter, 1977; Strayer & Strayer, 1976).

Leiter also noted that some children respond to a demanding initiation with teasing and rough-and-tumble play; this is a high-intensity response, but one which tends to turn a potential conflict situation into a playful interaction. DiPietro (1981) recently observed that while rough-and-tumble play is relatively common, expecially among boys, and is characterized by exuberant physical contact, angry or hostile aggression is rare. She reported that the 4-year-olds in her sample easily differentiated between hostile and playful aggressive exchanges. However, it is logical to hypothesize that hyperactive preschoolers would be likely to demonstrate less impulse control and that their tendency to become overexcited could easily result in the escalation of a toy struggle or other conflict situation once it bagan. Similarly, high-intensity, physical, rough-and-tumble play is more likely to deteriorate into serious aggression if one of the participants has difficulty regulating arousal and controlling impulses. Evidence from one study (Schleifer,

Weiss, Cohen, Elman, Cvejic, & Kruger, 1975) did indicate that hyperactive preschoolers were more aggressive than controls in a research nursery.

Aggressive behavior has been associated with negative peer ratings in several studies of preschoolers (Hartup, Glazer, & Charlesworth, 1967; Masters & Furman, 1981; Vaughn & Waters, 1981). Punishing behaviors, including verbal and physical aggression, tend not only to elicit similar behavior, but also lead to peer rejection. Vaughn and Waters (1981) reported that teasing and hostility were related to negative peer nominations, while object struggles and hostility expressed in the context of a game were not. These data suggest the importance of examining the quality of aggression, a point stressed by DiPietro (1981). For example, Moore (1967) hypothesized that unprovoked aggression may be more likely to lead to rejection by peers than aggression that is retaliatory. She also suggested that the intensity of aggressive acts may influence the degree of peer rejection. While researchers have not obtained popularity-unpopularity rankings of behavior problem preschoolers, these findings in nonclinical samples suggest that hyperactive preschoolers may well be less popular with age-mates.

The studies cited above suggest that aggression is rare relative to the number of prosocial interactions observed in preschool playgroups; the majority of social interactions tend to be positive and to elicit positive responses (DiPietro, 1981; Hartup et al., 1967; Leiter, 1977). Furthermore, studies of popularity among preschoolers have suggested that particular behaviors are valued by peers. For example, Hartup et al. (1967) reported that popular children were more positively reinforcing to others and that children who dispensed high rates of reinforcement—including positive attention, approval, and affection—also received more reinforcement from others. This study suggested a high degree of reciprocity among these 3- and 4-year-olds. A more recent study by Leiter (1977) likewise indicated that friendly overtures predominate and that they are responded to in kind. Other studies also demonstrated that friendliness and interactive play are associated with peer popularity (Moore, 1967; Vaughn & Waters, 1981). Moore (1967) noted that more popular children also tend to be more compliant with routines. She interpreted this as evidence that more popular children show emotional maturity and a willingness to regulate behavior to achieve group goals. Taken together, positive, cooperative, and reciprocal exchanges as well as attention to the needs and behaviors of others tend to characterize the social interactions of popular preschool children. It is likely that hyperactive preschoolers would show inadequate attention to others and tend not to regulate their behavior in concert with peers or teachers. In the only study to examine the peer interactions of hyperactive preschoolers, Schleifer et al. (1975) found that the amount of social participation did not differentiate hyperactive 4-year-olds from controls. However, data are lacking on the quality of contacts.

It seems logical to anticipate more problems among school-age youngsters with hyperactive symptomatology as games with rules become an integral aspect of peer contacts (Sutton-Smith, Rosenberg, & Morgan, 1963), as children's notions of friendship begin to involve more give and take (Damon, 1977), and as the nature of aggressive interactions changes (Hartup, 1974). Milich and Landau (1981) recently suggested that four general categories of behavior require study in relation to the peer problems of hyperactive youngsters: general prosocial behavior, aggressive and inappropriate behavior, cognitive and communicative skills, and classroom behavior. It has been demonstrated that these categories are relevant to the peer popularity of nonclinical samples of school-age children. Researchers have suggested that behaviors directed specifically to peers (Masters & Furman, 1981) and general competence and demeanor in the group (Bryan, 1974; Gottman, 1977) both influence popularity rankings. For example, children who are less attentive in class are more likely to be rejected (Gottman, 1977), as are children who show poorer school achievement (Bryan, 1974) and less communicative competence (Bryan, 1977).

Studies examining these behaviors in school-age hyperactive children are beginning to appear. There is accumulating evidence that hyperactive children are involved in more aggressive and disruptive behavior in the classroom (Klein & Young, 1979) and show less communicative competence (Whalen, Henker, Collins, McAuliffe, & Vaux, 1979) than controls. They are also less accepted by peers than their nonproblem classmates (Klein & Young, 1979). The specific friendships of hyperactive children have not been studied, but Weiss et al. (1971) noted that one-third of the hyperactive adolescents in their sample did not have a close friend. However, studies are needed that explore which specific aspects of the hyperactive youngster's symptoms get him or her into difficulty with peers. It is likely that high-intensity behavior, poor impulse control, and lack of attention to the needs, rights, and wants of others contribute to the hyperactive child's difficulties with peers in general and may interfere with the establishment of friendships. Several research programs are beginning to address some of these questions.

Activity Level in Preschoolers: Correlates and Continuity

Studies of nonclinical samples of preschoolers suggest that a high activity level is one manifestation of a relatively persistent behavioral style which influences the direction of both cognitive and social development. Halverson and Waldrop (1973, 1976) examined activity level and sociability in a sample af 2½-year-olds observed over time and across situations in a research nursery. Activity level was related to boisterous, vigorous play and to excitability. Factor analysis of observational data indicated that activity level and social participation formed two distinct factors, both reflecting intense behavior. The activity factor, however, included measures of gross motor activity, frequent shifts in play, and oppositional behavior with peers; the sociability factor included more directed play and positive peer interaction. Follow-up data obtained when children were 7½ years old (Halverson & Waldrop, 1976; Waldrop & Halverson, 1975) indicated continuity in both sociability and activity level. Despite the nonclinical nature of their sample, Halverson and Waldrop (1976) suggested that high activity and impulsivity tend to interfere with social and cognitive development. Higher activity level at both 2½ and 7½ years of age was associated with poorer cognitive functioning and with attempts to dominate peers at follow-up.

Other longitudinal studies of nonclinical samples likewise indicate that activity level represents a relatively stable aspect of personality and is associated with high-intensity behavior and involvement with peers. Battle and Lacey (1972) reanalyzed data from the Fels longitudinal study and noted that descriptions of impulsive, vigorous, and uncontrolled motor behavior in preschool were associated with high rates of social initiations, both positive and aggressive. Furthermore, activity level in boys tended to be relatively stable into elementary school and continued to be associated with attempts to dominate peers. Girls who had been more active in preschool, on the other hand, were more popular and achievement oriented in elementary school, but not more dominant or aggressive.

In a recent longitudinal study, Buss, Block, and Block (1980) collected independent teacher descriptions of children's behavior at ages 3, 4, and 7. They found that youngsters with high actometer scores in preschool were consistently described as vigorous, rapid in tempo, restless, attention seeking, and noncompliant. The peer interactions of more active youngsters were characterized as assertive, competitive, and aggressive. It is noteworthy that preschool activity level was associated with independent teacher ratings obtained 3 years later in elementary school, and that the more active youngsters in this sample were described as impulsive, inattentive, aggressive, and noncompliant at each age level. These behaviors appear to reflect a personality style that is relatively persistent and cuts across both cognitive and social domains. Block and Block (1980) used the term "ego-control" to describe an individual difference dimension which encompasses these behaviors and, at the extreme, "ego-undercontrol" appears to be similar to clinical hyperactivity.

Findings from other studies also indicate that maladaptive behavioral styles, which appear to overlap with hyperactivity, tend to be apparent in early childhood, to influence relationships with peers, to persist over time, and to be reflected in both cognitive functioning and psychological adjustment. Kohn and Parnes (1974) observed extreme groups of "apathetic-withdrawn" and "angry-defiant" preschoolers, selected from a large day care sample on the basis of teacher ratings. Angry-defiant youngsters engaged in more vocal and antagonistic interactions with peers than withdrawn children, who spent more time in solitary play. In a longitudinal study, Kohn (1977) reported that both anger-defiance and apathy-withdrawal, assessed in preschool, were associated with persistent difficulties in early elementary school and with some gaps in cognitive functioning. Angry-defiant behavior was particularly stable and was also associated with low task orientation, defined in terms of attentional problems and limited persistence.

Taken together, these longitudinal studies of nonclinical samples all indicate that behaviors related to self-regulation or ego-control (Block & Block, 1980)—including activity level, sustained and directed attention, and impulse control—are strongly interrelated and show persistence over time from preschool to school age. They also correlate with styles of relating to peers, responding to discipline, and coping with cognitive tasks. It appears that these findings have clear implications for clinical hyperactivity: they suggest that symptoms persist and influence behavior in a range of social and nonsocial situations.

Studies of Peer Relations in Clinical Groups

Very few studies have examined peer relations in clinical groups of children. Schleifer et al. (1975) studied preschool-age hyperactive and control youngsters in a research nursery. Observations indicated that hyperactive children were more aggressive with peers, but the groups did not differ in frequency of positive interactions. Although follow-up studies indicated that problems persisted in the clinical group (Campbell, Endman, & Bernfeld, 1977; Campbell, Schleifer, Weiss, & Perlman, 1977), aggression per se did not predict outcome for hyperactive children (Campbell, Schleifer, & Weiss, 1978). However, it is worth noting that preschool aggression was highly correlated with disruptive classroom behavior at age 7½ years for controls. Cohen, Sullivan, Minde, Novak, and Helwig (1981) studied hyperactive and control boys in kindergarten as part of a treatment and follow-up study. Hyperactive youngsters spent more time than controls in disruptive and solitary activities prior to the initiation of treatment. They continued to play alone more after several months of intervention; the 1-year follow-up study revealed that hyperactive boys continued to be rated as more disruptive and difficult to manage than controls.

Toddler and preschool groups of "emotionally disturbed" children attending a special hospital-based program were observed by Howes (Note 1) and compared to nonclinical groups. Friendships were defined on the basis of successful social initiations, reciprocal interactions, and positive affective exchanges. Dyads of disturbed children were less likely than control dyads to show patterns of interaction indicative of friendship; when they did, friendships were less likely to be maintained over time. Taken together, these few studies indicate that disturbed toddlers and preschoolers show different patterns of social initiation and social response than their more normally functioning peers. Furthermore, it seems that children with externalizing symptoms tend to be more aggressive with peers, while internalizing symptoms are associated with social withdrawal, as is the case in older children (Edelbrock & Achenbach, 1980).

Several recent studies of hyperactive school-age children also indicate that peer problems are prevalent (Campbell & Paulauskas, 1979) and that hyperactive children are more rejected by peers (Klein & Young, 1979). Furthermore, studies are beginning to delineate specific differences in the social behaviors of hyperactive and control children which provide some clues to the nature of the former's difficulties with peers. It is worth noting that the study of the social behavior of hyperactive children has been restricted almost exclusively to boys; only a small number of school-age girls are diagnosed as hyperactive (Bosco & Robin, 1980).

Whalen, Henker, and their colleagues (Whalen & Henker, 1980; Whalen et al., 1979) found that hyperactive boys in comparison to control boys, showed less communicative competence and were less responsive to the communications of their partners, assessed on a group decision-making task and on a referential communication task. Hyperactive youngsters were less likely to change their ongoing behavior in response to the changing role demands of the tasks and were more likely to engage in inappropriate and task-irrelevant conversation once they became acquainted with the situation. Cunningham, Siegel, and Offord (Note 2) also reported that hyperactive boys were less responsive to peers, often ignoring their verbal initiations, although they themselves were more talkative. Furthermore, during structured tasks, control boys became increasingly more directive and controlling, presumably because their hyperactive partner's irrelevant conversation and disruptive behavior interfered with task completion. Recent work by Pelham (Note 3) suggested that the inappropriate and disruptive behaviors that seem to set hyperactive children apart from peers are apparent fairly early in a social situation. Peers gave hyperactive youngsters lower acceptance ratings after only 1-2 hours of interaction. The teasing, boisterous, and aversive behaviors described by Pelham (Note 3) also characterized hyperactive youngsters in the classroom (Klein & Young, 1979) and were associated with peer rejection in nonclinical samples (Dodge, Note 4).

In summary, these studies suggest that hyperactive youngsters' intense and impulsive behaviors disrupt normal social exchange and their lack of responsiveness to others interferes with the development of a mutually rewarding reciprocal relationship (Mannarino, 1980). Pelham's results also suggest that the behavior of hyperactive boys may alienate peers during the initial acquaintanceship process and therefore interfere with the establishment of friendships (Furman & Childs, Note 5). Clearly, more research is needed on the peer networks of hyperactive children and on their behavior with friends as well as classmates. The relevance of these findings for intervention programs also remains to be examined (Milich & Landau, 1981).

A Study of Hyperactivity in Very Young Children

Research suggests that early problems persist (Richman, 1977; Westman, Rice, & Bermann, 1967) and that the focus on school-age hyperactive children may serve to exclude a rich source of developmental data and an excellent opportunity to provide early intervention. With this in mind, we have begun a study to identify, assess, treat, and follow a sample of very young children who are perceived as hyperactive by parents. Overall, we are concerned with whether we can identify a group of hyperactive, behavior problem toddlers and preschoolers (2-3½ years of age) from parent reports and whether these children actually differ from control children on a range of observational, cognitive, and historical variables. We are also interested in evaluating the effectiveness of parent training groups since we see ineffective child management and ignorance of normal child development as important aspects of parent perceptions of problem behavior in this age group. Finally, we are interested in the course of problem behaviors over time.

While our primary emphasis initially was on the child's performance on a variety of laboratory-based measures of attention, self-control, and tempo of play, consistent with the view that these problems reflect deficits in self-regulation (Douglas, 1980), initial intake data forced us to consider peer relations as an important component of the child's problem. Although parents contacted the project with complaints about a high activity level, a short attention span, demandingness, and discipline problems, poor peer relations were also an area of serious concern.

A number of mothers spontaneously commented on their child's aggressive and bossy behavior with peers. Furthermore, six children in the parent-identified hyperactive group had been withdrawn from at least one preschool program, five for aggressive and uncooperative behavior and one for problems with separation. No child in the control group had dropped out of preschool. Therefore, a short preschool observation was added to the research protocol in order to determine whether preschool attenders in the parent-referred group were really more aggressive and noncompliant than controls or whether parents, dealing with a child who was difficult to discipline, were exaggerating the severity of behaviors typical of children in the 2- to 3½-year-old age range. Our interest initially was merely in observing the preschool attenders in our sample in the natural environment while they were interacting with peers and with teachers. Since so little data exist on the behavior of referred children in this age range, and since our resources were limited, we began with a relatively short observation of behavior in preschool. This also permitted us to determine whether teachers saw the parent-referred group as significantly more difficult to handle than controls, thereby providing additional, independent data on the behavior of children in the real world. It also allowed for some examination of cross-situational consistency in behavior. Finally, since nearly one-half of our parent-referred problem group was female, we were also in a position to examine sex differences.

Subjects

The subjects in the present study included those children (N = 33) from the larger sample (N = 59) who were enrolled in a preschool or other peer group activity. This subsample included 13 control children (5 boys and 8 girls) who were recruited as volunteers from various sources in the community. They were not considered behavior problems by either parents or the research staff. The "hyperactive" group consisted of 12 boys and 8 girls whose parents contacted the project voicing concern about some or all of the target symptoms of overactivity, short attention span, inability to play alone, tantrums, and defiance. The project was publicized with posters in pediatricians' offices, preschools, and Mothers' Day Out groups.

While there were slightly more boys in the clinical group and more girls in the control group, this distribution was not unduly unbalanced, χ^2 (1) = < 1. All but one child observed in preschool were white. Thirty-two children were from intact families. Two "hyperactive" children had been adopted in early infancy.

Children ranged in age from 2 years, 1 month to 4 years, 3 months at the time of observation (mean age 3 years, 5 months). A 2 by 2 (sex by group) analysis of variance indicated that the groups were well matched on age (F < 1). It should be noted that children entered the project when they were between 2 and 3½ years old. However, some did not begin school until after enrolling in the project and they were not observed until they had been in school long enough to become assimilated into the peer group (Feldbaum, Christenson, & O'Neal, 1980). All children had been in school at least 6 weeks prior to observation. Three problem and three control children attended toddler groups with mothers present but on the sidelines. The remaining children were in regular preschool programs.

Demographic data indicated that the groups differed in socioeconomic status. Although all mothers had completed high school, mothers of problem youngsters were significantly lower in education level, F

(1, 29) = 13.55, p < .001, and fathers were lower in occupational level, F (1, 29) = 4.84, p < .05, than controls. The control subjects recruited to date have been predominantly middle class, while the clinical group ranges from working class to professional. However, children did not differ significantly in intelligence as measured by the Stanford-Binet (mean IQ was 112.63 for the problem group and 123.46 for the control group). One child in the clinical group refused to cooperate with the Binet administration.

Procedure

Teachers were contacted after written consent was obtained from parents. They were told only that the child was a participant in a research project on child development and that visit to the preschool was necessary to gather further information on the child's typical behavior. Each child was observed in preschool during 15 minutes of unstructured free play by one or two raters, at least one of whom was blind to the group designation of the child. In addition, the head teacher was asked to complete the Behar Preschool Behavior Questionnaire (BPBQ; Behar, 1977).

Observations

The purpose of the classroom observations was to obtain naturalistic data on the social behavior of parent-referred and control children as well as on other behavior which might reflect the poor impulse control typical of hyperactive youngsters. Therefore, several categories of behavior, similar to those used in other studies (Cohen et al., 1981; Feldbaum et al., 1980; Goggin, 1975), were defined and coded in 10-second blocks during one 15-minute observation period. Since preschools were scattered throughout the Pittsburgh area, it was feasible to observe each child only once. Categories are listed and defined in Table 14-1. General categories included play behaviors (alone and with peers), aggressive behaviors, and interaction with teacher.

Behaviors were coded for each 10-second interval in which they occurred. More than one category could be checked within each block if behaviors occurred either simultaneously or sequentially during an interval. Interobserver agreement was calculated as agreements divided by agreements plus disagreements on occurrence only. Two coders observed 15 children for the entire 15-minute period; interobserver agreement reached a mean of 89%.

It was predicted that problem youngsters would demonstrate more aggressive and noncompliant behavior in preschool and that they would spend more of their playtime wandering from activity to activity than nonproblem controls. Findings on the relationship between activity

Table 14-1. Definitions of Behaviors Observed in Preschool

Play behaviors

Cooperative interaction with peers: playing or talking with peers in a cooperative manner; nonaggressive responses to aggression from others

Solitary play: child is engaged with a toy or is involved in an activity by him- or herself; includes instances of "side-by-side" play when the child does not look at, talk to, or otherwise indicate awareness of another child in the immediate vicinity

Wandering-watching: child is not engaged in play alone or with others; includes staring at another child or the teacher and aimless wandering around the room

Aggression with peers

Verbal aggression toward peers: yelling, screaming, calling names, threatening, etc.

Physical aggression with peers: hitting, biting, and other destructive or harmful behaviors; includes knocking down, breaking, or taking away peers' toys or otherwise disrupting peers' play

Responds verbally to peer aggression: yelling, screaming, etc. in response to verbal or physical aggression from a peer

Responds physically to peer aggression: hitting, pushing, biting, kicking, etc. in response to verbal or physical aggression from a peer

Interaction with teacher

Compliance with direction: child responds by following directions when asked to modify or redirect an inappropriate behavior

Noncompliance with direction: child either ignores or responds negatively to the teacher when redirected

Positive interaction with teacher: child is engaged in conversation (other than compliance) or other positive interaction with the teacher, such as showing the teacher a toy or demonstrating an activity

level and play behavior in nonclinical samples (Goggin, 1975; Halverson & Waldrop, 1973) suggested that active youngsters are sociable with peers, but more disruptive and less goal directed. Goggin (1975) and Cohen et al. (1981) also found that more active boys engaged in more solitary play. We anticipated more solitary play and aimless wandering because we expected our parent-identified problem children to show less competence with peers and less sustained involvement with toys.

Teacher Ratings

As noted above, teachers were asked to complete the BPBQ (Behar, 1977), a 30-item checklist standardized on 3- to 6-year-olds. The BPBQ is scored on a 0 to 2 point scale; 0 indicates that the behavior in question "does not apply" to the child, 1 indicates it "sometimes applies," and 2 indicates it "certainly applies." This measure has demonstrated test-retest and interrater reliability. Furthermore, it discriminates referred from nonreferred preschoolers. A factor analysis of the BPBQ yielded three factors: hostile-aggressive, anxious-fearful, and hyper-active-distractible.

Results

Classroom Observations

The number of 10-second blocks in which each behavior occurred was summed for each subject. Since scores tended to be skewed and variances among groups were unequal, raw scores were subjected to a square root transformation to normalize the distribution prior to data analysis. In addition, since individual aggression categories occurred relatively infrequently, they were collapsed into a composite aggression variable which reflected all aggressive encounters. This composite variable was also subjected to a square root transformation. Data were then analyzed with group by sex analyses of variance.

As hypothesized, hyperactive children were more likely to be involved in aggressive encounters with peers, and this effect approached significance, $F (1,29) = 3.21, p = .08$. Boys, however, were not significantly more aggressive than girls, $F < 1$. Noncompliance with teacher directions showed a significant group by sex interaction, $F (1,29) = 10.90, p < .01$. Newman-Keuls post hoc comparisons indicated that problem boys were more likely to engage in noncompliant behavior than were problem girls or control children. Control children tended to engage in more positive interaction with the teacher, $F (1, 29) = 3.80, p = .06$. They tended to spontaneously approach their teachers and engage them in conversation, usually about a toys or some specific object that had held their attention. On the whole, teachers interacted more with boys than with girls, $F (1, 29) = 7.74, p < .01$, and boys, given more opportunity to interact, showed a trend toward more instances of compliance with teacher requests, $F (1, 29) = 3.60, p = .07$. This does not indicate that boys were more compliant, since unfortunately instances of compliance were not scored as a proportion of all requests; rather, boys and teachers interacted more, and often these interactions ended in the teacher redirecting the child or making a suggestion. Group differences are summarized in Table 14-2.

Hyperactive and control children did not differ in the amount of time spent in cooperative play with peers, $F < 1$, in solitary play, $F = 1.17$, or in watching others or wandering aimlessly around the classroom, $F < 1$, although there was a trend for girls to engage in more cooperative play than boys regardless of group, $F (1, 29) = 2.94, p = .10$. Even though all children spent most of their time during free-play observations engaged with a toy, both groups tended to devote more time to solitary play than to cooperative play with peers, probably because

Table 14-2. Maternal and Teacher Ratings on the BPBQ and Behaviors Observed for Hyperactive and Control Groups

Behaviors	Hyperactive (N = 20)	Control (N = 13)
Maternal ratings		
Hostile-aggressive	9.55[a](4.59)[b]	4.08 (2.40)
Anxious	4.45 (1.93)	3.62 (2.10)
Hyperactive	5.15 (1.73)	1.77 (1.24)
Total	23.65 (8.34)	11.92 (5.47)
Teacher ratings		
Hostile-aggressive	6.00 (5.30)	0.54 (1.39)
Anxious	3.40 (3.17)	1.62 (1.98)
Hyperactive	3.30 (2.58)	0.39 (0.65)
Total	16.20 (11.13)	3.39 (3.31)
Preschool observations		
Cooperative play[c]	14.70 (14.98)	18.00 (11.05)
Solitary play	50.10 (18.25)	44.39 (15.41)
Wandering	19.80 (12.25)	19.15 (9.85)
Aggression	3.35 (4.73)	0.62 (1.26)
Compliance	2.15 (2.58)	1.69 (1.97)
Noncompliance	1.75 (2.77)	0.15 (0.38)
Positive teacher interaction	15.75 (16.35)	21.08 (16.09)

[a]Means.
[b]Standard deviations appear in parentheses.
[c]Means and standard deviations of raw scores. Data were normalized prior to analysis.

these relatively young preschoolers had not yet accomplished the transition from solitary/parallel play to more involvement with peers (Mueller & Lucas, 1975; Rubin, 1980).

During the course of observation, 50 separate aggressive encounters were observed; 88% of these involved a problem child. Similarly, 26 instances of noncompliance with teacher requests were observed, and 92% of these involved a problem boy. Furthermore, boys in the problem group (N = 12) who were involved in more frequent aggressive interactions with peers were also more often noncompliant with the teacher (Spearman's ρ = .56, p < .05).

Teacher Ratings

Teacher ratings on the BPBQ consistently differentiated between the parent-referred problem group and the control children and confirmed parental ratings of behavior problems (Campbell, Gluck, & Ewing, Note 6). Teachers rated problem children as showing significantly more problems with hostility-aggression, F (1, 29) = 11.16, p < .002, and hyperactivity-distractibility, F (1, 29) = 13.11, $p < .001$, while ratings of anxiety-fearfulness fell short of statistical significance, F (1, 29) = 2.75. Total problem scores on the questionnaire also differentiated the groups, F (1, 29) = 13.50, $p < .001$, thus indicating that teachers viewed the problem children as having more behavior difficulties than their nonproblem peers. Neither main effects of sex nor sex by group interactions were significant, consistent with parental ratings. Thus, the problem boys were not perceived as more difficult than the problem girls.

It was also of interest to determine whether the children in the problem group who were seen as more active and aggressive by mothers were likewise seen as more problematic by teachers. Thus, maternal and teacher ratings on the aggression and hyperactivity factors of the BPBQ were correlated for the problem group only ($N = 20$). Since directional predictions were made, one-tailed tests were used. Maternal ratings of aggression at initial intake showed a moderate correlation with teacher ratings of aggression in preschool ($r = .48$, $p < .02$); similarly, problem children who were rated as more active and inattentive by mothers were also rated as more hyperactive by teachers ($r = .40$, $p < .05$).

The validity of teacher ratings as they applied to observed classroom behavior was also of interest. Classroom behaviors, therefore, which best reflected hyperactive symptomatology (i.e., aggression and noncompliance) were correlated with teacher ratings on the BPBQ factors for the problem subgroup only. Consistent with expectation, children who were observed to be more aggressive in preschool were rated as more hostile-aggressive, $r = .60$, $p < .01$, and hyperactive, $r = .56$, $p < .01$; likewise, observational measures of noncompliance were related to teacher ratings of hostility-aggression, $r = .37$, $p = .06$, and hyperactivity, $r = .38$, $p = .05$. In addition, teacher ratings of anxiety-fearfulness indicated some discriminative validity. Ratings were unrelated to observed aggression, $r = .15$ or noncompliance, $r = -.10$, indicating that teachers were not simply attributing more symptomatic behaviors to more difficult subjects because of a negative halo effect. Table 14-3.

Laboratory Measures

Finally, we were interested in the relationship between the problem behaviors observed in the classroom (aggression and noncompliance) and several laboratory measures that reflected problems with attention and impulse control. Children were observed during 15 minutes of free play in a laboratory playroom, and frequency of activity shifts was coded as one measure of attention deficit (Routh, Schroeder, O'Tuama, 1974). Nontoy contacts were also coded. This measure reflected the number of 10-second blocks in which the child was engaged with objects other than toys; these tended to be forbidden objects such as locked

Table 14-3. Correlations Between Problem Behaviors Observed in Preschool and Teacher Ratings and Laboratory Measures—Problem Subgroup Only ($N = 20$)

Ratings and measures	Preschool behaviors	
	Aggression	Noncompliance
Teacher ratings		
Hostile-aggressive	.60***	.37*
Anxious-fearful	.15	.10
Hyperactive	.56***	.38**
Laboratory measures[a]		
Activity shifts	.14	.62***
Nontoy contacts	.00	.51**
Impulsive responses	.33	.37*
Off-task	.42**	.29
Out of seat	.29	.38**

[a]The only laboratory measure to show a significant sex difference was the off-task measure.
*$p < .10$, one-tailed.
**$p < .05$, one-tailed.
***$p < .01$, one-tailed.

cabinets and doors to the videocamera and one-way mirrors. Children were also administered structured tasks and frequency of out-of-seat and off-task behaviors were calculated as number per minute of time on task, collapsed across three tasks. These measures reflect active and inattentive behavior. Finally, children were administered a delay task which required them to wait for a signal and then find a cookie hidden under one of three cups (Golden, Montare, & Bridger, 1977). Impulsive responses were scored when the child either picked up the cup or ate the cookie during the delay interval.

These five laboratory measures were correlated with classroom aggression and noncompliance for the hyperactive group only. As can be seen in Table 14-3, noncompliance in preschool was positively and significantly associated with four of five laboratory measures of short attention span and poor impulse control. Parent-identified problem children who were more aggressive in preschool were off-task more often during structured activities and tended to make more impulsive responses on the cookie delay task. Free-play behavior in the laboratory, however, was unrelated to preschool aggression.

Follow-up Data

All children are followed from 8 to 10 months after entry into the project. Of the 33 children observed in preschool, 10 hyperactive and 9 control children have been seen for follow-up thus far. Mothers of the problem children continue to perceive their children as significantly more hyperactive than do mothers of controls, F (1, 15) = 13.05, $p < .01$. However, a significant group by sex interaction, F (1, 15) = 11.34, $p < .01$, and post hoc comparisons indicate that hyperactive boys are rated as significantly more aggressive than referred girls or controls at follow-up ($p < .05$).

Discussion

The data indicate that these young parent-identified hyperactive children are indeed more aggressive in preschool than controls. Both problem boys and girls engage in more aggressive interactions; this finding is consistent with other studies of slightly older hyperactive children which either did not examine sex differences (Schleifer et al., 1975) or studied boys only (Cohen et al., 1981). Similarly, like Schleifer et al. (1975), we did not observe group differences in the frequency of social interactions with peers. Furthermore, boys in the parent-referred group were not only more negative with peers, but more noncompliant with teachers than controls or problem girls. Finally, teachers tended to engage in more positive interactions with boys than with girls, consistent with other studies (e.g., Serbin, O'Leary, Kent, & Tonick, 1973); these higher rates of teacher interaction may be a response to the more exuberant and attention-capturing play of boys (e.g., Carpenter & Huston-Stein, 1980).

In addition, within the hyperactive group, there was some evidence that active, inattentive, and noncompliant behavior was apparent across situations and that teacher ratings were consistent with observational data. Children in the problem group who were observed to be more aggressive and noncompliant in preschool were rated as more hyperactive and hostile-aggressive by teachers. Teachers and mothers showed moderate agreement in their hyperactivity and aggression ratings, indicating that difficult behavior was apparent both at home and at school. Furthermore, mothers reported that specific aggressive behaviors characterized the peer interactions of problem children, and these reports were confirmed by higher rates of observed aggression in preschool. Finally, problem children who were more noncompliant in preschool were less attentive and cooperative and more impulsive on several laboratory measures. Taken together, these data indicate that parent-referred problem children show less adaptive social behavior and that their difficulties with self-regulation show consistency across situations and observers.

Although our initial focus was on the short attention span and poor impulse control of the parent-referred young problem children, it became apparent that the difficulties in self-regulation exhibited by these youngsters were associated with aggressive peer interactions. Thus, an examination of peer relations was necessary for a comprehensive evaluation of the nature and extent of the behavior problems. Unfortunately, our coding system was admittedly crude and our observation period brief. More detailed narrative accounts of the nature of both aggressive and prosocial encounters with peers as well as observations over the course of several days would have helped us to answer questions which now appear to be of crucial importance to an understanding of the qualitative features of peer interaction in young children with behavior problems.

For example, it may be of importance to know the ratio of provoked to unprovoked aggressive encounters since unprovoked attacks on a peer are likely to have more negative implications for the child's ability to relate to peers and for peer acceptance (Moore, 1967). It would also be of interest to know the specific nature of a larger sample of aggressive interchanges: How many begin as possession struggles? As rough-and-tumble play? As fantasy play? Who initiates them? How do other children respond to the aggressive behavior of their hyperactive classmate? Do unprovoked aggressive interactions appear to be relatively random, the result of overexcitement and lack of control, or are they directed at specific targets?

While frequencies of aggressive exchanges differentiate hyperactive children from controls, frequencies of prosocial interactions do not. However, we know little about the quality of these prosocial acts: Who initiates them? Are they characteristically boisterous and vigorous? How do peers respond to the social initiations of hyperactive preschoolers? Do hyperactive youngsters have any special friends in preschool, and how do their friendship patterns differ from those of controls? These and other questions remain to be addressed.

While the description of the peer relations of hyperactive children sheds light on the nature and range of their symptomatology, the prognostic implications of peer problems are of particular importance. However, very little information is available on the prognosis of behavior problems in very young children or on the relative prognostic importance of various child and family characteristics. There is some evidence that peer problems in preschoolers are associated with a poor outcome in adolescence (Westman et al., 1967). Studies also indicate that aggressive and active behaviors in young children are relatively persistent and are associated with less competent social behavior among school-age children (Battle & Lacey, 1972; Block & Block, 1980; Kohn, 1977). Furthermore, follow-up studies of school-age hyperactive children indicate that higher rates of aggression are associated with poorer adjustment in adolescence (Milich & Loney, 1979). Taken together, these findings suggest that high rates of aggression observed in preschool may, in fact, predict continued hyperactive and aggressive symptomatology and concomitant peer problems in elementary school.

A more fine-grained analysis of aggressive encounters may also indicate that those youngsters who engage in more hostile and unprovoked aggression are at higher risk for continued difficulties. Children who lash out at more vulnerable targets may also be at higher risk. Several of the problem children were observed to show unprovoked aggression to smaller children; it was not clear at the time whether these were relatively random expressions of poor self-control or deliberate attacks on children who were less likely to retaliate. These subtle differences in the qualitative features of aggression in young children may well relate to outcome or to family characteristics that mediate outcome (Milich & Loney 1979). A related question concerns the nature of developmental change in the expression of aggression by normal (Hartup, 1974) as compared to behavior problem youngsters. Aggression in the context of other symptoms may show less developmental change than age-related aggression not associated with other deficits in impulse control.

It is also likely that aggression has different prognostic implications for behavior problem boys than for behavior problem girls. It is our clinical impression that the boys in the sample are likely to have more continuing difficulties than the girls. From the start we have been surprised both by the relatively large proportion of parent-referred girls and by the lack of sex differences on our measures. Problem girls were involved in more aggressive incidents in preschool than control children, but problem boys were even more likely to become aggressive (66% vs. 22% of aggressive incidents). Furthermore, the quality of the aggression among girls appeared to be less hostile and more object oriented (Feshbach & Feshbach, 1972).

Our follow-up data are consistent with the notion that there are sex differences in the quality and prognostic importance of preschool aggression. Although follow-up data have been analyzed for only a small proportion of the sample, and therefore, are very preliminary, it is worth noting that problem children continue to be rated as more hyperactive than controls at 8-month follow-up; however, only boys continue to be rated as more aggressive. Hartup (1974) noted that object-oriented aggression decreases with increasing age. These referred girls were apparently involved in more age-related aggression associated with difficulties in sharing toys a problem which decreased as they got older. Boys, on the other hand, were involved in a variety of aggressive exchanges, involving both provoked and unprovoked peer-oriented aggression. It may well be that these are the youngsters who continue to show aggressive behavior since their aggression reflects the core symptomatology of hyperactivity rather than the intensification of behavior typical of a developmental stage. Follow-up data on a larger sample as well as more detailed observations in kindergarten will begin to answer some of these questions. However, these preliminary findings are intriguing and are consistent with findings from nonclinical samples which suggest that the relationship between aggression and activity level may be more stable and have more prognostic significance for boys than for girls (Battle & Lacey, 1972; Halverson & Waldrop, 1973).

Clearly, longitudinal studies are needed which examine young behavior problem children over time and obtain measures of attention and self-control in a range of situations. Developmental changes in activity, attention, impulse control, aggression, and prosocial behaviors may begin to shed light on the vicissitudes of early symptomatology and on the predictive importance of particular symptoms. Family characteristics are also crucial, since it is clear that particular styles of child rearing exacerbate symptoms, while others can lead to a decrease in problem behavior (e.g., Thomas et al., 1968). However, research on behavior disorders in young children is only beginning, and little is understood about the nature, course, and correlates of early problems.

Acknowledgments

This research was supported in part by Grant R01 MH32735 from the National Institute of Mental Health to the first author. Thanks are due to Linda Ewing, Diane Gluck, Emily Szumowski, Anna Marie Breaux, and Susan Sandler for their invaluable help in all phases of this project.

Reference Notes

1. Howes, C. *Patterns of friendship in young children.* Paper presented at the biennial meeting of the Society for Research in Child Development, Boston, April 1981.
2. Cunningham, C. E., Siegel, L. S., & Offord, D. *The dose and age related effects of methylphenidate on the peer interactions of hyperactive boys.* Paper presented the annual meeting of the American Psychological Association, Montreal, 1980.
3. Pelham, W. *Peer relations and hyperactive children: Description and treatment effects.* Paper presented at the annual meeting of the American Psychological Association, Montreal, 1980.
4. Dodge, K. A. *Behavioral antecedents of peer social isolation and rejection.* Paper presented at the biennial meeting of the Society for Research in Child Development, Boston, April 1981.
5. Furman, W., & Childs, M. K. *A temporal perspective on children's friendships.* Paper presented at the biennial meeting of the Society for Research in Child Development, Boston, April 1981.
6. Campbell, S. B., Gluck, D. S., & Ewing, L. J. *"Hyperactivity" in toddlers: Behavioral and developmental differences between pervasive and situational subgroups.* Paper presented at the biennial meeting of the Society for Research in Child Development, Boston, April 1981.

References

American Psychiatric Association, *Diagnostic and statistical manual of mental disorders (DSM-III).* Washington, D.C.: 1980.
Anderson, S., & Messick, S. Social competency in young children. *Developmental Psychology*, 1974, *10*, 282-293.
Barkley, R. A review of stimulant drug research with hyperactive children. *Journal of Child Psychology and Psychiatry*, 1977, *18*, 137-165.

Barkley, R. A. Specific guidelines for defining hyperactivity (attention deficit disorder) in children. In B. Lahey & A. Kazdin (Eds.), *Advances in clinical child psychology* (Vol. 4). New York: Plenum Press, 1981.

Battle, E. S., & Lacey, B. A context for hyperactivity in children over time. *Child Development*, 1972, *43*, 757-773.

Behar, L. The Preschool Behavior Questionnaire. *Journal of Abnormal Child Psychology*, 1977, *5*, 265-276.

Block, J. H., & Block, J. The role of ego-control and ego-resiliency in the organization of behavior. In W. A. Collins (Ed.), *Minnesota symposia on child psychology* (Vol. 13). Hillsdale, N.J.: Erlbaum, 1980.

Bosco, J. J., & Robin, S. S. Hyperkinesis: Prevalence and treatment. In C. Whalen & B. Henker (Eds.), *Hyperactive children: The social ecology of identification and treatment.* New York: Academic Press, 1980.

Bowlby, J. *Attachment and loss* (Vol. 1): *Attachment.* New York: Basic Books, 1969.

Brazelton, T. B. *The Neonatal Behavioral Assessment Scale (Clinics in Developmental Medicine*, No. 50). Philadelphia: Lippincott, 1973.

Brazelton, T. B., Koslowski, B., & Main, M. The origins of reciprocity: The early Mother-infant interaction. In M. Lewis & L. Rosenblum (Eds.), *The effect of the infant on its caregiver.* New York: Wiley, 1974.

Bronson, W. Developments in behavior with age-mates during the second year of life. In M. Lewis & L. A. Rosenblum (Eds.), *Friendship and peer relations.* New York: Wiley, 1975.

Bryan, T. Peer popularity of learning disabled children. *Journal of Learning Disabilities*, 1974, *7*, 261-268.

Bryan, T. H. Learning disabled children's comprehension of nonverbal communication. *Journal of Learning Disabilities*, 1977, *10*, 36-41.

Buss, D. M., Block, J. H., & Block, J. Preschool activity level: Personality correlates and developmental implications. *Child Development*, 1980, *51*, 401-408.

Campbell, S. B. Hyperactivity: Course and treatment. In A. Davids (Ed.), *Child personality and psychopathology: Current topics* (Vol. 3). New York: Wiley, 1976.

Campbell, S. B. Developmental perspectives in child psychopathology. In T. Ollendick & M. Hersen (Eds.), *Handbook of child psychopathology.* New York: Plenum Press, in press.

Campbell, S. B., Endman, M., & Bernfeld, G. A three-year follow-up of hyperactive preschoolers into elementary school. *Journal of Child Psychology and Psychiatry*, 1977, *18*, 239-249.

Campbell, S. B., & Paulauskas, S. L. Peer relations in hyperactive children. *Journal of Child Psychology and Psychiatry*, 1979, *20*, 233-246.

Campbell, S. B., Schleifer, M., & Weiss, G. Continuities in maternal reports and child behaviors over time in hyperactive and comparison groups. *Journal of Abnormal Child Psychology*, 1978, *6*, 33-45.

Campbell, S. B., Schleifer, M., Weiss, G., & Perlman, T. A two-year follow-up of hyperactive preschoolers. *American Journal of Orthopsychiatry*, 1977, *47*, 149-162.

Carpenter, C. J., & Huston-Stein, A. Activity structure and sex-typed behavior in preschool children. *Child Development*, 1980, *51*, 862-872.

Cohen, N. J., Sullivan, J., Minde, K., Novak, C., & Helwig, C. Evaluation of the relative effectiveness of methylphenidate and cognitive behavior modification in the treatment of kindergarten-aged hyperactive children. *Journal of Abnormal Child Psychology*, 1981, *9*, 43-54.

Cowen, E. L., Pederson, A., Babigian, H., Izzo, L. D., & Trost, M. A. Long-term follow-up of early detected vulnerable children. *Journal of Consulting and Clinical Psychology*, 1973, *41*, 438-446.

Cowen, E. L., Trost, M. A., Izzo, L. D., Lorion, R. P., Dorr, D., & Isaacson, R. V. *New ways in school mental health. Early detection and prevention of school maladaptation.* New York: Human Sciences Press, 1975.

Damon, W. *The social world of the child.* San Francisco: Jossey-Bass, 1977.

DiPietro, J. A. Rough and tumble play: A function of gender. *Developmental Psychology*, 1981, *17*, 50-58.

Douglas, V. I. Treatment and training approaches to hyperactivity: Establishing external or internal control. In C. K. Whalen & B. Henker (Eds.), *Hyperactive children: The social ecology of identification and treatment.* New York: Academic Press, 1980.

Douglas, V. I., & Peters, K. Toward a clearer definition of the attentional deficit of hyperactive children. In G. Hale & M. Lewis (Eds.), *Attention and the development of cognitive skills.* New York: Plenum Press, 1979.

Edelbrock, C., & Achenbach, T. M. A typology of Child Behavior Profile patterns: Distribution and correlates for disturbed children aged 6-16. *Journal of Abnormal Child Psychology*, 1980, *8*, 441-470.

Feldbaum, C. L., Christenson, T. E., & O'Neal, E. C. An observational study of the assimilation of the newcomer to the preschool. *Child Development*, 1980, *51*, 497-507.

Feshbach, N., & Feshbach, S. Children's aggression. In W. W. Hartup (Ed.), *The young child: Reviews of research* (Vol. 2). Washington, D.C.: National Association for the Education of Young Children, 1972.

Freud, A. *Normality and pathology in childhood: Assessments of development.* New York: International Universities Press, 1965.

Goggin, J. E. Sex differences in the activity level of preschool children as a possible precursor of hyperactivity. *Journal of Genetic Psychology*, 1975, *127*, 75-81.

Golden, M., Montare, A., & Bridger, W. Verbal control of delay behavior in two year old boys as a function of social class. *Child Development*, 1977, *48*, 1107-1111.

Goldman, B. D., & Ross, H. S. Social skills in action: An analysis of early peer games. In J. A. Glick & K. A. Clarke-Stewart (Eds.), *Studies in social and cognitive development* (Vol. 1). New York: Gardner Press, 1978.

Gottman, J. M. Toward a definition of social isolation in children. *Child Development*, 1977, *48*, 513-517.

Green, K., Beck, S., Forehand, R., & Vosk, B. Validity of teacher nominations of child behavior problems. *Journal of Abnormal Child Psychology*, 1980, *8*, 397-404.

Halverson, C. F., & Waldrop, M. F. The relations of mechanically recorded activity level to varieties of preschool play behavior. *Child Development*, 1973, *44*, 678-681.

Halverson, C. F., & Waldrop, M. Relations between preschool activity and aspects of intellectual and social behavior at age 7½. *Developmental Psychology*, 1976, *12*, 107-112.

Hartup, W. W. Aggression in childhood: Developmental perspectives. *American Psychologist*, 1974, *29*, 336-341.

Hartup, W. W. Peer interaction and the behavioral development of the individual child. In E. Schopler & R. J. Reichler (Eds.), *Psychopathology and child development: Research and treatment.* New York: Plenum Press 1976.

Hartup, W. W. The social worlds of childhood. *American Psychologist,* 1979, *34,* 944-950.

Hartup, W. W., Glazer, J. A., & Charlesworth, R. Peer reinforcement and sociometric status. *Child Development,* 1967, *38,* 1017–1024.

Kagan, J. The concept of identification. *Psychological Review,* 1958, *65,* 296-305.

Klein, A. R., & Young, R. D. Hyperactive boys in their classroom: Assessment of teacher and peer perceptions, interaction, and classroom behaviors. *Journal of Abnormal Child Psychology,* 1979, *7,* 425-442.

Kohn, M. *Social competence, symptoms, and underachievement in childhood: A longitudinal perspective.* Washington, D. C.: Winston, 1977.

Kohn, M., & Parnes, B. Social interaction in the classroom—A comparison of apathetic-withdrawn and angry-defiant children. *Journal of Genetic Psychology,* 1974, *125,* 165-175.

Korner, A. F. Individual differences at birth: Implications for early experience and later development. *American Journal of Orthopsychiatry,* 1971, *41,* 608-619.

Lahey, B. B., Green, K. D., & Forehand, R. On the independence of ratings of hyperactivity, conduct problems, and attention deficits in children: A multiple regression analysis. *Journal of Consulting and Clinical Psychology,* 1980, *48,* 566-574.

Leiter, M. P. A study of reciprocity in preschool play groups. *Child Development,* 1977, *48,* 1288-1295.

Lewis, M., & Feiring, C. The child's social world. In R. Lerner & G. Spanier (Eds.), *Contributions of the child to marital quality and family interaction through the life-span.* New York: Academic Press, 1979.

Lieberman, A. F. Preschoolers' competence with a peer: Relations with attachment and peer experience. *Child Development,* 1977, *48,* 1277-1287.

Lytton, H. Disciplinary encounters between young boys and their mothers and fathers. Is there a contingency system? *Developmental Psychology,* 1979, *15,* 256-268.

Mannarino, A. P. The development of children's friendships. In H. C. Foot, A. J. Chapman, & J. R. Smith (Eds.), *Friendship and social relations in children.* New York: Wiley, 1980.

Masters, J. C., & Furman, W. Popularity, individual friendship selection, and specific peer interaction among children. *Developmental Psychology,* 1981, *17,* 344-350.

Milich, R., & Landau, S. Socialization and peer relations in hyperactive children. In K. D. Gadow & I. Bialer (Eds.), *Advances in learning and behavior disabilities* (Vol. 1). Greenwich, Conn.: JAI Press, 1981.

Milich, R., & Loney, J. The role of hyperactive and aggressive symptomatology in predicting adolescent outcome among hyperactive children. *Journal of Pediatric Psychology,* 1979, *4,* 93-112.

Moore, S. G. Correlates of peer acceptance in nursery school. In W. W. Hartup & N. L. Smothergill (Eds.), *The young child: Reviews of research,* Washington, D. C.: National Association for the Education of Young Children, 1967.

Mueller, E., & Lucas, T. A developmental analysis of peer interaction among toddlers. In M. Lewis & L. A. Rosenblum (Eds.), *Friendship and peer relations.* New York: Wiley, 1975.

Patterson, G. R., Littman, R. A., & Bricker, W. Assertive behavior in children: A step toward a theory of aggression. *Monographs of the Society for Research in Child Development*, 1967, *32* (5, Serial No. 113).

Richman, N. Short-term outcome of behavior problems in three year old children. In P. J. Graham (Ed.), *Epidemiological approaches in child psychiatry*. London: Academic Press, 1977.

Robins, L. N. *Deviant children grown up*. Baltimore: Williams & Wilkins, 1966.

Robins, L. N. Sturdy childhood predictors of adult antisocial behaviour: Replications from longitudinal studies. *Psychological Medicine*, 1978, *8*, 611-622.

Ross, A. O. *Psychological disorders of children*. New York: McGraw-Hill, 1974.

Routh, D., Schroeder, C., & O'Tuama, L. Development of activity level in children. *Developmental Psychology*, 1974, *10*, 163-168.

Rubin, Z. *Children's friendships*. Cambridge, Mass.: Harvard University Press, 1980.

Sandberg, S. T., Wieselberg, M., & Shaffer, D. Hyperkinetic and conduct problem children in a primary school population: Some epidemiological considerations. *Journal of Child Psychology and Psychiatry*, 1980, *21*, 293-312.

Schleifer, M., Weiss, G., Cohen, N. J., Elman, M., Cvejic, H., & Kruger, E. Hyperactivity in preschoolers and the effect of methylphenidate. *American Journal of Orthopsychiatry*, 1975, *45*, 38-50.

Serafica, F., & Harway, N. Social relations and self-esteem of children with learning disabilities. *Journal of Clinical Child Psychology*, 1979, *8*, 227-233.

Serbin, L. A., O'Leary, K. D., Kent, R. N., & Tonick, I. J. A comparison of teacher response to the preacademic and problem behavior of boys and girls. *Child Development*, 1973, *44*, 796-804.

Smith, P. K., & Green, M. Aggressive behavior in English nurseries and play groups: Sex differences and response of adults. *Child Development*, 1975, *46*, 211-214.

Sroufe, L. A. The coherence of individual development: Early care, attachment, and subsequent developmental issues. *American Psychologist*, 1979, *34*, 834-841.

Stern, D. Mother and infant at play: The dyadic interaction involving facial, vocal, and gaze behaviors. In M. Lewis & L. Rosenblum (Eds.), *The effect of the infant on its caregiver*. New York: Wiley, 1974.

Strayer, F. F., & Strayer, J. An ethological analysis of social agonism and dominance relations among preschool children. *Child Development*, 1976, *47*, 980-989.

Sutton-Smith, B., Rosenberg, G. G., & Morgan, E. The development of sex differences in play choices during preadolescence. *Child Development*, 1963, *34*, 119-126.

Thomas, A., Chess, S., & Birch, H. G. *Temperament and behavior disorders in children*. New York: New York University Press, 1968.

Vaughn, B. E., & Waters, E. Attention structure, sociometric status, and dominance: Interrelations, behavioral correlates, and relationships to social competence. *Developmental Psychology*, 1981, *17*, 275-288.

Waldrop, M. F., & Halverson, C. F. Intensive and extensive peer behavior: Longitudinal and cross-sectional analyses. *Child Development*, 1975, *46*, 19-26.

Waters, E., Wippman, J., & Sroufe, L. A. Attachment, positive affect, and competence in the peer group: Two studies in construct validation. *Child Development*, 1979, *50*, 821-829.

Weiss, G., Kruger, E., Danielson, U., & Elman, M. The effect of long-term treatment of hyperactive children with methylphenidate. *Canadian Medical Association Journal*, 1975, *112*, 159-164.

Weiss, G., Minde, K., Werry, J. S., Douglas, V., & Nemeth, E. Studies on the hyperactive child—VIII. Five year follow-up. *Archives of General Psychiatry*, 1971, *24*, 409-414.

Westman, J. C., Rice, D. L., & Bermann, E. Nursery school behavior and later school adjustment. *American Journal of Orthopsychiatry*, 1967, *37*, 725-731.

Whalen, C. K., & Henker, B. *Hyperactive children: The social ecology of identification and treatment.* New York: Academic Press, 1980.

Whalen, C., Henker, B., Collins, B., McAuliffe, S., & Vaux, A. Peer interaction in a structured communication task: Comparisons of normal and hyperactive boys and of methylphenidate (Ritalin) and placebo effects. *Child Development*, 1979, *50*, 388-401.

Winnicott, D. W. *Mother and child: A primer of first relationships.* New York: Basic Books, 1957.

Chapter 15

Social and Social–Cognitive Developmental Characteristics of Young Isolate, Normal, and Sociable Children

Kenneth H. Rubin

In the two decades since the full-scale introduction of early intervention programs in North America, the telling marker of programatic success has generally been the IQ score (Zigler & Trickett, 1978). Of course, most evaluation efforts have included other outcome measures; but the focus has clearly been on cognitive growth and development. During the past 5 years or so, however, there has been a growing movement to include social skills training and social-developmental measures in intervention programs and their evaluations (e.g., Kamii & DeVries, 1977; Shure & Spivack, 1980). Indeed, Zigler and Trickett recently (1978) wrote that "social competence, rather than IQ, should be the major source of intervention programs such as Head Start" (p. 793).

There has thus been a change of focus from the strictly cognitive to a more eclectic implementation and evaluation approach in early childhood intervention efforts. The turn toward social development appears to be the result of a number of significant findings from recent studies concerning the effects of peer relationships of the development of social skills. Moreover, some classical theories concerning the relation between peer interaction and social and social-cognitive development have begun to recapture the interest of researchers.

From the theoretical standpoint, one of the earliest psychological statements implicating peers in normal social development emanated from Piaget (1926, 1932). In his early work concerning communicative development and the growth of mature moral judgmental skills, Piaget noted that the cooperation and mutuality engendered in early peer relationships allows children to gain broader cognitive perspectives about their social worlds. He considered very young children to be egocentric and neither willing nor able to take the viewpoints, intentions, or feelings of their social partners into account. However, with the onset of peer play there is an opportunity not only to establish egalitarian and reciprocal relationships, but also to experience peer conflict and negotiation. Such conflict and negotiation could center around the acquisition of desirable objects or around different perspectives of the social world. In both cases he thought peer conflict and negotiation carry with them the power of eliciting compromise or reciprocity. To Piaget and others (Asher & Renshaw, 1981; Hartup, in press; Rubin & Pepler, 1980), children who have the opportunity to play with their peers eventually come to realize that positive and productive interaction is marked by compromise and by socialized thoughts.

Another theorist who considered peer relations to play a significant role in development was Sullivan (1953). He suggested that the foundations of mutual respect emanate from the child's peer, and more particularly from friendship relationships. He considered such relationships to provide a framework for the development of concepts of cooperation, mutual respect, and interpersonal sensitivity (cf. Berndt, Chapter 11, this volume; Smollar & Youniss, Chapter 12, this volume).

In addition to these classical theoretical statements, there have been a number of experimental training studies that clarify the significance of peer interaction. Working within neo-Piagetian frameworks, developmental psychologists have indicated that peer communication, conflict, and role playing can lead to improvements in perspective-taking skills and to decreases in aggression (Burns & Brainerd, 1979; Chandler, 1973; Iannotti, 1978; Rosen, 1974). Similar experimental interventions have succeeded also in promoting advances in the acquisition of knowledge concerning the impersonal world (Botvin & Murray, 1975; Miller & Brownell, 1975).

Learning and social-learning theorists and researchers also have indicated that children gain knowledge about their social worlds from their peers (Allen, 1976; Hartup, in press). Children can be taught directly (through tutelage and discussion) and indirectly (through observation) by their peers. Peers also provide each other with emotional support in threatening or novel situations (Schwarz, 1972; Ispa, Note 1).

Finally, and perhaps most relevant to the research described in this chapter, a body of data is accumulating that suggests that the quantity and quality of peer interaction during the early and middle years of childhood have some impact on later development. Bronson (1966) noted a correlational link between young children initially rated as "reserved-somber-shy" and later vulnerability, instability, and lack of dominance. Roff, Sells, and Golden (1972) and Cowen, Pederson, Babigian, Izzo, and Trost (1973) reported that ratings of peer rejection during the early elementary school years are predictive of school dropout, antisocial behavior, delinquency, sexual disorder, and psychopathology in adolescence and in the early years of adulthood.

Taken together, these theoretical and empirical perspectives lead to the conclusion that peer interaction is an important force in the development of social, cognitive, and social-cognitive competence. It is therefore unfortunate that not all children are equally likely to engage in peer interaction. The literature reviewed above indicated that the long-range prognosis for children who rarely play with their peers is not good. However, at this time we know little about the correlates of social withdrawal in early childhood. Moreover, procedures for identifying socially withdrawn children have not been well developed.

The purpose of the project described in this chapter was to develop an observational precedure to target preschool- and kindergarten-age children who rarely play with their peers; another aim was to examine some of the concurrent social, cognitive, and social-cognitive correlates of social withdrawal in early childhood. Do children as young as the preschool and kindergarten ages who do not play often with peers evidence deficits in social, cognitive, and social-cognitive development? Are "socially withdrawn" children rejected by their peers? These are some of the questions addressed in this study.

Targeting Socially Withdrawn Children

Approaches to Targeting

It is necessary to note that much of the extant research concerning correlates of social withdrawal or isolation in early childhood has not proven fruitful. Behavioral indices of social withdrawal typically have not been found to correlate with concurrent assessments of likeability by peers or with social cognitive development (Asher & Hymel, 1981; Asher, Markell, & Hymel, 1981). Consequently, some psychologists (most notably Asher and his colleagues) have argued against using rate-of-interaction approaches to identify young children who are at risk for later developmental problems. These writers suggested the use of sociometric rating scales of peer acceptance/rejection to identify children who are at risk.

Given that sociometric rating scales relate both concurrently (Rubin, 1972) and predictively (Cowen et al., 1973; Roff et al., 1972) to indices of social competence, the argument for using sociometric targeting procedures is well taken. The use of such procedures, however, does not allow examination of the *theoretically* based question concerning the significance of peer interaction for development. Theorists have speculated that peer interaction is a significant force in the development of social, cognitive, and social-cognitive competence; the classical theorists have not suggested that sociometric status plays a causal role in development. Since measures of sociometric status cannot be equated with measures of social participation, and since the purpose of this project was to discover correlates of social withdrawal, the targeting procedure employed was observational in nature.

One major criticism of the observational, rate-of-interaction approach to targeting at risk populations has concerned the rather variable and seemingly arbitrary criteria employed in the definition of "social isolation." If an investigator is truly interested in identifying at risk populations, it would be logical to target those children who fall at the extreme nonsocial end of the social interaction continuum. However, in previously published research, psychologists have attempted to maximize their sample sizes by choosing their "isolates" from small and select groups. For example, those children who fall in the bottom one-third of their class in terms of frequency of observed social behavior may constitute an "isolate" group. In such research, of a total sample of 60 children, 20 are identified as socially withdrawn.

In other cases, the isolate child has been defined as one who spends approximately 15% (Gottman, 1977), 33% (Furman, Rahe, & Hartup, 1979), or 50% (Keller & Carlson, 1974) of the time interacting with peers. On the average, an interaction rate of 25% or less has been used to define isolate status (Hops & Greenwood, 1981). It should be noted that in some cases isolate behavior is defined by all nonsocial activity (e.g., unoccupied, onlooker, solitary play, and parallel play), whereas in others only certain forms of nonsocial activity (e.g., unoccupied, onlooker, and solitary play) are included.

In the present study an "extreme-groups" targeting procedure was developed. The procedure involved identifying groups of children on the basis of normative distributions of observed social behavior both within each child's given age group and within his or her given class. The procedure employed to identify children who varied with respect to observed sociability is described below.

Targeting Procedure

The children were drawn from eight preschools and six kindergartens in southwestern Ontario. There were 123 preschoolers (mean age = 57.76 months, SD = 4.26) and 111 kindergarteners (mean age = 65.05 months, SD = 3.97); 71 of the preschoolers and 56 of the kindergarteners were females. The children were from predominately lower middle- to middle-class socioeconomic backgrounds. All children were of normal intelligence and English was the primary language in all homes.

Each child was observed during free play following procedures outlined elsewhere (Rubin, 1982).[1] Basically, each preschooler was observed for six 10-second time intervals each day over a 30-day period. The kindergarteners were observed for six 10-second intervals each day over only a 25-day period because of time constraints.

---

[1] A manual for coding free play behaviors is available from the author upon request.

Behaviors were coded on a checklist which included the cognitive play categories of Smilansky (1968); that is, functional-sensorimotor, constructive, and dramatic play and games with rules. The cognitive play categories were nested within the social participation categories originally described by Parten (1932) and revised by Rubin (in press): that is, solitary, parallel, and group activities. Thus, for example, if a given child was observed to construct a puzzle in close proximity, but not with another child, the activity was coded as parallel-constructive play. Other observational categories included unoccupied behavior, onlooker behavior, reading or being read to, rough-and-tumble play, exploration, active conversations with teachers or with peers, and transitional activities (moving from one activity to another or setting up).

After coding the child's play behavior, the observer noted the names of the focal child's play or conversational partners and who it was that initiated the group activity. The affective quality of each social interchange was coded as positive, neutral, or negative according to the criteria of Furman et al. (1979).

Four observers recorded the children's play behaviors. Each observer was trained by means of videotapes and observation of children's play in a laboratory preschool not used in the present study. Reliability was assessed by pairing each observer with every other observer for 30 minutes of observational coding each. The number of coding agreements per number of agreements plus disagreements exceeded 85% in each case.

The observational procedure described above was then used to target the children into one of three groups. *Isolates* were those children whose nonsocial behavior (unoccupied, onlooker, and solitary behavior) was 1 standard deviation above the entire age group mean and 10% above their class mean for nonsocial behavior. Moreover, isolates produced social behavior (i.e., group play and conversations) that was 1 standard deviation below the entire age group mean and 10% below their class means. These stringent criteria resulted in 17 preschoolers (6 males and 11 females) and 17 kindergarteners (6 males and 11 females) being identified as isolates.

Sociable children were those whose social behavior was 1 standard deviation above the entire age group mean and 10% above their class means. Moreover, sociable children produced nonsocial behavior that was 1 standard deviation below the entire age group mean and 10% below their class means. These criteria resulted in 17 preschoolers (9 males and 8 females) and 18 kindergarteners (11 males and 7 females) being identified as sociable children.

All other children (e.g., approximately 70% of the entire sample) were targeted as *normal.* Note that the preschool and kindergarten isolates engaged in peer-related social behavior only 10% and 13% of the time, respectively. These were clearly groups of children who did not often engage their classmates in social interaction.

Observed Classroom Differences Among the Three Groups

Means for the targeted groups of children are presented in Table 15-1. Grade-by-grade means are presented in Table 15-2. In preschool and kindergarten 18 and 23 children, respectively, were randomly selected from the "normal" populations for their age groups. These numbers were determined by the requirements of a dyadic peer relations study conducted after the original targeting phase of the research project.

Table 15-1. Classroom Behavior of the Three Target Groups (Mean Proportions)

Behavior	Isolate ($n = 34$)	Normal ($n = 41$)	Sociable ($n = 35$)
Onlooker	.19	.11	.09
Unoccupied	.07	.04	.04
Reading	.04	.04	.03
Conversations: peers	.08	.13	.21
Conversations: teachers	.02	.02	.02
Transitional	.13	.14	.13
Rough and Tumble	.01	.01	.02
Solitary play			
Functional	.08	.04	.02
Constructive	.11	.07	.03
Dramatic	.02	.01	.01
Games with rules	.00	.00	.00
Total	.21	.12	.06
Parallel play			
Functional	.10	.10	08
Constructive	.14	.18	.15
Dramatic	.01	.02	.04
Games with rules	.00	.00	.00
Total	.25	.30	.27
Group play			
Functional	.01	.02	.03
Constructive	.01	.01	.03
Dramatic	.01	.03	.05
Games with rules	.00	.01	.02
Total	.03	.07	.13
Total functional	.18	.16	.13
Total constructive	.26	.26	.21
Total dramatic	.04	.06	.11
No. Social initiations made	.04	.06	.11
No. Social initiations received	.02	.03	.06

Nonplay Behavior

The data in Tables 15-1 and 15-2 are presented as proportions because the preschoolers and kindergarteners were observed for different amounts of time. Prior to data analysis all values expressed as relative frequencies were normalized using the arcsin transformation to correct for the bimodal distribution inherent in proportional data (Winer, 1971). Grade (2) by sex (2) by target group (3) analyses of variance were computed for all nonplay behavior variables that appear in the tables. In addition, analyses of variance were computed for the following classifications of group interactive behavior: (a) the number of social

Table 15-2. Classroom Behavior of Each Group in Preschool and Kindergarten (Mean Proportions)

Behavior	Preschool			Kindergarten		
	I	N	S	I	N	S
Onlooker	.22	.13	.10	.16	.10	.07
Unoccupied	.07	.13	.03	.07	.06	.05
Reading	.04	.04	.04	.03	.04	.03
Conversations: peers	.06	.13	.22	.10	.13	.21
Conversations: teachers	.03	.03	.02	.01	.01	.02
Transitional	.10	.08	.07	.16	.18	.19
Rough and tumble	.01	.02	.03	.00	.01	.01
Solitary play						
Functional	.12	.08	.04	.03	.02	.01
Constructive	.07	.06	.02	.14	.09	.04
Dramatic	.02	.01	.01	.01	.00	.00
Games with rules	.00	.00	.00	.00	.00	.00
Total	.21	.15	.07	.18	.11	.05
Parallel play						
Functional	.15	.15	.13	.05	.06	.04
Constructive	.08	.13	.08	.20	.23	.21
Dramatic	.01	.02	.03	.02	.02	.04
Games with rules	.00	.00	.00	.00	.00	.00
Total	.24	.30	.24	.27	.31	.29
Group play						
Functional	.01	.03	.05	.01	.01	.01
Constructive	.01	.01	.05	.00	.01	.02
Dramatic	.02	.03	.07	.01	.03	.04
Games with rules	.00	.01	.02	.01	.01	.01
Total	.04	.09	.19	.03	.06	.08
Total functional	.28	.26	.22	.09	.09	.06
Total constructive	.16	.20	.15	.34	.33	.27
Total dramatic	.05	.07	.11	.04	.05	.08
No. Social initiations made	.03	.06	.10	.06	.07	.13
No. Social initiations received	.01	.01	.06	.02	.03	.06

initiations made; (b) the number of social initiations received; and (c) the proportions of interactions that were positive, neutral, and negative. Only those main effects or interactions that concern the three target groups are documented herein.

Significant main effects for target group (all df = 2,109) were found for onlooker behavior, F = 32.00, p < .001, unoccupied behavior, F = 3.00, p < .003, rough-and-tumble play, F = 4.48, p < .01, conversations with peers, F = 18.43, p < .001, the number of social initiations made, F = 21.31, p < .001, and the number of social initiations received from others, F = 16.67, p < .001. Post hoc, Newman-Keuls pairwise comparison tests (all p < .05 or better) indicated that isolate children produced significantly more onlooker and unoccupied behavior and fewer conversations with peers than the other two target groups. Normal children produced more onlooker behavior and fewer conversations with peers than sociable children. Sociable children emitted more social initiations and received more social initiations than did the other two groups. Sociable children also produced significantly more rough-and-tumble play than did isolate and normal children. No other multiple comparisons were significant.

There was one significant interaction. A significant grade by target group interaction was found for transitional behaviors, F (2,109) = 4.37, p < .01. Follow-up analyses indicated that isolate preschoolers were more likely to engage in transitional activities than both groups of their more sociable counterparts.

Play Behaviors

Analyses of play behaviors were computed by running a series of grade (2) by sex (2) by target group (3) by play type (4) analyses of variance. Solitary play, for example, included four different forms; functional, constructive, and dramatic play, and games. Similar analyses were computed for parallel and group play forms. In each case the play form was a within-groups factor.

Significant main effects for target group were, of course, found for solitary play, F (2, 98) = 22.06, p < .001, and group play, F (2, 98) = 26.50, p < .001. A significant effect for target group was also found for parallel play, F (2, 98) = 3.52, p < .03. Post hoc Newman-Keuls analyses indicated that the isolate children produced significantly more solitary play and less group play than did normal and sociable children. Normal children displayed significantly more parallel play than isolate children and less group play than sociable children.

More interesting, perhaps, were the significant grade by target group interactions concerning the play categories. A significant grade by target group by type of solitary play interaction was discovered, F (8, 392) = 2.01, p < .04. Follow-up analyses indicated that the solitary play patterns of the three target groups depended upon their grade levels. Preschool isolates were reliably more likely to produce solitary functional and solitary dramatic play than their kindergarten counterparts. This pattern of significant differences held true for preschool normal versus kindergarten normal children and for preschool sociable versus kindergarten sociable children (although it is important to note that the proportion of solitary dramatic play in the three target groups across both age groups ranged only from .00 to .02 of all play). Kindergarten isolates were more likely to emit solitary constructive play than preschool isolates. No such age differences in solitary constructive play were found between the normal and sociable groups.

Comparisons between target groups revealed that the preschool isolates were more likely to engage in solitary functional play than their more sociable age-mates. This was not the case for the kindergarteners. Preschool and kindergarten isolates were more likely to produce solitary constructive behavior than sociable children. Kindergarten isolates also produced more solitary constructive play than their normal counterparts. Finally, normal children, regardless of age, emitted significantly more solitary constructive play than the sociable targets.

Two conclusions may be drawn from these data. First, the frequency with which solitary functional and solitary dramatic play occur declines with age (see also Rubin & Krasnor, 1980; Rubin, Watson, & Jambor, 1978); the frequency of solitary constructive activity however, increases with age. Consequently, the former two types of solitary play may be considered less mature than solitary constructive play.

Second, the qualitative nature of social isolation changes from preschool to kindergarten. For preschoolers, social isolate status is more highly determined by the production of solitary functional play and, to a less extent, by solitary dramatic play. For kindergarteners, social isolate status is determined, for the most part, by solitary constructive activities. These findings suggest that kindergarteners who are targeted as isolates may vary with respect to the degree to which they are considered to be "at risk". Solitary constructive play has been considered a cognitively more mature form of play behavior than either solitary functional or solitary dramatic play. Moreover, the production of solitary functional and dramatic play has been found to correlate negatively with indices of social skill and cognitive development. Similar correlations between the production of solitary constructive play and social skills and cognitive development have not been found (Rubin, 1982). Thus, kindergarten isolates whose target status is determined by their production of solitary functional and dramatic play may be at greater risk than their isolate counterparts whose status is determined predominately by their constructive behaviors.

Another interaction effect relevant to the present study stemmed from analyses of the group play data. A group play by target group interaction was discovered, F (8, 392) = 4.58, $p < .001$. Follow-up analyses indicated that the sociable and normal children produced significantly more group dramatic play than the isolate children. Moreover, sociable children were more likely to engage in group constructive play than the other two target groups, and they produced more group games than the isolate children.

Put in a slightly different perspective, of the social interactive play that isolate children engaged in, only 33% consisted of the cognitively more mature forms of sociodramatic play and games with rules. For normal and sociable children, 57% and 54%, respectively, of their group interactive play was dramatic or game oriented. In short, in terms of proportional data, the quality of the isolate chidren's social activity was less cognitively mature than that of their more sociable counterparts. Moreover, not a single instance of spontaneously generated group games with rules was observed for any isolate child regardless of age. Given the significance that Piaget and others have attached to both sociodramatic play and social games for the development of sociocentered thought and mature moral thinking (see Rubin, Fein, & Vandenberg, in press, for a review of relevant theory and research), these findings may be expected to predict concurrent or future lags in these social-cognitive areas.

Finally, analyses of variance concerning the total amounts of functional, constructive, and dramatic play emitted by each group regardless of the social context resulted in a significant target group main effect for dramatic play, F (2, 98) = 10.88, $p < .001$. Post hoc comparisons indicated that the sociable and normal children were more likely than their isolate counterparts to engage in dramatic play, the sociable children produced significantly more dramatic play than the normal children. It is noteworthy that nearly one-half of the dramatic play of normal (43%) and sociable (45%) children was carried out in an interactive context. Only one-quarter of the dramatic play of isolates was social. As noted above, the apparent lack of sociodramatic behavior in the isolate children may not only reflect a current congitive and/or social-cognitive lag but may also predict deficits in the future.

Test Result Differences Among the Three Groups

Tests Administered

Each isolate, normal, and sociable child involved in this study was also administered a battery of tests designed to assess cognitive, social, and social-cognitive competency. The children were individually administered the following measures.

Peabody Picture Vocabulary Test. Each child was given this test, which is an index of receptive vocabulary that allows the computation of mental age.

Perspective taking. The "7-4" picture task, taken directly from Flavell (1968), was presented to each child. In this task, children were presented with a series of seven pictures which told a story about a young boy who was chased up an apple tree by a dog. Upon removal of three pictures, the story changed to one in which the boy ran up the tree to eat an apple. Each child was first shown the seven-picture story. The child was then asked to predict the story that someone who had only seen the four pictures would tell. The inclusion of information that only the subject child was privy to when telling the story from the viewpoint of the person who saw only the four-picture story was indicative of poor perspective-taking skills. A scoring procedure taken directly from Selman (1971) was employed. Scores ranged from 0 to 3, with a higher score indicative of socialized thought.

Social problem solving. Social problem-solving skill was assessed by administering an elaborated version of Spivack and Shure's (1974) Preschool Interpersonal Problem-Solving Test to each child. This modification, labeled the Social Problem-Solving Test, was designed to assess both quantitative and qualitative features of social problem solving. In general, each child was presented with a series of eight pictured problem situations in which one story character wants to play with a toy or use some material that another child has in his or her possession. The child was asked what the central character in the story could do or say so that he or she could gain access to the toy or material. The characters in the story varied in either age (same vs. different age characters), sex (same vs. different sex characters), or race (same vs. cross-race characters). For example, with regard to the three age-related picture stories, in one case two 4-year-old, same-sex, same-race characters were portrayed. In a second picture, sex and race were held constant, and the subject was told that a 4-year-old wanted to play with an object in the possession of a 6-year-old. In the third case, the 4-year-old wanted a toy being played with by a 2-year-old. Similar covariations occurred for the sex and race of the story characters.

After presentation of each picture and the associated story, the child was asked to tell the experimenter everything that the central character could do or say so that he or she could obtain the desired object. As in the Preschool Interpersonal Problem-Solving Test (Spivack & Shure, 1974), the number of relevant alternatives and the number of categories were computed. Moreover, following the first response, the experimenter asked, "if that didn't work, what else could X do or say so that he [she] could have Y?" A within-story flexibility score was computed as follows: 0, no further solution offered; 1, same category/ categories as in the first response; 2, modifications of the first response or completely novel alternatives provided.

In addition to the scoring procedures described above, the children's responses were coded as to the quality of the response. The number of responses falling into each of the following broad categories was computed:

1. *Prosocial*: ask; politeness; wait; command accompanied by a politeness marker; share or take turns; loan (e.g., "Can I have the ball please?").
2. *Agonistic*: direct imperatives; force or grab; physical attack on person; damage to property (e.g., "I would push him off the swing.").
3. *Authority intervention* (e.g., "Tell his mom to get the book for him.").
4. *Bribe, trade, or finagle* (e.g., "Say that she will give the boy a balloon if he lets her read the book.").
5. *Manipulate affect* (e.g., "If you give me that ball, I'll be real happy.").

The number of responses falling within each category was divided by total number of alternatives offered by each child. The resultant computations represented the proportion of the total number of alternatives accounted for by each category.

Sociometric popularity. Each child's sociometric status was ascertained by administering the peer rating scale developed by Asher, Singleton, Tinsley, and Hymel (1979). Each child was individually presented with color photographs of each of his or her classmates. The children were asked to assign each picture to one of three boxes on which there was drawn a happy face ("children you like a lot"), a neutral face ("children you kind of like"), and a sad face ("children you don't like"). As in Asher et al. (1979), children thus received a number of positive, neutral, and negative ratings. Since the number of children in each class varied, the number of positive, negative, and neutral ratings received by each child was divided by the number of children in each class to whom the sociometric test was administered. Furthermore, a total score was computed by according each "like a lot" rating a score of 3, each "kind of like" rating a score of 2, and each "don't like" rating a score of 1. These scores were summed and then divided by the number of children in each class who were given the sociometric test.

Differences Detected

Means for all assessments of interest are presented in Table 15-3. Grade (2) by sex (2) by target group (3) analyses of variance were conducted for mental age, the perspective-taking measure, and positive, neutral, negative, and total sociometric rating scores. Target main effects were found for mental age, F (, 98) = 7.57, $p < .001$, and for the number of *positive* ratings received on the sociometric test, F (2, 98) = 3.24, $p < .04$. Follow-up Newman-Keuls analyses indicated that the sociable and normal children had higher mental ages than the isolate children. In addition, the sociable children received significantly more positive sociometric ratings then both normal and isolate children. No other comparisons were significant.

Similar grade by sex by target analyses of variance were computed for each variable scored on the Social Problem-Solving Test: the total number of categories; the total number of alternatives; the total flexibility score; and the proportions of prosocial, agonistic, adult intervention, trade or bribe, and manipulate affect categories. The one significant main effect found for the target groups concerned the proportion of adult intervention strategies employed, F (2, 98) = 4.13, $p < .02$. A follow-up Newman-Keuls test showed that the isolate group was significantly more likely to employ this social problem-solving strategy than the other two groups.

There was one significant grade by sex by target interaction for the proportion of agonistic strategies, F (2, 98) = 5.56, $p < .005$. Follow-up comparisons indicated that male preschool isolates produced significantly more agonistic strategies than the male preschoolers in the other two groups. No such differences were found in kindergarten or for girls.

Table 15-3. Test Results for the Three Target Groups

Test	Isolates	Normal	Sociable
Mental age (mo.)	68.06	75.56	81.82
Perspective taking[a]	1.85	1.83	1.74
Sociometric status[b]			
Positive	.44	.46	.58
Neutral	.29	.25	.22
Negative	.27	.29	.20
Total	2.17	2.17	2.36
Social problem solving[c]			
Totals			
Categories	19.03	19.62	17.67
Relevant alternatives	13.19	13.43	13.09
Flexibility score	14.69	13.85	13.27
Categories (proportion)			
Prosocial	.70	.70	.76
Agonistic	.17	.11	.12
Adult intervention	.08	.04	.02
Trade	.03	.07	.05
Manipulate affect	.02	.08	.05

[a]Score on picture task taken from Flavell (1968).
[b]Score on peer rating scale from Asher et al.(1979).
[c]Results of Social Problem-Solving Test, modified from Spivack and Shure (1974).

Dyadic Play of Targeted Preschoolers

It is conceivable that many of the behavioral concomitants of child-hood maladjustment in general, and of social withdrawal in particular, cannot be identified from observations of free play within the class-room or from the administration of hypothetical-reflective social-cognitive tests in the laboratory. In the case of the former, time sampled observations may not allow sufficient in-depth analysis of children's social behaviors to provide researchers with possible explanations for social withdrawal or high sociability in the early years. Moreover, the behaviors of children in the classroom are produced under the watchful eye of adult supervisors. Children may display more adult-valued be-havior while they are in the classroom than when they are on their own.

Laboratory assessment may pose similar problems. Children, regard-less of targeted status, may provide the adult researcher with answers that he or she thinks the adult wants to hear in response to hypotheti-cally posed social problem-solving situations. For example, a typical item on hypothetical-reflective social problem-solving tasks is "How should Josh [a story character] get the ball that he wants from Tim? What should he say?" Children often respond by suggesting that Josh "say please"; however, children who offer these polite strategies rarely, if ever, employ such strategies when they face similar social problems in the natural setting. Indeed, there is little relation between what chil-dren say they would do to solve a given social problem and what they in fact do when faced with the same problem in the real world (Krasnor & Rubin, 1981).

In order to examine more closely the behaviors of isolate, normal, and sociable children that may reflect social competence and social-cognitive development, the unsupervised dyadic free-play behavior of some of the targeted children was videotaped. A first "cut" of the data corpus is presented below. In the following analysis, the private speech of the three target groups is examined.

Preliminary Analysis of Private Speech

In his early work, Piaget (1926) suggested that the ability to communi-cate effectively was causally linked to the child's opportunities for and engagement in peer interaction. As mentioned earlier, social inter-action was thought to confront children with alternative viewpoints of their worlds. Such confrontations were thought to result, ultimately, in a broadening of social-cognitive knowledge and social competence (cf. Asher & Renshaw, 1981). One off-shoot of peer interactive experi-ence and its consequences was the development of communicative com-petence and the decline of egocentric speech.

From this Piagetian perspective we hypothesized that children who do not play often with their peers would produce more egocentric or nonsocial speech in potentially social situations than their more sociable counterparts. Moreover, we expect the private speech of nonsocial children to be qualitatively different from that produced by their more sociable age-mates. For example, the private speech of nonsocial children in potentially social situations may be directed more often at inanimate or nonpresent others (Kohlberg, Yaeger, & Hjertholm, 1968) than that of the more sociable children; as such, the private speech may serve a social coping function for the isolate preschoolers.

In the first analysis of the videotape data, the quantity and quality of private speech emitted by preschool-age children who varied with respect to sociability was examined.

Methods

Five preschool children were randomly selected from each of the three original targeting groups. The children were paired with 15 other same-age, same-sex, nonfriend classmates. Friendship status was ascertained by referring to the sociometric data. Only pairs of mutually rated "like a little" (as opposed to "like a lot" and "don't like") children formed the dyads.

The dyads met in a small playroom set up in a laboratory trailer for 15 minutes on two occasions. The two sessions were separated by at least 1 week. In the room there was a child-size table with two chairs. Toys included two puzzles, a Fisher-Price Sesame Street Clubhouse (with an entire set of little Sesame Street characters), a small box of blocks, two trucks, two dolls (and doll clothes), and adult-size "dress-up" clothes.

A videocamera was placed behind a one-way mirror. Microphones hung from the ceiling of the playroom. The children were brought to the playroom by a female research assistant. The researcher told the children that they could do whatever they wanted in the playroom. She indicated that she had "a little work to do" and that when she had finished her work she would return to the room. The researcher then proceeded to videotape the children at play.

Each videotape was transcribed by the researcher who recorded the children's activities. The coding procedure was identical to that described in Rubin (1979). The unit of verbal coding was the *utterance*, or "that unit of speech separated from the following unit by a logical break in speech, a change in topic, and/or a one-second pause" (Rubin, 1979).

Utterances not addressed to the dyadic partner were coded as private utterances. Consequently, a refinement of Piaget's (1926) coefficient of egocentrism was computed by dividing the total number of private utterances by the total number of spontaneous utterances produced by the child.

Private utterances were then assigned to one of the following categories (Rubin, 1979):

1. *Self-regulatory, task-related speech*: directions to the self; feedback to the self concerning the appropriateness of one's own actions; asking questions of the self concerning some aspect of a task (e.g., puzzle construction).
2. *Description of own activity, non-task related*: comments about materials; description of own activity to the self; factual or feeling statements about the experimental situation, noises outside the playroom, or nonplay aspects of activity.
3. *Sound play and word repetition.*
4. *Fantasy statements*: holding a dialogue with an imaginary companion; speaking to inanimate objects; inventing a fantasy tale about the materials in the room.
5. *Exclamations.*

Once the utterances had been coded, a second experimenter recoded 10 randomly chosen transcripts to determine interrater reliability. Agreement concerning whether or not a given utterance was private was 88%. The two judges also coded private utterances into the particular categories of nonsocial speech. Agreement for each category ranged from 80.3% to 97.5%.

Results

Preliminary analyses indicated no within-groups differences in the expression of private speech between the two sessions. All data were thus pooled for subsequent analyses. In order to avoid the analysis of interdependent dyadic data, only the speech of one dyad member was coded and submitted to analysis. Thus, only the speech of the 15 children selected from the original target groups (5 isolate, 5 sociable, and 5 normal preschoolers) was coded and compared.

A between-groups analysis of variance indicated that the number of utterances produced by each group did not differ significantly from each other (utterances of isolates $M = 342.00$; normals, $M = 335.60$; sociables, $M = 338.13$). However, significant between-groups differences were found for the number of *private* utterances, $F (2, 12) = 4.54$, $p < .03$. Post hoc Newman-Keuls analyses ($p < .05$) revealed that the isolate children ($M = 104.80$) produced significantly more private utterances than either the normal ($M = 59.80$) or the sociable ($M = 29.40$) children. No other comparison was significant.

There was also a significant effect for the "coefficient of egocentrism," $F (2, 12) = 3.79, p < .05$. Follow-up multiple comparisons indicated that the isolate group had a higher coefficient of egocentrism ($M = .307$) than the normal ($M = .178$) and sociable ($M = .086$) groups.

There were no significant group differences for the number of self-regulatory utterances, utterances describing one's own activity, sound play utterances, and exclamations. The one qualitative difference in private speech produced by the three target groups concerned the number of fantasy statements, F (2, 12) = 5.63, $p < .02$. Follow-up Newman-Keuls comparisons indicated that isolate preschoolers ($M = 40.40$) were more likely to address comments to nonpresent or inanimate "others" than were their normal ($M = 17.20$) and sociable ($M = 9.60$) counterparts.

Conclusions

The purpose of the study reported in this chapter was to develop a procedure by which children who do not interact often with their peers can be identified. Another goal was to identify the play behaviors and the social, social-cognitive, and cognitive skills that differentiated socially withdrawn children from their more socially oriented counterparts.

In brief, the play of the isolate children was found to be less mature *cognitively* than that of the normal and sociable children. Socially withdrawn children engaged in fewer social games and in less dramatic play than their age-mates. Their play with others was less likely to consist of the higher cognitive level dramatic and game behaviors (see also Rubin et al., in press). Several theorists have suggested that the quality of children's play and games both reflects and causes social and cognitive skills required to engage in social games with rules. The latter skill was postulated to aid in the development of mature moral judgement and perspective-taking skills. Vygotsky (1967), Smilansky (1968), and many other theorists (see Rubin et al., in press, for a review) also suggested that dramatic and sociodramatic activities help children to develop cognitive, social, and creative skills.

Support for these contentions comes from both correlational and experimental sources. For example, Rubin and Maioni (1975) and, more recently, Connolly (Note 2) found that the incidence of dramatic play (particularly *socio*dramatic play) in preschoolers is positively correlated with indices of social, cognitive, and social-cognitive development. Experimental play-training research has indicated that sociodramatic activities can lead to social, cognitive, and social-cognitive development (e.g., Burns & Brainerd, 1978). In the present study, the less mature cognitive play patterns of the isolate children were associated with their lower mental ages in comparison to the other two groups. It is conceivable that the negative effects of not engaging in social pretense and games become increasingly apparent over time. A longitudinal study concerning the relations between social pretense, social and cognitive development, and target status is now in progress.

The isolate children did not differ significantly from their more sociable peers on the perspective-taking measure. Furthermore, few differences were found on the measure of social problem-solving. On the latter task, the socially withdrawn children were more likely to suggest that one seek adult intervention when faced with social difficulty with peers. Moreover, the preschool isolates were more likely than their age-mates to suggest agonistic (e.g., hit, grab) strategies to solve social problems. If these strategies are indeed employed by socially withdrawn children when they are faced with object-acquisition social problems, they probably do not endear themselves to their peers. At the time of writing, the object-acquisition strategies of the three target groups as observed during dyadic interaction is being analyzed. These data will provide information concerning the naturalistic assessment of social competence.

The sociometric data indicated that the isolate children were as popular (Asher total score) as their more sociable counterparts. Isolate children, because they tend to play on their own, may present somewhat of a problem to their peers who are asked to rate them sociometrically. It is probably quite difficult for peers to pass extremely positive or negative judgment on "wallflowers" or "invisible" children. In this manner, socially withdrawn children are quite different from more aggressive or hyperactive children who evidence the disruptive behaviors associated with peer rejection (Campbell & Cluss, Chapter 14 this volume).

Finally, from the private speech data it is quite clear that *preschool* children who do not play often with their peers in the classroom are more likely to speak to themselves when playing in dyadic settings. In short, their speech is more "egocentric" than that of their more sociable age-mates. This finding agrees nicely with the Piagetian speculation that peer interaction plays a significant role in the decline of nonsocial speech.

It is also important to note that the quality of private speech produced by isolate preschoolers differed to some degree from that of the other children. It would have been reasonable to predict that isolate children would prefer to engage in constructive, quiescent activities (puzzle construction or block building) rather than in social interactive endeavors when in the dyad; consequently, the quantity of self-guiding private speech (Rubin, 1979) would be greater for the isolate group. It was not; instead, the only qualitative difference concerned speech addressed to inanimate or nonpresent others. Although private speech researchers have generally considered the production of nonsocial verbalizations to inanimate "others" to be an immature form of the phenomenon (see Zivin, 1979, for reviews of the private speech literature), it may, in fact, serve an important coping function for those children who do not interact often with their peers. By producing such speech, the isolate child may provide him/herself with a "playmate" and may practice interpersonal communicative skills with that "playmate." Of course, the assumption being made is that nonsocial fantasy utterances are produced in response to the child's *recognition* of social isolation (or shyness or loneliness). Data remain to be gathered concerning the veracity of this assumption. Nevertheless, from the first analysis of the videotape data (similar data are available for the kindergarteners but they have not been coded and analyzed), it can be concluded that socially withdrawn preschoolers produce more egocentric speech in general, and more private speech to inanimate others than do their more sociable peers.

In conclusion, the present study did provide some initial support for the notion that a lack of social interaction in early childhood is accompanied by some developmental "costs." The children who interacted with their peers more often than normal for their age group appeared to be the most socially and cognitively competent. The sociable children initiated and received more social overtures than did their peers; this result may be taken as an index of observed popularity. These data are consistent with the finding that the sociable group also received a significantly greater number of positive ratings on the sociometric test than the other two groups.

Sociable children also engaged in more rough-and-tumble and dramatic play than their less sociable counterparts. In short, *observationally*, this group appears to be more playful and perhaps more creative (as evidenced by their greater production of nonliteral analogues to real-life behavior) than the other groups. Finally, members of the sociable group had higher mental ages than their peers.

With the present data base it is admittedly not possible to ascertain whether variations in children's sociability account for the between-groups differences found. Thus, it is premature to suggest that the quantity and quality of peer experience in early childhood determines social and cognitive development. One of the guiding premises for the present line of research is that the effects of social withdrawal have a comulative impact on development; that is, it is expected that differences between isolate children and their more sociable peers become increasingly apparent with age. To examine the causal relation between the effects of social isolation and development and to examine the veracity of the cumulative deficit hypothesis, the kindergarten children observed in this study will be followed throughout their elementary school years. It will no doubt be interesting to examine the long-term sequelae of sociability status in childhood; it may be possible to identify behavioral and cognitive determinants of sociability status and to use such information to implement ameliorative programs in early childhood.

Acknowledgments

This project was funded by the Ontario Mental Health Foundation and Ministry of Community and Social Services. I am grateful to Judy Mickle and Anne Emptage for their help in collecting, coding, and analyzing the data, and to the preschool and kindergarten children and teachers who kindly consented to participate in this project. Finally, Hildy Ross' constructive criticisms of an earlier draft are greatly appreciated.

Reference Notes

1. Ispa, J. *Familiar and unfamiliar peers as "havens of security" for Soviet nursery children*. Paper presented at the biennial meeting of the Society for Research in Child Development. New Orleans, March 1977.
2. Connolly, J. Social pretend play and social competence in preschoolers. Unpublished manuscript, Concordia University, 1982.

References

Allen, V. *Children as teachers.* New York: Academic Press, 1976.

Asher, S. R., & Hymel, S. Children's social competence in peer relations: Sociometric and behavioral assessment. In J. D. Wine & M. D. Smye (Eds.), *Social competence.* New York: Guilford Press, 1981.

Asher, S. R., Markell, R. A., & Hymel, S. Identifying children at risk in peer relations: A critique of the rate-of-interaction approach to assessment. *Child Development*, 1981, *4*, 1239-1245.

Asher, S. R., & Renshaw, P. D. Children without friends: Social knowledge and social skill training. In S. R. Asher & J. M. Gottman (Eds.), *The development of children's friendships.* New York: Cambridge University Press, 1981.

Asher, S. R., Singleton, L. C., Tinsley, B. R., & Hymel, S. A reliable sociometric measure for preschool children. *Developmental Psychology*, 1979, *15*, 443-444.

Botvin, G. J., & Murray, F. B. The efficacy of peer modeling and social conflict in the acquisition of conservation. *Child Development*, 1975, *46*, 796-799.

Bronson, W. C. Central orientations: A study of behavior organization from childhood to adolescence. *Child Development*, 1966, *37*, 125-155.

Burns, S., & Brainerd, C. J., Effects of constructive and dramatic play on perspective-taking in very young children. *Developmental Psychology*, 1979, *15*, 512-521.

Chandler, M. Egocentrism and antisocial behavior: The assessment and training of social perspective-taking skills. *Developmental Psychology*, 1973, *9*, 326-332.

Cowen, E. L., Pederson, A., Babigian, H., Izzo, L. D., & Trost, M. A. Long-term follow-up of early detected vulnerable children. *Journal of Consulting and Clinical Psychology*, 1973, *41*, 438-446.

Flavell, J. H. *The development of role-taking and communicative skills in children.* New York: Wiley, 1968.

Furman, W., Rahe, D. F., & Hartup, W. W. Rehabilitation of socially-withdrawn preschool children through mixed age and same-age socialization. *Child Development*, 1979, *50*, 915-922.

Hartup, W. W. The peer system. In E. M. Hetherington (Ed.), *Handbook of child psychology* (Vol. 3): *Social development.* New York: Wiley, in press.

Hops, H., & Greenwood, C. R. Social skills deficits. In E. J. Mash & G. Terdal (Eds.), *Behavioral assessment of childhood disorders.* New York: Guilford Press, In press.

Iannotti, R. J. Effects of role-taking experiences on role-taking, empathy, altruism, and aggression. *Developmental Psychology*, 1978, *14*, 119-124.

Kamii, C., & DeVries, R. Piaget for early education. In M. C. Day & R. K. Parker (Eds.), *The preschool in action.* Boston: Allyn & Bacon, 1977.

Keller, M. F., & Carlsen, P. M. The use of symbolic modeling to promote social skills in preschool children with low levels of social responsiveness. *Child Development*, 1974, *45*, 912-919.

Kohlberg, L., Yaeger, J., & Hjertholm, E. Private speech: Four studies and a review of theories. *Child Development*, 1968, *39*, 692-736.

Krasnor, L. R., & Rubin, K. H. Social problem-solving skills in young children. In T. Merluzzi, C. Glass, & M. Genest (Eds.), *Cognitive assessment.* New York: Guilford Press, 1981.

Miller, S. A., & Brownell, C. A. Peers, persuasion, and Piaget: Dyadic interaction between conservers and non-conservers. *Child Development*, 1975, *46*, 992-997.

Parten, M. B. Social participation among preschool children. *Journal of Abnormal and Social Psychology*, 1932, *27*, 243-269.

Piaget, J. *The language and thought of the child.* London: Routledge & Kegan Paul, 1926.

Piaget, J. *The moral judgment of the child.* Glencoe: Free Press, 1932.

Piaget, J. *Play, dreams and imitation in childhood.* New York: Norton, 1951.

Roff, M., Sells, S. B., & Golden, M. M. *Social adjustment and personality development in children.* Minneapolis: University of Minnesota Press, 1972.

Rosen, C. E. The effects of sociodramatic play on problem-solving behavior among culturally disadvantaged children. *Child Development*, 1974, *45*, 920-927.

Rubin, K. H. Relationship between egocentric communication and popularity among peers. *Developmental Psychology*, 1972, *7*, 364.

Rubin, K. H. The impact of the natural setting on private speech. In G. Zivin (Ed.), *The development of self-regulation through private speech.* New York: Wiley, 1979.

Rubin, K. H. Non-social play in early childhood: Necessarily evil? *Child Development*, 1982, *53*, 651-658.

Rubin, K. H., Fein, G. G., & Vandenberg, B. Play. In E. M Hetherington (Ed.), *Handbook of child psychology* (Vol. 3): *Social development.* New York: Wiley, in press.

Rubin, K. H., & Krasnor, L. R. Changes in the play behaviors of preschoolers: A short-term longitudinal investigation. *Canadian Journal of Behavioral Science*, 1980, *12*, 278-282.

Rubin, K. H., & Maioni, R. L. Play preference and its relationship to egocentrism, popularity and classification skills in preschoolers. *Merrill-Palmer Quarterly*, 1975, *21*, 171-179.

Rubin, K. H., & Pepler, D. J. The relationship of child's play to social-cognitive development. In H. Foot, T. Chapman, & J. Smith (Eds.), *Friendship and childhood relationships.* London: Wiley, 1980.

Rubin, K. H., Watson, K., & Jambor, T. Free-play behaviors in preschool and kindergarten children. *Child Development*, 1978, *49*, 534-536.

Schwarz, J. C. Effects of peer familiarity on the behavior of preschoolers in a novel situation. *Journal of Personality and Social Psychology*, 1972, *24*, 276-284.

Selman, R. L. Taking another's perspective: Role-taking development in early childhood, *Child Development*, 1971, *42*, 1721-1734.

Shure, M. B. & Spivack, G. Interpersonal problem-solving as a mediator of behavioral adjustment in preschool and kindergarten children. *Journal of Applied Developmental Psychology*, 1980, *1*, 29-44.

Smilansky, S. *The effects of sociodramatic play on disadvantaged preschool children.* New York: Wiley, 1968.

Spivack, G., & Shure, M. B. *Social adjustment in young children.* San Francisco: Jossey-Bass, 1974.

Sullivan, J. S. *The interpersonal theory of psychiatry.* New York: Norton, 1953.

Vygotsky, L. Play and its role in the mental development of the child. *Soviet Psychology*, 1967, *12*, 62-76.

Winer, B. J. *Statistical principles in experimental design.* New York: McGraw-Hill, 1971.

Zigler, E., & Trickett, P. I.Q., social competence, and evaluation of early childhood intervention programs. *American Psychologist*, 1978, *33*, 789-798.

Zivin, G. (ed.). *The development of self-regulation through private speech.* New York: Wiley, 1979.

Chapter 16

Social Competence and Peer Status: The Distinction Between Goals and Strategies

Peter D. Renshaw and Steven R. Asher

Sociometric status in the peer group is a fairly stable phenomenon (Asher, Singleton, Tinsley, & Hymel, 1979; Roff, Sells, & Golden, 1972), and longitudinal research suggests that low status is predictive of later life adjustment (Cowen, Pederson, Babigian, Izzo, & Trost, 1973; Roff et al., 1972; Ullmann, 1957). However, the reasons for poor acceptance by the peer group are not well understood. Several explanations have been advanced since the 1930s to explain why certain children are unpopular. One group of researchers has focused on the characteristics of the group itself and examined how group roles and responsibilities are distributed (Jennings, 1959; Moreno, 1934). From this perspective, unpopular children are those who have been temporarily assigned, either formally or informally, to a marginal group role. In order to assist unpopular children, these researchers suggest that a new group structure be engineering by reassigning roles or creating new responsibilities for marginal group members (Jennings, 1959).

A contrasting perspective emphasizes the contribution of individual children's social competence to their status in the peer group. Adopting the latter perspective, in this chapter we focus on the social competence of popular and unpopular children. This focus has been productive in furthering our understanding of the reasons certain children are isolated or rejected and in designing intervention efforts to help children without friends. An extensive body of work has emerged that points to social skill deficits as a basis for peer relationship problems. In this chapter, we describe the evidence that leads to this conclusion.

Beyond this, we advance the proposition that a focus on social competence requires attention to multiple processes that underly the phenomenon. To date, researchers examining the competence correlates of status in the peer group have focused primarily on children's social behavior but have not considered in sufficient detail the processes that contribute to adaptive versus maladaptive behavior. In particular, an important distinction can be made between children's knowledge of social interaction strategies and children's goals for social interaction. Research over nearly five decades (Gottman, Gonso, & Rasmussen, 1975; Hartup, Glazer, & Charlesworth, 1967; Koch, 1933; Lippitt, 1941; Marshall & McCandless, 1957; Putallaz & Gottman, 1981) has emphasized children's ability to behave appropriately (e.g., to cooperate or play constructively) in social contexts. However, children might behave maladaptively not necessarily because they lack strategic knowledge of appropriate behavior, but because their social goals lead inexorably to behaviors that cause difficulties with other children; that is, children may sometimes construe situations in ways that lead to goals that are dysfunctional in terms of initiating or maintaining positive social relationships with others. In this chapter, we advance the hypothesis that popular and unpopular children differ not only in their social interaction strategies, but in the nature of their interpersonal goals as well.

Social Skill Basis of Sociometric Status

Differences in the social interaction style of popular versus unpopular children have been found repeatedly (see Asher & Hymel, 1981, for a review). These differences appear in both naturalistic settings (Goldman, Corsini, & DeUrioste, 1980; Hartup et al., 1967; Koch, 1933; Moore & Updegraff, 1964; Rubin & Hayvren, 1981) and in contrived, or analogue, settings (Putallaz & Gottman, 1981). Furthermore, differences exist across a variety of interpersonal situations. In general, low-status children seem to be less effective at initiating relationships, maintaining relationships, and resolving potentially disruptive interpersonal conflicts (see Asher, Renshaw, & Hymel, 1982, for a review).

Until recently, however, a fundamental question remained to be answered concerning the causal relationship between social behavior and sociometric status. Are the observed behavioral differences the cause of children's low status or the consequence of low status? This issue has long been recognized as central. For example, Moore (1967) stated:

> To know that popular children perform a preponderance of friendly behaviors is not to say that their friendliness is the 'cause' of their popularity. It is just as reasonable to hypothesize that being well liked inspires a child to perform friendly behaviors as it is to hypothesize that performing these behaviors causes the child to be well liked. (p. 236)

The possibility that low status causes incompetent behavior should not be dismissed lightly. A child who is trapped in the role of a marginal group member probably will behave in ways that do not reflect the child's true competence. Even as adults, most of us sometimes experience situations in which we feel disliked or ignored. These feelings in turn can lead to insecurity or anger, and the behavior that results may be maladaptive. Thus it is conceivable that low status causes ineffective behavior and that the relationship between interaction style and sociometric status is, at the least, bidirectional. When the research design only involves observing children interacting with their established peer group, inferences about the direction of causality are risky.

Particular research designs are needed to establish that social skill deficits cause low status. One method is to examine whether children's interaction style predicts their status in a new group of previously unfamiliar peers. Another research strategy is to teach social skills to low-status children and observe whether an improved sociometric status results. A third method involves interviewing children about hypothetical situations to assess social knowledge apart from the context of the child's everyday peer group; if unpopular children truly lack social knowledge, then this should be revealed when children are interviewed independently of their current social group. Recently, each of these methods have been used; the results are reviewed next.

Children's Interaction Style in New Groups

Despite 50 years of research on the behavioral correlates of sociometric status, until recently no one had investigated whether interaction style in a new group of previously unfamiliar peers predicts sociometric status. Within the past year, however, several researchers have done this type of study (Putallaz, 1981; Coie & Kupersmidt, Note 1; Dodge, Note 2). The research designs differ somewhat from one investigation to the next, but each is an ambitious undertaking that reveals provocative and important findings.

In the Coie and Kupersmidt (Note 1) study, 10 four-person groups of fourth-grade boys were formed on the basis of sociometric data collected in the children's class. In each group, one child was popular, one was rejected, one was neglected, and one was average in status. Rejected children were those who received many negative nominations from peers and few positive nominations; neglected children were those who received few of either type of nomination and were thus ignored rather than overtly disliked. In one-half of the groups the children knew one another and in the other half the group members came from different schools and thus were unfamiliar with one another. This allowed the investigators to compare the maintenance versus the emergence of sociometric status.

The boys met once a week for 40 minutes over a 6-week period. After each session, each child was driven home and informally questioned concerning the child's feelings toward the other group members. Results for the first two weeks indicated that sociometric status in the new unfamiliar groups was not significantly correlated with status in the child's school. However, by the third week the correlation was significant ($r = .54$) and it increased over the remaining sessions (e.g., sixth week, $r = .74$). This study shows that sociometric status in an established peer group is predictive of status in a new group. Further examination by Coie and Kupersmidt (Note 1) qualified this picture somewhat: rejected children became rejected in both familiar and unfamiliar groups, but neglected children achieved a satisfactory social position in the unfamiliar group. Apparently, children who are neglected in one group can make a fresh start when placed in a new group. Postexperimental reports from peers indicated that neglected children were perceived as shy in the familiar group but not in the unfamiliar group. This may mean that neglected children's behavior is the outcome and not the cause of their status; or it may mean that children who become neglected in classroom-size groups can cope more effectively in small groups.

On the other hand, rejected children do seem to bring about their status. Coie and Kupersmidt videotaped their groups and examined the behaviors of the different groups of children. Rejected children were more possessive of toys, more verbally abusive, and more physically aggressive than popular children. This pattern fits with earlier research suggesting that rejected children have a more negative interaction style (Gronlund & Anderson, 1957; Hartup et al., 1967).

The results for popular children indicated interesting differences in their behavior in unfamiliar and familiar groups. In unfamiliar groups, popular children did less "bossing" of others, were less possessive of toys, and displayed almost no aversive behavior. Indeed, they were sometimes viewed as shy. In familiar groups, by contrast, popular children were much more freewheeling. They asserted themselves more and behaved in ways that could be viewed as bossy, although nonviolently so. As Coie and Kupersmidt commented, it appears that in familiar groups popular children had a certain amount of license for assertive and potentially aversive acts without jeopardizing their status.

Dodge (Note 2) also brought children together who were previously unfamiliar with one another. In this study, six playgroups were formed, each composed of eight 7-year-old boys. The children in each group came from eight different schools and thus did not know one another. The groups met for eight play sessions; the purpose was to identify behaviors that led to different types of status within the new groups. Thus, sociometric data were collected at the end of the last play session.

The findings fit with the pattern of previous research. Popular children engaged in cooperative play and social conversation more than rejected children, and the differences became more pronounced over play sessions. Rejected children were more likely to engage in physical aggression and in hostile verbalizations (insults, contentious statements, exclusion of peers from play). Children who became rejected were also more likely to engage in various types of rule violations (e.g., standing on the table, grabbing, and eating toys). This study highlights the variety of behaviors that can lead to rejection. As in Coie and Kupersmidt's study, disruption of the ongoing flow of the group's life seems to be implicated.

Putallaz (1981) also had children enter a new group, but in this case the group consisted of two child confederates of the experimenter whose behavior was carefully scripted. The purpose was to learn whether children's style of entry and their reactions to particular group events are predictive of their later sociometric status. The subjects were kindergarten children and their entry behavior was observed during the summer prior to beginning first grade. Sociometric data were collected four months later, when the children were back in school. Thus target subjects' behavior with unfamiliar confederates was used to predict to their sociometric status in a completely different group several months later.

The study built upon an earlier investigation in which children entered a dyad of familiar peers. In that study, Putallaz and Gottman (1981) found that when unpopular children entered a group they were less likely to take the frame of reference of the group members. Thus, unpopular children were more likely to call attention to themselves and less likely to get into the ongoing flow of conversation. Putallaz (1981) examined this issue further by coding children's entry style in terms of whether children overtly interfered with the flow of events. Results supported the frame-of-reference hypothesis. For example, the proportion of relevant comments children made was significantly correlated with the number of positive sociometric nominations children received four months later in first grade. In many ways, this is a remarkable finding. Children's social skillfulness was assessed in only one relatively brief contrived situation, the sociometric data were collected four months later, and the group members during the entry situation were different from the children who would later be first-grade classmates. The Putallaz findings, in combination with the earlier Putallaz and Gottman (1981) study, provide strong evidence that unpopular children are less skillful at entering groups.

In summary, three recent studies were designed to learn whether less effective interaction styles cause low sociometric status, rather than vice versa. The evidence from these studies indicates that a negative interaction style predicts low status, that being rejected in one group predicts being rejected in a completely new group, and that failure to adopt the frame of reference or norms of the group characterizes rejected children's negative interaction style.

Social Skill Training Studies

If low status is caused by social skill deficits, then teaching social skills to low-status children should lead to greater acceptance by the peer group. Within the past decade several studies have been reported in which unpopular children were taught social skills and sociometric status was used as an outcome measure (Gottman, Gonso, & Schuler, 1976; Gresham & Nagle, 1980; Hymel & Asher, 1977; Ladd, 1981; LaGreca & Santogrossi, 1980; Oden & Asher, 1977). The typical strategy in these studies was to verbally instruct children in major social interaction concepts (e.g., being cooperative, being supportive), provide children with play opportunities to practice the ideas, and then have children evaluate their own play behavior in light of the ideas. Four of these six studies produced clear support for a social skill deficit interpretation, in that gains in sociometric status resulting from social skill instruction exceeded gains of attention-control groups or groups of children who got to play with others but received no instruction (Gottman et al., 1976; Gresham & Nagle, 1980; Ladd, 1981; Oden & Asher, 1977). Two studies produced more equivocal results. LaGreca & Santogrossi (1980) found behavioral change but no sociometric change. Hymel & Asher (1977) found that trained children gained in sociometric status, but so did a group of children who received play opportunities but no verbal instruction. The absence of a no-treatment control group in this study makes interpretation difficult.

An interesting finding in this set of studies is the specificity of the sociometric outcomes that have been achieved. Both Gresham and Nagle (1980) and Oden and Asher (1977) found that classmates expressed significantly greater willingness to play with a trained child but did not show greater interest in working with the child. This makes sense in light of the content of the training programs and the play context in which skills were taught. Moreover, the training seems to have greater impact on children's general acceptance in class than on their number of best friends. Three studies included a limited-choice peer-nomination measure (e.g., "Name your three best friends in this class") as well as a rating-scale measure (Gresham & Nagle, 1980; Hymel & Asher, 1977; Oden & Asher, 1977). Gains on the nomination measure were smaller than on the rating-scale measure and typically nonsignificant. The reason might be that the content of the training programs emphasized skills related to the criterion of acceptance rather than making or maintaining friends. Teaching children friendship-making skills per se might involve teaching them how to initiate afterschool activities or emphasizing values central to the development of friendship (e.g., loyalty, trust). These types of program content have not been included to date.

Another noteworthy feature of coaching studies is that successful training programs have had rather different program content. For example, Oden and Asher (1977) taught four general concepts: participation, communication, cooperation, and being validating or supportive of others. Ladd (1981), in contrast, taught three verbal skills: asking positive questions, offering useful suggestions or directions, and offering supportive statements. Nonetheless, different programs may affect similar underlying processes. Children might acquire new goals for social interaction, gain confidence in their ability to affect positive social outcomes, and learn to monitor their own and other's social behavior (Asher & Renshaw, 1981; Dweck, 1981). These processes could contribute to the success of skill-training efforts that emphasize somewhat different skills.

Although important questions about underlying processes remain, the contributions of skill-training research to date have been considerable. Unpopular children are making gains in peer acceptance that last well beyond the end of the intervention. Furthermore, from the perspective of this chapter, training studies have helped demonstrate that social interaction style can be the cause of low sociometric status rather than simply its consequence.

Children's Social Knowledge

Studies in which children are placed into new groups and studies in which children are directly taught social skills support the notion that unpopular children lack social skills. Nevertheless, by design, these studies are unable to address a fundamental issue concerning the exact nature of the deficit. Are the ineffective strategies displayed by unpopular children due to performance deficits or deficits in competence (Flavell & Wohlwill, 1969)? Similarly, are the effects of intervention due to impact on performance variables or competence variables? A child may have knowledge of the appropriate social strategies to use in a particular peer situation (competence) but fail to implement the strategies (performance) because of anxiety, expectations of failure, fear of rejection by peers, and so on. These performance variables could certainly be at work in new group situations. Similarly, the intervention studies reviewed above were designed to have impact on performance as well as competence variables. In terms of competence, each training procedure explicitly taught concepts about social interaction that some unpopular children may not have known. In terms of performance, each training procedure provided for behavioral rehearsal and feedback that may have reduced some children's anxiety, dispelled fears of peer rejection, and increased expectations for future success in peer interaction. It is not clear from the studies reviewed thus far whether unpopular children lack competence, in the sense that they do not know how to interact, or whether they have performance problems, in the sense that they have knowledge of how to behave but fail to behave skillfully for other reasons, such as anxiety or fear of rejection.

One means of determining whether unpopular children have deficits in their social knowledge is to provide a task that directly assesses children's knowledge as opposed to their real-life behavior. This has been done in several recent studies by presenting children with hypothetical social situations and eliciting their ideas about what they would do in each situation. The responses of children may be verbal or may be enacted in a role play. In studies using this methodology, unpopular children have been found to be lacking in knowledge of effective interaction strategies.

There are a number of research traditions in the domain of children's social knowledge that have employed the hypothetical-situations methodology. In addition to those studies concerned with unpopular children (Asher & Renshaw, 1981; Gottman et al., 1975; Ladd & Oden, 1979), three other traditions have focused on various aspects of social knowledge. First, there are a growing number of studies on the development of children's persuasive tactics (Clark & Delia, 1976; Piché, Rubin, & Michlin, 1978; Finley & Humphreys, Note 3; Howie-Day, Note 4). These studies have successfully employed the hypothetical-situations methodology to explore a variety of developmental issues, such as age-related changes in children's use of sanctions, the degree of accommodation children make to a listener's perspective, and the degree to which children adjust their persuasive appeals to specific situational demands.

Second, there is growing interest in children's social scripts (Abelson, 1976; Nelson & Gruendel, in press; Stein & Goldman, 1981; Goldman, Note 5; Nelson & Gruendel, Note 6). Children's knowledge of recurrent social events (social scripts) has been explored by asking them to recount in general terms how they would be friendly toward a peer, how they would complete daily chores, or how they would participate in a birthday party. This method of eliciting hypothetical responses has enabled researchers to describe children's knowledge and organization of real-life events. The goal of this research, as Stein and Goldman (1981) point out, is to demonstrate how "[social] knowledge is the source of the child's content and evaluative inferences during . . . actual social events" (p. 318). This is a recent but expanding field and promises to extend our understanding of children's social knowledge and the link between social knowledge and behavior.

The third domain of research of children's social knowledge is the cognitive-developmental perspective, which is reflected in the recent research of Damon (1977) and Selman (1980, 1981). The purpose of much of this research has remained strictly developmental, that is, to describe age-related changes in children's reasoning about social relationships. However, in recent research Selman (1980) is attempting to extend the developmental approach to the study of individual differences in a clinical setting. Here, again, the study of children's social knowledge by means of hypothetical-situations methodology is being extended to establish links between level of knowledge and social behavior.

The investigation of popular and unpopular children's social knowledge has been guided by the hypothesis that children's behavior is regulated by the ideas they have about what to do in various situations. In a study designed to relate children's friendship-making strategies to sociometric status, Gottman et al. (1975) noted that children tended to use a four-stage sequence in their role play of making friends: offering a greeting, asking for information, extending inclusion, and giving information. However, not all children included all the steps in the sequence. When children were divided into two groups based on the number of friendship nominations they received, it was found that the low-friends group scored significantly lower on the knowledge measure than the high-friends group. These data suggest that knowledge of how to make friends is more advanced in children of higher sociometric status.

In a subsequent study, Ladd and Oden (1979) examined the relationship between peer acceptance and children's knowledge of how to be helpful to a child in need. Third- and fifth-grade children were individually interviewed concerning a set of simple cartoon drawings and an accompanying commentary. Three helping situations were depicted: being teased by peers, being yelled at by a peer, and having a schoolwork problem in class. Children's helping strategies were coded into 12 general categories (e.g., order-command, console-comfort, instruct). The large number of categories needed to capture children's ideas about helpfulness suggested that there was wide variation in what children thought was appropriate. However, an additional calculation from the data presented by Ladd and Oden (1979, p. 406) suggests that there was a fairly high level of consensus in children's responses. The three most common categories of responses of third-grade children account for over 70% of the children's responses. At the fifth-grade level, the percentage exceeds 60%. These data indicate that children have a rather widely shared view of the appropriate ways to help a peer in need.

Nonetheless, it may be that unpopular children do not fully share this normative knowledge of how to be helpful. Ladd and Oden's analyses relating social knowledge to sociometric status confirmed this. They calculated a uniqueness measure for each subject. A response was counted as unique if no other same-sex classmate suggested that category, or if the response was judged as noncategorizable. In a regression analysis, the uniqueness variable predicted sociometric status for both boys and girls: As the number of unique responses increased, the sociometric status of the children decreased. This finding highlights the nonnormativeness of unpopular children's ideas about helping a peer, and suggests that unpopular children lack knowledge of how to interact appropriately with peers.

The utility of the hypothetical-situations methodology is demonstrated in the two studies reviewed above. However, only one type of social situation (being helpful, making a new friend) was used in each study. It may be that unpopular children have effective strategies for some types of social settings, but are at a loss in other settings. For example, some children might be effective at initiating relationships but have difficulty maintaining them. What is required, therefore, is a sampling of the social settings and social tasks that confront children in their everyday encounters with peers.

More attention to the actual content of children's ideas would also be useful. Ladd and Oden (1979) coded the responses of children into different content categories in order to create their content-free measure of uniqueness; thus their emphasis was not on the actual content of children's strategies. Nevertheless, they commented that inspection of unique responses suggested that many responses were situationally inappropriate, including bossy and verbally or physically aggressive strategies. This comment suggests the importance of examining the actual content of children's ideas. Some researchers (Jack, 1934; Shure, Note 7), however, have actually advocated content-free analysis of children's social strategies. They argue that there are inherent difficulties in judging the appropriateness and value of alternative strategies because the appropriateness of alternative strategies varies with the cultural background of the children. For example, is demanding a toy from another child more appropriate than snatching it? Examination of the content of children's social strategies is very likely to lead to such value judgments, especially when groups of children are being compared (e.g., popular vs. unpopular; economically advantaged vs. disadvantaged; normal vs. disturbed).

Adopting a content-free approach would, however, unduly restrict our understanding of children's social knowledge. To illustrate, Shure and Spivack (1972) compared the social problem-solving strategies of normal and disturbed children, 10-12 years old. Quantitatively, they found that the disturbed children suggested significantly fewer means (strategies) for attaining a specified goal. If no further analysis had been performed, one could conclude that the disturbed children simply needed to be taught more ways of solving problems. However, content analysis more precisely indicated the nature of the deficit. The disturbed children tended to use more aggressive and pragmatically direct strategies in attaining their goals. In contrast, the normal children suggested indirect strategies that Shure and Spivack (1972, pp. 351-352) described as involving planning, foresight, and sophisticated use of other people. The social knowledge deficit of the disturbed children, therefore, appears to be an inability to plan their future actions and include other people as participants in their plans, rather than simply a general lack of ideas.

The two extensions of the hypothetical situations methodology—sampling more social settings and paying more attention to the content of children's ideas—were incorporated in a recent study with popular and unpopular kindergarten children (Asher & Renshaw, 1981). Children were interviewed about nine hypothetical social situations. The purpose was to examine the content of popular and unpopular children's ideas for three types of social situations: initiating relationships or interaction with other children (getting to know children at a new school, making a new friend, joining a game); maintaining relationships with other children (e.g., cooperating with a friend, helping a friend); and dealing with conflicts with peers (responding when a peer tries to take a toy away, responding when a guest turns the television channel without asking). Children's responses for each social situation were recorded, transcribed, and divided into separate idea units. The idea units were subsequently used to create a set of categories which captured the range of ideas suggested by the children.

The high degree of consensus in elementary school children's responses found by both Gottman et al. (1975) and Ladd and Oden (1979) was replicated with the kindergarten children. Asher and Renshaw (1981) found that 70% of the three most common strategies suggested by the popular children were also among the top three strategies suggested by the unpopular group. However, examination of those ideas suggested exclusively by either the popular or unpopular children provided useful insights into the knowledge deficits of unpopular children. First, in those situations that involved initiating or maintaining relationships with others, some unpopular children appeared at a loss in that they suggested vague responses, such as "he could play," "he could help," or "he could be friends," when the task was to specify how these goals could be achieved. Other responses from unpopular children were inexplicably negative in tone. In contrast, the exclusive ideas of the popular children showed both specificity and a high level of prosocial content. For example, some popular children were prepared to give their sled to a friend without one, to give a ride to a friend whose bicycle was broken, and to help the friend carry books. In situations in which peer conflict occurred, unpopular children's exclusive ideas were highly aggressive, involving both general physical attack and destruction of the objects (toy or television). The exclusive ideas of popular children for the same situations were assertive but sophisticated and nonaggressive, involving the use of persuasive strategies and appeals to social norms.

In order to describe children's responses across situations, Asher and Renshaw (1981) had two judges, blind to the sociometric status of the children, rate all the strategies on three dimensions: effectiveness, relationship enhancement, and assertiveness. No differences were found on assertiveness, but popular children's ideas were rated as more effective and more relationship enhancing.

Thus, social knowledge interviews, like the research strategies discussed earlier, implicate social skill deficits as a basis for low status in the peer group. The convergence of evidence across research strategies strongly supports a focus on social competence as a basis for understanding and facilitating children's peer relations. Unpopular children not only behave inappropriately, they also seem to lack knowledge about what is appropriate in various situations.

Children's Goals for Social Interaction

Research to date has focused primarily on differences in children's social interaction strategies and differences in underlying knowledge of appropriate social behavior. Clearly this has been a productive perspective. However, further progress may depend on attending to important components of social skillfulness in addition to knowledge of appropriate interaction strategies. Particular attention needs to be directed to the contribution of children's goals for social interaction. Our hypothesis is that part of the social skill deficit of unpopular children consists of their selection of goals that are inappropriate to particular social situations (Asher & Renshaw, 1981). If children pursue inappropriate goals in social situations, then their strategies will likewise appear inappropriate, even though they may know appropriate strategies for achieving particular goals.

In everyday social interaction, children are confronted with many situations in which the goals are ill defined or at least complex. As Greene (1976) has pointed out, the distinguishing feature of social problems (as compared to cognitive problems) is that they are ill structured. Thus the first step in solving such problems is to center on an appropriate goal for the situation, or coordinate a series of goals. Take, for example, the case of two children who are playing a board game. What might their goals be here? To win the game? To maintain or enhance their relationship? To get better at the game? If one child was excessively preoccupied with the first goal he or she might engage in dysfunctional social behavior such as cheating or dominating the game. The child might know how to play cooperatively but fail to do so because of certain goal commitments in the situation.

It seems essential, then, that in assessing and modifying children's social competence, a distinction be made between social goals and social strategies. We are not the first to make this distinction. It appears in the cognitive problem-solving literature (Miller, Galanter, & Pribram, 1960; Schank & Abelson, 1977; Simon, 1976) and has been made recently in the social problem-solving literature, as well. Krasnor and Rubin (1981) define the process of social problem solving as the choice of social goals and the social behaviors which are selected as means to achieve these goals. However, when Krasnor and Rubin (1981) translated the problem-solving model into components for assessment, assumptions were made that led to the neglect of goals: "As in the information-processing approach to cognitive or nonsocial problem solving (Newell & Simon, 1972), we will assume that the child has selected a goal (e.g., to obtain an object). We further assume that the child has the motivation to act on this goal" (p. 468). These assumptions are particularly appropriate when the purpose is to study children's strategies. By presenting all children with the same goal, it is possible to study individual differences in children's tactics or means of attaining the goal. However, presenting children with goals ignores the fact that social situations are ill defined and that the selection of social goals may be a particularly important aspect of children's social problem solving.

If the situations employed in previous hypothetical-situations research are examined carefully, it can be seen how a social goal has been imposed on an essentially ill-defined social context. For example, Asher and Renshaw (1981) and Ladd and Oden (1979) presented a number of incidents to children: a child being teased; a child being yelled at; a child with a flat tire on his bike; or a child having a schoolwork problem. There is a range of social goals that children may pursue in these situations: The interviewer in these studies provided the goal of being helpful, but instead children may want to avoid the situation, may want to join in the teasing or yelling, or may simply want to find out more information about the situation. The situation itself does not define the goal for the children. They must formulate, however tentatively or even unconsciously, some social goal to pursue in the situation.

Attention to children's goals could inform our understanding of research discussed earlier in this chapter. Consider first the experiments in which children were brought together in a new group. Coie and Kupersmidt (Note 1) found that popular children initially engaged in verbal give and take but in a way that was relatively unassertive. Only in later sessions did children exhibit more assertive and even bossy behavior. Rejected children, by contrast, entered the group more forcefully and exhibited bossy behavior and even physical aggression in early as well as later stages. It may be that popular and rejected children have different goals when entering a new group. Popular children may have the goal of being liked or gaining acceptance. As Coie and Kupersmidt put it, they avoid giving offense. As time passes and they gain acceptance and confidence, popular children's goals may shift somewhat to include the goal of having influence over the group's direction. Hence, they begin to evidence strong leadership, even bossiness. For rejected children, the goal upon entering a group may be less to gain acceptance than it is to influence or control events, or even to draw attention to the self. These goals would lead to bossy behavior early in the group's life and to behavior that singled out the child in some way.

Children, like adults, typically feel apprehensive when entering an unfamiliar group (McGrew, 1972). It seems plausible that children's goals upon entry would include reducing their level of discomfort. For popular children, gaining acceptance would serve that function. Given popular children's style of not giving offense, they are likely to be successful in becoming comfortable in the group. By contrast, the style of unpopular children is less likely to be successful; instead, it is likely to lead to counterinfluence attempts, physical aggression, and rejection. The result, we suspect, is that rejected children often feel quite uncomfortable when in groups.

A focus on children's goals can also inform our understanding of why social skill training studies are effective. In Oden and Asher's (1977) coaching procedure, for example, the coach teaches certain social interaction concepts (participating, communicating, cooperating, and being validating or supportive) and suggests that using the ideas may make games fun to play. Repeatedly, the coach emphasizes the goal of both play partners having a good time ("Did the ideas we talked about help you and Billy to have a good time?"). We suspect that this message may have influenced some children who might otherwise focus exclusively on the goal of winning games and ignore the goal of creating or maintaining an enjoyable relationship with the other child. Popular children may coordinate a complex set of goals, whereas unpopular children may tend to focus their attention primarily on winning and thereby engage in dysfunctional social behavior.

Differences in goals may also underly differences in strategies found in hypothetical-situations interviews. For example, in our kindergarten interview study (Asher & Renshaw, 1981) children were shown a situation in which the guest (a child new to the neighborhood) suddenly changes the television channel to another station. Our subjects were asked what the host child could do. As noted earlier, some children responded to this type of item with physically aggressive strategies, whereas others were cooperative or accommodating. Still others were verbally assertive but nonviolent. It seems plausible that different goals may underly these different strategies. The aggressive child may be focusing on the goal of maintaining his or her integrity or territory ("He's not going to push me around—this is my house."); the accommodating child may be focusing on the goal of developing a relationship with the new neighbor, or on the goal of avoiding a hassle. The verbally assertive but nonaggressive child ("Please turn that back. We'll watch what you want later.") may be simultaneously focusing on two goals: protecting his or her own rights and not doing damage to a potential relationship.

In summary, we are suggesting that the ill-defined or ambiguous nature of many social situations allows for multiple goal constructions, and hence the possibility of marked individual differences in the goals children construe for specific situations. These individual differences in goal construal processes could underly observed behavioral differences as well as revealed differences in hypothetical-situations interviews. Furthermore, it seems possible that the positive results of previous social skill training studies may be due in part to effects of intervention on the way children construe their goals in social interaction situations.

A Study of Children's Goals and Strategies

In this section we describe a study by Renshaw (1981) that was an initial attempt to assess children's goals in social situations and to relate children's goals to their status in the peer group. The study was conducted with third- through sixth-grade children who were classified as popular or unpopular based on their sociometric status in class. A mean split was used to make the classification—children above the mean in sociometric status were classified as popular and children below the mean were classified as unpopular. As in Asher and Renshaw (1981), the study involved a range of situations and focused on the actual content of children's ideas. In addition, it went beyond this earlier effort by focusing on children's goals as well as their strategies.

The first part of the interview was designed to elicit from children their strategies and goals for four hypothetical social situations. The hypothetical situations needed to be carefully structured so that both the social goals and strategies of children could be assessed. The story grammar schemes proposed by Stein (1980) was very useful in this regard. Each hypothetical situation was structured so that a social *setting* was described, and an *initiating event* was proposed. In Stein's story grammar scheme the initiating event immediately precedes goal formulation. We left the story without an explicit goal to allow children to formulate their own goals for the social situation. The initiating event demands some response from the child, but the goal of the response is not clearly defined. The four hypothetical social situations used by Renshaw (1981) are presented below:

1. *First day at a new school*
   Your parents have moved to a new town.
   This is your first day at a new school. (*setting*)
   As recess begins, the kids go out to play. (*initiating event*)
2. *Rebuffed at gaining entry*
   One free period you have nothing to do.
   Then you see two kids getting out a game of monopoly. (*setting*)
   You go over to them to play and they say "Heh, we didn't ask you." (*initiating event*)
3. *Friend with disliked other*
   You play with your friend at recess most of the time. (*setting*)

One day at recess you see your friend with a kid that you dislike.
(*initiating event*)
4. *Other child changes channel*
You ask a kid who is new to the neighborhood to watch cartoons one
Saturday morning. (*setting*)
After about 10 minutes, the kid changes the channel without asking.
(*initiating event*)

These four hypothetical social situations were presented in random
order to the children. The first probe used by the interviewer was
designed to elicit children's strategies. Thus, the interviewer asked,
"What would you say or do if that happened?" Following the children's
answer to the strategy probe, the interviewer asked them the goal probe,
"Why would you do (or say) those things?" An alternative goal probe
was also used: "What are you trying to do by doing (or saying) those
things?" If children were unable to answer, or said that they didn't
understand the question, the interviewer said, "Well, kids might do different things here. I'm trying to work out why you'd do that rather
than something else."

The goals that children suggested for the four situations were categorized according to how friendly and assertive they were as rated by
two adult raters. Five general types of social goals were identified:
positive-outgoing, positive-accommodating, rule-oriented, avoidance,
and hostile. *Positive-outgoing goals* were highly friendly and assertive
and included such goals as wanting to make friends, join in group
activities, or maintain existing relationships with peers. *Positive-accommodating goals* were highly friendly but average in assertiveness and
focused on preserving the rights of other children in the situation and
accommodating or building peer relationships slowly. These goals,
like the positive-outgoing goals, were basically friendly, but they
were also somewhat more restrained or cautious. *Avoidance goals*
(average on friendliness and low on assertiveness) focused on the possibility of experiencing negative emotions in the situation and the desire
to escape from the situation. These avoidance goals reflected a sense of
helplessness and the desire to avoid even trying to find a solution to the
problematic situation. *Hostile goals* were low on friendliness and high
on assertiveness and focused on repaying perceived injury or unkindness
and breaking established friendships. These goals were elicited only in
those situations in which there was some incident that could be used to
justify a hostile intention. *Rule-oriented goals* were average on friendliness and high on assertiveness and were neither particularly friendly nor
hostile, but focused on the material rights and interests of the children
in the situation and emphasized upholding these rights and interests.

These five goal types were used to classify the responses of children
to each of the four situations. The results indicated a clear and statistically significant age-related trend in children's social goals. Older chil-

dren (fifth and sixth graders) were more likely to suggest positive-outgoing, and positive-accommodating goals, whereas younger children
(third and fourth graders) were more likely to suggest hostile goals. This
developmental trend is particularly highlighted by considering the children's goals for the situation in which the other child changes the television channel. This situation was structured so that two opposing perspectives could be evoked. On the one hand, the child in the hypothetical situation was described as "new to the neighborhood." This information could have been used by the children to create a role for themselves that focused on helping the new child settle in and being con-
siderate so that a positive relationship could develop between them. On
the other hand, the new child behaved badly by changing the television
channel without asking. This information could be used by the children
to justify the rejection and exclusion of the new child. The results indicated that the older children were significantly more likely than the
younger children to suggest the goal of wanting to be sympathetic and
companionable toward the new child. In contrast, the younger children
were significantly more likely than the older group to focus on their
own needs and preferences regarding the television program. The older
children, therefore, placed more value on the interpersonal relationship
between themselves and the new child, whereas the younger children
tended to ignore the interpersonal relationship and focused on their
own individual interests.

Children below average in sociometric status were expected to be less
friendly in their goal orientation than high-status children and were
expected to formulate more avoidance-type goals or hostile goals in
problematic social situations. The results supported only the former
hypothesis: high-status children suggested significantly more positive-
outgoing goals; however, the high- and low-status children suggested
avoidance goals and hostile goals with similar frequences. Thus the low-
status children were not overtly unfriendly in their orientation to social
interaction, they simply were somewhat less positive and outgoing.

Renshaw (1981) also included a recognition task in which children
were presented with four types of goals for each situation (friendly and
assertive, friendly but unassertive, unfriendly and unassertive, and
unfriendly and assertive). Children were asked to rank order each goal
in terms of which goals they would choose. Results here indicated a
striking similarity between high- and low-status children and between
younger and older children. All groups of children ranked the positive
goals above the avoidance and hostile goals. Thus unpopular children
and younger children seem to recognize appropriate goals even though
they do not always produce them.

Viewed in total, the findings provide some support for the notion
that low-status children differ in their social goals from high-status children. It is true that the differences were modest overall; however, we

suspect that the differences would have been larger had an extreme-groups design been utilized. The low-status children were defined as below the mean in peer acceptance; thus children who were only somewhat below average in peer acceptance were included with children who would be classified as rejected or neglected. These different groups of low-status children may have contrasting goal orientations. Children slightly below average in status may be quite positive in their social orientation but more accommodating and subservient; rejected children may focus on their own needs even at the expense of others; and neglected children may be anxious to avoid problematic social situations. Future research, therefore, should provide a more differentiated grouping of the children who are below average in status.

Another issue worthy of further research is the context in which children's goals are assessed. The methodology used by Renshaw (1981) involves a reflective reasoning task (Selman, 1981)—children were asked to reflect on what they might do in a variety of hypothetical situations. This type of task minimizes pressure on the child and is likely to elicit a more competent response than would be obtained in real-life situations. There is a need to study children's reasoning in action. The focus here would be on how children's goals are developed and modified during actual social episodes. We suspect that differences in children's goal construal processes will be even more evident once the focus moves from hypothetical to real situations.

Conclusions

The study of children's social competence has traditionally emphasized children's overt behavioral interaction style, and more recently children's knowledge of social interaction strategies. These emphases are in keeping with the generally accepted view of social competence as the child's ability to affect interpersonal outcomes or goals. However, this view, and the research approach it implies, ignores the possibility that children's selection of goals—that is, their decisions about which interpersonal outcomes to pursue—may be the foundation of the behavior that they subsequently carry out. Thus the process of construing situations and selecting goals should be viewed as being at the center of children's social competence insofar as these processes can dictate the general direction of children's social behavior.

We believe that the study of how children formulate and coordinate complex goals will prove to be very fruitful. Although challenging methodological problems remain, consideration of children's goals should help us to understand and facilitate the social development of children who are experiencing serious peer relationship problems.

Reference Notes

1. Coie, J. D., & Kupersmidt, J. *A behavioral analysis of emerging social status in boys' groups.* Paper presented at the biennial meeting of the Society for Research in Child Development, Boston, 1981.
2. Dodge, K. A. *Behavioral antecedents of peer social rejection and isolation.* Paper presented at the biennial meeting of the Society for Research in Child Development, Boston, 1981.
3. Finley, G. E., & Humphreys, C. A. *Egocentrism and the development of persuasive skills.* Paper presented at the biennial meeting of the Society for Research in Child Development, Minneapolis, 1971.
4. Howie-Day, A. M. *Metapersuasion: The development of reasoning about persuasive strategies.* Paper presented at the biennial meeting of the Society for Research in Child Development, San Francisco, 1979.
5. Goldman, S. R. *The development of semantic knowledge systems for realistic goals.* Paper presented at the biennial meeting of the Society for Research in Child Development, San Francisco, 1979.
6. Nelson, K., & Gruendel, J. M. *From personal episode to social script: Two dimensions in the development of event knowledge.* Paper presented at the biennial meeting of the Society for Research in Child Development, San Francisco, 1979.
7. Shure, M. *The problem-solving approach to social development.* Paper presented at the biennial meeting of the Society for Research in Child Development, San Francisco, 1979.

References

Abelson, R. P. Script processing in attitude formation and decision making. In J. S. Carroll & J. W. Payne (Eds.), *Cognition and social behavior*. Hillsdale, N.J.: Erlbaum, 1976.

Asher, S. R., & Hymel, S. Children's social competence in peer relations: Sociometric and behavioral assessment. In J. D. Wine & M. D. Smye (Eds.), *Social competence*. New York: Guilford Press, 1981.

Asher, S. R., & Renshaw, P. D. Children without friends: Social knowledge and social skill training. In S. R. Asher & J. M. Gottman (Eds.), *The development of children's friendships*. New York: Cambridge University Press, 1981.

Asher, S. R., Renshaw, P. D., & Hymel, S. Peer relations and the development of social skills. In S. G. Moore & C. R. Cooper (Eds.), *The young child: Reviews of research* (Vol. 3). Washington, D.C.: National Association for the Education of Young Children, 1982.

Asher, S. R., Singleton, L. C., Tinsley, B. R., & Hymel, S. A reliable sociometric measure for preschool children. *Developmental Psychology*, 1979, *15*, 443-444.

Clark, R. A., & Delia, J. G. The development of functional persuasive skills in childhood and early adolescence. *Child Development*, 1976, *47*, 1008-1014.

Cowen, E. L., Pederson, A., Babigian, H., Izzo, L. D., & Trost, M. A. Long-term follow-up of early detected vulnerable children. *Journal of Consulting and Clinical Psychology*, 1973, *41*, 438-446.

Damon, W. *The social world of the child*. San Francisco: Jossey-Bass, 1977.

Dweck, C. S. Social-cognitive processes in children's friendships. In S. R. Asher & J. M. Gottman (Eds.), *The development of children's friendships*. New York: Cambridge University Press, 1981.

394   Peter D. Renshaw and Steven R. Asher

Flavell, J. H., & Wohlwill, J. F. Formal and functional aspects of cognitive develop-
ment. In D. Elkind & J. H. Flavell (Eds.), *Studies in cognitive development:
Essays in honor of Jean Piaget*. New York: Oxford University Press, 1969.
Goldman, J. A., Corsini, D. A., & DeUrioste, R. Implications of positive and nega-
tive sociometric status for assessing the social competency of young children.
Journal of Applied Developmental Psychology, 1980, *1*, 209-220.
Gottman, J., Gonso, J., & Rasmussen, B. Social interaction, social competence, and
friendship in children. *Child Development*, 1975, *46*, 709-718.
Gottman, J. M., Gonso, J., & Schuler, P. Teaching social skills to isolated children.
Journal of Abnormal Child Psychology, 1976, *4*, 179-197.
Greene, D. Social perception as problem solving. In J. S. Carroll & J. W. Payne
(Eds.), *Cognition and social behavior*. Hillsdale, N.J.: Erlbaum, 1976.
Gresham, F. M., & Nagle, R. J. Social skills training with children: Responsiveness
to modeling and coaching as a function of peer orientation. *Journal of Consult-
ing and Clinical Psychology*, 1980, *18*, 718-729.
Gronlund, N. E., & Anderson, L. Personality characteristics of socially accepted,
socially neglected, and socially rejected junior high school pupils. *Educational
Administration and Supervision*, 1957, *43*, 329-338.
Hartup, W. W., Glazer, J. A., & Charlesworth, R. Peer reinforcement and sociometric
status. *Child Development*, 1967, *38*, 1017-1024.
Hymel, S., & Asher, S. R. *Assessment and training of isolated children's social
skills*. Paper presented at the biennial meeting of the Society for Research in
Child Development, New Orleans, 1977. (ERIC Document Reproduction Service
No. ED 136 930)
Jack, L. M. An experimental study of ascendant behavior in preschool children.
University of Iowa Studies in Child Welfare, 1934, *9*(3), 9-65.
Jennings, H. *Sociometry in group relations: A manual for teachers*. Washington,
D.C.: American Council on Education, 1959.
Koch, H. L. Popularity in preschool children: Some related factors and a technique
for its measurement. *Child Development*, 1933, *4*, 164-175.
Krasnor, L. R., & Rubin, K. H. The assessment of social problem-solving skills in
young children. In T. Merluzzi, C. Glass, & M. Genest (Eds.), *Cognitive assess-
ment*. New York: Guilford Press, 1981.
Ladd, G. W. Effectiveness of a social learning method for enhancing children's social
interaction and peer acceptance. *Child Development*, 1981, *52*, 171-178.
Ladd, G. W., & Oden, S. L. The relationship between peer acceptance and children's
ideas about helpfulness. *Child Development*, 1979, *50*, 402-408.
LaGreca, A. M., & Santogrossi, D. A. Social skills training with elementary school
students: A behavioral group approach. *Journal of Consulting and Clinical Psy-
chology*, 1980, *48*, 220-227.
Lippitt, R. Popularity among preschool children. *Child Development*, 1941, *12*,
305-332.
Marshall, H. R., & McCandless, B. R. A study in prediction of social behavior of
preschool children. *Child Development*, 1957, *28*, 149-159.
McGrew, W. C. *An ethological study of children's behavior*. New York: Academic
Press, 1972.
Miller, G. A., Galanter, E., & Pribram, K. H. *Plans and the structure of behavior*.
New York: Holt, Rinehart & Winston, 1960.
Moore, S. G. Correlates of peer acceptance in nursery school children. In W. W.

Hartup & N. L. Smothergill (Eds.), *The young child*. Washington, D.C.: National Association for the Education of Young Children, 1967.

Moore, S. G., & Updegraff, R. Sociometric status of preschool children related to age, sex, nurturance giving, and dependency. *Child Development*, 1964, *35*, 519-524.

Moreno, J. L. *Who shall survive? A new approach to the problem of human inter-relations*. Washington, D.C.: Nervous and Mental Disease Publishing, 1934.

Nelson, K., & Gruendel, J. M. At morning it's lunchtime: A scriptal view of children's dialogues. *Discourse Processes*, in press.

Newell, A., & Simon, H. *Human problem solving*. Englewood Cliffs, N.J.: Prentice-Hall, 1972.

Oden, S., & Asher, S. R. Coaching children in social skills for friendship making. *Child Development*, 1977, *48*, 495-506.

Piché, G., Rubin, D., & Michlin, M. Age and social class in children's use of persuasive communicative appeals. *Child Development*, 1978, *49*, 773-780.

Putallaz, M. *Predicting children's sociometric status from their behavior*. Unpublished doctoral dissertation, University of Illinois, 1981.

Putallaz, M., & Gottman, J. M. Social skills and group acceptance. In S. R. Asher & J. M. Gottman (Eds.), *The development of children's friendships*. New York: Cambridge University Press, 1981.

Renshaw, P. D. *Social knowledge and sociometric status: Children's goals and strategies for peer interaction*. Unpublished doctoral dissertation, University of Illinois, 1981.

Roff, M., Sells, S. B., & Golden, M. W. *Social adjustment and personality development in children*. Minneapolis: University of Minnesota Press, 1972.

Rubin, K. H., & Hayvren, M. The social and cognitive play of preschool-age children differing with regard to sociometric status. *Journal of Research and Development in Education*, 1981, *14*, 116-122.

Schank, R. C., & Abelson, R. P. *Scripts, plans, goals and understanding: An inquiry into human knowledge structures*. Hillsdale, N.J.: Erlbaum, 1977.

Selman, R. L. *The growth of interpersonal understanding*. New York: Academic Press, 1980.

Selman, R. L. The child as a friendship philosopher. In S. R. Asher & J. M. Gottman (Eds.), *The development of children's friendships*. New York: Cambridge University Press, 1981.

Shure, M. B., & Spivack, G. Means-ends thinking, adjustment and social class among elementary school-aged children. *Journal of Consulting and Clinical Psychology*, 1972, *38*, 348-353.

Simon, H. Identifying basic abilities underlying intelligent performance on complex tasks. In L. Resnick (Ed.), *The nature of intelligence*. Hillsdale, N.J.: Erlbaum, 1976.

Stein, N. L. How children understand stories: A developmental analysis. In L. G. Katz (Ed.), *Current topics in early childhood education* (Vol. 2). Hillsdale, N.J.: Ablex, 1980.

Stein, N. L., & Goldman, S. R. Children's knowledge about social situations: From causes to consequences. In S. R. Asher & J. M. Gottman (Eds.), *The development of children's friendships*. New York: Cambridge University Press, 1981.

Ullmann, C. A. Teachers, peers, and tests as predictors of adjustment. *Journal of Educational Psychology*, 1957, *48*, 257-267.

Author Index

Subject Index